Machine Learning Using TensorFlow Cookbook

Over 60 recipes on machine learning using deep
learning solutions from Kaggle Masters and Google
Developer Experts

Alexia Audevart

Konrad Banachewicz

Luca Massaron

BIRMINGHAM - MUMBAI

Machine Learning Using TensorFlow Cookbook

Producer: Tushar Gupta

Acquisition Editor – Peer Reviews: Divya Mudaliar

Content Development Editor: Alex Patterson

Technical Editor: Aditya Sawant

Project Editor: Parvathy Nair

Copy Editor: Safis Editing

Proofreader: Safis Editing

Indexer: Priyanka Dhadke

Presentation Designer: Pranit Padwal

First published: February 2021

Production reference: 1030221

Published by Packt Publishing Ltd.
Livery Place
35 Livery Street
Birmingham B3 2PB, UK.

ISBN 978-1-80020-886-5

www.packt.com

Contributors

About the authors

Alexia Audevart, "Data & Enthusiasm," is a **Google Developer Expert (GDE)** in machine learning and the founder of datactik.

She is a data scientist and helps her clients solve business problems by making their applications smarter. Her goal is to create insights from data.

As a trainer and speaker, she works with professionals as well as universities and has even done her own TEDx talk.

Her first book is a collaboration on Artificial Intelligence and Neuroscience.

Thanks first to Max and Maxime, who took time out of their busy lives to review my chapters with such care.

I am also grateful to all the data enthusiasts I have met throughout my life, from whom I have learned a lot. Special thanks to our GDE coordinators, Paige Bailey, Jozef Vodicka, Justyna Politanska-Pyszko, and Soonson Kwon.

Many thanks to Théo, Léane, Lucas, Joséphine, Mélissa, Bastein, and my wonderful extended family.

Last but not least, special thanks go to my parents, Guy and Christine, and my brother, Ludovic; your support has meant more than you will ever know.

Konrad Banachewicz holds a PhD in statistics from Vrije Universiteit Amsterdam. During his period in academia, he focused on problems of extreme dependency modeling in credit risk. In addition to his research activities, Konrad was a tutor, supervising Masters-level students. Starting with classical statistics, he slowly moved toward data mining and machine learning before the terms "data science" and "big data" became ubiquitous.

In the decade since his PhD, Konrad has worked in a variety of financial institutions on a wide array of quantitative data analysis problems. In the process, he became an expert on the entire lifetime of a data product cycle: from translating business requirements ("what do they really need?"), through data acquisition ("spreadsheets and flat files? really?"), wrangling, modeling and testing (the actually fun part), all the way to presenting the results to people allergic to mathematical terminology (which is the majority of business). He has covered different ends of the frequency spectrum in finance (from high-frequency trading to credit risk, and everything in between), predicted potato prices, and analyzed anomalies in the performance of large-scale industrial equipment.

As a person who himself has stood on the shoulders of giants, Konrad believes in sharing knowledge with others: it is very important to know how to approach practical problems with data science methods, but equally important to know how not to do it.

Konrad seems addicted to data analysis, so in his spare time he competes on Kaggle ("the home of data science").

I would like to thank my wife – her patience (in listening to me talk about experience replay) and support (I run on tea the same way cars need gasoline) were invaluable. Thank you, honey.

Luca Massaron is a data scientist with more than a decade of experience in transforming data into smarter artifacts, in solving real-world problems, and in generating value for businesses and stakeholders. He is the author of best-selling books on AI, machine learning, and algorithms. Luca is also a Kaggle Master who reached no. 7 in the worldwide user rankings for his performance in data science competitions and a **Google Developer Expert** (**GDE**) in machine learning.

My warmest thanks go to my family, Yukiko and Amelia, for their support and loving patience.

I also want to thank our GDE coordinators, Paige Bailey, Jozef Vodicka, Justyna Politanska-Pyszko, and Soonson Kwon, and all the members of this fantastic community of experts created by Google.

About the reviewer

Karthik Muthuswamy graduated from NTU Singapore with a doctorate in computer science, specifically in the field of computer vision. He has co-authored many journal and conference papers as well as submitted patent applications in the field of machine learning.

He works for SAP, in Germany, as a Senior Data Scientist, to research and develop enterprise applications that could leverage machine learning. He has also co-authored books and online courses on different topics of machine learning, and is a contributor to many open-source software projects. He teaches machine learning to the software development community with an aim of reducing the barriers of entry to learning about machine learning.

Table of Contents

Preface

TensorFlow 2.x, developed by Google, is an end-to-end open source platform for machine learning. It has a comprehensive, flexible ecosystem of tools, libraries, and community resources that lets researchers push state-of-the-art ML and developers easily build and deploy ML-powered applications.

The independent recipes in this book will teach you how to use TensorFlow for complex data computations and allow you to dig deeper and gain more insights into your data than ever before. With the help of this book, you will work with recipes for training models, model evaluation, regression analysis, tabular data, image and text processing and prediction, and much more. You will explore RNNs, CNNs, GANs, and reinforcement learning, each using the latest version of Google's machine learning library, TensorFlow. Through real-world examples, you will get hands-on experience with various data problems and solving techniques using TensorFlow. Once you are familiar and comfortable with the TensorFlow ecosystem, you will be shown how to take it to production.

By the end of the book, you will be proficient in the field of machine learning using TensorFlow 2.x. You will also have good insight into deep learning and be capable of implementing machine learning algorithms in real-world scenarios.

Who this book is for

This book is meant for data scientists, machine learning developers, deep learning researchers, and developers with a basic statistical background who want to work with neural networks and discover the TensorFlow structure and its new features. A working knowledge of the Python programming language is required to get the most out of the book.

What this book covers

Chapter 1, Getting Started with TensorFlow 2.x, covers the main objects and concepts in TensorFlow. We introduce tensors, variables, and placeholders. We also show how to work with matrices and various mathematical operations in TensorFlow. At the end of the chapter, we show how to access the data sources used in the rest of the book.

Chapter 2, The TensorFlow Way, establishes how to connect all the algorithm components from *Chapter 1, Getting Started with TensorFlow*, into a computational graph in multiple ways to create a simple classifier. Along the way, we cover computational graphs, loss functions, backpropagation, and training with data.

Chapter 3, Keras, focuses on the high-level TensorFlow API named Keras. After having introduced the layers that are the building blocks of the models, we will cover the Sequential, Functional, and Sub-Classing APIs to create Keras models.

Chapter 4, Linear Regression, focuses on using TensorFlow for exploring various linear regression techniques, such as Lasso and Ridge, ElasticNet, and logistic regression. We conclude extending linear models with Wide & Deep. We show how to implement each model using estimators.

Chapter 5, Boosted Trees, discusses the TensorFlow implementation of boosted trees – one of the most popular models for tabular data. We demonstrate the functionality by addressing a business problem of predicting hotel booking cancellations.

Chapter 6, Neural Networks, covers how to implement neural networks in TensorFlow, starting with the operational gates and activation function concepts. We then show a shallow neural network and how to build up various different types of layers. We end the chapter by teaching a TensorFlow neural network to play tic tac toe.

Chapter 7, Predicting with Tabular Data, this chapter extends the previous one by demonstrating how to use TensorFlow for tabular data. We show how to process data handling missing values, binary, nominal, ordinal, and date features. We also introduce activation functions like GELU and SELU (particularly effective for deep architectures) and the correct usage of cross-validation in order to validate your architecture and parameters when you do not have enough data available.

Chapter 8, Convolutional Neural Networks, expands our knowledge of neural networks by illustrating how to use images with convolutional layers (and other image layers and functions). We show how to build a shortened CNN for MNIST digit recognition and extend it to color images in the CIFAR-10 task. We also illustrate how to extend prior-trained image recognition models for custom tasks. We end the chapter by explaining and demonstrating the StyleNet/neural style and DeepDream algorithms in TensorFlow.

Chapter 9, Recurrent Neural Networks, introduces a powerful architecture type (RNN) that has been instrumental in achieving state-of-the-art results on different modes of sequential data; applications presented include time-series prediction and text sentiment analysis.

Chapter 10, Transformers, is dedicated to Transformers – a new class of deep learning models that have revolutionized the field of **Natural Language Processing** (**NLP**). We demonstrate how to leverage their strength for both generative and discriminative tasks.

Chapter 11, Reinforcement Learning with TensorFlow and TF-Agents, presents the TensorFlow library dedicated to reinforcement learning. The structured approach allows us to handle problems ranging from simple games to content personalization in e-commerce.

Chapter 12, Taking TensorFlow to Production, gives tips and examples on moving TensorFlow to a production environment and how to take advantage of multiple processing devices (for example, GPUs) and setting up TensorFlow distributed on multiple machines. We also show the various uses of TensorBoard, and how to view computational graph metrics and charts. We end the chapter by showing an example of setting up an RNN model on TensorFlow serving an API.

To get the most out of this book

You need to have a basic understanding of neural networks, but this is not mandatory since the topics will be covered from a practical point of view and theoretical information will be provided where needed.

A working knowledge of basic machine learning algorithms and technicalities is a plus. You need a good working knowledge of Python 3. You should already know how to install packages using `pip`, as well as how to set up your working environment to work with TensorFlow.

The environment setup will be covered in *Chapter 1, Getting Started with TensorFlow 2.x.*

Download the example code files

The code bundle for the book is hosted on GitHub at `https://github.com/PacktPublishing/ Machine-Learning-Using-TensorFlow-Cookbook`. We also have other code bundles from our rich catalog of books and videos available at `https://github.com/PacktPublishing/`. Check them out!

Download the color images

We also provide a PDF file that has color images of the screenshots/diagrams used in this book. You can download it here: `https://static.packt-cdn.com/ downloads/9781800208865_ColorImages.pdf`.

Conventions used

There are a number of text conventions used throughout this book.

`CodeInText`: Indicates code words in text, database table names, folder names, filenames, file extensions, pathnames, dummy URLs, user input, and Twitter handles. For example; "The `truncated_normal()` function always picks normal values within two standard deviations of the specified mean."

A block of code is set as follows:

```
import TensorFlow as tf
import NumPy as np
```

Any command-line input or output is written as follows:

```
pip install tensorflow-datasets
```

Bold: Indicates a new term, an important word, or words that you see on the screen, for example, in menus or dialog boxes, also appear in the text like this. For example: "TF-Agents is a library for **reinforcement learning** (**RL**) in TensorFlow."

 Warnings or important notes appear like this.

 Tips and tricks appear like this.

Get in touch

Feedback from our readers is always welcome.

General feedback: Email feedback@packtpub.com, and mention the book's title in the subject of your message. If you have questions about any aspect of this book, please email us at questions@packtpub.com.

Errata: Although we have taken every care to ensure the accuracy of our content, mistakes do happen. If you have found a mistake in this book we would be grateful if you would report this to us. Please visit, http://www.packtpub.com/submit-errata, selecting your book, clicking on the Errata Submission Form link, and entering the details.

Piracy: If you come across any illegal copies of our works in any form on the Internet, we would be grateful if you would provide us with the location address or website name. Please contact us at copyright@packtpub.com with a link to the material.

If you are interested in becoming an author: If there is a topic that you have expertise in and you are interested in either writing or contributing to a book, please visit http://authors. packtpub.com.

Reviews

Please leave a review. Once you have read and used this book, why not leave a review on the site that you purchased it from? Potential readers can then see and use your unbiased opinion to make purchase decisions, we at Packt can understand what you think about our products, and our authors can see your feedback on their book. Thank you!

For more information about Packt, please visit packtpub.com.

1
Getting Started with TensorFlow 2.x

Google's TensorFlow engine has a unique way of solving problems, allowing us to solve machine learning problems very efficiently. Nowadays, machine learning is used in almost all areas of life and work, with famous applications in computer vision, speech recognition, language translations, healthcare, and many more. We will cover the basic steps to understand how TensorFlow operates and eventually build up to production code techniques later in the pages of this book. For the moment, the fundamentals presented in this chapter are paramount in order to provide you with a core understanding for the recipes found in the rest of this book.

In this chapter, we'll start by covering some basic recipes and helping you to understand how TensorFlow 2.x works. You'll also learn how to access the data used to run the examples in this book, and how to get additional resources. By the end of this chapter, you should have knowledge of the following:

- ▶ Understanding how TensorFlow 2.x works
- ▶ Declaring and using variables and tensors
- ▶ Working with matrices
- ▶ Declaring operations
- ▶ Implementing activation functions
- ▶ Working with data sources
- ▶ Finding additional resources

Without any further ado, let's begin with the first recipe, which presents in an easy fashion the way TensorFlow deals with data and computations.

How TensorFlow works

Started as an internal project by researchers and engineers from the Google Brain team, initially named **DistBelief**, an open source framework for high performance numerical computations was released in November 2015 under the name TensorFlow (tensors are a generalization of scalars, vectors, matrices, and higher dimensionality matrices). You can read the original paper on the project here: http://download.tensorflow.org/paper/ whitepaper2015.pdf. After the appearance of version 1.0 in 2017, last year, Google released TensorFlow 2.0, which continues the development and improvement of TensorFlow by making it more user-friendly and accessible.

Production-oriented and capable of handling different computational architectures (CPUs, GPUs, and now TPUs), TensorFlow is a framework for any kind of computation that requires high performance and easy distribution. It excels at deep learning, making it possible to create everything from shallow networks (neural networks made of a few layers) to complex deep networks for image recognition and natural language processing.

In this book, we're going to present a series of recipes that will help you use TensorFlow for your deep learning projects in a more efficient way, cutting through complexities and helping you achieve both a wider scope of applications and much better results.

At first, computation in TensorFlow may seem needlessly complicated. But there is a reason for it: because of how TensorFlow deals with computation, when you become accustomed to TensorFlow style, developing more complicated algorithms becomes relatively easy. This recipe will guide us through the pseudocode of a TensorFlow algorithm.

Getting ready

Currently, TensorFlow is tested and supported on the following 64-bit systems: Ubuntu 16.04 or later, macOS 10.12.6 (Sierra) or later (no GPU support, though), Raspbian 9.0 or later, and Windows 7 or later. The code for this book has been developed and tested on an Ubuntu system, but it should run fine on any other system as well. The code for the book is available on GitHub at https://github.com/PacktPublishing/Machine-Learning-Using-TensorFlow-Cookbook, which acts as the book repository for all the code and some data.

Throughout this book, we'll only concern ourselves with the Python library wrapper of TensorFlow, although most of the original core code for TensorFlow is written in C++. TensorFlow operates nicely with Python, ranging from version 3.7 to 3.8. This book will use Python 3.7 (you can get the plain interpreter at https://www.python.org) and TensorFlow 2.2.0 (you can find all the necessary instructions to install it at https://www.tensorflow.org/install).

While TensorFlow can run on the CPU, most algorithms run faster if processed on a GPU, and it is supported on graphics cards with Nvidia Compute Capability 3.5 or higher (preferable when running complex networks that are more computationally intensive).

 All the recipes you'll find in the book are compatible with TensorFlow 2.2.0. Where necessary, we'll point out the differences in syntax and execution with the previous 2.1 and 2.0 versions.

Popular GPUs for running scripts based on TensorFlow on a workstation are Nvidia Titan RTX and Nvidia Quadro RTX models, whereas in data centers, we instead commonly find Nvidia Tesla architectures with at least 24 GB of memory (for instance, Google Cloud Platform offers GPU Nvidia Tesla K80, P4, T4, P100 and V100 models). To run properly on a GPU, you will also need to download and install the Nvidia CUDA toolkit, version 5.x+ (`https://developer.nvidia.com/cuda-downloads`).

Some of the recipes in this chapter will rely on an installation of the current versions of SciPy, NumPy, and Scikit-learn Python packages. These accompanying packages are also included in the Anaconda package (`https://www.anaconda.com/products/individual#Downloads`).

How to do it...

Here, we'll introduce the general flow of TensorFlow algorithms. Most recipes will follow this outline:

1. **Import or generate datasets**: All of our machine learning algorithms will depend on datasets. In this book, we'll either generate data or use an outside source of datasets. Sometimes, it's better to rely on generated data because we can control how to vary and verify the expected outcome. Most of the time, we will access public datasets for the given recipe. The details on accessing these datasets can be found in the *Additional resources* recipe at the end of this chapter:

```
import tensorflow as tf
import tensorflow_datasets as tfds
import numpy as np

data = tfds.load("iris", split="train")
```

2. **Transform and normalize data**: Generally, input datasets do not come in the exact form we want for what we intend to achieve. TensorFlow expects us to transform the data into the accepted shape and data type. In fact, the data is usually not in the correct dimension or type that our algorithms expect, and we will have to transform it properly before we can use it. Most algorithms also expect normalized data (which implies variables whose mean is zero and whose standard deviation is one) and we will look at how to accomplish this here as well. TensorFlow offers built-in functions that can load your data, split your data into batches, and allow you to transform variables and normalize each batch using simple NumPy functions, including the following:

```
for batch in data.batch(batch_size, drop_remainder=True):
    labels = tf.one_hot(batch['label'], 3)
    X = batch['features']
    X = (X - np.mean(X)) / np.std(X)
```

3. **Partition the dataset into training, test, and validation sets**: We generally want to test our algorithms on different sets that we have trained on. Many algorithms also require hyperparameter tuning, so we set aside a validation set for determining the best set of hyperparameters.

4. **Set algorithm parameters (hyperparameters)**: Our algorithms usually have a set of parameters that we hold constant throughout the procedure. For example, this could be the number of iterations, the learning rate, or other fixed parameters of our choice. It's considered good practice to initialize these together using global variables, so that the reader or user can easily find them, as follows:

```
epochs = 1000
batch_size = 32
input_size = 4
output_size = 3
learning_rate = 0.001
```

5. **Initialize variables**: TensorFlow depends on knowing what it can and cannot modify. TensorFlow will modify/adjust the variables (model weights/biases) during optimization to minimize a loss function. To accomplish this, we feed in data through input variables. We need to initialize both variables and placeholders with size and type so that TensorFlow knows what to expect. TensorFlow also needs to know the type of data to expect. For most of this book, we will use float32. TensorFlow also provides float64 and float16 data types. Note that more bytes are used for precision results in slower algorithms, but fewer bytes results in less precision of the resulting algorithm. Refer to the following code for a simple example of how to set up an array of weights and a vector of biases in TensorFlow:

```
weights = tf.Variable(tf.random.normal(shape=(input_size,
                                              output_size),
                                    dtype=tf.float32))
```

```
biases  = tf.Variable(tf.random.normal(shape=(output_size,),
                                        dtype=tf.float32))
```

6. **Define the model structure**: After we have the data, and have initialized our variables, we have to define the model. This is done by building a computational graph. The model for this example will be a logistic regression model (logit $E(Y) = bX + a$):

```
logits = tf.add(tf.matmul(X, weights), biases)
```

7. **Declare the loss functions**: After defining the model, we must be able to evaluate the output. This is where we declare the loss function. The loss function is very important as it tells us how far off our predictions are from the actual values. The different types of loss function are explored in greater detail in the *Implementing Backpropagation* recipe in *Chapter 2, The TensorFlow Way*. Here, as an example, we implement the cross entropy with logits, which computes softmax cross entropy between logits and labels:

```
loss = tf.reduce_mean(
    tf.nn.softmax_cross_entropy_with_logits(labels, logits))
```

8. **Initialize and train the model**: Now that we have everything in place, we need to create an instance of our graph, feed in the data, and let TensorFlow change the variables to predict our training data better. Here is one way to initialize the computational graph and, by means of multiple iterations, converge the weights in the model structure using the SDG optimizer:

```
optimizer = tf.optimizers.SGD(learning_rate)

with tf.GradientTape() as tape:
    logits = tf.add(tf.matmul(X, weights), biases)
    loss = tf.reduce_mean(
        tf.nn.softmax_cross_entropy_with_logits(labels, logits))
gradients = tape.gradient(loss, [weights, biases])
optimizer.apply_gradients(zip(gradients, [weights, biases]))
```

9. **Evaluate the model**: Once we've built and trained the model, we should evaluate the model by looking at how well it does with new data through some specified criteria. We evaluate on the training and test set, and these evaluations will allow us to see whether the model is under or overfitting. We will address this in later recipes. In this simple example, we evaluate the final loss and compare the fitted values against the ground truth training ones:

```
print(f"final loss is: {loss.numpy():.3f}")
preds = tf.math.argmax(tf.add(tf.matmul(X, weights), biases),
axis=1)
ground_truth = tf.math.argmax(labels, axis=1)
```

```
for y_true, y_pred in zip(ground_truth.numpy(), preds.numpy()):
    print(f"real label: {y_true} fitted: {y_pred}")
```

10. **Tune hyperparameters**: Most of the time, we will want to go back and change some of the hyperparameters, checking the model's performance based on our tests. We then repeat the previous steps with different hyperparameters and evaluate the model on the validation set.

11. **Deploy/predict new outcomes**: It is also a key requirement to know how to make predictions on new and unseen data. We can achieve this easily with TensorFlow with all of our models once we have them trained.

How it works...

In TensorFlow, we have to set up the data, input variables, and model structure before we can tell the program to train and tune its weights to improve predictions. TensorFlow accomplishes this through computational graphs. These computational graphs are directed graphs with no recursion, which allows for computational parallelism.

To do this, we need to create a loss function for TensorFlow to minimize. TensorFlow accomplishes this by modifying the variables in the computational graph. TensorFlow knows how to modify the variables because it keeps track of the computations in the model and automatically computes the variable gradients (how to change each variable) to minimize the loss. Because of this, we can see how easy it can be to make changes and try different data sources.

See also

► For a further introduction to TensorFlow and more on its resources, refer to the official documentation and tutorials at TensorFlow's official page: `https://www.tensorflow.org/`

► Within the official pages, a more encyclopedic place to start with is the official Python API documentation, `https://www.tensorflow.org/api_docs/python/`, where you will find all the possible commands enumerated

► There are also tutorials available: `https://www.tensorflow.org/tutorials/`

► Besides that, an unofficial collection of TensorFlow tutorials, projects, presentations, and code repositories can be found here: `https://github.com/dragen1860/TensorFlow-2.x-Tutorials`

Declaring variables and tensors

Tensors are the primary data structure that TensorFlow uses to operate on the computational graph. Even if now, in TensorFlow 2.x, this aspect is hidden, the data flow graph is still operating behind the scenes. This means that the logic of building a neural network doesn't change all that much between TensorFlow 1.x and TensorFlow 2.x. The most eye-catching aspect is that you no longer have to deal with placeholders, the previous entry gates for data in a TensorFlow 1.x graph.

Now, you simply declare tensors as variables and proceed to building your graph.

A *tensor* is a mathematical term that refers to generalized vectors or matrices. If vectors are one-dimensional and matrices are two-dimensional, a tensor is *n*-dimensional (where *n* could be 1, 2, or even larger).

We can declare these tensors as variables and use them for our computations. To do this, first, we must learn how to create tensors.

Getting ready

When we create a tensor and declare it as a variable, TensorFlow creates several graph structures in our computation graph. It is also important to point out that just by creating a tensor, TensorFlow is not adding anything to the computational graph. TensorFlow does this only after running an operation to initialize the variables. See the next section, on variables and placeholders, for more information.

How to do it...

Here, we will cover the four main ways in which we can create tensors in TensorFlow.

We will not be unnecessarily exhaustive in this recipe or others. We will tend to illustrate only the mandatory parameters of the different API calls, unless you might find it interesting for the recipe to cover any optional parameter; when that happens, we'll justify the reasoning behind it.

1. Fixed size tensors:
    - ❏ In the following code, we create a zero-filled tensor:
      ```
      row_dim, col_dim = 3, 3
      zero_tsr = tf.zeros(shape=[row_dim, col_dim], dtype=tf.float32)
      ```

❑ In the following code, we create a one-filled tensor:

```
ones_tsr = tf.ones([row_dim, col_dim])
```

❑ In the following code, we create a constant-filled tensor:

```
filled_tsr = tf.fill([row_dim, col_dim], 42)
```

❑ In the following code, we create a tensor out of an existing constant:

```
constant_tsr = tf.constant([1,2,3])
```

 Note that the `tf.constant()` function can be used to broadcast a value into an array, mimicking the behavior of `tf.fill()` by writing `tf.constant(42, [row_dim, col_dim])`.

2. **Tensors of similar shape**: We can also initialize variables based on the shape of other tensors, as follows:

```
zeros_similar = tf.zeros_like(constant_tsr)
ones_similar = tf.ones_like(constant_tsr)
```

 Note that since these tensors depend on prior tensors, we must initialize them in order. Attempting to initialize the tensors in a random order will result in an error.

3. **Sequence tensors**: In TensorFlow, all parameters are documented as tensors. Even when scalars are required, the API mentions these as zero-dimensional scalars. It won't therefore be a surprise that TensorFlow allows us to specify tensors that contain defined intervals. The following functions behave very similarly to NumPy's `linspace()` outputs and `range()` outputs (for reference: `https://docs.scipy.org/doc/numpy/reference/generated/numpy.linspace.html`). See the following function:

```
linear_tsr = tf.linspace(start=0.0, stop=1.0, num=3)
```

 Note that the start and stop parameters should be float values, and that num should be an integer.

The resultant tensor has a sequence of [0.0, 0.5, 1.0] (the `print(linear_tsr)` command will provide the necessary output). Note that this function includes the specified stop value. See the following `tf.range` function for comparison:

```
integer_seq_tsr = tf.range(start=6, limit=15, delta=3)
```

The result is the sequence [6, 9, 12]. Note that this function does not include the limit value and it can operate with both integer and float values for the start and limit parameters.

4. **Random tensors**: The following generated random numbers are from a uniform distribution:

```
randunif_tsr = tf.random.uniform([row_dim, col_dim],
                                  minval=0, maxval=1)
```

Note that this random uniform distribution draws from the interval that includes `minval` but not `maxval` (`minval <= x < maxval`). Therefore, in this case, the output range is [0, 1). If, instead, you need to draw only integers and not floats, just add the `dtype=tf.int32` parameter when calling the function.

To get a tensor with random draws from a normal distribution, you can run the following code:

```
randnorm_tsr = tf.random.normal([row_dim, col_dim],
                                mean=0.0, stddev=1.0)
```

There are also times where we want to generate normal random values that are assured within certain bounds. The `truncated_normal()` function always picks normal values within two standard deviations of the specified mean:

```
runcnorm_tsr = tf.random.truncated_normal([row_dim, col_dim],
                                          mean=0.0, stddev=1.0)
```

We might also be interested in randomizing entries of arrays. To accomplish this, two functions can help us: `random.shuffle()` and `image.random_crop()`. The following code performs this:

```
shuffled_output = tf.random.shuffle(input_tensor)
cropped_output = tf.image.random_crop(input_tensor, crop_size)
```

Later on in this book, we'll be interested in randomly cropping images of size (height, width, 3) where there are three-color spectrums. To fix a dimension in `cropped_output`, you must give it the maximum size in that dimension:

```
height, width = (64, 64)
my_image = tf.random.uniform([height, width, 3], minval=0,
        maxval=255, dtype=tf.int32)
cropped_image = tf.image.random_crop(my_image,
        [height//2, width//2, 3])
```

This code snippet will generate random noise images that will be cropped, halving both the height and width, but the depth dimension will be untouched because you fixed its maximum value as a parameter.

How it works...

Once we have decided how to create the tensors, we may also create the corresponding variables by wrapping the tensor in the `Variable()` function, as follows:

```
my_var = tf.Variable(tf.zeros([row_dim, col_dim]))
```

There's more on this in the following recipes.

There's more...

We are not limited to the built-in functions: we can convert any NumPy array into a Python list, or a constant into a tensor using the `convert_to_tensor()` function. Note that this function also accepts tensors as an input in case we wish to generalize a computation inside a function.

Using eager execution

When developing deep and complex neural networks, you need to continuously experiment with architectures and data. This proved difficult in TensorFlow 1.0 because you always need to run your code from the beginning to end in order to check whether it worked. TensorFlow 2.x works in eager execution mode as default, which means that you develop and check your code step by step as you progress into your project. This is great news; now we just have to understand how to experiment with eager execution, so we can use this TensorFlow 2.x feature to our advantage. This recipe will provide you with the basics to get started.

Getting ready

TensorFlow 1.x performed optimally because it executed its computations after compiling a static computational graph. All computations were distributed and connected into a graph as you compiled your network and that graph helped TensorFlow to execute computations, leveraging the available resources (multi-core CPUs of multiple GPUs) in the best way, and splitting operations between the resources in the most timely and efficient way. That also meant, in any case, that once you defined and compiled your graph, you could not change it at runtime but had to instantiate it from scratch, thereby incurring some extra work.

In TensorFlow 2.x, you can still define your network, compile it, and run it optimally, but the team of TensorFlow developers has now favored, by default, a more experimental approach, allowing immediate evaluation of operations, thus making it easier to debug and to try network variations. This is called eager execution. Operations now return concrete values instead of pointers to parts of a computational graph to be built later. More importantly, you can now have all the functionality of the host language available while your model is executing, making it easier to write more complex and sophisticated deep learning solutions.

How to do it...

You basically don't have to do anything; eager execution is the default way of operating in TensorFlow 2.x. When you import TensorFlow and start using its functions, you operate in eager execution since you can perform checks when executing:

```
tf.executing_eagerly()
True
```

That's all you need to do.

How it works...

Just run TensorFlow operations and the results will return immediately:

```
x = [[2.]]
m = tf.matmul(x, x)
print("the result is {}".format(m))
the result is [[4.]]
```

That's all there is to it!

There's more...

As TensorFlow is now set on eager execution as default, you won't be surprised to hear that tf.Session has been removed from the TensorFlow API. You no longer need to build a computational graph before running a computation; all you have to do now is build your network and test it along the way. This opens the road to common software best practices, such as documenting the code, using object-oriented programming when scripting your code, and organizing it into reusable self-contained modules.

Working with matrices

Understanding how TensorFlow works with matrices is very important when developing the flow of data through computational graphs. In this recipe, we will cover the creation of matrices and the basic operations that can be performed on them with TensorFlow.

It is worth emphasizing the importance of matrices in machine learning (and mathematics in general): machine learning algorithms are computationally expressed as matrix operations. Knowing how to perform matrix computations is a plus when working with TensorFlow, though you may not need it often; its high-end module, Keras, can deal with most of the matrix algebra stuff behind the scenes (more on Keras in *Chapter 3, Keras*).

This book does not cover the mathematical background on matrix properties and matrix algebra (linear algebra), so the unfamiliar reader is strongly encouraged to learn enough about matrices to be comfortable with matrix algebra. In the *See also* section, you can find a couple of resources to help you to revise your calculus skills or build them from scratch, and get even more out of TensorFlow.

Getting ready

Many algorithms depend on matrix operations. TensorFlow gives us easy-to-use operations to perform such matrix calculations. You just need to import TensorFlow and follow this section to the end; if you're not a matrix algebra expert, please first have a look at the *See also* section of this recipe for resources to help you to get the most out of the following recipe.

How to do it...

We proceed as follows:

1. **Creating matrices**: We can create two-dimensional matrices from NumPy arrays or nested lists, as described in the *Declaring and using variables and tensors* recipe at the beginning of this chapter. We can use the tensor creation functions and specify a two-dimensional shape for functions such as `zeros()`, `ones()`, and `truncated_normal()`. TensorFlow also allows us to create a diagonal matrix from a one-dimensional array or list using the `diag()` function, as follows:

```
identity_matrix = tf.linalg.diag([1.0, 1.0, 1.0])
A = tf.random.truncated_normal([2, 3])
B = tf.fill([2,3], 5.0)
C = tf.random.uniform([3,2])
D = tf.convert_to_tensor(np.array([[1., 2., 3.],
                                   [-3., -7., -1.],
                                   [0., 5., -2.]]),
                         dtype=tf.float32)

print(identity_matrix)

[[ 1.  0.  0.]
 [ 0.  1.  0.]
 [ 0.  0.  1.]]

print(A)

[[ 0.96751703  0.11397751 -0.3438891 ]
 [-0.10132604 -0.8432678   0.29810596]]
```

```
print(B)

[[ 5.   5.   5.]
 [ 5.   5.   5.]]

print(C)

[[ 0.33184157  0.08907614]
 [ 0.53189191  0.67605299]
 [ 0.95889051 0.67061249]]
```

 Please note that the C tensor is created in a random way, and it will probably differ in your session from what is represented in this book.

```
print(D)

[[ 1.   2.   3.]
 [-3. -7. -1.]
 [ 0.   5. -2.]]
```

2. **Addition, subtraction, and multiplication**: To add, subtract, or multiply matrices of the same dimension, TensorFlow uses the following function:

```
print(A+B)

[[ 4.61596632  5.39771316  4.4325695 ]
 [ 3.26702736  5.14477345  4.98265553]]

print(B-B)

[[ 0.   0.   0.]
 [ 0.   0.   0.]]

print(tf.matmul(B, identity_matrix))

[[ 5.   5.   5.]
 [ 5.   5.   5.]]
```

It is important to note that the `matmul()` function has arguments that specify whether or not to transpose the arguments before multiplication (the Boolean parameters, `transpose_a` and `transpose_b`), or whether each matrix is sparse (`a_is_sparse` and `b_is_sparse`).

If, instead, you need element-wise multiplication between two matrices of the same shape and type (this is very important or you will get an error), you just use the `tf.multiply` function:

```
print(tf.multiply(D, identity_matrix))

[[ 1.  0.  0.]
 [-0. -7. -0.]
 [ 0.  0. -2.]]
```

 Note that matrix division is not explicitly defined. While many define matrix division as multiplying by the inverse, it is fundamentally different from real-numbered division.

3. **The transpose**: Transpose a matrix (flip the columns and rows) as follows:

```
print(tf.transpose(C))

[[0.33184157 0.53189191 0.95889051]
 [0.08907614 0.67605299 0.67061249]]
```

Again, it is worth mentioning that reinitializing gives us different values than before.

4. **Determinant:** To calculate the determinant, use the following code:

```
print(tf.linalg.det(D))

-38.0
```

5. **Inverse**: To find the inverse of a square matrix, see the following:

```
print(tf.linalg.inv(D))

[[-0.5        -0.5        -0.5       ]
 [ 0.15789474  0.05263158  0.21052632]
 [ 0.39473684  0.13157895  0.02631579]]
```

The inverse method is based on Cholesky decomposition only if the matrix is symmetric positive definite. If the matrix is not symmetric positive definite, then it is based on LU decomposition.

6. **Decompositions**: For Cholesky decomposition, use the following code:

```
print(tf.linalg.cholesky(identity_matrix))

[[ 1.  0.  1.]
 [ 0.  1.  0.]
 [ 0.  0.  1.]]
```

7. **Eigenvalues and eigenvectors**: For eigenvalues and eigenvectors, use the following code:

```
print(tf.linalg.eigh(D))

[[-10.65907521  -0.22750691   2.88658212]
 [  0.21749542   0.63250104  -0.74339638]
 [  0.84526515   0.2587998    0.46749277]
 [ -0.4880805    0.73004459   0.47834331]]
```

Note that the `tf.linalg.eigh()` function outputs two tensors: in the first, you find the **eigenvalues** and, in the second tensor, you have the **eigenvectors**. In mathematics, such an operation is known as the **eigendecomposition** of a matrix.

How it works...

TensorFlow provides all the tools for us to get started with numerical computations and adding these computations to our neural networks.

See also

If you need to build your calculus skills quickly and understand more about TensorFlow operations, we suggest the following resources:

▶ The free book *Mathematics for Machine Learning*, which can be found here: `https://mml-book.github.io/`. This contains everything you need to know if you want to operate successfully with machine learning in general.

▶ For an even more accessible source, watch the lessons about vectors and matrices from the Kahn Academy (`https://www.khanacademy.org/math/precalculus`) to get to work with the most basic data elements of a neural network.

Declaring operations

Apart from matrix operations, there are hosts of other TensorFlow operations we must at least be aware of. This recipe will provide you with a quick and essential glance at what you really need to know.

Getting ready

Besides the standard arithmetic operations, TensorFlow provides us with more operations that we should be aware of. We should acknowledge them and learn how to use them before proceeding. Again, we just import TensorFlow:

```
import tensorflow as tf
```

Now we're ready to run the code to be found in the following section.

How to do it...

TensorFlow has the standard operations on tensors, that is, `add()`, `subtract()`, `multiply()`, and `division()` in its `math` module. Note that all of the operations in this section will evaluate the inputs elementwise, unless specified otherwise:

1. TensorFlow provides some variations of `division()` and the relevant functions.

2. It is worth mentioning that `division()` returns the same type as the inputs. This means that it really returns the floor of the division (akin to Python 2) if the inputs are integers. To return the Python 3 version, which casts integers into floats before dividing and always returns a float, TensorFlow provides the `truediv()` function, as follows:

    ```
    print(tf.math.divide(3, 4))

    0.75

    print(tf.math.truediv(3, 4))

    tf.Tensor(0.75, shape=(), dtype=float64)
    ```

3. If we have floats and want integer division, we can use the `floordiv()` function. Note that this will still return a float, but it will be rounded down to the nearest integer. This function is as follows:

    ```
    print(tf.math.floordiv(3.0,4.0))

    tf.Tensor(0.0, shape=(), dtype=float32)
    ```

4. Another important function is mod(). This function returns the remainder after division. It is as follows:

```
print(tf.math.mod(22.0, 5.0))


tf.Tensor(2.0, shape=(), dtype=float32)
```

5. The cross product between two tensors is achieved by the cross() function. Remember that the cross product is only defined for two three-dimensional vectors, so it only accepts two three-dimensional tensors. The following code illustrates this use:

```
print(tf.linalg.cross([1., 0., 0.], [0., 1., 0.]))


tf.Tensor([0. 0. 1.], shape=(3,), dtype=float32)
```

6. Here's a compact list of the more common math functions. All of these functions operate elementwise:

Function	Operation
tf.math.abs()	Absolute value of one input tensor
tf.math.ceil()	Ceiling function of one input tensor
tf.math.cos()	Cosine function of one input tensor
tf.math.exp()	Base e exponential of one input tensor
tf.math.floor()	Floor function of one input tensor
tf.linalg.inv()	Multiplicative inverse (1/x) of one input tensor
tf.math.log()	Natural logarithm of one input tensor
tf.math.maximum()	Elementwise maximum of two tensors
tf.math.minimum()	Elementwise minimum of two tensors
tf.math.negative()	Negative of one input tensor
tf.math.pow()	The first tensor raised to the second tensor elementwise
tf.math.round()	Rounds one input tensor
tf.math.rsqrt()	The reciprocal of the square root of one tensor
tf.math.sign()	Returns -1, 0, or 1, depending on the sign of the tensor
tf.math.sin()	Sine function of one input tensor
tf.math.sqrt()	Square root of one input tensor
tf.math.square()	Square of one input tensor

7. **Specialty mathematical functions**: There are some special math functions that are often used in machine learning that are worth mentioning, and TensorFlow has built-in functions for them. Again, these functions operate elementwise, unless specified otherwise:

`tf.math.digamma()`	Psi function, the derivative of the `lgamma()` function
`tf.math.erf()`	Gaussian error function, element-wise, of one tensor
`tf.math.erfc()`	Complementary error function of one tensor
`tf.math.igamma()`	Lower regularized incomplete gamma function
`tf.math.igammac()`	Upper regularized incomplete gamma function
`tf.math.lbeta()`	Natural logarithm of the absolute value of the beta function
`tf.math.lgamma()`	Natural logarithm of the absolute value of the gamma function
`tf.math.squared_difference()`	Computes the square of the differences between two tensors

How it works...

It is important to know which functions are available to us so that we can add them to our computational graphs. We will mainly be concerned with the preceding functions. We can also generate many different custom functions as compositions of the preceding, as follows:

```
# Tangent function (tan(pi/4)=1)
def pi_tan(x):
    return tf.tan(3.1416/x)


print(pi_tan(4))


tf.Tensor(1.0000036, shape=(), dtype=float32)
```

The complex layers that constitute a deep neural network are just composed of the preceding functions, so now, thanks to this recipe, you have all the basics you need to create anything you want.

There's more...

If we wish to add other operations to our graphs that are not listed here, we must create our own from the preceding functions. Here is an example of an operation that wasn't used previously that we can add to our graph. We can add a custom polynomial function, *3 * x^2 - x + 10*, using the following code:

```
def custom_polynomial(value):
    return tf.math.subtract(3 * tf.math.square(value), value) + 10
print(custom_polynomial(11))


tf.Tensor(362, shape=(), dtype=int32)
```

There's no limit to the custom functions you can create now, though I always recommend that you first consult the TensorFlow documentation. Often, you don't need to reinvent the wheel; you can find that what you need has already been coded.

Implementing activation functions

Activation functions are the key for neural networks to approximate non-linear outputs and adapt to non-linear features. They introduce non-linear operations into neural networks. If we're careful as to which activation functions are selected and where we put them, they're very powerful operations that we can tell TensorFlow to fit and optimize.

Getting ready

When we start to use neural networks, we'll use activation functions regularly because activation functions are an essential part of any neural network. The goal of an activation function is just to adjust weight and bias. In TensorFlow, activation functions are non-linear operations that act on tensors. They are functions that operate in a similar way to the previous mathematical operations. Activation functions serve many purposes, but the main concept is that they introduce a non-linearity into the graph while normalizing the outputs.

How to do it...

The activation functions live in the **neural network** (**nn**) library in TensorFlow. Besides using built-in activation functions, we can also design our own using TensorFlow operations. We can import the predefined activation functions (from `tensorflow import nn`) or be explicit and write nn in our function calls. Here, we'll choose to be explicit with each function call:

1. The rectified linear unit, known as ReLU, is the most common and basic way to introduce non-linearity into neural networks. This function is just called $max(0,x)$. It is continuous, but not smooth. It appears as follows:

    ```
    print(tf.nn.relu([-3., 3., 10.]))


    tf.Tensor([ 0.  3. 10.], shape=(3,), dtype=float32)
    ```

2. There are times where we'll want to cap the linearly increasing part of the preceding ReLU activation function. We can do this by nesting the `max(0,x)` function in a `min()` function. The implementation that TensorFlow has is called the ReLU6 function. This is defined as `min(max(0,x),6)`. This is a version of the hard-sigmoid function, is computationally faster, and does not suffer from vanishing (infinitesimally near zero) or exploding values. This will come in handy when we discuss deeper neural networks in later chapters on convolutional neural networks and recurrent ones. It appears as follows:

```
print(tf.nn.relu6([-3., 3., 10.]))

tf.Tensor([ 0.  3. 6.], shape=(3,), dtype=float32)
```

3. The sigmoid function is the most common continuous and smooth activation function. It is also called a logistic function and has the form *1 / (1 + exp(-x))*. The sigmoid function is not used very often because of its tendency to zero-out the backpropagation terms during training. It appears as follows:

```
print(tf.nn.sigmoid([-1., 0., 1.]))

tf.Tensor([0.26894143 0.5 0.7310586 ], shape=(3,), dtype=float32)
```

 We should be aware that some activation functions, such as the sigmoid, are not zero-centered. This will require us to zero-mean data prior to using it in most computational graph algorithms.

4. Another smooth activation function is the hyper tangent. The hyper tangent function is very similar to the sigmoid except that instead of having a range between 0 and 1, it has a range between -1 and 1. This function has the form of the ratio of the hyperbolic sine over the hyperbolic cosine. Another way to write this is as follows:

```
((exp(x) - exp(-x))/(exp(x) + exp(-x))
```

This activation function is as follows:

```
print(tf.nn.tanh([-1., 0., 1.]))

tf.Tensor([-0.7615942  0. 0.7615942], shape=(3,), dtype=float32)
```

5. The `softsign` function is also used as an activation function. The form of this function is *x/(|x| + 1)*. The `softsign` function is supposed to be a continuous (but not smooth) approximation to the sign function. See the following code:

```
print(tf.nn.softsign([-1., 0., -1.]))

tf.Tensor([-0.5 0.  -0.5], shape=(3,), dtype=float32)
```

6. Another function, the `softplus` function, is a smooth version of the ReLU function. The form of this function is *log(exp(x) + 1)*. It appears as follows:

```
print(tf.nn.softplus([-1., 0., -1.]))

tf.Tensor([0.31326166 0.6931472  0.31326166], shape=(3,),
dtype=float32)
```

 The `softplus` function goes to infinity as the input increases, whereas the `softsign` function goes to 1. As the input gets smaller, however, the `softplus` function approaches zero and the `softsign` function goes to -1.

7. The **Exponential Linear Unit** (**ELU**) is very similar to the softplus function except that the bottom asymptote is -1 instead of 0. The form is *(exp(x) + 1)* if *x < 0*, else *x*. It appears as follows:

```
print(tf.nn.elu([-1., 0., -1.]))

tf.Tensor([-0.63212055 0. -0.63212055], shape=(3,), dtype=float32)
```

8. Now, from this recipe, you should understand the basic key activations. Our list of the existing activation functions is not exhaustive, and you may discover that for certain problems, you need to try some of the lesser known among them. Apart from the activations from this recipe, you can find even more activations on the Keras activation pages: `https://www.tensorflow.org/api_docs/python/tf/keras/activations`

How it works...

These activation functions are ways that we can introduce non-linearity in neural networks or other computational graphs in the future. It is important to note where in our network we are using activation functions. If the activation function has a range between 0 and 1 (sigmoid), then the computational graph can only output values between 0 and 1. If the activation functions are inside and hidden between nodes, then we want to be aware of the effect that the range can have on our tensors as we pass them through. If our tensors were scaled to have a mean of zero, we will want to use an activation function that preserves as much variance as possible around zero.

This would imply that we want to choose an activation function such as the **hyperbolic tangent** (**tanh**) or the **softsign**. If the tensors were all scaled to be positive, then we would ideally choose an activation function that preserves variance in the positive domain.

There's more...

We can even easily create custom activations such as the Swish, which is $x*sigmoid(x)$ (see *Swish: a Self-Gated Activation Function*, Ramachandran et al., 2017, `https://arxiv.org/abs/1710.05941`), which can be used as a more performing replacement for ReLU activations in image and tabular data problems:

```
def swish(x):
    return x * tf.nn.sigmoid(x)

print(swish([-1., 0., 1.]))

tf.Tensor([-0.26894143  0.  0.7310586 ], shape=(3,), dtype=float32)
```

After having tried the activations proposed by TensorFlow, your next natural step will be to replicate the ones you find on deep learning papers or that you create by yourself.

Working with data sources

For most of this book, we will rely on the use of datasets to fit machine learning algorithms. This section has instructions on how to access each of these datasets through TensorFlow and Python.

 Some of the data sources rely on the maintenance of outside websites so that you can access the data. If these websites change or remove this data, then some of the following code in this section may need to be updated. You can find the updated code on this book's GitHub page:

`https://github.com/PacktPublishing/Machine-Learning-Using-TensorFlow-Cookbook`

Getting ready

Throughout the book, the majority of the datasets that we will be using are accessible using TensorFlow Datasets, whereas some others will require some extra effort by using a Python script to download, or by manually downloading them through the internet.

TensorFlow Datasets (**TFDS**) is a collection of datasets ready to use (you can find the complete list here: `https://www.tensorflow.org/datasets/catalog/overview`). It automatically handles downloading and preparation of the data and, being a wrapper around `tf.data`, constructs efficient and fast data pipelines.

In order to install TFDS, just run the following installation command on your console:

```
pip install tensorflow-datasets
```

We can now move on to explore the core datasets that you will be using in this book (not all of these datasets are included here, just the most common ones. Some other very specific datasets will be introduced in different chapters throughout the book).

How to do it...

1. **Iris data**: This dataset is arguably the classic structured dataset used in machine learning and perhaps in all examples of statistics. It is a dataset that measures sepal length, sepal width, petal length, and petal width of three different types of iris flowers: *Iris setosa, Iris virginica,* and *Iris versicolor*. There are 150 measurements in total, which means that there are 50 measurements for each species. To load the dataset in Python, we will use TFDS functions, as follows:

```
import tensorflow_datasets as tfds
iris = tfds.load('iris', split='train')
```

 When you are importing a dataset for the first time, a bar will point out where you are as you download the dataset. If you prefer, you can deactivate it if you type the following:

```
tfds.disable_progress_bar()
```

2. **Birth weight data**: This data was originally from Baystate Medical Center, Springfield, Mass, 1986. This dataset contains measurements including childbirth weight and other demographic and medical measurements of the mother and the family history. There are 189 observations of eleven variables. The following code shows you how you can access this data as `tf.data.dataset`:

```
import tensorflow_datasets as tfds

birthdata_url = 'https://raw.githubusercontent.com/PacktPublishing/
TensorFlow-2-Machine-Learning-Cookbook-Third-Edition/master/
birthweight.dat'
path = tf.keras.utils.get_file(birthdata_url.split("/")[-1],
birthdata_url)

def map_line(x):
```

```
        return tf.strings.to_number(tf.strings.split(x))


birth_file = (tf.data
                .TextLineDataset(path)
                .skip(1)      # Skip first header line
                .map(map_line)
              )
```

3. **Boston housing data**: Carnegie Mellon University maintains a library of datasets in their `StatLib` Library. This data is easily accessible via The University of California at Irvine's machine learning repository (`https://archive.ics.uci.edu/ml/index.php`). There are 506 observations of house worth, along with various demographic data and housing attributes (14 variables). The following code shows you how to access this data in TensorFlow:

```
import tensorflow_datasets as tfds


housing_url = 'http://archive.ics.uci.edu/ml/machine-learning-
databases/housing/housing.data'
path = tf.keras.utils.get_file(housing_url.split("/")[-1], housing_
url)


def map_line(x):
    return tf.strings.to_number(tf.strings.split(x))


housing = (tf.data
              .TextLineDataset(path)
              .map(map_line)
           )
```

4. **MNIST handwriting data**: The **Mixed National Institute of Standards and Technology** (**MNIST**) dataset is a subset of the larger NIST handwriting database. The MNIST handwriting dataset is hosted on Yann LeCun's website (`http://yann.lecun.com/exdb/mnist/`). It is a database of 70,000 images of single-digit numbers (0-9), with about 60,000 annotated for a training set and 10,000 for a test set. This dataset is used so often in image recognition that TensorFlow provides built-in functions to access this data. In machine learning, it is also important to provide validation data to prevent overfitting (target leakage). Because of this, TensorFlow sets aside 5,000 images of the training set in a validation set. The following code shows you how to access this data in TensorFlow:

```
import tensorflow_datasets as tfds


mnist = tfds.load('mnist', split=None)
mnist_train = mnist['train']
mnist_test = mnist['test']
```

5. **Spam-ham text data**. UCI's machine learning dataset library also holds a spam-ham text message dataset. We can access this `.zip` file and get the spam-ham text data as follows:

```
import tensorflow_datasets as tfds


zip_url = 'http://archive.ics.uci.edu/ml/machine-learning-
databases/00228/smsspamcollection.zip'
path = tf.keras.utils.get_file(zip_url.split("/")[-1], zip_url,
extract=True)


path = path.replace("smsspamcollection.zip", "SMSSpamCollection")


def split_text(x):
    return tf.strings.split(x, sep='\t')


text_data = (tf.data
                .TextLineDataset(path)
                .map(split_text)
             )
```

6. **Movie review data**: Bo Pang from Cornell has released a movie review dataset that classifies reviews as good or bad. You can find the data on the Cornell University website: http://www.cs.cornell.edu/people/pabo/movie-review-data/. To download, extract, and transform this data, we can run the following code:

```
import tensorflow_datasets as tfds


movie_data_url = 'http://www.cs.cornell.edu/people/pabo/movie-
review-data/rt-polaritydata.tar.gz'
path = tf.keras.utils.get_file(movie_data_url.split("/")[-1], movie_
data_url, extract=True)


path = path.replace('.tar.gz', '')


with open(path+filename, 'r', encoding='utf-8', errors='ignore') as
movie_file:
    for response, filename in enumerate(['\\rt-polarity.neg', '\\rt-
polarity.pos']):
        with open(path+filename, 'r') as movie_file:
            for line in movie_file:
                review_file.write(str(response) + '\t' + line.
encode('utf-8').decode())


def split_text(x):
    return tf.strings.split(x, sep='\t')
```

```
movies = (tf.data
          .TextLineDataset('movie_reviews.txt')
          .map(split_text)
          )
```

7. **CIFAR-10 image data**: The Canadian Institute for Advanced Research has released an image set that contains 80 million labeled colored images (each image is scaled to 32 x 32 pixels). There are 10 different target classes (airplane, automobile, bird, and so on). CIFAR-10 is a subset that includes 60,000 images. There are 50,000 images in the training set, and 10,000 in the test set. Since we will be using this dataset in multiple ways, and because it is one of our larger datasets, we will not run a script each time we need it. To get this dataset, just execute the following code to download the CIFAR-10 dataset (this may take a long time):

```
import tensorflow_datasets as tfds

ds, info = tfds.load('cifar10', shuffle_files=True, with_info=True)

print(info)

cifar_train = ds['train']
cifar_test = ds['test']
```

8. **The works of Shakespeare text data**: Project Gutenberg is a project that releases electronic versions of free books. They have compiled all of the works of Shakespeare together. The following code shows you how to access this text file through TensorFlow:

```
import tensorflow_datasets as tfds

shakespeare_url = 'https://raw.githubusercontent.com/
PacktPublishing/TensorFlow-2-Machine-Learning-Cookbook-Third-
Edition/master/shakespeare.txt'
path = tf.keras.utils.get_file(shakespeare_url.split("/")[-1],
shakespeare_url)

def split_text(x):
    return tf.strings.split(x, sep='\n')

shakespeare_text = (tf.data
                    .TextLineDataset(path)
                    .map(split_text)
                    )
```

9. **English-German sentence translation data**: The Tatoeba project (http://tatoeba.org) collects sentence translations in many languages. Their data has been released under the Creative Commons license. From this data, ManyThings.org (http://www.manythings.org) has compiled sentence-to-sentence translations in text files that are available for download. Here, we will use the English-German translation file, but you can change the URL to whichever languages you would like to use:

```python
import os
import pandas as pd
from zipfile import ZipFile
from urllib.request import urlopen, Request
import tensorflow_datasets as tfds

sentence_url = 'https://www.manythings.org/anki/deu-eng.zip'

r = Request(sentence_url, headers={'User-Agent': 'Mozilla/5.0 (X11;
U; Linux i686) Gecko/20071127 Firefox/2.0.0.11'})
b2 = [z for z in sentence_url.split('/') if '.zip' in z][0] #gets
just the '.zip' part of the url

with open(b2, "wb") as target:
    target.write(urlopen(r).read()) #saves to file to disk

with ZipFile(b2) as z:
    deu = [line.split('\t')[:2] for line in z.open('deu.txt').
read().decode().split('\n')]

os.remove(b2) #removes the zip file

# saving to disk prepared en-de sentence file
with open("deu.txt", "wb") as deu_file:
    for line in deu:
        data = ",".join(line)+'\n'
        deu_file.write(data.encode('utf-8'))

def split_text(x):
    return tf.strings.split(x, sep=',')

text_data = (tf.data
            .TextLineDataset("deu.txt")
            .map(split_text)
            )
```

With this last dataset, we have completed our review of the datasets that you will most frequently encounter when using the recipes you will find in this book. At the start of each recipe, we'll remind you how to download the relevant dataset and explain why it is relevant for the recipe in question.

How it works...

When it comes to using one of these datasets in a recipe, we'll refer you to this section and assume that the data is loaded in the ways we've just described. If further data transformation or preprocessing is necessary, then that code will be provided in the recipe itself.

Usually, the approach will simply be as follows when we use data from TensorFlow datasets:

```
import tensorflow_datasets as tfds

dataset_name = "..."
data = tfds.load(dataset_name, split=None)
train = data['train']
test = data['test']
```

In any case, depending on the location of the data, it may turn out to be necessary to download it, extract it, and transform it.

See also

Here are some additional references for the data resources we use in this book:

▶ Hosmer, D.W., Lemeshow, S., and Sturdivant, R. X. (2013) *Applied Logistic Regression: 3rd Edition*

▶ Lichman, M. (2013). *UCI machine learning repository*: http://archive.ics.uci.edu/ml. Irvine, CA: University of California, School of Information and Computer Science

▶ Bo Pang, Lillian Lee, and Shivakumar Vaithyanathan, *Thumbs up? Sentiment classification using machine learning techniques*, Proceedings of EMNLP 2002: http://www.cs.cornell.edu/people/pabo/movie-review-data/

▶ Krizhevsky. (2009). *Learning Multiple Layers of Features from Tiny Images*: http://www.cs.toronto.edu/~kriz/cifar.html

▶ *Project Gutenberg. Accessed* April 2016: http://www.gutenberg.org/

Additional resources

In this section, you will find additional links, documentation sources, and tutorials that will be of great assistance when learning and using TensorFlow.

Getting ready

When learning how to use TensorFlow, it helps to know where to turn for assistance or pointers. This section lists some resources to get TensorFlow running and to troubleshoot problems.

How to do it...

Here is a list of TensorFlow resources:

- ▶ The code for this book is available online at the Packt repository: `https://github.com/PacktPublishing/Machine-Learning-Using-TensorFlow-Cookbook`

- ▶ The official TensorFlow Python API documentation is located at `https://www.tensorflow.org/api_docs/python`. Here, there is documentation and examples of all of the functions, objects, and methods in TensorFlow.

- ▶ TensorFlow's official tutorials are very thorough and detailed. They are located at `https://www.tensorflow.org/tutorials/index.html`. They start covering image recognition models, and work through Word2Vec, RNN models, and sequence-to-sequence models. They also have additional tutorials for generating fractals and solving PDE systems. Note that they are continually adding more tutorials and examples to this collection.

- ▶ TensorFlow's official GitHub repository is available via `https://github.com/tensorflow/tensorflow`. Here, you can view the open source code and even fork or clone the most current version of the code if you want. You can also see current filed issues if you navigate to the `issues` directory.

- ▶ A public Docker container that is kept up to date by TensorFlow is available on Dockerhub at `https://hub.docker.com/r/tensorflow/tensorflow/`.

- ▶ A great source for community help is Stack Overflow. There is a tag for TensorFlow. This tag seems to be growing in interest as TensorFlow is gaining in popularity. To view activity on this tag, visit `http://stackoverflow.com/questions/tagged/Tensorflow`.

▶ While TensorFlow is very agile and can be used for many things, the most common use of TensorFlow is deep learning. To understand the basis of deep learning, how the underlying mathematics works, and to develop more intuition on deep learning, Google has created an online course that's available on Udacity. To sign up and take this video lecture course, visit `https://www.udacity.com/course/deep-learning--ud730`.

▶ TensorFlow has also made a site where you can visually explore training a neural network while changing the parameters and datasets. Visit `http://playground.tensorflow.org/` to explore how different settings affect the training of neural networks.

▶ Andrew Ng teaches an online course called Neural Networks and Deep Learning : `https://www.coursera.org/learn/neural-networks-deep-learning`

▶ Stanford University has an online syllabus and detailed course notes for *Convolutional Neural Networks for Visual Recognition*: `http://cs231n.stanford.edu/`

2

The TensorFlow Way

In *Chapter 1, Getting Started with TensorFlow 2.x* we introduced how TensorFlow creates tensors and uses variables. In this chapter, we'll introduce how to put together all these objects using eager execution, thus dynamically setting up a computational graph. From this, we can set up a simple classifier and see how well it performs.

 Also, remember that the current and updated code from this book is available online on GitHub at https://github.com/PacktPublishing/Machine-Learning-Using-TensorFlow-Cookbook.

Over the course of this chapter, we'll introduce the key components of how TensorFlow operates. Then, we'll tie it together to create a simple classifier and evaluate the outcomes. By the end of the chapter, you should have learned about the following:

- ▶ Operations using eager execution
- ▶ Layering nested operations
- ▶ Working with multiple layers
- ▶ Implementing loss functions
- ▶ Implementing backpropagation
- ▶ Working with batch and stochastic training
- ▶ Combining everything together

Let's start working our way through more and more complex recipes, demonstrating the TensorFlow way of handling and solving data problems.

Operations using eager execution

Thanks to *Chapter 1*, Getting Started with TensorFlow 2.x we can already create objects such as variables in TensorFlow. Now we will introduce operations that act on such objects. In order to do so, we'll return to eager execution with a new basic recipe showing how to manipulate matrices. This recipe, and the following ones, are still basic ones, but over the course of the chapter, we'll combine these basic recipes into more complex ones.

Getting ready

To start, we load TensorFlow and NumPy, as follows:

```
import TensorFlow as tf
import NumPy as np
```

That's all we need to get started; now we can proceed.

How to do it...

In this example, we'll use what we have learned so far, and send each number in a list to be computed by TensorFlow commands and print the output.

First, we declare our tensors and variables. Here, out of all the various ways we could feed data into the variable using TensorFlow, we will create a NumPy array to feed into our variable and then use it for our operation:

```
x_vals = np.array([1., 3., 5., 7., 9.])
x_data = tf.Variable(x_vals, dtype=tf.float32)
m_const = tf.constant(3.)
operation = tf.multiply(x_data, m_const)
for result in operation:
    print(result.NumPy())
```

The output of the preceding code is as follows:

```
3.0
9.0
15.0
21.0
27.0
```

Once you get accustomed to working with TensorFlow variables, constants, and functions, it will become natural to start from NumPy array data, progress to scripting data structures and operations, and test their results as you go.

How it works...

Using eager execution, TensorFlow immediately evaluates the operation values, instead of manipulating the symbolic handles referred to the nodes of a computational graph to be later compiled and executed. You can therefore just iterate through the results of the multiplicative operation and print the resulting values using the `.NumPy` method, which returns a NumPy object from a TensorFlow tensor.

Layering nested operations

In this recipe, we'll learn how to put multiple operations to work; it is important to know how to chain operations together. This will set up layered operations to be executed by our network. In this recipe, we will multiply a placeholder by two matrices and then perform addition. We will feed in two matrices in the form of a three-dimensional NumPy array.

This is another easy-peasy recipe to give you ideas about how to code in TensorFlow using common constructs such as functions or classes, improving readability and code modularity. Even if the final product is a neural network, we're still writing a computer program, and we should abide by programming best practices.

Getting ready

As usual, we just need to import TensorFlow and NumPy, as follows:

```
import TensorFlow as tf
import NumPy as np
```

We're now ready to move forward with our recipe.

How to do it...

We will feed in two NumPy arrays of size *3* x *5*. We will multiply each matrix by a constant of size *5* x *1,* which will result in a matrix of size *3* x *1*. We will then multiply this by a *1* x *1* matrix resulting in a *3* x *1* matrix again. Finally, we add a *3* x *1* matrix at the end, as follows:

1. First, we create the data to feed in and the corresponding placeholder:

```
my_array = np.array([[1., 3., 5., 7., 9.],
                     [-2., 0., 2., 4., 6.],
                     [-6., -3., 0., 3., 6.]])
x_vals = np.array([my_array, my_array + 1])
x_data = tf.Variable(x_vals, dtype=tf.float32)
```

2. Next, we create the constants that we will use for matrix multiplication and addition:

```
m1 = tf.constant([[1.], [0.], [-1.], [2.], [4.]])
m2 = tf.constant([[2.]])
a1 = tf.constant([[10.]])
```

3. Now, we declare the operations to be eagerly executed. As good practice, we create functions that execute the operations we need:

```
def prod1(a, b):
    return tf.matmul(a, b)

def prod2(a, b):
    return tf.matmul(a, b)

def add1(a, b):
    return tf.add(a, b)
```

4. Finally, we nest our functions and display the result:

```
result = add1(prod2(prod1(x_data, m1), m2), a1)
print(result.NumPy())

[[ 102.]
 [  66.]
 [  58.]]
[[ 114.]
 [  78.]
 [  70.]]
```

Using functions (and also classes, as we are going to cover) will help you write clearer code. That makes debugging more effective and allows easy maintenance and reuse of code.

How it works...

Thanks to eager execution, there's no longer a need to resort to the "kitchen sink" programming style (meaning that you put almost everything in the global scope of the program; see https://stackoverflow.com/questions/33779296/what-is-exact-meaning-of-kitchen-sink-in-programming) that was so common when using TensorFlow 1.x. At the moment, you can adopt either a functional programming style or an object-oriented one, such as the one we present in this brief example, where you can arrange all your operations and computations in a more logical and understandable way:

```
class Operations():
    def __init__(self, a):
        self.result = a
```

```
    def apply(self, func, b):
        self.result = func(self.result, b)
        return self

operation = (Operations(a=x_data)
                .apply(prod1, b=m1)
                .apply(prod2, b=m2)
                .apply(add1, b=a1))


print(operation.result.NumPy())
```

Classes can help you organize your code and reuse it better than functions, thanks to class inheritance.

There's more...

In all the examples in this recipe, we've had to declare the data shape and know the outcome shape of the operations before we run the data through the operations. This is not always the case. There may be a dimension or two that we do not know beforehand or some that can vary during our data processing. To take this into account, we designate the dimension or dimensions that can vary (or are unknown) as value **None**.

For example, to initialize a variable to have an unknown amount of rows, we would write the following line and then we can assign values of arbitrary row numbers:

```
v = tf.Variable(initial_value=tf.random.normal(shape=(1, 5)),
                shape=tf.TensorShape((None, 5)))


v.assign(tf.random.normal(shape=(10, 5)))
```

It is fine for matrix multiplication to have flexible rows because that won't affect the arrangement of our operations. This will come in handy in later chapters when we are feeding data in multiple batches of varying batch sizes.

> While the use of *None* as a dimension allows us to use variably-sized dimensions, I always recommend that you be as explicit as possible when filling out dimensions. If the size of our data is known in advance, then we should explicitly write that size as the dimensions. The use of **None** as a dimension is recommended to be limited to the batch size of the data (or however many data points we are computing on at once).

Working with multiple layers

Now that we have covered multiple operations, we will cover how to connect various layers that have data propagating through them. In this recipe, we will introduce how to best connect various layers, including custom layers. The data we will generate and use will be representative of small random images. It is best to understand this type of operation with a simple example and see how we can use some built-in layers to perform calculations. The first layer we will explore is called a **moving window**. We will perform a small moving window average across a 2D image and then the second layer will be a custom operation layer.

Moving windows are useful for everything related to time series. Though there are layers specialized for sequences, a moving window may prove useful when you are analyzing, for instance, MRI scans (neuroimages) or sound spectrograms.

Moreover, we will see that the computational graph can get large and hard to look at. To address this, we will also introduce ways to name operations and create scopes for layers.

Getting ready

To start, you have to load the usual packages – NumPy and TensorFlow – using the following:

```
import TensorFlow as tf
import NumPy as np
```

Let's now progress to the recipe. This time things are getting more complex and interesting.

How to do it...

We proceed with the recipe as follows.

First, we create our sample 2D image with NumPy. This image will be a *4 x 4* pixel image. We will create it in four dimensions; the first and last dimensions will have a size of 1 (we keep the batch dimension distinct, so you can experiment with changing its size). Note that some TensorFlow image functions will operate on four-dimensional images. Those four dimensions are image number, height, width, and channel, and to make it work with one channel, we explicitly set the last dimension to 1, as follows:

```
batch_size = [1]
x_shape = [4, 4, 1]
x_data = tf.random.uniform(shape=batch_size + x_shape)
```

To create a moving window average across our *4 x 4* image, we will use a built-in function that will convolute a constant across a window of the shape *2 x 2*. The function we will use is conv2d(); this function is quite commonly used in image processing and in TensorFlow.

This function takes a piecewise product of the window and a filter we specify. We must also specify a stride for the moving window in both directions. Here, we will compute four moving window averages: the upper-left, upper-right, lower-left, and lower-right four pixels. We do this by creating a *2 x 2* window and having strides of length 2 in each direction. To take the average, we will convolute the *2 x 2* window with a constant of 0.25, as follows:

```
def mov_avg_layer(x):
    my_filter = tf.constant(0.25, shape=[2, 2, 1, 1])
    my_strides = [1, 2, 2, 1]
    layer = tf.nn.conv2d(x, my_filter, my_strides,
                         padding='SAME', name='Moving_Avg_Window')
    return layer
```

Note that we are also naming this layer `Moving_Avg_Window` by using the name argument of the function.

To figure out the output size of a convolutional layer, we can use the following formula: Output = $(W – F + 2P)/S + 1)$, where W is the input size, F is the filter size, P is the padding of zeros, and S is the stride.

Now, we define a custom layer that will operate on the *2 x 2* output of the moving window average. The custom function will first multiply the input by another *2 x 2* matrix tensor, and then add 1 to each entry. After this, we take the sigmoid of each element and return the *2 x 2* matrix. Since matrix multiplication only operates on two-dimensional matrices, we need to drop the extra dimensions of our image that are of size 1. TensorFlow can do this with the built-in `squeeze()` function. Here, we define the new layer:

```
def custom_layer(input_matrix):
    input_matrix_sqeezed = tf.squeeze(input_matrix)
    A = tf.constant([[1., 2.], [-1., 3.]])
    b = tf.constant(1., shape=[2, 2])
    temp1 = tf.matmul(A, input_matrix_sqeezed)
    temp = tf.add(temp1, b) # Ax + b
    return tf.sigmoid(temp)
```

Now, we have to arrange the two layers in the network. We will do this by calling one layer function after the other, as follows:

```
first_layer = mov_avg_layer(x_data)
second_layer = custom_layer(first_layer)
```

Now, we just feed in the *4 x 4* image into the functions. Finally, we can check the result, as follows:

```
print(second_layer)

tf.Tensor(
[[0.9385519  0.90720266]
 [0.9247799  0.82272065]], shape=(2, 2), dtype=float32)
```

Let's now understand more in depth how it works.

How it works...

The first layer is named `Moving_Avg_Window`. The second is a collection of operations called `Custom_Layer`. Data processed by these two layers is first collapsed on the left and then expanded on the right. As shown by the example, you can wrap all the layers into functions and call them, one after the other, in a way that later layers process the outputs of previous ones.

Implementing loss functions

For this recipe, we will cover some of the main loss functions that we can use in TensorFlow. Loss functions are a key aspect of machine learning algorithms. They measure the distance between the model outputs and the target (truth) values.

In order to optimize our machine learning algorithms, we will need to evaluate the outcomes. Evaluating outcomes in TensorFlow depends on specifying a loss function. A loss function tells TensorFlow how good or bad the predictions are compared to the desired result. In most cases, we will have a set of data and a target on which to train our algorithm. The loss function compares the target to the prediction (it measures the distance between the model outputs and the target truth values) and provides a numerical quantification between the two.

Getting ready

We will first start a computational graph and load `matplotlib`, a Python plotting package, as follows:

```
import matplotlib.pyplot as plt
import TensorFlow as tf
```

Now that we are ready to plot, let's proceed to the recipe without further ado.

How to do it...

First, we will talk about loss functions for regression, which means predicting a continuous dependent variable. To start, we will create a sequence of our predictions and a target as a tensor. We will output the results across 500 x values between -1 and 1. See the *How it works...* section for a plot of the outputs. Use the following code:

```
x_vals = tf.linspace(-1., 1., 500)
target = tf.constant(0.)
```

The L2 norm loss is also known as the Euclidean loss function. It is just the square of the distance to the target. Here, we will compute the loss function as if the target is zero. The L2 norm is a great loss function because it is very curved near the target and algorithms can use this fact to converge to the target more slowly the closer it gets to zero. We can implement this as follows:

```
def l2(y_true, y_pred):
    return tf.square(y_true - y_pred)
```

> TensorFlow has a built-in form of the L2 norm, called `tf.nn.l2_loss()`. This function is actually half the L2 norm. In other words, it is the same as the previous one but divided by 2.

The L1 norm loss is also known as the **absolute loss function**. Instead of squaring the difference, we take the absolute value. The L1 norm is better for outliers than the L2 norm because it is not as steep for larger values. One issue to be aware of is that the L1 norm is not smooth at the target, and this can result in algorithms not converging well. It appears as follows:

```
def l1(y_true, y_pred):
    return tf.abs(y_true - y_pred)
```

Pseudo-Huber loss is a continuous and smooth approximation to the **Huber loss function**. This loss function attempts to take the best of the L1 and L2 norms by being convex near the target and less steep for extreme values. The form depends on an extra parameter, `delta`, which dictates how steep it will be. We will plot two forms, *delta1 = 0.25* and *delta2 = 5*, to show the difference, as follows:

```
def phuber1(y_true, y_pred):
    delta1 = tf.constant(0.25)
    return tf.multiply(tf.square(delta1), tf.sqrt(1. +
                       tf.square((y_true - y_pred)/delta1)) - 1.)

def phuber2(y_true, y_pred):
```

```
    delta2 = tf.constant(5.)
    return tf.multiply(tf.square(delta2), tf.sqrt(1. +
                    tf.square((y_true - y_pred)/delta2)) - 1.)
```

Now, we'll move on to loss functions for classification problems. Classification loss functions are used to evaluate loss when predicting categorical outcomes. Usually, the output of our model for a class category is a real-value number between 0 and 1. Then, we choose a cutoff (0.5 is commonly chosen) and classify the outcome as being in that category if the number is above the cutoff. Next, we'll consider various loss functions for categorical outputs.

To start, we will need to redefine our predictions (x_vals) and target. We will save the outputs and plot them in the next section. Use the following:

```
x_vals = tf.linspace(-3., 5., 500)
target = tf.fill([500,], 1.)
```

Hinge loss is mostly used for support vector machines but can be used in neural networks as well. It is meant to compute a loss among two target classes, 1 and -1. In the following code, we are using the target value 1, so the closer our predictions are to 1, the lower the loss value:

```
def hinge(y_true, y_pred):
    return tf.maximum(0., 1. - tf.multiply(y_true, y_pred))
```

Cross-entropy loss for a binary case is also sometimes referred to as the **logistic loss function**. It comes about when we are predicting the two classes 0 or 1. We wish to measure a distance from the actual class (0 or 1) to the predicted value, which is usually a real number between 0 and 1. To measure this distance, we can use the cross-entropy formula from information theory, as follows:

```
def xentropy(y_true, y_pred):
    return (- tf.multiply(y_true, tf.math.log(y_pred)) -
            tf.multiply((1. - y_true), tf.math.log(1. - y_pred)))
```

Sigmoid cross-entropy loss is very similar to the previous loss function except we transform the x values using the sigmoid function before we put them in the cross-entropy loss, as follows:

```
def xentropy_sigmoid(y_true, y_pred):
    return tf.nn.sigmoid_cross_entropy_with_logits(labels=y_true,
                                                    logits=y_pred)
```

Weighted cross-entropy loss is a weighted version of sigmoid cross-entropy loss. We provide a weight on the positive target. For an example, we will weight the positive target by 0.5, as follows:

```
def xentropy_weighted(y_true, y_pred):
    weight = tf.constant(0.5)
```

```
    return tf.nn.weighted_cross_entropy_with_logits(labels=y_true,
                                                    logits=y_pred,
                                               pos_weight=weight)
```

Softmax cross-entropy loss operates on non-normalized outputs. This function is used to measure a loss when there is only one target category instead of multiple. Because of this, the function transforms the outputs into a probability distribution via the softmax function and then computes the loss function from a true probability distribution, as follows:

```
def softmax_xentropy(y_true, y_pred):
    return tf.nn.softmax_cross_entropy_with_logits(labels=y_true,
                                                   logits=y_pred)

unscaled_logits = tf.constant([[1., -3., 10.]])
target_dist = tf.constant([[0.1, 0.02, 0.88]])
print(softmax_xentropy(y_true=target_dist,
                       y_pred=unscaled_logits))

[ 1.16012561]
```

Sparse softmax cross-entropy loss is almost the same as softmax cross-entropy loss, except instead of the target being a probability distribution, it is an index of which category is true. Instead of a sparse all-zero target vector with one value of 1, we just pass in the index of the category that is the `true` value, as follows:

```
def sparse_xentropy(y_true, y_pred):
    return tf.nn.sparse_softmax_cross_entropy_with_logits(
                                                   labels=y_true,
                                                   logits=y_pred)

unscaled_logits = tf.constant([[1., -3., 10.]])
sparse_target_dist = tf.constant([2])
print(sparse_xentropy(y_true=sparse_target_dist,
                      y_pred=unscaled_logits))

[ 0.00012564]
```

Now let's understand better how such loss functions operate by plotting them on a graph.

How it works...

Here is how to use `matplotlib` to plot the regression loss functions:

```
x_vals = tf.linspace(-1., 1., 500)
target = tf.constant(0.)
```

```
funcs = [(l2, 'b-', 'L2 Loss'),
         (l1, 'r--', 'L1 Loss'),
         (phuber1, 'k-.', 'P-Huber Loss (0.25)'),
         (phuber2, 'g:', 'P-Huber Loss (5.0)')]

for func, line_type, func_name in funcs:
    plt.plot(x_vals, func(y_true=target, y_pred=x_vals),
             line_type, label=func_name)

plt.ylim(-0.2, 0.4)
plt.legend(loc='lower right', prop={'size': 11})
plt.show()
```

We get the following plot as output from the preceding code:

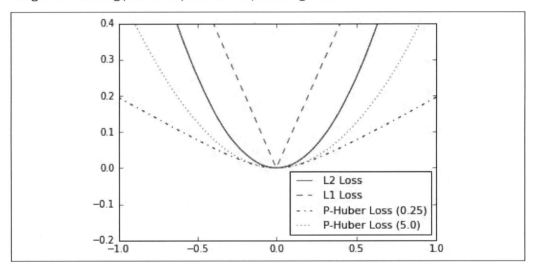

Figure 2.1: Plotting various regression loss functions

Here is how to use `matplotlib` to plot the various classification loss functions:

```
x_vals = tf.linspace(-3., 5., 500)
target = tf.fill([500,], 1.)

funcs = [(hinge, 'b-', 'Hinge Loss'),
         (xentropy, 'r--', 'Cross Entropy Loss'),
         (xentropy_sigmoid, 'k-.', 'Cross Entropy Sigmoid Loss'),
         (xentropy_weighted, 'g:', 'Weighted Cross Enropy Loss
(x0.5)')]

for func, line_type, func_name in funcs:
```

```
        plt.plot(x_vals, func(y_true=target, y_pred=x_vals),
                 line_type, label=func_name)
plt.ylim(-1.5, 3)
plt.legend(loc='lower right', prop={'size': 11})
plt.show()
```

We get the following plot from the preceding code:

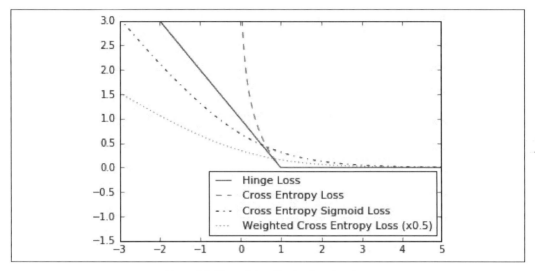

Figure 2.2: Plots of classification loss functions

Each of these loss curves provides different advantages to the neural network optimizing it. We are now going to discuss this a little bit more.

There's more...

Here is a table summarizing the properties and benefits of the different loss functions that we have just graphically described:

Loss function	Use	Benefits	Disadvantages
L2	Regression	More stable	Less robust
L1	Regression	More robust	Less stable
Pseudo-Huber	Regression	More robust and stable	One more parameter
Hinge	Classification	Creates a max margin for use in SVM	Unbounded loss affected by outliers
Cross-entropy	Classification	More stable	Unbounded loss, less robust

The remaining classification loss functions all have to do with the type of cross-entropy loss. The cross-entropy sigmoid loss function is for use on unscaled logits and is preferred over computing the sigmoid loss and then the cross-entropy loss, because TensorFlow has better built-in ways to handle numerical edge cases. The same goes for softmax cross-entropy and sparse softmax cross-entropy.

Most of the classification loss functions described here are for two-class predictions. This can be extended to multiple classes by summing the cross-entropy terms over each prediction/target.

There are also many other metrics to look at when evaluating a model. Here is a list of some more to consider:

Model metric	Description
R-squared (coefficient of determination)	For linear models, this is the proportion of variance in the dependent variable that is explained by the independent data. For models with a larger number of features, consider using adjusted R-squared.
Root mean squared error	For continuous models, this measures the difference between prediction and actual via the square root of the average squared error.
Confusion matrix	For categorical models, we look at a matrix of predicted categories versus actual categories. A perfect model has all the counts along the diagonal.
Recall	For categorical models, this is the fraction of true positives over all predicted positives.
Precision	For categorical models, this is the fraction of true positives over all actual positives.
F-score	For categorical models, this is the harmonic mean of precision and recall.

In your choice of the right metric, you have to both evaluate the problem you have to solve (because each metric will behave differently and, depending on the problem at hand, some loss minimization strategies will prove better than others for our problem), and to experiment with the behavior of the neural network.

Implementing backpropagation

One of the benefits of using TensorFlow is that it can keep track of operations and automatically update model variables based on backpropagation. In this recipe, we will introduce how to use this aspect to our advantage when training machine learning models.

Getting ready

Now, we will introduce how to change our variables in the model in such a way that a loss function is minimized. We have learned how to use objects and operations, and how to create loss functions that will measure the distance between our predictions and targets. Now, we just have to tell TensorFlow how to backpropagate errors through our network in order to update the variables in such a way to minimize the loss function. This is achieved by declaring an optimization function. Once we have an optimization function declared, TensorFlow will go through and figure out the backpropagation terms for all of our computations in the graph. When we feed data in and minimize the loss function, TensorFlow will modify our variables in the network accordingly.

For this recipe, we will do a very simple regression algorithm. We will sample random numbers from a normal distribution, with mean 1 and standard deviation 0.1. Then, we will run the numbers through one operation, which will be to multiply them by a weight tensor and then adding a bias tensor. From this, the loss function will be the L2 norm between the output and the target. Our target will show a high correlation with our input, so the task won't be too complex, yet the recipe will be interestingly demonstrative, and easily reusable for more complex problems.

The second example is a very simple binary classification algorithm. Here, we will generate 100 numbers from two normal distributions, $N(-3,1)$ and $N(3,1)$. All the numbers from $N(-3, 1)$ will be in target class 0, and all the numbers from $N(3, 1)$ will be in target class 1. The model to differentiate these classes (which are perfectly separable) will again be a linear model optimized accordingly to the sigmoid cross-entropy loss function, thus, at first operating a sigmoid transformation on the model result and then computing the cross-entropy loss function.

While specifying a good learning rate helps the convergence of algorithms, we must also specify a type of optimization. From the preceding two examples, we are using standard gradient descent. This is implemented with the `tf.optimizers.SGD` TensorFlow function.

How to do it...

We'll start with the regression example. First, we load the usual numerical Python packages that always accompany our recipes, `NumPy` and `TensorFlow`:

```
import NumPy as np
import TensorFlow as tf
```

Next, we create the data. In order to make everything easily replicable, we want to set the random seed to a specific value. We will always repeat this in our recipes, so we exactly obtain the same results; check yourself how chance may vary the results in the recipes, by simply changing the seed number.

Moreover, in order to get assurance that the target and input have a good correlation, plot a scatterplot of the two variables:

```
np.random.seed(0)
x_vals = np.random.normal(1, 0.1, 100).astype(np.float32)
y_vals = (x_vals * (np.random.normal(1, 0.05, 100) - 0.5)).astype(np.
float32)

plt.scatter(x_vals, y_vals)
plt.show()
```

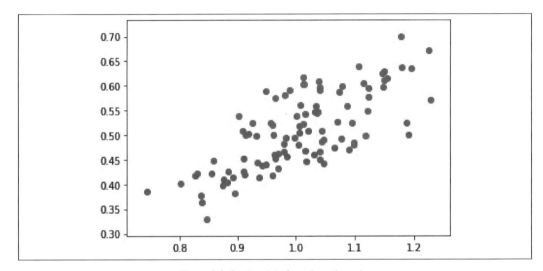

Figure 2.3: Scatterplot of x_vals and y_vals

We add the structure of the network (a linear model of the type *bX + a*) as a function:

```
def my_output(X, weights, biases):
    return tf.add(tf.multiply(X, weights), biases)
```

Next, we add our L2 Loss function to be applied to the results of the network:

```
def loss_func(y_true, y_pred):
    return tf.reduce_mean(tf.square(y_pred - y_true))
```

Now, we have to declare a way to optimize the variables in our graph. We declare an optimization algorithm. Most optimization algorithms need to know how far to step in each iteration. Such a distance is controlled by the learning rate. Setting it to a correct value is specific to the problem we are dealing with, so we can figure out a suitable setting only by experimenting. Anyway, if our learning rate is too high, our algorithm might overshoot the minimum, but if our learning rate is too low, our algorithm might take too long to converge.

The learning rate has a big influence on convergence and we will discuss it again at the end of the section. While we're using the standard gradient descent algorithm, there are many other alternative options. There are, for instance, optimization algorithms that operate differently and can achieve a better or worse optimum depending on the problem. For a great overview of different optimization algorithms, see the paper by Sebastian Ruder in the *See also* section at the end of this recipe:

```
my_opt = tf.optimizers.SGD(learning_rate=0.02)
```

There is a lot of theory on which learning rates are best. This is one of the harder things to figure out in machine learning algorithms. Good papers to read about how learning rates are related to specific optimization algorithms are listed in the *See also* section at the end of this recipe.

Now we can initialize our network variables (`weights` and `biases`) and set a recording list (named `history`) to help us visualize the optimization steps:

```
tf.random.set_seed(1)
np.random.seed(0)
weights = tf.Variable(tf.random.normal(shape=[1]))
biases = tf.Variable(tf.random.normal(shape=[1]))
history = list()
```

The final step is to loop through our training algorithm and tell TensorFlow to train many times. We will do this 100 times and print out results every 25th iteration. To train, we will select a random x and y entry and feed it through the graph. TensorFlow will automatically compute the loss, and slightly change the weights and biases to minimize the loss:

```
for i in range(100):
    rand_index = np.random.choice(100)
    rand_x = [x_vals[rand_index]]
    rand_y = [y_vals[rand_index]]
    with tf.GradientTape() as tape:
        predictions = my_output(rand_x, weights, biases)
        loss = loss_func(rand_y, predictions)
    history.append(loss.NumPy())
    gradients = tape.gradient(loss, [weights, biases])
    my_opt.apply_gradients(zip(gradients, [weights, biases]))
    if (i + 1) % 25 == 0:
        print(f'Step # {i+1} Weights: {weights.NumPy()} Biases: {biases.
NumPy()}')
        print(f'Loss = {loss.NumPy()}')


Step # 25 Weights: [-0.58009654] Biases: [0.91217995]
```

```
Loss = 0.13842473924160004
Step # 50 Weights: [-0.5050226] Biases: [0.9813488]
Loss = 0.006441597361117601
Step # 75 Weights: [-0.4791306] Biases: [0.9942327]
Loss = 0.01728087291121483
Step # 100 Weights: [-0.4777394] Biases: [0.9807473]
Loss = 0.05371852591633797
```

In the loops, `tf.GradientTape()` allows TensorFlow to track the computations and calculate the gradient with respect to the observed variables. Every variable that is within the `GradientTape()` scope is monitored (please keep in mind that constants are not monitored, unless you explicitly state it with the command `tape.watch(constant)`). Once you've completed the monitoring, you can compute the gradient of a target in respect of a list of sources (using the command `tape.gradient(target, sources)`) and get back an eager tensor of the gradients that you can apply to the minimization process. The operation is automatically concluded with the updating of your sources (in our case, the `weights` and `biases` variables) with new values.

When the training is completed, we can visualize how the optimization process operates over successive gradient applications:

```python
plt.plot(history)
plt.xlabel('iterations')
plt.ylabel('loss')
plt.show()
```

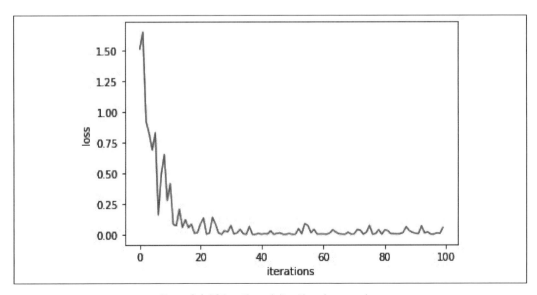

Figure 2.4: L2 loss through iterations in our recipe

At this point, we will introduce the code for the simple classification example. We can use the same TensorFlow script, with some updates. Remember, we will attempt to find an optimal set of weights and biases that will separate the data into two different classes.

First, we pull in the data from two different normal distributions, N(-3, 1) and N(3, 1). We will also generate the target labels and visualize how the two classes are distributed along our predictor variable:

```
np.random.seed(0)
x_vals = np.concatenate((np.random.normal(-3, 1, 50),
                         np.random.normal(3, 1, 50))
                        ).astype(np.float32)
y_vals = np.concatenate((np.repeat(0., 50), np.repeat(1., 50))).astype(np.
float32)

plt.hist(x_vals[y_vals==1], color='b')
plt.hist(x_vals[y_vals==0], color='r')
plt.show()
```

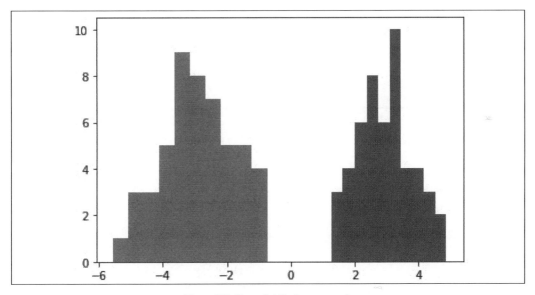

Figure 2.5: Class distribution on x_vals

Because the specific loss function for this problem is sigmoid cross-entropy, we update our loss function:

```
def loss_func(y_true, y_pred):
    return tf.reduce_mean(
        tf.nn.sigmoid_cross_entropy_with_logits(labels=y_true,
                                                logits=y_pred))
```

Next, we initialize our variables:

```
tf.random.set_seed(1)
np.random.seed(0)
weights = tf.Variable(tf.random.normal(shape=[1]))
biases = tf.Variable(tf.random.normal(shape=[1]))
history = list()
```

Finally, we loop through a randomly selected data point several hundred times and update the `weights` and `biases` variables accordingly. As we did before, every 25 iterations we will print out the value of our variables and the loss:

```
for i in range(100):
    rand_index = np.random.choice(100)
    rand_x = [x_vals[rand_index]]
    rand_y = [y_vals[rand_index]]
    with tf.GradientTape() as tape:
        predictions = my_output(rand_x, weights, biases)
        loss = loss_func(rand_y, predictions)
    history.append(loss.NumPy())
    gradients = tape.gradient(loss, [weights, biases])
    my_opt.apply_gradients(zip(gradients, [weights, biases]))
    if (i + 1) % 25 == 0:
        print(f'Step {i+1} Weights: {weights.NumPy()} Biases: {biases.
NumPy()}')
        print(f'Loss = {loss.NumPy()}')


Step # 25 Weights: [-0.01804185] Biases: [0.44081175]
Loss = 0.5967269539833069
Step # 50 Weights: [0.49321094] Biases: [0.37732077]
Loss = 0.3199256658554077
Step # 75 Weights: [0.7071932] Biases: [0.32154965]
Loss = 0.03642747551202774
Step # 100 Weights: [0.8395616] Biases: [0.30409005]
Loss = 0.028119442984461784
```

A plot, also in this case, will reveal how the optimization proceeded:

```
plt.plot(history)
plt.xlabel('iterations')
plt.ylabel('loss')
plt.show()
```

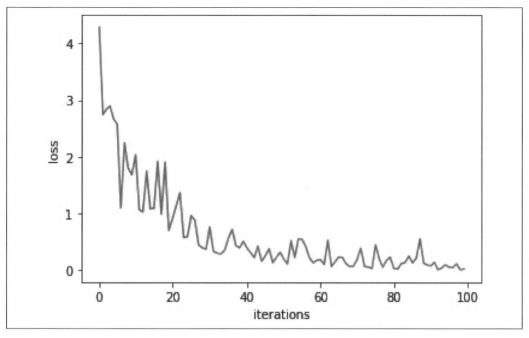

Figure 2.6: Sigmoid cross-entropy loss through iterations in our recipe

The directionality of the plot is clear, though the trajectory is a bit bumpy because we are learning one example at a time, thus making the learning process decisively stochastic. The graph could also point out the need to try to decrease the learning rate a bit.

How it works...

For a recap and explanation, for both examples, we did the following:

1. We created the data. Both examples needed to load data into specific variables used by the function that computes the network.

2. We initialized variables. We used some random Gaussian values, but initialization is a topic on its own, since much of the final results may depend on how we initialize our network (just change the random seed before initialization to find it out).

3. We created a loss function. We used the L2 loss for regression and the cross-entropy loss for classification.

4. We defined an optimization algorithm. Both algorithms used gradient descent.

5. We iterated across random data samples to iteratively update our variables.

There's more...

As we mentioned before, the optimization algorithm is sensitive to the choice of learning rate. It is important to summarize the effect of this choice in a concise manner:

Learning rate size	Advantages/disadvantages	Uses
Smaller learning rate	Converges slower but more accurate results	If the solution is unstable, try lowering the learning rate first
Larger learning rate	Less accurate, but converges faster	For some problems, helps prevent solutions from stagnating

Sometimes, the standard gradient descent algorithm can be stuck or slow down significantly. This can happen when the optimization is stuck in the flat spot of a saddle. To combat this, the solution is taking into account a momentum term, which adds on a fraction of the prior step's gradient descent value. You can access this solution by setting the momentum and the Nesterov parameters, along with your learning rate, in `tf.optimizers.SGD` (see `https://www.TensorFlow.org/api_docs/python/tf/keras/optimizers/SGD` for more details).

Another variant is to vary the optimizer step for each variable in our models. Ideally, we would like to take larger steps for smaller moving variables and shorter steps for faster changing variables. We will not go into the mathematics of this approach, but a common implementation of this idea is called the **Adagrad algorithm**. This algorithm takes into account the whole history of the variable gradients. The function in TensorFlow for this is called `AdagradOptimizer()` (`https://www.TensorFlow.org/api_docs/python/tf/keras/optimizers/Adagrad`).

Sometimes, Adagrad forces the gradients to zero too soon because it takes into account the whole history. A solution to this is to limit how many steps we use. This is called the **Adadelta algorithm**. We can apply this by using the `AdadeltaOptimizer()` function (`https://www.TensorFlow.org/api_docs/python/tf/keras/optimizers/Adadelta`).

There are a few other implementations of different gradient descent algorithms. For these, refer to the TensorFlow documentation at `https://www.TensorFlow.org/api_docs/python/tf/keras/optimizers`.

See also

For some references on optimization algorithms and learning rates, see the following papers and articles:

► Recipes from this chapter, as follows:

❑ The Implementing Loss Functions section.

❑ The Implementing Backpropagation section.

► **Kingma, D., Jimmy, L. Adam**: *A Method for Stochastic Optimization. ICLR* 2015 `https://arxiv.org/pdf/1412.6980.pdf`

► **Ruder, S.** *An Overview of Gradient Descent Optimization Algorithms.* 2016 `https://arxiv.org/pdf/1609.04747v1.pdf`

► **Zeiler, M.** *ADADelta: An Adaptive Learning Rate Method.* 2012 `https://arxiv.org/pdf/1212.5701.pdf`

Working with batch and stochastic training

While TensorFlow updates our model variables according to backpropagation, it can operate on anything from a one-datum observation (as we did in the previous recipe) to a large batch of data at once. Operating on one training example can make for a very erratic learning process, while using too large a batch can be computationally expensive. Choosing the right type of training is crucial for getting our machine learning algorithms to converge to a solution.

Getting ready

In order for TensorFlow to compute the variable gradients for backpropagation to work, we have to measure the loss on a sample or multiple samples. Stochastic training only works on one randomly sampled data-target pair at a time, just as we did in the previous recipe. Another option is to put a larger portion of the training examples in at a time and average the loss for the gradient calculation. The sizes of the training batch can vary, up to and including the whole dataset at once. Here, we will show how to extend the prior regression example, which used stochastic training, to batch training.

We will start by loading `NumPy`, `matplotlib`, and `TensorFlow`, as follows:

```
import matplotlib as plt
import NumPy as np
import TensorFlow as tf
```

Now we just have to script our code and test our recipe in the *How to do it...* section.

How to do it...

We start by declaring a batch size. This will be how many data observations we will feed through the computational graph at one time:

```
batch_size = 20
```

Next, we just apply small modifications to the code used before for the regression problem:

```
np.random.seed(0)
x_vals = np.random.normal(1, 0.1, 100).astype(np.float32)
y_vals = (x_vals * (np.random.normal(1, 0.05, 100) - 0.5)).astype(np.
float32)

def loss_func(y_true, y_pred):
    return tf.reduce_mean(tf.square(y_pred - y_true))

tf.random.set_seed(1)
np.random.seed(0)
weights = tf.Variable(tf.random.normal(shape=[1]))
biases = tf.Variable(tf.random.normal(shape=[1]))
history_batch = list()

for i in range(50):
    rand_index = np.random.choice(100, size=batch_size)
    rand_x = [x_vals[rand_index]]
    rand_y = [y_vals[rand_index]]
    with tf.GradientTape() as tape:
        predictions = my_output(rand_x, weights, biases)
        loss = loss_func(rand_y, predictions)
    history_batch.append(loss.NumPy())
    gradients = tape.gradient(loss, [weights, biases])
    my_opt.apply_gradients(zip(gradients, [weights, biases]))
    if (i + 1) % 25 == 0:
        print(f'Step # {i+1} Weights: {weights.NumPy()} \
            Biases: {biases.NumPy()}')
        print(f'Loss = {loss.NumPy()}')
```

Since our previous recipe, we have learned how to use matrix multiplication in our network and in our cost function. At this point, we just need to deal with inputs that are made of more rows as batches instead of single examples. We can even compare it with the previous approach, which we can now name stochastic optimization:

```
tf.random.set_seed(1)
np.random.seed(0)
weights = tf.Variable(tf.random.normal(shape=[1]))
biases = tf.Variable(tf.random.normal(shape=[1]))
history_stochastic = list()

for i in range(50):
    rand_index = np.random.choice(100, size=1)
    rand_x = [x_vals[rand_index]]
```

```
    rand_y = [y_vals[rand_index]]
    with tf.GradientTape() as tape:
        predictions = my_output(rand_x, weights, biases)
        loss = loss_func(rand_y, predictions)
    history_stochastic.append(loss.NumPy())
    gradients = tape.gradient(loss, [weights, biases])
    my_opt.apply_gradients(zip(gradients, [weights, biases]))
    if (i + 1) % 25 == 0:
        print(f'Step # {i+1} Weights: {weights.NumPy()} \
              Biases: {biases.NumPy()}')
        print(f'Loss = {loss.NumPy()}')
```

Just running the code will retrain our network using batches. At this point, we need to evaluate the results, get some intuition about how it works, and reflect on the results. Let's proceed to the next section.

How it works...

Batch training and stochastic training differ in their optimization methods and their convergence. Finding a good batch size can be difficult. To see how convergence differs between batch training and stochastic training, you are encouraged to change the batch size to various levels.

A visual comparison of the two approaches will explain better how using batches for this problem resulted in the same optimization as stochastic training, though there were fewer fluctuations during the process. Here is the code to produce the plot of both the stochastic and batch losses for the same regression problem. Note that the batch loss is much smoother and the stochastic loss is much more erratic:

```
plt.plot(history_stochastic, 'b-', label='Stochastic Loss')
plt.plot(history_batch, 'r--', label='Batch Loss')
plt.legend(loc='upper right', prop={'size': 11})
plt.show()
```

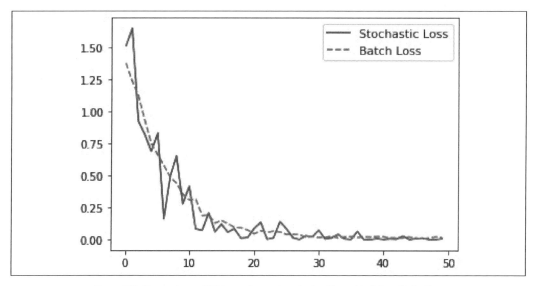

Figure 2.7: Comparison of L2 loss when using stochastic and batch optimization

Now our graph displays a smoother trend line. The persistent presence of bumps could be solved by reducing the learning rate and adjusting the batch size.

There's more...

Type of training	Advantages	Disadvantages
Stochastic	Randomness may help move out of local minimums	Generally needs more iterations to converge
Batch	Finds minimums quicker	Takes more resources to compute

Combining everything together

In this section, we will combine everything we have illustrated so far and create a classifier for the iris dataset. The iris dataset is described in more detail in the *Working with data sources* recipe in *Chapter 1, Getting Started with TensorFlow*. We will load this data and make a simple binary classifier to predict whether a flower is the species Iris setosa or not. To be clear, this dataset has three species, but we will only predict whether a flower is a single species, Iris setosa or not, giving us a binary classifier.

Getting ready

We will start by loading the libraries and data and then transform the target accordingly. First, we load the libraries needed for our recipe. For the Iris dataset, we need the TensorFlow Datasets module, which we haven't used before in our recipes. Note that we also load `matplotlib` here, because we would like to plot the resultant line afterward:

```
import matplotlib.pyplot as plt
import NumPy as np
import TensorFlow as tf
import TensorFlow_datasets as tfds
```

How to do it...

As a starting point, let's first declare our batch size using a global variable:

```
batch_size = 20
```

Next, we load the iris data. We will also need to transform the target data to be just 1 or 0, whether the target is setosa or not. Since the iris dataset marks setosa as a 0, we will change all targets with the value 0 to 1, and the other values all to 0. We will also only use two features, petal length and petal width. These two features are the third and fourth entry in each row of the dataset:

```
iris = tfds.load('iris', split='train[:90%]', W)
iris_test = tfds.load('iris', split='train[90%:]', as_supervised=True)

def iris2d(features, label):
    return features[2:], tf.cast((label == 0), dtype=tf.float32)

train_generator = (iris
                    .map(iris2d)
                    .shuffle(buffer_size=100)
                    .batch(batch_size)
                  )

test_generator = iris_test.map(iris2d).batch(1)
```

As shown in the previous chapter, we use the TensorFlow dataset functions to both load and operate the necessary transformations by creating a data generator that can dynamically feed our network with data, instead of keeping it in an in-memory NumPy matrix. As a first step, we load the data, specifying that we want to split it (using the parameters `split='train[:90%]'` and `split='train[90%:]'`). This allows us to reserve a part (10%) of the dataset for the model evaluation, using data that has not been part of the training phase.

We also specify the parameter, `as_supervised=True`, that will allow us to access the data as tuples of features and labels when iterating from the dataset.

Now we transform the dataset into an iterable generator by applying successive transformations. We shuffle the data, we define the batch to be returned by the iterable, and, most important, we apply a custom function that filters and transforms the features and labels returned from the dataset at the same time.

Then, we define the linear model. The model will take the usual form *bX+a*. Remember that TensorFlow has loss functions with the sigmoid built in, so we just need to define the output of the model prior to the sigmoid function:

```
def linear_model(X, A, b):
    my_output = tf.add(tf.matmul(X, A), b)
    return tf.squeeze(my_output)
```

Now, we add our sigmoid cross-entropy loss function with TensorFlow's built-in `sigmoid_cross_entropy_with_logits()` function:

```
def xentropy(y_true, y_pred):
    return tf.reduce_mean(
        tf.nn.sigmoid_cross_entropy_with_logits(labels=y_true,
                                                logits=y_pred))
```

We also have to tell TensorFlow how to optimize our computational graph by declaring an optimizing method. We will want to minimize the cross-entropy loss. We will also choose `0.02` as our learning rate:

```
my_opt = tf.optimizers.SGD(learning_rate=0.02)
```

Now, we will train our linear model with 300 iterations. We will feed in the three data points that we require: petal length, petal width, and the target variable. Every 30 iterations, we will print the variable values:

```
tf.random.set_seed(1)

np.random.seed(0)
A = tf.Variable(tf.random.normal(shape=[2, 1]))
b = tf.Variable(tf.random.normal(shape=[1]))
history = list()

for i in range(300):
    iteration_loss = list()
    for features, label in train_generator:
        with tf.GradientTape() as tape:
            predictions = linear_model(features, A, b)
```

```
        loss = xentropy(label, predictions)
      iteration_loss.append(loss.NumPy())
      gradients = tape.gradient(loss, [A, b])
      my_opt.apply_gradients(zip(gradients, [A, b]))
   history.append(np.mean(iteration_loss))
   if (i + 1) % 30 == 0:
      print(f'Step # {i+1} Weights: {A.NumPy().T} \
          Biases: {b.NumPy()}')
      print(f'Loss = {loss.NumPy()}')


Step # 30 Weights: [[-1.1206311  1.2985772]] Biases: [1.0116111]
Loss = 0.4503694772720337
...
Step # 300 Weights: [[-1.5611029   0.11102282]] Biases: [3.6908474]
Loss = 0.10326375812292099
```

If we plot the loss against the iterations, we can acknowledge from the smoothness of the reduction of the loss over time how the learning has been quite an easy task for the linear model:

```
plt.plot(history)
plt.xlabel('iterations')
plt.ylabel('loss')
plt.show()
```

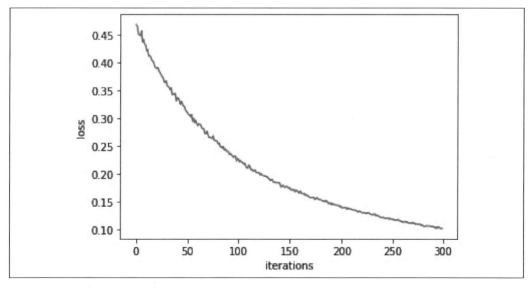

Figure 2.8: Cross-entropy error for the Iris setosa data

We'll conclude by checking the performance on our reserved test data. This time we just take the examples from the test dataset. As expected, the resulting cross-entropy value is analogous to the training one:

```
predictions = list()
labels = list()
for features, label in test_generator:
    predictions.append(linear_model(features, A, b).NumPy())
    labels.append(label.NumPy()[0])


test_loss = xentropy(np.array(labels), np.array(predictions)).NumPy()
print(f"test cross-entropy is {test_loss}")


test cross-entropy is 0.10227929800748825
```

The next set of commands extracts the model variables and plots the line on a graph:

```
coefficients = np.ravel(A.NumPy())
intercept = b.NumPy()


# Plotting batches of examples
for j, (features, label) in enumerate(train_generator):
    setosa_mask = label.NumPy() == 1
    setosa = features.NumPy()[setosa_mask]
    non_setosa = features.NumPy()[~setosa_mask]
    plt.scatter(setosa[:,0], setosa[:,1], c='red', label='setosa')
    plt.scatter(non_setosa[:,0], non_setosa[:,1], c='blue', label='Non-
setosa')
    if j==0:
        plt.legend(loc='lower right')


# Computing and plotting the decision function
a = -coefficients[0] / coefficients[1]
xx = np.linspace(plt.xlim()[0], plt.xlim()[1], num=10000)
yy = a * xx - intercept / coefficients[1]
on_the_plot = (yy > plt.ylim()[0]) & (yy < plt.ylim()[1])
plt.plot(xx[on_the_plot], yy[on_the_plot], 'k--')


plt.xlabel('Petal Length')
plt.ylabel('Petal Width')
plt.show()
```

The resultant graph is in the *How it works...* section, where we also discuss the validity and reproducibility of the obtained results.

How it works...

Our goal was to fit a line between the Iris setosa points and the other two species using only petal width and petal length. If we plot the points, and separate the area of the plot where classifications are zero from the area where classifications are one with a line, we see that we have achieved this:

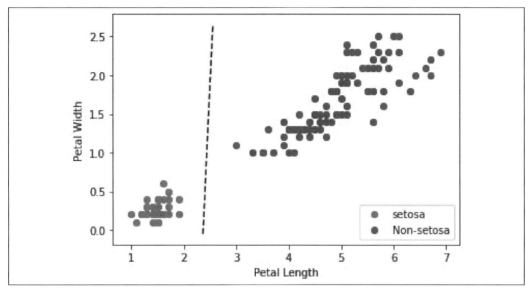

Figure 2.9: Plot of Iris setosa and non-setosa for petal width versus petal length; the solid line is the linear separator that we achieved after 300 iterations

The way the separating line is defined depends on the data, the network architecture, and the learning process. Different starting situations, even due to the random initialization of the neural network's weights, may provide you with a slightly different solution.

There's more...

While we achieved our objective of separating the two classes with a line, it may not be the best model for separating two classes. For instance, after adding new observations, we may realize that our solution badly separates the two classes. As we progress into the next chapter, we will start dealing with recipes that address these problems by providing testing, randomization, and specialized layers that will increase the generalization capabilities of our recipes.

See also

▶ For information about the Iris dataset, see the documentation at `https://archive.ics.uci.edu/ml/datasets/iris`.

▶ If you want to understand more about decision boundaries drawing for machine learning algorithms, we warmly suggest this excellent Medium article from Navoneel Chakrabarty: `https://towardsdatascience.com/decision-boundary-visualization-a-z-6a63ae9cca7d`

3
Keras

In this chapter, we will focus on the high-level TensorFlow API named Keras.

By the end of this chapter, you should have a better understanding of:

- ▶ The Keras Sequential API
- ▶ The Keras Functional API
- ▶ The Keras Subclassing API
- ▶ The Keras Preprocessing API

Introduction

In the previous chapter, we covered TensorFlow's fundamentals, and we are now able to set up a computational graph. This chapter will introduce Keras, a high-level neural network API written in Python with multiple backends. TensorFlow is one of them. François Chollet, a French software engineer and AI researcher currently working at Google, created Keras for his own personal use before it was open-sourced in 2015. Keras's primary goal is to provide an easy-to-use and accessible library to enable fast experiments.

TensorFlow v1 suffers from usability issues; in particular, a sprawling and sometimes confusing API. For example, TensorFlow v1 offers two high-level APIs:

- ▶ The Estimator API (added in release 1.1) is used for training models on localhost or distributed environments
- ▶ The Keras API was then added later (release 1.4.0) and intended to be used for fast prototyping

With TensorFlow v2, Keras became the official high-level API. Keras can scale and suit various user profiles, from research to application development and from model training to deployment. Keras provides four key advantages: it's user-friendly (without sacrificing flexibility and performance), modular, composable, and scalable.

The TensorFlow Keras APIs are the same as the Keras API. However, the implementation of Keras in its TensorFlow version of the backend has been optimized for TensorFlow. It integrates TensorFlow-specific functionality, such as eager execution, data pipelines, and Estimators.

The difference between Keras, the independent library, and Keras' implementation as integrated with TensorFlow is only the way to import it.

Here is the command to import the Keras API specification:

```
import keras
```

Here is TensorFlow's implementation of the Keras API specification:

```
import tensorflow as tf
from tensorflow import keras
```

Now, let's start by discovering the basic building blocks of Keras.

Understanding Keras layers

Keras layers are the fundamental building blocks of Keras models. Each layer receives data as input, does a specific task, and returns an output.

Keras includes a wide range of built-in layers:

- **Core layers:** Dense, Activation, Flatten, Input, Reshape, Permute, RepeatVector, SpatialDropOut, and many more.

- **Convolutional layers for Convolutional Neural Networks:** Conv1D, Conv2D, SeparableConv1D, Conv3D, Cropping2D, and many more.

- **Pooling** layers that perform a downsampling operation to reduce feature maps: MaxPooling1D, AveragePooling2D, and GlobalAveragePooling3D.

- **Recurrent layers for recurrent neural networks to process recurrent or sequence data:** RNN, SimpleRNN, GRU, LSTM, ConvLSTM2D, etc.

- **The embedding layer**, only used as the first layer in a model and turns positive integers into dense vectors of fixed size.

- ▶ **Merge layers:** Add, Subtract, Multiply, Average, Maximum, Minimum, and many more.
- ▶ **Advanced activation layers:** LeakyReLU, PReLU, Softmax, ReLU, etc.
- ▶ **The batch normalization layer**, which normalizes the activation of the previous layer at each batch.
- ▶ **Noise layers:** GausianNoise, GausianDropout, and AlphaDropout.
- ▶ **Layer wrappers:** TimeDistributed applies a layer to every temporal slice of an input and bidirectional wrapper for RNNs.
- ▶ **Locally-connected layers:** LocallyConnected1D and LocallyConnected2D. They work like Conv1D or Conv2D without sharing their weights.

We can also write our Keras layers as explained in the Keras Subclassing API section of this chapter.

Getting ready

To start, we'll review some methods that are common in all Keras layers. These methods are very useful to know the configuration and the state of a layer.

How to do it...

1. Let's start with the layer's weights. The weights are possibly the most essential concept in a layer; it decides how much influence the input will have on the output. It represents the state of a layer. The `get_weights()` function returns the weights of the layer as a list of NumPy arrays:

```
layer.get_weights()
```

The `set_weights()` method fixes the weights of the layer from a list of Numpy arrays:

```
layer.set_weights(weights)
```

2. As we'll explain in the Keras Functional API recipe, sometimes neural network topology isn't linear. In this case, a layer can be used several times in the network (shared layer). We can easily get the inputs and outputs of a layer by using this command if the layer is a single node (no shared layer):

```
layer.input
layer.output
```

Or this one, if the layer has multiple nodes:

```
layer.get_input_at(node_index)
layer.get_output_at(node_index)
```

3. We can also easily get the layer's input and output shapes by using this command if a layer is a single node (no shared layer):

```
layer.input_shape
layer.output_shape
```

Or this one, if the layer has multiple nodes:

```
layer.get_input_shape_at(node_index)
layer.get_output_shape_at(node_index)
```

4. Now, we'll be discussing the layer's configuration. As the same layer could be instantiating several times, the configuration doesn't include the weights or connectivity information. The `get_config()` function returns a dictionary containing the configuration of the layer:

```
layer.get_config()
```

The `from_config()` method instantiates a layer's configuration:

```
layer.from_config(config)
```

Note that the layer configuration is stored in an associative array (Python dictionary), a data structure that maps keys to values.

How it works...

The layers are the building blocks of the models. Keras offers a wide range of building layers and useful methods to know more about what's happening and get inside the models.

With Keras, we can build models in three ways: with the Sequential, the Functional, or the Subclassing API. We'll later see that only the last two APIs allow access to the layers.

See also

For some references on the Keras Layers API, see the following documentation:

▶ Keras layers API documentation: `https://keras.io/layers/about-keras-layers/`
▶ TensorFlow Keras layers API documentation: `https://www.tensorflow.org/api_docs/python/tf/keras/layers`

Using the Keras Sequential API

The main goal of Keras is to make it easy to create deep learning models. The Sequential API allows us to create Sequential models, which are a linear stack of layers. Models that are connected layer by layer can solve many problems. To create a Sequential model, we have to create an instance of a Sequential class, create some model layers, and add them to it.

We will go from the creation of our Sequential model to its prediction via the compilation, training, and evaluation steps. By the end of this recipe, you will have a Keras model ready to be deployed in production.

Getting ready

This recipe will cover the main ways of creating a Sequential model and assembling layers to build a model with the Keras Sequential API.

To start, we load TensorFlow and NumPy, as follows:

```
import tensorflow as tf
from tensorflow import keras
from keras.layers import Dense
import numpy as np
```

We are ready to proceed with an explanation of how to do it.

How to do it...

1. First, we will create a Sequential model. Keras offers two equivalent ways of creating a Sequential model. Let's start by passing a list of layer instances as an array to the constructor. We'll build a multi-class classifier (10 categories) fully connected model, aka a multi-layer perceptron, by entering the following code.

```
model = tf.keras.Sequential([
    # Add a fully connected layer with 1024 units to the model
    tf.keras.layers.Dense(1024, input_dim=64),
    # Add an activation layer with ReLU activation function
    tf.keras.layers.Activation('relu'),
    # Add a fully connected layer with 256 units to the model
    tf.keras.layers.Dense(256),
    # Add an activation layer with ReLU activation function
    tf.keras.layers.Activation('relu'),
    # Add a fully connected layer with 10 units to the model
    tf.keras.layers.Dense(10),
    # Add an activation layer with softmax activation function
```

```
        tf.keras.layers.Activation('softmax')
])
```

Another way to create a Sequential model is to instantiate a Sequential class and then add layers via the `.add()` method.

```
model = tf.keras.Sequential()
# Add a fully connected layer with 1024 units to the model
model.add(tf.keras.layers.Dense(1024, input_dim=64))
# Add an activation layer with ReLU activation function
model.add(tf.keras.layers.Activation(relu))
# Add a fully connected layer with 256 units to the model
model.add(tf.keras.layers.Dense(256))
# Add an activation layer with ReLU activation function
model.add(tf.keras.layers.Activation('relu'))
# Add a fully connected layer with 10 units to the model
model.add(tf.keras.layers.Dense(10))
# Add an activation layer with softmax activation function
model.add(tf.keras.layers.Activation('softmax'))
```

2. Let's take a closer look at the layer configuration. The `tf.keras.layers` API offers a lot of built-in layers and also provides an API to create our layers. In most of them, we can set these parameters to the layer's constructor:

   ❑ We can add an activation function by specifying the name of a built-in function or as a callable object. This function decides whether a neuron should be activated or not. By default, a layer has no activation function. Below are the two ways to create a layer with an activation function. Note that you don't have to run the following code; these layers are not assigned to variables.

   ```
   # Creation of a dense layer with a sigmoid activation
   function:
   Dense(256, activation='sigmoid')
   # Or:
   Dense(256, activation=tf.keras.activations.sigmoid)
   ```

   ❑ We can also specify an initialization strategy for the initial weights (kernel and bias) by passing the string identifier of built-in initializers or a callable object. The kernel is by default set to the "Glorot uniform" initializer, and the bias is set to zeros.

   ```
   # A dense layer with a kernel initialized to a truncated
   normal distribution:
   Dense(256, kernel_initializer='random_normal')
   # A dense layer with a bias vector initialized with a
   constant value of 5.0:
   ```

```
Dense(256, bias_initializer=tf.keras.initializers.
Constant(value=5))
```

❑ We can also specify regularizers for kernel and bias, such as L1 (also called Lasso) or L2 (also called Ridge) regularization. By default, no regularization is applied. A regularizer aims to prevent overfitting by penalizing a model for having large weights. These penalties are incorporated in the loss function that the network optimizes.

```
# A dense layer with L1 regularization of factor 0.01 applied
to the kernel matrix:
Dense(256, kernel_regularizer=tf.keras.regularizers.l1(0.01))
# A dense layer with L2 regularization of factor 0.01 applied
to the bias vector:
Dense(256, bias_regularizer=tf.keras.regularizers.l2(0.01))
```

3. In Keras, it's strongly recommended to set the input shape for the first layer. Yet, contrary to appearances, the input layer isn't a layer but a tensor. Its shape must be the same as our training data. The following layers perform automatic shape inference; their shapes are calculated based on the unit of the previous layer.

Each type of layer requires input with a certain number of dimensions, so there are different ways to specify the input shape depending on the kind of layer. Here, we'll focus on the Dense layer, so we'll use the `input_dim` parameter. Since the shape of the weights depends on the input size, if the input shape isn't specified in advance, the model has no weights: the model is not built. In this case, you can't call any methods of the Layer class such as `summary`, `layers`, `weights`, and so on.

In this recipe, we'll create datasets with 64 features, and we'll process batches of 10 samples. The shape of our input data is (10,64), aka (`batch_size, number_of_features`). By default, a Keras model is defined to support any batch size, so the batch size isn't mandatory. We just have to specify the number of features through the `input_dim` parameter to our first layer.

```
Dense(256, input_dim=(64))
```

However, we can force the batch size for efficiency reasons with the `batch_size` argument.

```
Dense(256, input_dim=(64), batch_size=10)
```

4. Before the learning phase, our model needs to be configured. This is done by the `compile` method. We have to specify:

❑ An optimization algorithm for the training of our neural network. We can pass an optimizer instance from the `tf.keras.optimizers` module. For example, we can use an instance of `tf.keras.optimizers.RMSprop` or `'RMSprop'`, which is an optimizer that implements the RMSprop algorithm.

❏ A loss function called an objective function or optimization score function aims at minimizing the model. It can be the name of an existing loss function (such as `categorical_crossentropy` or `mse`), a symbolic TensorFlow loss function (`tf.keras.losses.MAPE`), or a custom loss function, which takes as input two tensors (true tensors and predicted tensors) and returns a scalar for each data point.

❏ A list of metrics used to judge our model's performance that aren't used in the model training process. We can either pass the string names or callables from the `tf.keras.metrics` module.

❏ If you want to be sure that the model trains and evaluates eagerly, we can set the argument `run_eagerly` to true.

Note that the graph is finalized with the `compile` method.

Now, we'll compile the model using the Adam optimizer for categorical cross-entropy loss and display the accuracy metric.

```
model.compile(
    optimizer="adam",
    loss="categorical_crossentropy",
    metrics=["accuracy"]
)
```

5. Now, we'll generate three toy datasets of **64** features with random values. One will be used to train the model (2,000 samples), another one to validate (500 samples), and the last one to test (500 samples).

```
data = np.random.random((2000, 64))
labels = np.random.random((2000, 10))
val_data = np.random.random((500, 64))
val_labels = np.random.random((500, 10))
test_data = np.random.random((500, 64))
test_labels = np.random.random((500, 10))
```

6. After the model has been configured, the learning phase begins by calling the `fit` method. The training configuration is done by these three arguments:

❏ We have to set the number of epochs, aka the number of iterations over the entire input data.

❏ We have to specify the number of samples per gradient, called the `batch_size` argument. Note that the last batch may be smaller if the total number of samples is not divisible by the batch size.

❏ We can specify a validation dataset by setting the `validation_data` argument (a tuple of inputs and labels). This dataset makes it easy to monitor the performance of the model. The loss and metrics are computed in inference mode at the end of each epoch.

Now, we'll train the model on our toy datasets by calling the `fit` method:

```
model.fit(data, labels, epochs=10, batch_size=50,
          validation_data=(val_data, val_labels))
```

7. Then, we'll evaluate our model on the test dataset. We'll call the `model.evaluate` function, which predicts the loss value and the metric values of the model in test mode. Computation is done in batches. It has three important arguments: the input data, the target data, and the batch size. This function predicts the output for a given input. Then, it computes the `metrics` function (specified in the `model.compile` based on the target data) and the model's prediction and returns the computed metric value as the output.

```
model.evaluate(data, labels, batch_size=50)
```

8. We can also just use the model to make a prediction. The `tf.keras.Model.predict` method takes as input only data and returns a prediction. And here's how to predict the output of the last layer of inference for the data provided, as a NumPy array:

```
result = model.predict(data, batch_size=50)
```

Analyzing this model's performance is of no interest in this recipe because we randomly generated a dataset.

Now, let's move on to an analysis of this recipe.

How it works...

Keras provides the Sequential API to create models composed of a linear stack of layers. We can either pass a list of layer instances as an array to the constructor or use the add method.

Keras provides different kinds of layers. Most of them share some common constructor arguments such as `activation`, `kernel_initializer` and `bias_initializer`, and `kernel_regularizer` and `bias_regularizer`.

Take care with the delayed-build pattern: if no input shape is specified on the first layer, the model gets built the first time the model is called on some input data or when methods such as `fit`, `eval`, `predict`, and `summary` are called. The graph is finalized with the `compile` method, which configures the model before the learning phase. Then, we can evaluate the model or make predictions.

See also

For some references on the Keras Sequential API, visit the following websites:

▶   tf.keras.Sequential model API documentation: `https://www.tensorflow.org/api_docs/python/tf/keras/Sequential`

> ▶ Keras Sequential model API documentation: `https://keras.io/models/sequential/`

Using the Keras Functional API

The Keras Sequential API is great for developing deep learning models in most situations. However, this API has some limitations, such as a linear topology, that could be overcome with the Functional API. Note that many high-performing networks are based on a non-linear topology such as Inception, ResNet, etc.

The Functional API allows defining complex models with a non-linear topology, multiple inputs, multiple outputs, residual connections with non-sequential flows, and shared and reusable layers.

The deep learning model is usually a directed acyclic graph (DAG). The Functional API is a way to build a graph of layers and create more flexible models than the `tf.keras.Sequential` API.

Getting ready

This recipe will cover the main ways of creating a Functional model, using callable models, manipulating complex graph topologies, sharing layers, and finally introducing the concept of the layer "node" with the Keras Sequential API.

As usual, we just need to import TensorFlow as follows:

```
import tensorflow as tf
from tensorflow import keras
from keras.layers import Input, Dense, TimeDistributed
import keras.models
```

We are ready to proceed with an explanation of how to do it.

How to do it...

Let's go and make a Functional model for recognizing the MNIST dataset of handwritten digits. We will predict the handwritten digits from grayscale images.

Creating a Functional model

1. First, we will load the MNIST dataset.

    ```
    mnist = tf.keras.datasets.mnist
    (X_mnist_train, y_mnist_train), (X_mnist_test, y_mnist_test) =
    mnist.load_data()
    ```

2. Then, we will create an input node with a 28x28 dimensional shape. Remember that in Keras, the input layer is not a layer but a tensor, and we have to specify the input shape for the first layer. This tensor must have the same shape as our training data. By default, a Keras model is defined to support any batch size, so the batch size isn't mandatory. `Input()` is used to instantiate a Keras tensor.

```
inputs = tf.keras.Input(shape=(28,28))
```

3. Then, we will flatten the images of size (28,28) using the following command. This will produce an array of 784 pixels.

```
flatten_layer = keras.layers.Flatten()
```

4. We'll add a new node in the graph of layers by calling the `flatten_layer` on the `inputs` object:

```
flatten_output = flatten_layer(inputs)
```

The "layer call" action is like drawing an arrow from `inputs` to the `flatten_layer`. We're "passing" the inputs to the flatten layer, and as a result, it produces outputs. A layer instance is callable (on a tensor) and returns a tensor.

5. Then, we'll create a new layer instance:

```
dense_layer = tf.keras.layers.Dense(50, activation='relu')
```

6. We'll add a new node:

```
dense_output = dense_layer(flatten_output)
```

7. To build a model, multiple layers are stacked. In this example, we will add another `dense` layer to do a classification task between 10 classes:

```
predictions = tf.keras.layers.Dense(10, activation='softmax')(dense_output)
```

8. Input tensor(s) and output tensor(s) are used to define a model. The model is a function of one or more input layers and one or more output layers. The model instance formalizes the computational graph on how the data flows from input(s) to output(s).

```
model = keras.Model(inputs=inputs, outputs=predictions)
```

9. Now, we'll print the summary.

```
model.summary()
```

10. This results in the following output:

```
Model: "functional_1"

Layer (type)                    Output Shape              Param #
=================================================================
input_1 (InputLayer)            [(None, 28, 28)]          0

flatten (Flatten)               (None, 784)               0

dense (Dense)                    (None, 50)                39250

dense_1 (Dense)                  (None, 10)                510
=================================================================
Total params: 39,760
Trainable params: 39,760
Non-trainable params: 0
```

Figure 3.1: Summary of the model

11. Such a model can be trained and evaluated by the same `compile`, `fit`, `evaluate`, and `predict` methods used in the Keras Sequential model.

```
model.compile(optimizer='sgd',
              loss='sparse_categorical_crossentropy',
              metrics=['accuracy'])
model.fit(X_mnist_train, y_mnist_train,
          validation_data=(X_mnist_train, y_mnist_train),
          epochs=10)
```

In this recipe, we have built a model using the Functional API.

Using callable models like layers

Let's go into the details of the Functional API with callable models.

1. With the Functional API, it is easy to reuse trained models: any model can be treated as a layer, by calling it on a tensor. We will reuse the model defined in the previous section as a layer to see this in action. It's a classifier for 10 categories. This model returns 10 probabilities: 1 for each category. It's called a 10-way softmax. So, by calling the model defined above, the model will predict for each input one of the 10 classes.

```
x = Input(shape=(784,))
# y will contain the prediction for x
y = model(x)
```

Note that by calling a model, we are not just reusing the model architecture, we are also reusing its weights.

2. If we're facing a sequence problem, creating a model will become very easy with the Functional API. For example, instead of processing one image, we want to process a video composed of many images. We could turn an image classification model into a video classification model in just one line using the `TimeDistributed` layer wrapper. This wrapper applies our previous model to every temporal slice of the input sequence, or in other words, to each image of our video.

```
from keras.layers import TimeDistributed

# Input tensor for sequences of 50 timesteps,
# Each containing a 28x28 dimensional matrix.
input_sequences = tf.keras.Input(shape=(10, 28, 28))

# We will apply the previous model to each sequence so one for each
timestep.
# The MNIST model returns a vector with 10 probabilities (one for
each digit).
# The TimeDistributed output will be a sequence of 50 vectors of
size 10.
processed_sequences = tf.keras.layers.TimeDistributed(model)(input_
sequences)
```

We have seen that models are callable like layers. Now, we'll learn how to create complex models with a non-linear topology.

Creating a model with multiple inputs and outputs

The Functional API makes it easy to manipulate a large number of intertwined datastreams with multiple inputs and outputs and non-linear connectivity topologies. These cannot be handled with the Sequential API, which isn't able to create a model with layers that aren't connected sequentially or with multiple inputs or outputs.

Let's go with an example. We're going to build a system for predicting the price of a specific house and the elapsed time before its sale.

The model will have two inputs:

❏ Data about the house such as the number of bedrooms, house size, air conditioning, fitted kitchen, etc.

❏ A recent picture of the house

This model will have two outputs:

- ❑ The elapsed time before the sale (two categories – slow or fast)
- ❑ The predicted price

1. To build this system, we'll start by building the first block to process tabular data about the house.

```
house_data_inputs = tf.keras.Input(shape=(128,), name='house_data')
x = tf.keras.layers.Dense(64, activation='relu')(house_data_inputs)
block_1_output = tf.keras.layers.Dense(32, activation='relu')(x)
```

2. Then, we'll build the second block to process the house image data.

```
house_picture_inputs = tf.keras.Input(shape=(128,128,3),
name='house_picture')
x = tf.keras.layers.Conv2D(64, 3, activation='relu', padding='same')
(house_picture_inputs)
x = tf.keras.layers.Conv2D(64, 3, activation='relu', padding='same')
(x)
block_2_output = tf.keras.layers.Flatten()(x)
```

3. Now, we'll merge all available features into a single large vector via concatenation.

```
x = tf.keras.layers.concatenate([block_1_output, block_2_output])
```

4. Then, we'll stick a logistic regression for price prediction on top of the features.

```
price_pred = tf.keras.layers.Dense(1, name='price',
activation='relu')(x)
```

5. And, we'll stick a time classifier on top of the features.

```
time_elapsed_pred = tf.keras.layers.Dense(2, name='elapsed_time',
activation='softmax')(x)
```

6. Now, we'll build the model.

```
model = keras.Model([house_data_inputs, house_picture_inputs],
                    [price_pred, time_elapsed_pred],
                    name='toy_house_pred')
```

7. Now, we'll plot the model.

```
keras.utils.plot_model(model, 'multi_input_and_output_model.png',
show_shapes=True)
```

8. This results in the following output:

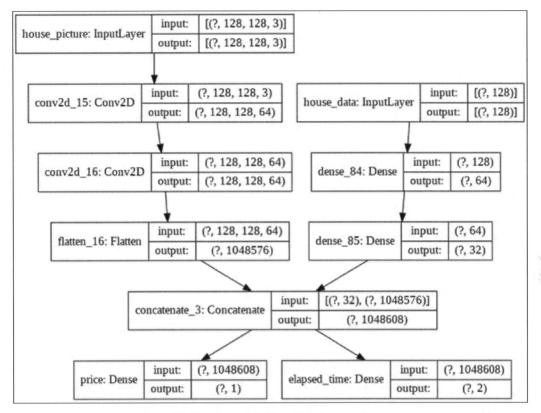

Figure 3.2: Plot of a model with multiple inputs and outputs

In this recipe, we have created a complex model using the Functional API with multiple inputs and outputs that predicts the price of a specific house and the elapsed time before its sale. Now, we'll introduce the concept of shared layers.

Shared layers

Some models reuse the same layer multiple times inside their architecture. These layer instances learn features that correspond to multiple paths in the graph of layers. Shared layers are often used to encode inputs from similar spaces.

To share a layer (weights and all) across different inputs, we only need to instantiate the layer once and call it on as many inputs as we want.

Let's consider two different sequences of text. We will apply the same embedding layer to these two sequences, which feature similar vocabulary.

```
# Variable-length sequence of integers
text_input_a = tf.keras.Input(shape=(None,), dtype='int32')

# Variable-length sequence of integers
text_input_b = tf.keras.Input(shape=(None,), dtype='int32')

# Embedding for 1000 unique words mapped to 128-dimensional vectors
shared_embedding = tf.keras.layers.Embedding(1000, 128)

# Reuse the same layer to encode both inputs
encoded_input_a = shared_embedding(text_input_a)
encoded_input_b = shared_embedding(text_input_b)
```

In this recipe, we have learned how to reuse a layer multiple times in the same model. Now, we'll introduce the concept of extracting and reusing a layer.

Extracting and reusing nodes in the graph of layers

In the first recipe of this chapter, we saw that a layer is an instance that takes a tensor as an argument and returns another tensor. A model is composed of several layer instances. These layer instances are objects that are chained one to another by their layer input and output tensors. Each time we instantiate a layer, the output of the layer is a new tensor. By adding a "node" to the layer, we link the input to the output tensor.

The graph of layers is a static data structure. With the Keras Functional API, we can easily access and inspect the model.

The `tf.keras.application` module contains canned architectures with pre-trained weights.

1. Let's go to download the ResNet 50 pre-trained model.
    ```
    resnet = tf.keras.applications.resnet.ResNet50()
    ```

2. Then, we'll display the intermediate layers of the model by querying the graph data structure:
    ```
    intermediate_layers = [layer.output for layer in resnet.layers]
    ```

3. Then, we'll display the top 10 intermediate layers of the model by querying the graph data structure:
    ```
    intermediate_layers[:10]
    ```

4. This results in the following output:

```
[<tf.Tensor 'input_7:0' shape=(None, 224, 224, 3) dtype=float32>,
<tf.Tensor 'conv1_pad/Pad:0' shape=(None, 230, 230, 3)
dtype=float32>,
<tf.Tensor 'conv1_conv/BiasAdd:0' shape=(None, 112, 112, 64)
dtype=float32>,
<tf.Tensor 'conv1_bn/cond/Identity:0' shape=(None, 112, 112, 64)
dtype=float32>,
<tf.Tensor 'conv1_relu/Relu:0' shape=(None, 112, 112, 64)
dtype=float32>,
<tf.Tensor 'pool1_pad/Pad:0' shape=(None, 114, 114, 64)
dtype=float32>,
<tf.Tensor 'pool1_pool/MaxPool:0' shape=(None, 56, 56, 64)
dtype=float32>,
<tf.Tensor 'conv2_block1_1_conv/BiasAdd:0' shape=(None, 56, 56, 64)
dtype=float32>,
<tf.Tensor 'conv2_block1_1_bn/cond/Identity:0' shape=(None, 56, 56,
64) dtype=float32>,
<tf.Tensor 'conv2_block1_1_relu/Relu:0' shape=(None, 56, 56, 64)
dtype=float32>]
```

5. Now, we'll select all the feature layers. We'll go into the details in the convolution neural network chapter.

```
feature_layers = intermediate_layers[:-2]
```

6. Then, we'll reuse the nodes in order to create our feature-extraction model.

```
feat_extraction_model = keras.Model(inputs=resnet.input,
outputs=feature_layers)
```

One of the interesting benefits of a deep learning model is that it can be reused partly or wholly on similar predictive modeling problems. This technique is called "transfer learning": it significantly improves the training phase by decreasing the training time and the model's performance on a related problem.

The new model architecture is based on one or more layers from a pre-trained model. The weights of the pre-trained model may be used as the starting point for the training process. They can be either fixed or fine-tuned, or totally adapted during the learning phase. The two main approaches to implement transfer learning are weight initialization and feature extraction. Don't worry, we'll go into the details later in this book.

In this recipe, we have loaded a pretrained model based on the VGG19 architecture. We have extracted nodes from this model and reused them in a new model.

How it works...

The Keras Sequential API is appropriate in the vast majority of cases but is limited to creating layer-by-layer models. The Functional API is more flexible and allows extracting and reusing nodes, sharing layers, and creating non-linear models with multiple inputs and multiple outputs. Note that many high-performing networks are based on a non-linear topology.

In this recipe, we have learned how to build models using the Keras Functional API. These models are trained and evaluated by the same `compile`, `fit`, `evaluate`, and `predict` methods used by the Keras Sequential model.

We have also viewed how to reuse trained models as a layer, how to share layers, and also how to extract and reuse nodes. This last approach is used in transfer learning techniques that speed up training and improve performance.

There's more...

As we can access every layer, models built with the Keras Functional API have specific features such as model plotting, whole-model saving, etc.

Models built with the Functional API could be complex, so here are some tips to consider to avoid pulling your hair out during the process:

- ▶ Name the layers: It will be quite useful when we display summaries and plots of the model graph.
- ▶ Separate submodels: Consider each submodel as being like a Lego brick that we will combine together with the others at the end.
- ▶ Review the layer summary: Use the `summary` method to check the outputs of each layer.
- ▶ Review graph plots: Use the `plot` method to display and check the connection between the layers.
- ▶ Consistent variable names: Use the same variable name for the input and output layers. It avoids copy-paste mistakes.

See also

For some references on the Keras Functional API, visit the following websites:

- ▶ Keras Functional API documentation: `https://keras.io/getting-started/functional-api-guide/`
- ▶ `tf.keras.Model` API: `https://www.tensorflow.org/api_docs/python/tf/keras/Model`

- ▶ Machine Learning Mastery: `https://machinelearningmastery.com/keras-functional-api-deep-learning/`
- ▶ Inside TensorFlow: tf.Keras by François Chollet (part1) `https://www.youtube.com/watch?v=UYRBHFAvLSs`
- ▶ Inside TensorFlow: tf.Keras (part2) `https://www.youtube.com/watch?v=uhzGTijaw8A`

Using the Keras Subclassing API

Keras is based on object-oriented design principles. So, we can subclass the `Model` class and create our model architecture definition.

The Keras Subclassing API is the third way proposed by Keras to build deep neural network models.

This API is fully customizable, but this flexibility also brings complexity! So, hold on to your hats, it's harder to use than the Sequential or Functional API.

But you're probably wondering why we need this API if it's so hard to use. Some model architectures and some custom layers can be extremely challenging. Some researchers and some developers hope to have full control of their models and the way to train them. The Subclassing API provides these features. Let's go into the details.

Getting ready

Here, we will cover the main ways of creating a custom layer and a custom model using the Keras Subclassing API.

To start, we load TensorFlow, as follows:

```
import tensorflow as tf
from tensorflow import keras
```

We are ready to proceed with an explanation of how to do it.

How to do it...

Let's start by creating our layer.

Creating a custom layer

As explained in the *Understanding Keras layers* section, Keras provides various built-in layers such as dense, convolutional, recurrent, and normalization layers through its layered API.

All layers are subclasses of the Layer class and implement these methods:

▶ The build method, which defines the weights of the layer.

▶ The call method, which specifies the transformation from inputs to outputs done by the layer.

▶ The compute_output_shape method, if the layer modifies the shape of its input. This allows Keras to perform automatic shape inference.

▶ The get_config and from_config methods, if the layer is serialized and deserialized.

1. Let's put the theory into action. First, we'll make a subclass layer for a custom dense layer:

```python
class MyCustomDense(tf.keras.layers.Layer):
    # Initialize this class with the number of units
    def __init__(self, units):
        super(MyCustomDense, self).__init__()
        self.units = units

    # Define the weights and the bias
    def build(self, input_shape):
        self.w = self.add_weight(shape=(input_shape[-1], self.
units),
                                 initializer='random_normal',
                                 trainable=True)
        self.b = self.add_weight(shape=(self.units,),
                                 initializer='random_normal',
                                 trainable=True)

    # Applying this layer transformation to the input tensor
    def call(self, inputs):
        return tf.matmul(inputs, self.w) + self.b

    # Function to retrieve the configuration
    def get_config(self):
        return {'units': self.units}
```

2. Then, we'll create a model using the `MyCustomDense` layer created in the previous step:

```
# Create an input layer
inputs = keras.Input((12,4))

# Add an instance of MyCustomeDense layer
outputs = MyCustomDense(2)(inputs)

# Create a model
model = keras.Model(inputs, outputs)

# Get the model config
config = model.get_config()
```

3. Next, we will reload the model from the config:

```
new_model = keras.Model.from_config(config,
                            custom_objects={'MyCustomDense':
MyCustomDense})
```

In this recipe, we have created our `Layer` class. Now, we'll create our model.

Creating a custom model

By subclassing the `tf.keras.Model` class, we can build a fully customizable model.

We define our layers in the __init__ method, and we can have full, complete control over the forward pass of the model by implementing the `call` method. The `training` Boolean argument can be used to specify different behavior during the training or inference phase.

1. First, we will load the MNIST dataset and normalize the grayscale:

```
mnist = tf.keras.datasets.mnist
(X_mnist_train, y_mnist_train), (X_mnist_test, y_mnist_test) =
mnist.load_data()

train_mnist_features = X_mnist_train/255
test_mnist_features = X_mnist_test/255
```

2. Let's go and make a subclass `Model` for recognizing MNIST data:

```
class MyMNISTModel(tf.keras.Model):
    def __init__(self, num_classes):
        super(MyMNISTModel, self).__init__(name='my_mnist_model')
        self.num_classes = num_classes

        self.flatten_1 = tf.keras.layers.Flatten()
        self.dropout = tf.keras.layers.Dropout(0.1)
        self.dense_1 = tf.keras.layers.Dense(50, activation='relu')

        self.dense_2 = tf.keras.layers.Dense(10,
activation='softmax')

    def call(self, inputs, training=False):

        x = self.flatten_1(inputs)

        # Apply dropout only during the training phase
        x = self.dense_1(x)
        if training:
            x = self.dropout(x, training=training)
        return self.dense_2(x)
```

3. Now, we are going to instantiate the model and process the training:

```
my_mnist_model = MyMNISTModel(10)
# Compile
my_mnist_model.compile(optimizer='sgd',
                       loss='sparse_categorical_crossentropy',
                       metrics=['accuracy'])
# Train
my_mnist_model.fit(train_features, y_train,
                   validation_data=(test_features, y_test),
                   epochs=10)
```

How it works...

The Subclassing API is a way for deep learning practitioners to build their layers or models using object-oriented Keras design principles. We recommend using this API only if your model cannot be achieved using the Sequential or the Functional API. Although this way can be complicated to implement, it remains useful in a few cases, and it is interesting for all developers and researchers to know how layers and models are implemented in Keras.

See also

For some references on the Keras Subclassing API, see the following tutorials, papers, and articles:

- ▶ Writing custom layers and models with Keras: `https://www.tensorflow.org/guide/keras/custom_layers_and_models`
- ▶ Writing your own Keras layers: `https://keras.io/layers/writing-your-own-keras-layers/`

Using the Keras Preprocessing API

The Keras Preprocessing API gathers modules for data processing and data augmentation. This API provides utilities for working with sequence, text, and image data. Data preprocessing is an essential step in machine learning and deep learning. It converts, transforms, or encodes raw data into an understandable, useful, and efficient format for learning algorithms.

Getting ready

This recipe will cover some preprocessing methods provided by Keras for sequence, text, and image data.

As usual, we just need to import TensorFlow as follows:

```
import tensorflow as tf
from tensorflow import keras
import numpy as np
from tensorflow.keras.preprocessing.sequence import TimeseriesGenerator,
pad_sequences, skipgrams, make_sampling_table
from tensorflow.keras.preprocessing.text import text_to_word_sequence, one_
hot, hashing_trick, Tokenizer
from tensorflow.keras.models import Sequential
from tensorflow.keras.layers import Dense
```

We are ready to proceed with an explanation of how to do it.

How to do it...

Let's start with the sequence data.

Sequence preprocessing

Sequence data is data where the order matters, such as text or a time series. So, a time series is defined by a series of data points ordered by time.

Time series generator

Keras provides utilities for preprocessing sequence data such as time series data. It takes in consecutive data points and applies transformations using time series parameters such as stride, length of history, etc., to return a TensorFlow dataset instance.

1. Let's go with a toy time series dataset of 10 integer values:

   ```
   series = np.array([i for i in range(10)])
   print(series)
   ```

2. This results in the following output:

   ```
   array([0, 1, 2, 3, 4, 5, 6, 7, 8, 9])
   ```

3. We want to predict the next value from the last five lag observations. So, we'll define a generator with the `length` argument set to 5. This argument specifies the length of the output sequences in a number of timesteps:

   ```
   generator = TimeseriesGenerator(data = series,
                                   targets = series,
                                   length=5,
                                   batch_size=1,
                                   shuffle=False,
                                   reverse=False)
   ```

4. We want to generate samples composed of 5 lag observations for one prediction and the toy time series dataset contains 10 values. So, the number of samples generated is 5:

   ```
   # number of samples
   print('Samples: %d' % len(generator))
   ```

5. Then, we'll display the inputs and output of each sample and check that the data is well prepared:

   ```
   for i in range(len(generator)):
       x, y = generator[i]
       print('%s => %s' % (x, y))
   ```

6. This results in the following output:

   ```
   [[0 1 2 3 4]] => [5]
   [[1 2 3 4 5]] => [6]
   [[2 3 4 5 6]] => [7]
   ```

```
[[3 4 5 6 7]] => [8]
[[4 5 6 7 8]] => [9]
```

7. Now, we'll create and compile a model:

    ```
    model = Sequential()
    model.add(Dense(10, activation='relu', input_dim=5))
    model.add(Dense(1))
    model.compile(optimizer='adam', loss='mse')
    ```

8. And we'll train the model by giving the generator as input data:

    ```
    model.fit(generator, epochs=10)
    ```

Preparing time series data for modeling with deep learning methods can be very challenging. But fortunately, Keras provides a generator that will help us transform a univariate or multivariate time series dataset into a data structure ready to train models. This generator offers many options to prepare the data, such as the shuffle, the sampling rate, the start and end offsets, etc. We recommend consulting the official Keras API to get more details.

Now, we'll focus on how to prepare data for variable-length input sequences.

Padding sequences

When processing sequence data, each sample often has different lengths. In order for all the sequences to fit the desired length, the solution is to pad them. Sequences shorter than the defined sequence length are padded with values at the end (by default) or the beginning of each sequence. Otherwise, if the sequence is greater than the desired length, the sequence is truncated.

1. Let's start with four sentences:

    ```
    sentences = [["What", "do", "you", "like", "?"],
                 ["I", "like", "basket-ball", "!"],
                 ["And", "you", "?"],
                 ["I", "like", "coconut", "and", "apple"]]
    ```

2. First, we'll build the vocabulary lookup table. We'll create two dictionaries to go from the words to integer identifiers and vice versa.

    ```
    text_set = set(np.concatenate(sentences))
    vocab_to_int = dict(zip(text_set, range(len(text_set))))
    int_to_vocab = {vocab_to_int[word]:word for word in vocab_to_int.
    keys()}
    ```

3. Then after building the vocabulary lookup table, we'll encode the sentences as integer arrays.

```
encoded_sentences = []
for sentence in sentences:
    encoded_sentence = [vocab_to_int[word] for word in sentence]
    encoded_sentences.append(encoded_sentence)
encoded_sentences
```

4. This results in the following output:

```
[[8, 4, 7, 6, 0], [5, 6, 2, 3], [10, 7, 0], [5, 6, 1, 9, 11]]
```

5. Now, we'll use the pad_sequences function to truncate and pad sequences to a common length easily. The pre-sequence padding is activated by default.

```
pad_sequences(encoded_sentences)
```

6. This results in the following output:

```
array([[ 8,  4,  7,  6,  0],
       [ 0,  5,  6,  2,  3],
       [ 0,  0, 10,  7,  0],
       [ 5,  6,  1,  9, 11]], dtype=int32)
```

7. Then, we'll activate the post-sequence padding and set the maxlen argument to the desired length – here, 7.

```
pad_sequences(encoded_sentences, maxlen = 7)
```

8. This results in the following output:

```
array([[ 0,  0,  8,  4,  7,  6,  0],
       [ 0,  0,  0,  5,  6,  2,  3],
       [ 0,  0,  0,  0, 10,  7,  0],
       [ 0,  0,  5,  6,  1,  9, 11]], dtype=int32)
```

9. The length of the sequence can also be trimmed to the desired length – here, 3. By default, this function removes timesteps from the beginning of each sequence.

```
pad_sequences(encoded_sentences, maxlen = 3)
```

10. This results in the following output:

```
array([[ 7,  6,  0],
       [ 6,  2,  3],
       [10,  7,  0],
       [ 1,  9, 11]], dtype=int32)
```

11. Set the truncating argument to `post` to remove timesteps from the end of each sequence.

```
pad_sequences(encoded_sentences, maxlen = 3, truncating='post')
```

12. This results in the following output:

```
array([[ 8,  4,  7],
       [ 5,  6,  2],
       [10,  7,  0],
       [ 5,  6,  1]], dtype=int32)
```

Padding is very useful when we want all sequences in a list to have the same length.

In the next section, we will cover a very popular technique for preprocessing text.

Skip-grams

Skip-grams is one of the unsupervised learning techniques in natural language processing. It finds the most related words for a given word and predicts the context word for this given word.

Keras provides the `skipgrams` pre-processing function, which takes in an integer-encoded sequence of words and returns the relevance for each pair of words in the defined window. If the pair of words is relevant, the sample is positive, and the associated label is set to 1. Otherwise, the sample is considered negative, and the label is set to 0.

An example is better than thousands of words. So, let's take this sentence, `"I like coconut and apple,"` select the first word as our "context word," and use a window size of two. We make pairs of the context word "I" with the word covered in the specified window. So, we have two pairs of words (`I, like`) and (`I, coconut`), both of which equal 1.

Let's put the theory into action:

1. First, we'll encode a sentence as a list of word indices:

```
sentence = "I like coconut and apple"
encoded_sentence = [vocab_to_int[word] for word in sentence.split()]
vocabulary_size = len(encoded_sentence)
```

2. Then, we'll call the `skipgrams` function with a window size of 1:

```
pairs, labels = skipgrams(encoded_sentence,
                          vocabulary_size,
                          window_size=1,
                          negative_samples=0)
```

3. Now, we'll print the results:

```
for i in range(len(pairs)):
    print("({:s} , {:s} ) -> {:d}".format(
        int_to_vocab[pairs[i][0]],
        int_to_vocab[pairs[i][1]],
        labels[i]))
```

4. This results in the following output:

```
(coconut , and ) -> 1
(apple , ! ) -> 0
(and , coconut ) -> 1
(apple , and ) -> 1
(coconut , do ) -> 0
(like , I ) -> 1
(and , apple ) -> 1
(like , coconut ) -> 1
(coconut , do ) -> 0
(I , like ) -> 1
(coconut , like ) -> 1
(and , do ) -> 0
(like , coconut ) -> 0
(I , ! ) -> 0
(like , ! ) -> 0
(and , coconut ) -> 0
```

Note that the non-word is defined by index 0 in the vocabulary and will be skipped. We recommend that readers consult the Keras API to find more details about padding.

Now, let's introduce some tips to preprocess text data.

Text preprocessing

In deep learning, we cannot feed raw text directly into our network. We have to encode our text as numbers and provide integers as input. Our model will generate integers as output. This module provides utilities for preprocessing text input.

Split text to word sequence

Keras provides the text_to_word_sequence method, which transforms a sequence into a list of words or tokens.

1. Let's go with this sentence:

```
sentence = "I like coconut , I like apple"
```

2. Then, we'll call the method that converts a sentence into a list of words. By default, this method splits the text on whitespace.

```
text_to_word_sequence(sentence, lower=False)
```

3. This results in the following output:

```
['I', 'like', 'coconut', 'I', 'like', 'apple']
```

4. Now, we'll set the `lower` argument to `True`, and the text will be converted to lower case:

```
text_to_word_sequence(sentence, lower=True, filters=[])
```

5. This results in the following output:

```
['i', 'like', 'coconut', ',', 'i', 'like', 'apple']
```

Note that by default, the `filter` argument filters out a list of characters such as punctuation. In our last code execution, we removed all the predefined filters.

Let's continue with a method to encode words or categorical features.

Tokenizer

The `Tokenizer` class is the utility class for text tokenization. It's the preferred approach for preparing text in deep learning.

This class takes as inputs:

▶ The maximum number of words to keep. Only the most common words will be kept based on word frequency.

▶ A list of characters to filter out.

▶ A boolean to convert the text into lower case, or not.

▶ The separator for word splitting.

1. Let's go with this sentence:

```
sentences = [["What", "do", "you", "like", "?"],
             ["I", "like", "basket-ball", "!"],
             ["And", "you", "?"],
             ["I", "like", "coconut", "and", "apple"]]
```

2. Now, we will create a `Tokenizer` instance and fit it on the previous sentences:

```
# create the tokenizer
t = Tokenizer()
# fit the tokenizer on the documents
t.fit_on_texts(sentences)
```

3. The tokenizer creates several pieces of information about the document. We can get a dictionary containing the count for each word.

```
print(t.word_counts)
```

4. This results in the following outputs:

```
OrderedDict([('what', 1), ('do', 1), ('you', 2), ('like', 3), ('?',
2), ('i', 2), ('basket-ball', 1), ('!', 1), ('and', 2), ('coconut',
1), ('apple', 1)])
```

5. We can also get a dictionary containing, for each word, the number of documents in which it appears:

```
print(t.document_count)
```

6. This results in the following outputs:

```
4
```

7. A dictionary contains, for each word, its unique integer identifier:

```
print(t.word_index)
```

8. This results in the following outputs:

```
{'like': 1, 'you': 2, '?': 3, 'i': 4, 'and': 5, 'what': 6, 'do': 7,
'basket-ball': 8, '!': 9, 'coconut': 10, 'apple': 11}
```

9. The number of unique documents that were used to fit the `Tokenizer`.

```
print(t.word_docs)
```

10. This results in the following outputs:

```
defaultdict(<class 'int'>, {'do': 1, 'like': 3, 'what': 1, 'you': 2,
'?': 2, '!': 1, 'basket-ball': 1, 'i': 2, 'and': 2, 'coconut': 1,
'apple': 1})
```

11. Now, we are ready to encode our documents, thanks to the `texts_to_matrix` function. This function provides four different document encoding schemes to compute the coefficient for each token.

    Let's start with the binary mode, which returns whether or not each token is present in the document.

```
t.texts_to_matrix(sentences, mode='binary')
```

12. This results in the following outputs:

```
[[0. 1. 1. 1. 0. 0. 1. 1. 0. 0. 0. 0.]
 [0. 1. 0. 0. 1. 0. 0. 0. 1. 1. 0. 0.]
 [0. 0. 1. 1. 0. 1. 0. 0. 0. 0. 0. 0.]
 [0. 1. 0. 0. 1. 1. 0. 0. 0. 0. 1. 1.]]
```

13. The `Tokenizer` API offers another mode based on word count – it returns the count of each word in the document:

```
t.texts_to_matrix(sentences, mode='count')
```

14. This results in the following outputs:

```
[[0. 1. 1. 1. 0. 0. 1. 1. 0. 0. 0. 0.]
 [0. 1. 0. 0. 1. 0. 0. 0. 1. 1. 0. 0.]
 [0. 0. 1. 1. 0. 1. 0. 0. 0. 0. 0. 0.]
 [0. 1. 0. 0. 1. 1. 0. 0. 0. 0. 1. 1.]]
```

Note that we can also use the `tfidf` mode or the frequency mode. The first returns the term frequency-inverse document frequency score for each word, and the second returns the frequency of each word in the document related to the total number of words in the document.

The `Tokenizer` API can fit the training dataset and encode text data in the training, validation, and test datasets.

In this section, we have covered a few techniques to prepare text data before training and prediction.

Now, let's go on to prepare and augment images.

Image preprocessing

The data preprocessing module provides a set of tools for real-time data augmentation on image data.

In deep learning, the performance of a neural network is often improved by the number of examples available in the training dataset.

The `ImageDataGenerator` class in the Keras preprocessing API allows the creation of new data from the training dataset. It isn't applied to the validation or test dataset because it aims to expand the number of examples in the training datasets with plausible new images. This technique is called data augmentation. Beware not to confuse data preparation with data normalization or image resizing, which is applied to all data in interaction with the model. Data augmentation includes many transformations from the field of image manipulation, such as rotation, horizontal and vertical shift, horizontal and vertical flip, brightness, and much more.

The strategy may differ depending on the task to realize. For example, in the MNIST dataset, which contains images of handwritten digits, applying a horizontal flip doesn't make sense. Except for the figure 8, this transformation isn't appropriate.

While in the case of a baby picture, applying this kind of transformation makes sense because the image could have been taken from the left or right.

1. Let's put the theory into action and perform a data augmentation on the `CIFAR10` dataset. We will start by downloading the `CIFAR` dataset.

    ```
    # Load CIFAR10 Dataset
    (x_cifar10_train, y_cifar10_train), (x_cifar10_test, y_cifar10_test)
    = tf.keras.datasets.cifar10.load_data()
    ```

2. Now, we'll create an image data generator that applies a horizontal flip, a random rotation between 0 and 15, and a shift of 3 pixels on the width and on the height.

    ```
    datagen = tf.keras.preprocessing.image.ImageDataGenerator(
        rotation_range=15,
        width_shift_range=3,
        height_shift_range=3,
        horizontal_flip=True)
    ```

3. Create an iterator on the train dataset.

    ```
    it= datagen.flow(x_cifar10_train, y_cifar10_train, batch_size = 32)
    ```

4. Create a model and compile it.

    ```
    model = tf.keras.models.Sequential([
        tf.keras.layers.Conv2D(filters=32, kernel_size=3, padding="same",
    activation="relu", input_shape=[32, 32, 3]),
        tf.keras.layers.Conv2D(filters=32, kernel_size=3, padding="same",
    activation="relu"),
        tf.keras.layers.MaxPool2D(pool_size=2),
        tf.keras.layers.Conv2D(filters=64, kernel_size=3, padding="same",
    activation="relu"),
        tf.keras.layers.Conv2D(filters=64, kernel_size=3, padding="same",
    activation="relu"),
        tf.keras.layers.MaxPool2D(pool_size=2),
        tf.keras.layers.Flatten(),
        tf.keras.layers.Dense(128, activation="relu"),
        tf.keras.layers.Dense(10, activation="softmax")
    ])

    model.compile(loss="sparse_categorical_crossentropy",
                    optimizer=tf.keras.optimizers.SGD(lr=0.01),
                    metrics=["accuracy"])
    ```

5. And process the training by calling the `fit` method. Take care to set the `step_per_epoch` argument, which specifies the number of sample batches comprising an epoch.

```
history = model.fit(it, epochs=10,
                    steps_per_epoch=len(x_cifar10_train) / 32,
                    validation_data=(x_cifar10_test,
                                     y_cifar10_test))
```

With the image data generator, we have extended the size of our original dataset by creating new images. With more images, the training of a deep learning model can be improved.

How it works...

The Keras Preprocessing API allows transforming, encoding, and augmenting data for neural networks. It makes it easier to work with sequence, text, and image data.

First, we introduced the Keras Sequence Preprocessing API. We used the time series generator to transform a univariate or multivariate time series dataset into a data structure ready to train models. Then, we focused on the data preparation for variable-length input sequences, aka padding. And we finished this first part with the skip-gram technique, which finds the most related words for a given word and predicts the context word for that given word.

Then, we covered the Keras Text Preprocessing API, which offers a complete turnkey solution to process natural language. We learned how to split text into words and tokenize the words using binary, word count, `tfidf`, or frequency mode.

Finally, we focused on the Image Preprocessing API using the `ImageDataGenerator`, which is a real advantage to increase the size of your training dataset and to work with images.

See also

For some references on the Keras Preprocessing API, visit the following websites:

- Sequence Preprocessing Keras API: http://keras.io/preprocessing/sequence/
- Text Processing Keras API: https://keras.io/preprocessing/text/
- More about syntactic and semantic word similarities: Tomas Mikolov and Kai Chen and Greg Corrado and Jeffrey Dean. (2013). Efficient Estimation of Word Representations in Vector Space https://arxiv.org/pdf/1301.3781v3.pdf
- Image Preprocessing Keras API: http://keras.io/preprocessing/image/
- More examples of data image augmentation: https://machinelearningmastery.com/how-to-configure-image-data-augmentation-when-training-deep-learning-neural-networks/

4

Linear Regression

Linear regression may be one of the most important algorithms in statistics, machine learning, and science in general. It's one of the most widely used algorithms, and it is very important to understand how to implement it and its various flavors. One of the advantages that linear regression has over many other algorithms is that it is very interpretable. We end up with a number (a coefficient) for each feature and such a number directly represents how that feature influences the target (the so-called dependent variable).

For instance, if you had to predict the selling value of a house and you obtained a dataset of historical sales comprising house characteristics (such as the lot size, indicators of the quality and condition of the house, and the distance from the city center), you could easily apply a linear regression. You could obtain a reliable estimator in a few steps and the resulting model would be easy to understand and explain to others, too. A linear regression, in fact, first estimates a baseline value, called the intercept, and then estimates a multiplicative coefficient for each feature. Each coefficient can transform each feature into a positive and negative part of the prediction. By summing the baseline and all the coefficient-transformed features, you get your final prediction. Therefore, in our house sale price prediction problem, you could get a positive coefficient for the lot size, implying that larger lots will sell for more, and a negative coefficient for the distance from the city center, an indicator that estates located in the outskirts have less market value.

Computing such kinds of models with TensorFlow is fast, suitable for big data, and much easier to put into production because it will be accessible to general interpretation by inspection of a weights vector.

In this chapter, we will introduce you to recipes explaining how linear regression is implemented in TensorFlow, via Estimators or Keras, and then move on to providing solutions that are even more practical. In fact, we will explain how to tweak it using different loss functions, how to regularize coefficients in order to achieve feature selection in your models, and how to use regression for classification, for non-linear problems, and when you have categorical variables with high-cardinality (high-cardinality means variables with many unique values).

 Remember that all the code is available on GitHub at `https://github.com/PacktPublishing/Machine-Learning-Using-TensorFlow-Cookbook`.

In this chapter, we will cover recipes involving linear regression. We start with the mathematical formulation for solving linear regression with matrices, before moving on to implementing standard linear regression and variants with the TensorFlow paradigm. We will cover the following topics:

- ▶ Learning the TensorFlow way of regression
- ▶ Turning a Keras model into an Estimator
- ▶ Understanding loss functions in linear regression
- ▶ Implementing Lasso and Ridge regression
- ▶ Implementing logistic regression
- ▶ Resorting to non-linear solutions
- ▶ Using Wide & Deep models

By the end of the chapter, you will find that creating linear models (and some non-linear ones, too) using TensorFlow is easy using the recipes provided.

Learning the TensorFlow way of linear regression

The statistical approach in linear regression, using matrices and decomposition methods on data, is very powerful. In any event TensorFlow has another means to solve for the coefficients of a slope and an intercept in a regression problem. TensorFlow can achieve a result in such problems iteratively, that is, gradually learning the best linear regression parameters that will minimize the loss, as we have seen in the recipes in previous chapters.

The interesting fact is that you actually don't have to write all the code from scratch when dealing with a regression problem in TensorFlow: Estimators and Keras can assist you in doing that. Estimators are to be found in `tf.estimator`, a high-level API in TensorFlow.

Estimators were introduced in TensorFlow 1.3 (see `https://github.com/tensorflow/tensorflow/releases/tag/v1.3.0-rc2`) as **"canned Estimators"**, pre-made specific procedures (such as regression models or basic neural networks) created to simplify training, evaluation, predicting, and the exporting of models for serving. Using pre-made procedures aids development in an easier and more intuitive way, leaving the low-level API for customized or research solutions (for instance, when you want to test the solutions you found in a paper or when your problem requires a completely customized approach). Moreover, Estimators are easily deployed on CPUs, GPUs, or TPUs, as well as on a local host or on a distributed multi-server environment, without any further code changes on your model, making them suitable for ready-to-production use cases. That is the reason why Estimators are absolutely not going away anytime soon from TensorFlow, even if Keras, as presented in the previous chapter, is the main high-level API for TensorFlow 2.x. On the contrary, more and more support and development will be made to integrate between Keras and Estimators and you will soon realize in our recipes how easily you can turn Keras models into your own custom Estimators.

Four steps are involved in developing an Estimator model:

1. Acquire your data using `tf.data` functions
2. Instantiate the feature column(s)
3. Instantiate and train the Estimator
4. Evaluate the model's performance

In our recipes, we will explore all four steps providing you with reusable solutions for each.

Getting ready

In this recipe, we will loop through batches of data points and let TensorFlow update the slope and y intercept. Instead of generated data, we will use the Boston Housing dataset.

Originating in the paper by Harrison, D. and Rubinfeld, D.L. *Hedonic Housing Prices and the Demand for Clean Air* (J. Environ. Economics & Management, vol.5, 81-102, 1978), the Boston Housing dataset can be found in many analysis packages (such as in scikit-learn) and is present at the UCI Machine Learning Repository, as well as at the original StatLib archive (http://lib.stat.cmu.edu/datasets/boston). It is a classical dataset for regression problems, but not a trivial one. For instance, the samples are ordered and if you do not shuffle the examples randomly, you may produce ineffective and biased models when you make a train/test split.

Going into the details, the dataset is made up of 506 census tracts of Boston from the 1970 census and it features 21 variables regarding various aspects that could affect real estate value. The target variable is the median monetary value of the houses, expressed in thousands of USD. Among the available features, there are a number of obvious ones, such as the number of rooms, the age of the buildings, and the crime levels in the neighborhood, and some others that are a bit less obvious, such as the pollution concentration, the availability of nearby schools, the access to highways, and the distance from employment centers.

Getting back to our solution, specifically, we will find an optimal of the features that will assist us in estimating the house prices in Boston. Before talking more about the effects of different loss functions on this problem in the next section, we are also going to show you how to create a regression Estimator in TensorFlow starting from Keras functions, which opens up important customizations for solving different problems.

How to do it...

We proceed with the recipe as follows:

We start by loading the necessary libraries, and then load the data in-memory using pandas functions. We will also separate predictors from targets (the MEDV, median house values) and divide the data into training and test sets:

```python
import tensorflow as tf
import numpy as np
import pandas as pd
import tensorflow_datasets as tfds
tfds.disable_progress_bar()

housing_url = 'http://archive.ics.uci.edu/ml/machine-learning-databases/
housing/housing.data'
path = tf.keras.utils.get_file(housing_url.split("/")[-1], housing_url)

columns = ['CRIM', 'ZN', 'INDUS', 'CHAS', 'NOX', 'RM', 'AGE',
           'DIS', 'RAD', 'TAX', 'PTRATIO', 'B', 'LSTAT', 'MEDV']
data = pd.read_table(path, delim_whitespace=True,
                     header=None, names=columns)

np.random.seed(1)
train = data.sample(frac=0.8).copy()
y_train = train['MEDV']
train.drop('MEDV', axis=1, inplace=True)

test = data.loc[~data.index.isin(train.index)].copy()
y_test = test['MEDV']
test.drop('MEDV', axis=1, inplace=True)
```

We then declare two key functions for our recipe:

1. `make_input_fn`, which is a function that creates a `tf.data` dataset from a pandas DataFrame turned into a Python dictionary of pandas Series (the features are the keys, the values are the feature vectors). It also provides batch size definition and random shuffling.

2. `define_feature_columns`, which is a function that maps each column name to a specific `tf.feature_column` transformation. `tf.feature_column` is a TensorFlow module (https://www.tensorflow.org/api_docs/python/tf/feature_column) offering functions that can process any kind of data in a suitable way for being inputted into a neural network.

The `make_input_fn` function is used to instantiate two data functions, one for training (the data is shuffled, with a batch size of 256 and set to consume 1,400 epochs), and one for test (set to a single epoch, no shuffling, so the ordering is the original one).

The `define_feature_columns` function is used to map the numeric variables using the `numeric_column` function (https://www.tensorflow.org/api_docs/python/tf/feature_column/numeric_column) and the categorical ones using `categorical_column_with_vocabulary_list` (https://www.tensorflow.org/api_docs/python/tf/feature_column/categorical_column_with_vocabulary_list). Both will signal to our Estimator how to handle such data in the optimal manner:

```python
learning_rate = 0.05
def make_input_fn(data_df, label_df, num_epochs=10,
                  shuffle=True, batch_size=256):

    def input_function():
        ds = tf.data.Dataset.from_tensor_slices((dict(data_df), label_df))
        if shuffle:
            ds = ds.shuffle(1000)
        ds = ds.batch(batch_size).repeat(num_epochs)
        return ds

    return input_function

def define_feature_columns(data_df, categorical_cols, numeric_cols):
    feature_columns = []

    for feature_name in numeric_cols:
        feature_columns.append(tf.feature_column.numeric_column(
            feature_name, dtype=tf.float32))

    for feature_name in categorical_cols:
        vocabulary = data_df[feature_name].unique()
```

```
        feature_columns.append(

    tf.feature_column.categorical_column_with_vocabulary_list(
                                    feature_name, vocabulary))

        return feature_columns

categorical_cols = ['CHAS', 'RAD']
numeric_cols = ['CRIM', 'ZN', 'INDUS',  'NOX', 'RM', 'AGE', 'DIS', 'TAX',
'PTRATIO', 'B', 'LSTAT']
feature_columns = define_feature_columns(data, categorical_cols, numeric_
cols)

train_input_fn = make_input_fn(train, y_train, num_epochs=1400)
test_input_fn = make_input_fn(test, y_test, num_epochs=1, shuffle=False)
```

As a next step, we pass to instantiate the Estimator for a linear regression model. We will just recall the formula for the linear model, $y = aX + b$, which implies that there is a coefficient for the intercept value and then a coefficient for each feature or feature transformation (for instance, categorical data is one-hot encoded, so you have a single coefficient for each value of the variable):

```
linear_est = tf.estimator.LinearRegressor(feature_columns=feature_columns)
```

Now, we just have to train the model and evaluate its performance. The metric used is the root mean squared error (the less the better):

```
linear_est.train(train_input_fn)
result = linear_est.evaluate(test_input_fn)

print(result)
```

Here are the reported results:

```
INFO:tensorflow:Loss for final step: 25.013594.
...
INFO:tensorflow:Finished evaluation at 2020-05-11-15:48:16
INFO:tensorflow:Saving dict for global step 2800: average_loss = 32.715736,
global_step = 2800, label/mean = 22.048513, loss = 32.715736, prediction/
mean = 21.27578
```

Here is a good place to note how to see whether the model is overfitting or underfitting the data. If our data is broken into test and training sets, and the performance is greater on the training set and lower on the test set, then we are overfitting the data. If the accuracy is still increasing on both the test and training sets, then the model is underfitting and we should continue training.

In our case, the training ended with an average loss of 25.0. Our test average is instead 32.7, implying we have probably overfitted and we should reduce the training iterations.

We can visualize the performances of the Estimator as it trains the data and as it is compared to the test set results. This requires the use of TensorBoard (`https://www.tensorflow.org/tensorboard/`), TensorFlow's visualization kit, which will be explained in more detail later in the book.

In any event, you can just replicate the visualizations by using the `4. Linear Regression with TensorBoard.ipynb` notebook instead of the `4. Linear Regression.ipynb` version. Both can be found in the book's GitHub repository at `https://github.com/PacktPublishing/Machine-Learning-Using-TensorFlow-Cookbook`.

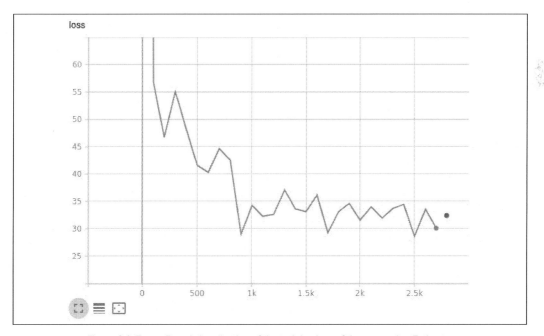

Figure 4.1: TensorBoard visualization of the training loss of the regression Estimator

The visualization shows that the Estimator fitted the problem quickly, reaching an optimal value after 1,000 observed batches. Afterward, it oscillated near the minimum loss value reached. The test performance, represented by a blue dot, is near the best reached value, thereby proving that the model is performing and stable even with unseen examples.

How it works...

The Estimator that calls the proper TensorFlow functionalities, sifts the data from the data functions, and converts the data into the proper form based on the matched feature name and `tf.feature_column` function does the entire job. All that remains is to check the fitting. Actually, the optimal line found by the Estimator is not guaranteed to be the line of best fit. Convergence to the line of best fit depends on the number of iterations, batch size, learning rate, and loss function. It is always good practice to observe the loss function over time as this can help you troubleshoot problems or hyperparameter changes.

There's more...

If you want to increase the performance of your linear model, interactions could be the key. This means that you create a combination between two variables and that combination can explain the target better than the features taken singularly. In our Boston Housing dataset, combining the average room number in a house and the proportion of the lower income population in an area can reveal more about the type of neighborhood and help infer the housing value of the area. We combine the two just by pointing them out to the `tf.feature_column.crossed_column` function.The Estimator, also receiving this output among the features, will automatically create the interaction:

```
def create_interactions(interactions_list, buckets=5):
    interactions = list()
    for (a, b) in interactions_list:
        interactions.append(tf.feature_column.crossed_column([a, b], hash_
bucket_size=buckets))
    return interactions


derived_feature_columns = create_interactions([['RM', 'LSTAT']])
linear_est = tf.estimator.LinearRegressor(feature_columns=feature_
columns+derived_feature_columns)
linear_est.train(train_input_fn)
result = linear_est.evaluate(test_input_fn)

print(result)
```

Here is the plot of the training loss and the resulting test set result.

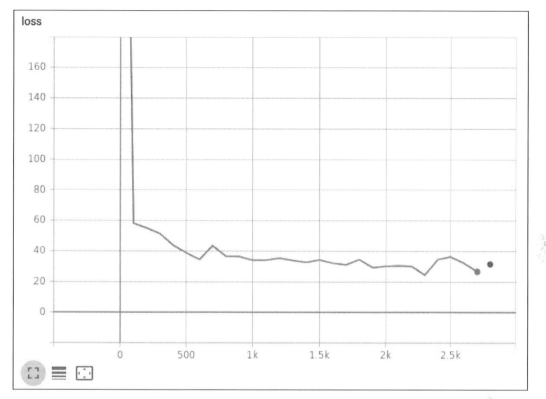

Figure 4.2: TensorBoard plot of the regression model with interactions

Observe how the fitting is now faster and much more stable than before, indicating that we provided more informative features to the model (the interactions).

Another useful recipe function is suitable for handling predictions: the Estimator returns them as a dictionary. A simple function will convert everything into a more useful array of predictions:

```
def dicts_to_preds(pred_dicts):
    return np.array([pred['predictions'] for pred in pred_dicts])

preds = dicts_to_preds(linear_est.predict(test_input_fn))
print(preds)
```

Having your predictions as an array will help you to reuse and export the results in a more convenient way than a dictionary could.

Turning a Keras model into an Estimator

Up to now, we have worked out our linear regression models using specific Estimators from the `tf.estimator` module. This has clear advantages because our model is mostly run automatically and we can easily deploy it in a scalable way on the cloud (such as Google Cloud Platform, offered by Google) and on different kinds of servers (CPU-, GPU-, and TPU-based). Anyway, by using Estimators, we may lack the flexibility in our model architecture as required by our data problem, which is instead offered by the Keras modular approach that we discussed in the previous chapter. In this recipe, we will remediate this by showing how we can transform Keras models into Estimators and thus take advantage of both the Estimators API and Keras versatility at the same time.

Getting ready

We will use the same Boston Housing dataset as in the previous recipe, while also making use of the `make_input_fn` function. As before, we need our core packages to be imported:

```
import tensorflow as tf
import numpy as np
import pandas as pd
import tensorflow_datasets as tfds
tfds.disable_progress_bar()
```

We will also need to import the Keras module from TensorFlow.

```
import tensorflow.keras as keras
```

Importing `tf.keras` as `keras` will also allow you to easily reuse any previous script that you wrote using the standalone Keras package.

How to do it...

Our first step will be to redefine the function creating the feature columns. In fact, now we have to specify an input to our Keras model, something that was not necessary with native Estimators since they just need a `tf.feature` function mapping the feature:

```
def define_feature_columns_layers(data_df, categorical_cols, numeric_cols):
    feature_columns = []
    feature_layer_inputs = {}

    for feature_name in numeric_cols:
        feature_columns.append(tf.feature_column.numeric_column(feature_
name, dtype=tf.float32))
```

```
        feature_layer_inputs[feature_name] = tf.keras.Input(shape=(1,),
    name=feature_name)

        for feature_name in categorical_cols:
            vocabulary = data_df[feature_name].unique()
            cat = tf.feature_column.categorical_column_with_vocabulary_
    list(feature_name, vocabulary)
            cat_one_hot = tf.feature_column.indicator_column(cat)
            feature_columns.append(cat_one_hot)
            feature_layer_inputs[feature_name] = tf.keras.Input(shape=(1,),
    name=feature_name, dtype=tf.int32)

        return feature_columns, feature_layer_inputs
```

The same goes for interactions. Here, too, we need to define the input that will be used by our Keras model (in this case, one-hot encoding):

```
def create_interactions(interactions_list, buckets=5):
    feature_columns = []

    for (a, b) in interactions_list:
        crossed_feature = tf.feature_column.crossed_column([a, b], hash_
bucket_size=buckets)
        crossed_feature_one_hot = tf.feature_column.indicator_
column(crossed_feature)
        feature_columns.append(crossed_feature_one_hot)

    return feature_columns
```

After preparing the necessary inputs, we can proceed to the model itself. The inputs will be collected in a feature layer that will pass the data to a `batchNormalization` layer, which will automatically standardize it. After that the data will be directed to the output node, which will produce the numeric output.

```
def create_linreg(feature_columns, feature_layer_inputs, optimizer):

    feature_layer = keras.layers.DenseFeatures(feature_columns)
    feature_layer_outputs = feature_layer(feature_layer_inputs)
    norm = keras.layers.BatchNormalization()(feature_layer_outputs)
    outputs = keras.layers.Dense(1, kernel_initializer='normal',
activation='linear')(norm)

    model = keras.Model(inputs=[v for v in feature_layer_inputs.values()],
outputs=outputs)
    model.compile(optimizer=optimizer, loss='mean_squared_error')
    return model
```

At this point, having set all the necessary inputs, new functions are created and we can run them:

```
categorical_cols = ['CHAS', 'RAD']
numeric_cols = ['CRIM', 'ZN', 'INDUS', 'NOX', 'RM', 'AGE', 'DIS', 'TAX',
'PTRATIO', 'B', 'LSTAT']
feature_columns, feature_layer_inputs = define_feature_columns_layers(data,
categorical_cols, numeric_cols)
interactions_columns = create_interactions([['RM', 'LSTAT']])

feature_columns += interactions_columns

optimizer = keras.optimizers.Ftrl(learning_rate=0.02)
model = create_linreg(feature_columns, feature_layer_inputs, optimizer)
```

We have now obtained a working Keras model. We can convert it into an Estimator using the `model_to_estimator` function. This requires the establishment of a temporary directory for the Estimator's outputs:

```
import tempfile

def canned_keras(model):
    model_dir = tempfile.mkdtemp()
    keras_estimator = tf.keras.estimator.model_to_estimator(
        keras_model=model, model_dir=model_dir)
    return keras_estimator
estimator = canned_keras(model)
```

Having canned the Keras model into an Estimator, we can proceed as before to train the model and evaluate the results.

```
train_input_fn = make_input_fn(train, y_train, num_epochs=1400)
test_input_fn = make_input_fn(test, y_test, num_epochs=1, shuffle=False)

estimator.train(train_input_fn)
result = estimator.evaluate(test_input_fn)

print(result)
```

When we plot the fitting process using TensorBoard, we will observehow the training trajectory is quite similar to the one obtained by previous Estimators:

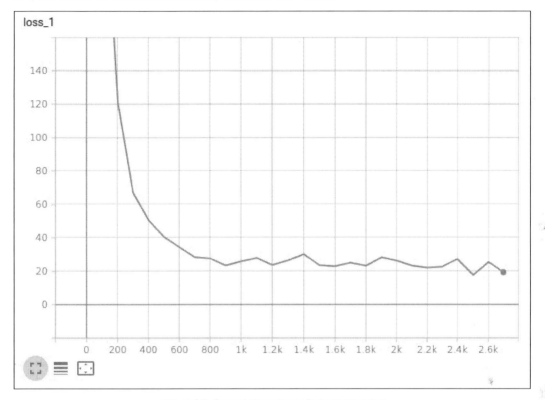

Figure 4.3: Canned Keras linear Estimator training

Canned Keras Estimators are indeed a quick and robust way to bind together the flexibility of user-defined solutions by Keras and the high-performance training and deployment from Estimators.

How it works...

The `model_to_estimator` function is not a wrapper of your Keras model. Instead, it parses your model and transforms it into a static TensorFlow graph, allowing distributed training and scaling for your model.

There's more...

One great advantage of using linear models is to be able to explore their weights and get an idea of what feature is producing the result we obtained. Each coefficient will tell us, given the fact that the inputs are standardized by the batch layer, how that feature is impacted with respect to the others (the coefficients are comparable in terms of absolute value) and whether it is adding or subtracting from the result (given a positive or negative sign):

```
weights = estimator.get_variable_value('layer_with_weights-1/kernel/.
ATTRIBUTES/VARIABLE_VALUE')
print(weights)
```

Anyway, if we extract the weights from our model we will find out that we cannot easily interpret them because they have no labels and the dimensionality is different since the tf.feature functions have applied different transformations.

We need a function that can extract the correct labels from our feature columns as we mapped them prior to feeding them to our canned Estimator:

```
def extract_labels(feature_columns):
    labels = list()
    for col in feature_columns:
        col_config = col.get_config()
        if 'key' in col_config:
            labels.append(col_config['key'])
        elif 'categorical_column' in col_config:
            if
col_config['categorical_column']['class_name']=='VocabularyListCategoricalC
olumn':
                key = col_config['categorical_column']['config']['key']
                for item in
col_config['categorical_column']['config']['vocabulary_list']:
                    labels.append(key+'_val='+str(item))
            elif
col_config['categorical_column']['class_name']=='CrossedColumn':
                keys =
col_config['categorical_column']['config']['keys']
                for bucket in
range(col_config['categorical_column']['config']['hash_bucket_size']):
                    labels.append('x'.join(keys)+'_bkt_'+str(bucket))
    return labels
```

This function only works with TensorFlow version 2.2 or later because in earlier TensorFlow 2.x versions the get_config method was not present in tf.feature objects.

Now we can extract all the labels and meaningfully match each weight in the output to its respective feature:

```
labels = extract_labels(feature_columns)

for label, weight in zip(labels, weights):
    print(f"{label:15s} : {weight[0]:+.2f}")
```

Once you have the weights, you can easily get the contribution of each feature to the result by observing the sign and the magnitude of each coefficient. The scale of the feature can, however, influence the magnitude unless you previously statistically standardized the features by subtracting the mean and dividing by the standard deviation.

Understanding loss functions in linear regression

It is important to know the effect of loss functions in algorithm convergence. Here, we will illustrate how the L1 and L2 loss functions affect convergence and predictions in linear regression. This is the first customization that we are applying to our canned Keras Estimator. More recipes in this chapter will enhance that initial Estimator by adding more functionality.

Getting ready

We will use the same Boston Housing dataset as in the previous recipe, as well as utilize the following functions:

```
* define_feature_columns_layers
* make_input_fn
* create_interactions
```

However, we will change our loss functions and learning rates to see how convergence changes.

How to do it...

We proceed with the recipe as follows:

The start of the program is the same as the last recipe. We therefore load the necessary packages and also we download the Boston Housing dataset, if it is not already available:

```
import tensorflow as tf
import tensorflow.keras as keras
import numpy as np
import pandas as pd
import tensorflow_datasets as tfds
tfds.disable_progress_bar()
```

After that, we need to redefine our create_linreg by adding a new parameter controlling the type of loss. The default is still the mean squared error (L2 loss), but now it can be easily changed when instantiating the canned Estimator:

```
def create_linreg(feature_columns, feature_layer_inputs, optimizer,
                  loss='mean_squared_error',
                  metrics=['mean_absolute_error']):

    feature_layer = keras.layers.DenseFeatures(feature_columns)
    feature_layer_outputs = feature_layer(feature_layer_inputs)
    norm = keras.layers.BatchNormalization()(feature_layer_outputs)
    outputs = keras.layers.Dense(1, kernel_initializer='normal',
                                 activation='linear')(norm)

    model = keras.Model(inputs=[v for v in feature_layer_inputs.values()],
                        outputs=outputs)
    model.compile(optimizer=optimizer, loss=loss, metrics=metrics)
    return model
```

After doing so, we can train our model explicitly using the `Ftrl` optimizer with a different learning rate, more suitable for an L1 loss (we set the loss to mean absolute error):

```
categorical_cols = ['CHAS', 'RAD']
numeric_cols = ['CRIM', 'ZN', 'INDUS',  'NOX', 'RM', 'AGE', 'DIS', 'TAX',
'PTRATIO', 'B', 'LSTAT']
feature_columns, feature_layer_inputs = define_feature_columns_layers(data,
categorical_cols, numeric_cols)
interactions_columns = create_interactions([['RM', 'LSTAT']])

feature_columns += interactions_columns

optimizer = keras.optimizers.Ftrl(learning_rate=0.02)
model = create_linreg(feature_columns, feature_layer_inputs, optimizer,
                    loss='mean_absolute_error',
                    metrics=['mean_absolute_error',
                            'mean_squared_error'])

estimator = canned_keras(model)

train_input_fn = make_input_fn(train, y_train, num_epochs=1400)
test_input_fn = make_input_fn(test, y_test, num_epochs=1, shuffle=False)

estimator.train(train_input_fn)
result = estimator.evaluate(test_input_fn)

print(result)
```

Here are the results that we obtained by switching to an L1 loss:

```
{'loss': 3.1208777, 'mean_absolute_error': 3.1208777, 'mean_squared_error':
27.170328, 'global_step': 2800}
```

We can now visualize the training performances along iterations using TensorBoard:

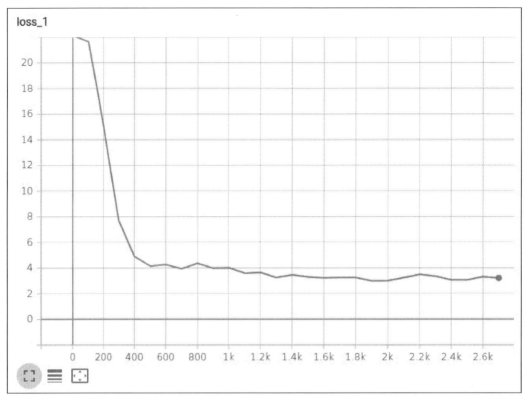

Figure 4.4: Mean absolute error optimization

The resulting plot shows a nice descent of the mean absolute error, which simply slows down after 400 iterations and tends to stabilize in a plateau after 1,400 iterations.

How it works...

When choosing a loss function, we must also choose a corresponding learning rate that will work with our problem. Here, we test two situations, the first in which L2 is adopted and the second in which L1 is preferred.

If our learning rate is small, our convergence will take more time. However, if our learning rate is too large, we will have issues with our algorithm never converging.

There's more...

To understand what is happening, we should look at how a large learning rate and small learning rate act on **L1 norms** and **L2 norms**. If the rate is too large, L1 can get stuck at a suboptimal result, whereas L2 can achieve an even worse performance. To visualize this, we will look at a one-dimensional representation of learning steps on both norms, as follows:

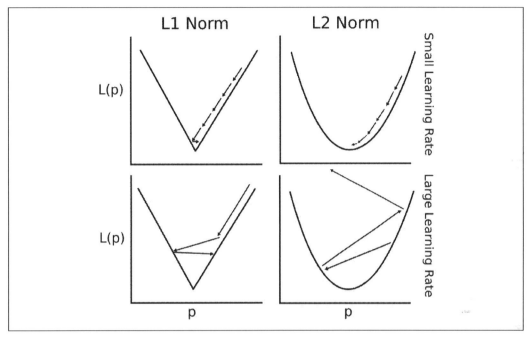

Figure 4.5: What can happen with the L1 and L2 norm with larger and smaller learning rates

Small learning rates, as depicted in the preceding diagram, are indeed a guarantee of a better optimization in any case. Larger rates do not really work with L2, but may prove just suboptimal with L1 by stopping further optimizations after a while, without causing any further damage.

Implementing Lasso and Ridge regression

There are ways to limit the influence of coefficients on the regression output. These methods are called regularization methods, and two of the most common regularization methods are Lasso and Ridge regression. We cover how to implement both of these in this recipe.

Getting ready

Lasso and Ridge regression are very similar to regular linear regression, except that we add regularization terms to limit the slopes (or partial slopes) in the formula. There may be multiple reasons for this, but a common one is that we wish to restrict the number of features that have an impact on the dependent variable.

How to do it...

We proceed with the recipe as follows:

We will use the Boston Housing dataset again and set up our functions in the same way as in the previous recipes. In particular we need `define_feature_columns_layers`, `make_input_fn`, and `create_interactions`. We again first load the libraries, and then we define a new `create_ridge_linreg` where we set a new Keras model using `keras.regularizers.l2` as the `regularizer` of our dense layer:

```python
import tensorflow as tf
import tensorflow.keras as keras
import numpy as np
import pandas as pd
import tensorflow_datasets as tfds
tfds.disable_progress_bar()

def create_ridge_linreg(feature_columns, feature_layer_inputs, optimizer,
                        loss='mean_squared_error',
                        metrics=['mean_absolute_error'],
                        l2=0.01):

    regularizer = keras.regularizers.l2(l2)

    feature_layer = keras.layers.DenseFeatures(feature_columns)
    feature_layer_outputs = feature_layer(feature_layer_inputs)
    norm = keras.layers.BatchNormalization()(feature_layer_outputs)
    outputs = keras.layers.Dense(1,
                                 kernel_initializer='normal',
                                 kernel_regularizer = regularizer,
                                 activation='linear')(norm)

    model = keras.Model(inputs=[v for v in feature_layer_inputs.values()],
                        outputs=outputs)
    model.compile(optimizer=optimizer, loss=loss, metrics=metrics)
    return model
```

Once this is done, we can again run our previous linear model with L1 loss and see the results improve:

```
categorical_cols = ['CHAS', 'RAD']
numeric_cols = ['CRIM', 'ZN', 'INDUS',  'NOX', 'RM', 'AGE', 'DIS', 'TAX',
'PTRATIO', 'B', 'LSTAT']
feature_columns, feature_layer_inputs = define_feature_columns_layers(data,
categorical_cols, numeric_cols)
interactions_columns = create_interactions([['RM', 'LSTAT']])


feature_columns += interactions_columns


optimizer = keras.optimizers.Ftrl(learning_rate=0.02)
model = create_ridge_linreg(feature_columns, feature_layer_inputs,
optimizer,
                    loss='mean_squared_error',
                    metrics=['mean_absolute_error',
                            'mean_squared_error'],
                        l2=0.01)


estimator = canned_keras(model)


train_input_fn = make_input_fn(train, y_train, num_epochs=1400)
test_input_fn = make_input_fn(test, y_test, num_epochs=1, shuffle=False)


estimator.train(train_input_fn)
result = estimator.evaluate(test_input_fn)


print(result)
```

Here are the Ridge regression results:

```
{'loss': 25.903751, 'mean_absolute_error': 3.27314, 'mean_squared_error':
25.676477, 'global_step': 2800}
```

In addition, here is the plot of the training using TensorBoard:

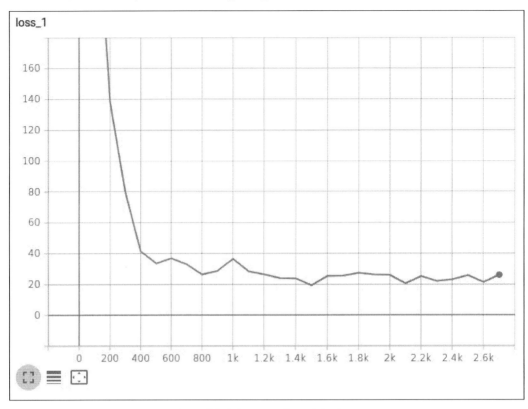

Figure 4.6: Ridge regression training loss

We can also replicate that for L1 regularization by creating a new function:

```
create_lasso_linreg.
def create_lasso_linreg(feature_columns, feature_layer_inputs, optimizer,
                        loss='mean_squared_error', metrics=['mean_absolute_
error'],
                        l1=0.001):

    regularizer = keras.regularizers.l1(l1)

    feature_layer = keras.layers.DenseFeatures(feature_columns)
    feature_layer_outputs = feature_layer(feature_layer_inputs)
    norm = keras.layers.BatchNormalization()(feature_layer_outputs)
    outputs = keras.layers.Dense(1,
                                 kernel_initializer='normal',
                                 kernel_regularizer = regularizer,
                                 activation='linear')(norm)
```

```
    model = keras.Model(inputs=[v for v in feature_layer_inputs.values()],
outputs=outputs)
    model.compile(optimizer=optimizer, loss=loss, metrics=metrics)
    return model


categorical_cols = ['CHAS', 'RAD']
numeric_cols = ['CRIM', 'ZN', 'INDUS',  'NOX', 'RM', 'AGE', 'DIS', 'TAX',
'PTRATIO', 'B', 'LSTAT']
feature_columns, feature_layer_inputs = define_feature_columns_layers(data,
categorical_cols, numeric_cols)
interactions_columns = create_interactions([['RM', 'LSTAT']])


feature_columns += interactions_columns


optimizer = keras.optimizers.Ftrl(learning_rate=0.02)
model = create_lasso_linreg(feature_columns, feature_layer_inputs,
optimizer,
                    loss='mean_squared_error',
                    metrics=['mean_absolute_error',
                            'mean_squared_error'],
                    l1=0.001)


estimator = canned_keras(model)


train_input_fn = make_input_fn(train, y_train, num_epochs=1400)
test_input_fn = make_input_fn(test, y_test, num_epochs=1, shuffle=False)


estimator.train(train_input_fn)
result = estimator.evaluate(test_input_fn)


print(result)
```

Here are the results obtained from the L1 Lasso regression:

```
{'loss': 24.616476, 'mean_absolute_error': 3.1985352, 'mean_squared_error':
24.59167, 'global_step': 2800}
```

In addition, here is the plot of the training loss:

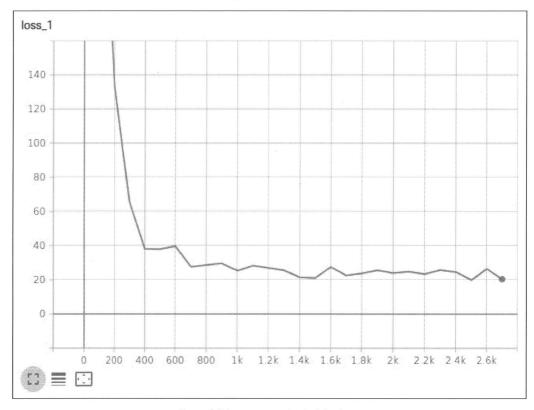

Figure 4.7: Lasso regression training loss

Comparing the Ridge and Lasso approach, we notice that they are not too dissimilar in terms of training loss, but the test result favors Lasso. This could be explained by a noisy variable that had to be excluded in order for the model to improve, since Lasso routinely excludes non-useful variables from the prediction estimation (by assigning a zero coefficient to them), whereas Ridge just down-weights them.

How it works...

We implement Lasso regression by adding a continuous Heaviside step function to the loss function of linear regression. Owing to the steepness of the step function, we have to be careful with step size. Too big a step size and it will not converge. For Ridge regression, see the change required in the next section.

There's more...

Elastic net regression is a type of regression that combines Lasso regression with Ridge regression by adding L1 and L2 regularization terms to the loss function.

Implementing elastic net regression is straightforward following the previous two recipes, because you just need to change the regularizer.

We just create a `create_elasticnet_linreg` function, which picks up as parameters the values of L1 and L2 strengths:

```
def create_elasticnet_linreg(feature_columns, feature_layer_inputs,
                             optimizer,
                             loss='mean_squared_error',
                             metrics=['mean_absolute_error'],
                             l1=0.001, l2=0.01):

    regularizer = keras.regularizers.l1_l2(l1=l1, l2=l2)

    feature_layer = keras.layers.DenseFeatures(feature_columns)
    feature_layer_outputs = feature_layer(feature_layer_inputs)
    norm = keras.layers.BatchNormalization()(feature_layer_outputs)
    outputs = keras.layers.Dense(1,
                                 kernel_initializer='normal',
                                 kernel_regularizer = regularizer,
                                 activation='linear')(norm)

    model = keras.Model(inputs=[v for v in feature_layer_inputs.values()],
                        outputs=outputs)
    model.compile(optimizer=optimizer, loss=loss, metrics=metrics)
    return model
```

Finally, we re-run the complete steps for training from data and obtain an evaluation of the model's performances:

```
categorical_cols = ['CHAS', 'RAD']
numeric_cols = ['CRIM', 'ZN', 'INDUS', 'NOX', 'RM', 'AGE', 'DIS', 'TAX',
'PTRATIO', 'B', 'LSTAT']
feature_columns, feature_layer_inputs = define_feature_columns_layers(data,
categorical_cols, numeric_cols)
interactions_columns = create_interactions([['RM', 'LSTAT']])


feature_columns += interactions_columns


optimizer = keras.optimizers.Ftrl(learning_rate=0.02)
model = create_elasticnet_linreg(feature_columns, feature_layer_inputs,
                                 optimizer,
                                 loss='mean_squared_error',
                                 metrics=['mean_absolute_error',
                                          'mean_squared_error'],
                                 l1=0.001, l2=0.01)


estimator = canned_keras(model)


train_input_fn = make_input_fn(train, y_train, num_epochs=1400)
test_input_fn = make_input_fn(test, y_test, num_epochs=1, shuffle=False)


estimator.train(train_input_fn)
result = estimator.evaluate(test_input_fn)


print(result)
```

Here are the results:

```
{'loss': 24.910872, 'mean_absolute_error': 3.208289, 'mean_squared_error':
24.659771, 'global_step': 2800}
```

Here is the training loss plot for the ElasticNet model:

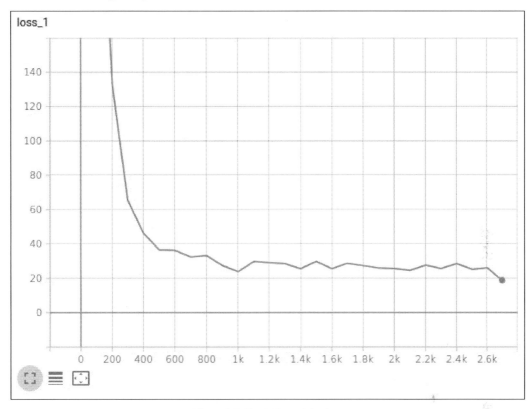

Figure 4.8: ElasticNet training loss

The test results obtained do not differ too much from Ridge and Lasso, landing somewhere between them. As stated previously, the problem involves removing variables from the dataset in order to improve the performances, and as we've now seen the Lasso model is the best for doing so.

Implementing logistic regression

For this recipe, we will implement logistic regression to predict the probability of breast cancer using the Breast Cancer Wisconsin dataset (`https://archive.ics.uci.edu/ml/datasets/Breast+Cancer+Wisconsin+(Diagnostic)`). We will be predicting the diagnosis from features that are computed from a digitized image of a **fine needle aspiration** (**FNA**) of a breast mass. An FNA is a common breast cancer test, consisting of a small tissue biopsy that can be examined under a microscope.

The dataset can immediately be used for a classification model, without further transformations, since the target variable consists of 357 benign cases and 212 malignant ones. The two classes do not have the exact same consistency (an important requirement when doing binary classification with regression models), but they are not extremely different, allowing us to build a straightforward example and evaluate it using plain accuracy.

Please remember to check whether your classes are balanced (in other words, having approximately the same number of cases), otherwise you will have to apply specific recipes to balance the cases, such as applying weights, or your model may provide inaccurate predictions (you can refer to the following Stack Overflow question if you just need further details: `https://datascience.stackexchange.com/questions/13490/how-to-set-class-weights-for-imbalanced-classes-in-keras`).

Getting ready

Logistic regression is a way to turn linear regression into a binary classification. This is accomplished by transforming the linear output into a sigmoid function that scales the output between zero and one. The target is a zero or one, which indicates whether a data point is in one class or another. Since we are predicting a number between zero and one, the prediction is classified into class value 1 if the prediction is above a specified cut-off value, and class 0 otherwise. For the purpose of this example, we will specify that cutoff to be 0.5, which will make the classification as simple as rounding the output.

When classifying, anyway, sometimes you need to control the kinds of mistakes you make, and this is especially true for medical applications (such as the example we are proposing), but it may be a sensible problem for other ones, too (for example, in the case of fraud detection in the insurance or banking sectors). In fact, when you classify, you get correct guesses, but also **false positives** and **false negatives**. False positives are the errors the model makes when it predicts a positive (class 1), but the true label is negative. False negatives, on the other hand, are cases labeled by the model as negative when they are actually positive.

When using a 0.5 threshold for deciding the class (positive or negative class), you are actually equating the expectations for false positives and false negatives. In reality, according to your problem, false positive and false negative errors may have different consequences. In the case of detecting cancer, clearly you absolutely do not want false negatives because that would mean predicting a patient as healthy when they are instead facing a life-threatening situation.

By setting the classification threshold higher or lower, you can trade-off false positives for false negatives. Higher thresholds will have more false negatives than false positives. Lower ones will have fewer false negatives but more false positives. For our recipe, we will just use the 0.5 threshold, but please be aware that the threshold is also something you have to consider for your model's real-world applications.

How to do it...

We proceed with the recipe as follows:

We start by loading the libraries and recovering the data from the internet:

```
import tensorflow as tf
import tensorflow.keras as keras
import numpy as np
import pandas as pd
import tensorflow_datasets as tfds
tfds.disable_progress_bar()

breast_cancer = 'https://archive.ics.uci.edu/ml/machine-learning-databases/
breast-cancer-wisconsin/breast-cancer-wisconsin.data'
path = tf.keras.utils.get_file(breast_cancer.split("/")[-1], breast_cancer)

columns = ['sample_code', 'clump_thickness', 'cell_size_uniformity',
           'cell_shape_uniformity',
           'marginal_adhesion', 'single_epithelial_cell_size',
           'bare_nuclei', 'bland_chromatin',
           'normal_nucleoli', 'mitoses', 'class']

data = pd.read_csv(path, header=None, names=columns, na_values=[np.nan,
'?'])
data = data.fillna(data.median())

np.random.seed(1)
train = data.sample(frac=0.8).copy()
y_train = (train['class']==4).astype(int)
train.drop(['sample_code', 'class'], axis=1, inplace=True)

test = data.loc[~data.index.isin(train.index)].copy()
y_test = (test['class']==4).astype(int)
test.drop(['sample_code', 'class'], axis=1, inplace=True)
```

Next, we specify the logistic regression function. The main modification with respect to our linear regression model is that we change the activation in the single output neuron from `linear` to `sigmoid`, which is enough to obtain a logistic regression because our output will be a probability expressed in the range 0.0 to 1.0:

```python
def create_logreg(feature_columns, feature_layer_inputs, optimizer,
                  loss='binary_crossentropy', metrics=['accuracy'],
                  l2=0.01):

    regularizer = keras.regularizers.l2(l2)

    feature_layer = keras.layers.DenseFeatures(feature_columns)
    feature_layer_outputs = feature_layer(feature_layer_inputs)
    norm = keras.layers.BatchNormalization()(feature_layer_outputs)
    outputs = keras.layers.Dense(1,
                          kernel_initializer='normal',
                          kernel_regularizer = regularizer,
                          activation='sigmoid')(norm)

    model = keras.Model(inputs=[v for v in feature_layer_inputs.values()],
outputs=outputs)
    model.compile(optimizer=optimizer, loss=loss, metrics=metrics)
    return model
```

Finally, we run our procedure:

```python
categorical_cols = []
numeric_cols = ['clump_thickness', 'cell_size_uniformity',
                'cell_shape_uniformity',
                'marginal_adhesion', 'single_epithelial_cell_size',
                'bare_  nuclei', 'bland_chromatin',
                'normal_nucleoli', 'mitoses']

feature_columns, feature_layer_inputs = define_feature_columns_layers(data,
categorical_cols, numeric_cols)

optimizer = keras.optimizers.Ftrl(learning_rate=0.007)
model = create_logreg(feature_columns, feature_layer_inputs, optimizer,
l2=0.01)

estimator = canned_keras(model)

train_input_fn = make_input_fn(train, y_train, num_epochs=300, batch_
size=32)
test_input_fn = make_input_fn(test, y_test, num_epochs=1, shuffle=False)
```

```
estimator.train(train_input_fn)
result = estimator.evaluate(test_input_fn)

print(result)
```

Here is the reported accuracy of our logistic regression:

```
{'accuracy': 0.95, 'loss': 0.16382739, 'global_step': 5400}
```

In addition, here you can find the loss plot:

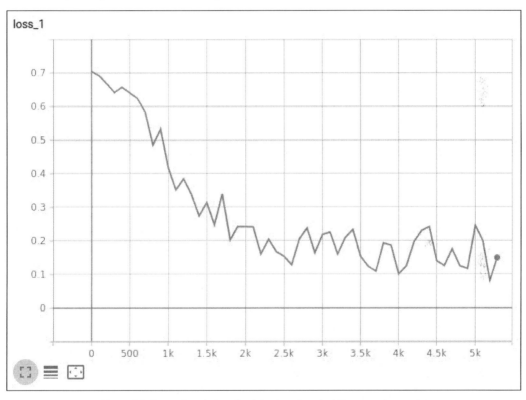

Figure 4.9: TensorBoard plot of training loss for a logistic regression model

Using a few commands, we achieved a good result in terms of accuracy and loss for this problem, in spite of a slightly unbalanced target class (more benign cases than malignant ones).

How it works...

Logistic regression predictions are based on the sigmoid curve and, to modify our previous linear model accordingly, we just need to switch to a sigmoid activation.

There's more...

When you are predicting a multi-class or multi-label you don't need to extend the binary model using different kinds of **One Versus All** (**OVA**) strategies, but you just need to extend the number of output nodes to match the number of classes you need to predict. Using multiple neurons with sigmoid activation, you will obtain a multi-label approach, while using a softmax activation, you'll get a multi-class prediction. You will find more recipes in the later chapters of this book that indicate how to do this using simple Keras functions.

Resorting to non-linear solutions

Linear models are approachable and interpretable, given the one-to-one relation between feature columns and regression coefficients. Sometimes, anyway, you may want to try non-linear solutions in order to check whether models that are more complex can model your data better and solve your prediction problem in a more expert manner. **Support Vector Machines** (**SVMs**) are an algorithm that rivaled neural networks for a long time and they are still a viable option thanks to recent developments in terms of random features for large-scale kernel machines (Rahimi, Ali; Recht, Benjamin. Random features for large-scale kernel machines. In: *Advances in neural information processing systems*. 2008. pp. 1177-1184). In this recipe, we demonstrate how to leverage Keras and obtain a non-linear solution to a classification problem.

Getting ready

We will still be using functions from the previous recipes, including define_feature_columns_layers and make_input_fn. As in the logistic regression recipe, we will continue using the breast cancer dataset. As before, we need to load the following packages:

```
import tensorflow as tf
import tensorflow.keras as keras
import numpy as np
import pandas as pd
import tensorflow_datasets as tfds
tfds.disable_progress_bar()
```

At this point we are ready to proceed with the recipe.

How to do it...

In addition to the previous packages, we also specifically import the `RandomFourierFeatures` function, which can apply a non-linear transformation to the input. Depending on the loss function, a `RandomFourierFeatures` layer can approximate kernel-based classifiers and regressors. After this, we just need to apply our usual single-output node and get our predictions.

Depending on the TensorFlow 2.x version you are using you may need to import it from different modules:

```
try:
    from tensorflow.python.keras.layers.kernelized import
RandomFourierFeatures
except:
    # from TF 2.2
    from tensorflow.keras.layers.experimental import RandomFourierFeatures
```

Now we develop the `create_svc` function. It contains an L2 regularizer for the final dense node, a batch normalization layer for the input, and a `RandomFourierFeatures` layer inserted among them. In this intermediate layer non-linearities are generated and you can set the `output_dim` parameter in order to determine the number of non-linear interactions that will be produced by the layers. Naturally, you can contrast the overfitting caused after setting higher `output_dim` values by raising the L2 regularization value, thereby achieving more regularization:

```
def create_svc(feature_columns, feature_layer_inputs, optimizer,
               loss='hinge', metrics=['accuracy'],
               l2=0.01, output_dim=64, scale=None):

    regularizer = keras.regularizers.l2(l2)

    feature_layer = keras.layers.DenseFeatures(feature_columns)
    feature_layer_outputs = feature_layer(feature_layer_inputs)
    norm = keras.layers.BatchNormalization()(feature_layer_outputs)
    rff = RandomFourierFeatures(output_dim=output_dim, scale=scale, kernel_
initializer='gaussian')(norm)
    outputs = keras.layers.Dense(1,
                                 kernel_initializer='normal',
                                 kernel_regularizer = regularizer,
                                 activation='sigmoid')(rff)

    model = keras.Model(inputs=[v for v in feature_layer_inputs.values()],
```

```
    outputs=outputs)
        model.compile(optimizer=optimizer, loss=loss, metrics=metrics)
        return model
```

As in the previous recipes, we define the different columns, we set the model and the optimizer, we prepare the input function, and finally we train and evaluate the results:

```
categorical_cols = []
numeric_cols = ['clump_thickness', 'cell_size_uniformity',
                'cell_shape_uniformity',
                'marginal_adhesion', 'single_epithelial_cell_size',
                'bare_nuclei', 'bland_chromatin',
                'normal_nucleoli', 'mitoses']

feature_columns, feature_layer_inputs = define_feature_columns_layers(data,
categorical_cols, numeric_cols)

optimizer = keras.optimizers.Adam(learning_rate=0.00005)
model = create_svc(feature_columns, feature_layer_inputs, optimizer,
                   loss='hinge', l2=0.001, output_dim=512)

estimator = canned_keras(model)

train_input_fn = make_input_fn(train, y_train, num_epochs=500, batch_
size=512)
test_input_fn = make_input_fn(test, y_test, num_epochs=1, shuffle=False)

estimator.train(train_input_fn)
result = estimator.evaluate(test_input_fn)

print(result)
```

Here is the reported accuracy. For an even better result, you have to try different combinations of the output dimension of the RandomFourierFeatures layer and the regularization term:

```
{'accuracy': 0.95 'loss': 0.7390725, 'global_step': 1000}
```

Here is the loss plot from TensorBoard:

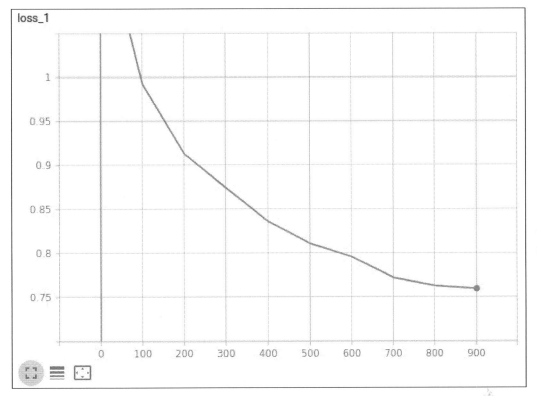

Figure 4.10: Loss plot for the RandomFourierFeatures-based model

The plot is indeed quite nice, thanks to the fact that we used a larger batch than usual. Given the complexity of the task, due to the large number of neurons to be trained, a larger batch generally works better than a smaller one.

How it works...

Random Fourier features are a way to approximate the work done by SVM kernels, thereby achieving a lower computational complexity and making such an approach also feasible for a neural network implementation. If you require a more in-depth explanation, you can read the original paper, quoted at the beginning of the recipe, or you can take advantage of this very clear answer on Stack Exchange: `https://stats.stackexchange.com/questions/327646/how-does-a-random-kitchen-sink-work#327961`.

There's more...

Depending on the loss function, you can obtain different non-linear models:

- ▶ **Hinge loss** sets your model in an SVM
- ▶ **Logistic loss** turns your model into kernel logistic regression (classification performance is almost the same as SVM, but kernel logistic regression can provide class probabilities)
- ▶ **Mean squared error** transforms your model into a kernel regression

It is up to you to decide what loss to try first, and decide how to set the dimension of the output from the random Fourier transformation. By way of a general suggestion you could start with a large number of output nodes and iteratively test whether shrinking their number improves the result.

Using Wide & Deep models

Linear models can boast a great advantage over complex models: they are efficient and easily interpretable, even when you work with many features and with features that interact with each other. Google researchers mentioned this aspect as the power of **memorization** because your linear model records the association between the features and the target into single coefficients. On the other hand, neural networks are blessed with the power of **generalization**, because in their complexity (they use multiple layers of weights and they interrelate each input), they can manage to approximate the general rules that govern the outcome of a process.

Wide & Deep models, as conceived by Google researchers (`https://arxiv.org/abs/1606.07792`), can blend memorization and generalization because they combine a linear model, applied to numeric features, together with generalization, applied to sparse features, such as categories encoded into a sparse matrix. Therefore, **wide** in their name implies the regression part, and **deep** the neural network aspect:

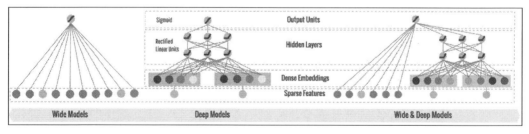

Figure 4.11: How wide models (linear models) blend with neural networks in Wide & Deep models
(from the paper by Cheng, Heng-Tze, et al. "Wide & deep learning for recommender systems."
Proceedings of the 1st workshop on deep learning for recommender systems. 2016)

Such a blend can achieve the best results when working on recommender system problems (such as the one featured in Google Play). Wide & Deep models work the best in recommendation problems because each part handles the right kind of data. The **wide** part handles the features relative to the user's characteristics (dense numeric features, binary indicators, or their combination in interaction features) that are more stable over time, whereas the **deep** part processes feature strings representing previous software downloads (sparse inputs on very large matrices), which instead are more variable over time and so require a more sophisticated kind of representation.

Getting ready

Actually, Wide & Deep models also work fine with many other data problems, recommender systems being their speciality, and such models are readily available among Estimators (see https://www.tensorflow.org/api_docs/python/tf/estimator/DNNLinearCombinedEstimator). In this recipe we will use a mixed data dataset, the **Adult dataset** (https://archive.ics.uci.edu/ml/datasets/Adult). Also widely known as the **Census dataset**, the purpose of this dataset is to predict whether your income exceeds $50K/annum based on census data. The available features are quite varied, from continuous values related to age to variables with a large number of classes, including occupation. We will then use each different type of feature to feed the correct part of the Wide & Deep model.

How to do it...

We start by downloading the Adult dataset from the UCI archive:

```
census_dir = 'https://archive.ics.uci.edu/ml/machine-learning-databases/
adult/'
train_path = tf.keras.utils.get_file('adult.data', census_dir + 'adult.
data')
test_path = tf.keras.utils.get_file('adult.test', census_dir + 'adult.
test')

columns = ['age', 'workclass', 'fnlwgt', 'education', 'education_num',
           'marital_status', 'occupation', 'relationship', 'race',
           'gender', 'capital_gain', 'capital_loss', 'hours_per_week',
           'native_country', 'income_bracket']

train_data = pd.read_csv(train_path, header=None, names=columns)
test_data = pd.read_csv(test_path, header=None, names=columns, skiprows=1)
```

Then, we select a subset of features for our purposes and we extract the target variable and transform it from the string type to the int type:

```
predictors = ['age', 'workclass', 'education', 'education_num',
              'marital_status', 'occupation', 'relationship', 'gender']

y_train = (train_data.income_bracket==' >50K').astype(int)
y_test = (test_data.income_bracket==' >50K.').astype(int)

train_data = train_data[predictors]
test_data = test_data[predictors]
```

This dataset requires additional manipulation since some fields present missing values. We treat them by replacing missing values with a mean value. As a general rule, we have to impute all missing data before feeding it into a TensorFlow model:

```
train_data[['age', 'education_num']] = train_data[['age', 'education_
num']].fillna(train_data[['age', 'education_num']].mean())
test_data[['age', 'education_num']] = test_data[['age', 'education_num']].
fillna(train_data[['age', 'education_num']].mean())
```

Now, we can proceed to define columns by means of the proper `tf.feature_column` function:

- ▶ **Numeric columns**: dealing with numeric values (such as the age)
- ▶ **Categorical columns**: dealing with categorical values when the unique categories are just a few in number (such as the gender)
- ▶ **Embeddings**: dealing with categorical values when unique categories are many in number by mapping categorical values into a dense, low-dimensional, numeric space

We also define the function that faciliates the interaction of categorical and numeric columns:

```
def define_feature_columns(data_df, numeric_cols, categorical_cols,
categorical_embeds, dimension=30):
    numeric_columns = []
    categorical_columns = []
    embeddings = []

    for feature_name in numeric_cols:
        numeric_columns.append(tf.feature_column.numeric_column(feature_
name, dtype=tf.float32))

    for feature_name in categorical_cols:
        vocabulary = data_df[feature_name].unique()
        categorical_columns.append(tf.feature_column.categorical_column_
with_vocabulary_list(feature_name, vocabulary))
```

```
    for feature_name in categorical_embeds:
        vocabulary = data_df[feature_name].unique()
        to_categorical =
tf.feature_column.categorical_column_with_vocabulary_list(feature_name,
                                                    vocabulary)
embeddings.append(tf.feature_column.embedding_column(to_categorical,

dimension=dimension))

    return numeric_columns, categorical_columns, embeddings

def create_interactions(interactions_list, buckets=10):
    feature_columns = []

    for (a, b) in interactions_list:
        crossed_feature = tf.feature_column.crossed_column([a, b],
                                    hash_bucket_size=buckets)
        crossed_feature_one_hot = tf.feature_column.indicator_column(
                                            crossed_feature)
        feature_columns.append(crossed_feature_one_hot)

    return feature_columns
```

Now that all the functions have been defined, we map the different columns and add some meaningful interaction (such as crossing education with occupation). We map high-dimensional categorical features into a fixed lower-dimensional numeric space of 32 dimensions by setting the dimension parameter:

```
numeric_columns, categorical_columns, embeddings = define_feature_
columns(train_data,

numeric_cols=['age', 'education_num'],

categorical_cols=['gender'],

categorical_embeds=['workclass', 'education',

'marital_status', 'occupation',

'relationship'],

dimension=32)

interactions = create_interactions([['education', 'occupation']],
buckets=10)
```

Having mapped the features, we then input them into our estimator (see `https://www.tensorflow.org/api_docs/python/tf/estimator/DNNLinearCombinedClassifier`), specifying the feature columns to be handled by the wide part and those by the deep part. For each part we also specify an optimizer (usually Ftrl for the linear part and Adam for the deep part) and, for the deep part, we specify the architecture of hidden layers as a list of numbers of neurons:

```
estimator = tf.estimator.DNNLinearCombinedClassifier(
    # wide settings
    linear_feature_columns=numeric_columns+categorical_
columns+interactions,
    linear_optimizer=keras.optimizers.Ftrl(learning_rate=0.0002),
    # deep settings
    dnn_feature_columns=embeddings,
    dnn_hidden_units=[1024, 256, 128, 64],
    dnn_optimizer=keras.optimizers.Adam(learning_rate=0.0001))
```

We then proceed to define the input function (no different to what we have done in the other recipes presented in this chapter):

```
def make_input_fn(data_df, label_df, num_epochs=10, shuffle=True, batch_
size=256):

    def input_function():
        ds = tf.data.Dataset.from_tensor_slices((dict(data_df), label_df))
        if shuffle:
            ds = ds.shuffle(1000)
        ds = ds.batch(batch_size).repeat(num_epochs)
        return ds

    return input_function
```

Finally, we train the Estimator for 1,500 steps and evaluate the results on the test data:

```
train_input_fn = make_input_fn(train_data, y_train,
                               num_epochs=100, batch_size=256)
test_input_fn = make_input_fn(test_data, y_test,
                              num_epochs=1, shuffle=False)
estimator.train(input_fn=train_input_fn, steps=1500)
results = estimator.evaluate(input_fn=test_input_fn)
print(results)
```

We obtain an accuracy of about 0.83 on our test set, as reported using the evaluate method on the Estimator:

```
{'accuracy': 0.83391684, 'accuracy_baseline': 0.76377374, 'auc':
0.88012385, 'auc_precision_recall': 0.68032277, 'average_loss': 0.35969484,
'label/mean': 0.23622628, 'loss': 0.35985297, 'precision': 0.70583993,
'prediction/mean': 0.21803579, 'recall': 0.5091004, 'global_step': 1000}
```

Here is the plot of the training loss and the test estimate (the blue dot):

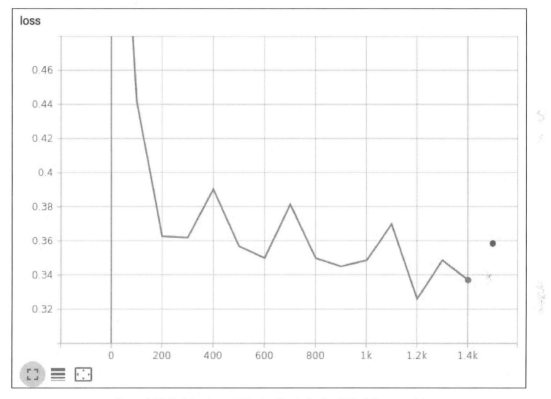

Figure 4.12: Training loss and test estimate for the Wide & Deep model

For full prediction probabilities, we just extract them from the dictionary data type used by the Estimator. The predict_proba function will return a NumPy array with the probabilities for the positive (income in excess of USD 50K) and negative classes in distinct columns:

```
def predict_proba(predictor):
    preds = list()
    for pred in predictor:
        preds.append(pred['probabilities'])
    return np.array(preds)

predictions =
predict_proba(estimator.predict(input_fn=test_input_fn))
```

How it works...

Wide & Deep models represent a way to handle linear models together with a more complex approach involving neural networks. As for other Estimators, this Estimator is also quite straightforward and easy to use. The keys for the success of the recipe in terms of other applications definitely rest upon defining an input data function and mapping the features with the more suitable functions from tf.features_columns.

5

Boosted Trees

In this chapter, we describe boosted trees: the **TensorFlow** (**TF**) approach to gradient boosting. It is a class of ML algorithms that produce a prediction model in the form of an ensemble of weak prediction models, typically decision trees. The model is constructed in a stage-wise fashion and generalized by utilizing an arbitrary (differentiable) loss function. Gradient boosted trees are an extremely popular class of algorithms, as they can be parallelized (at the tree construction stage), can natively handle missing values and outliers, and require minimal data preprocessing.

Introduction

In this chapter, we briefly demonstrate how to approach a binary classification problem using `BoostedTreesClassifier`. We will apply the technique to solve a realistic business problem using a popular educational dataset: predicting which customers are likely to cancel their bookings. The data for this problem – and several other business problems – comes in tabular format, and typically contains a mixture of different feature types: numeric, categorical, dates, and so on. In the absence of sophisticated domain knowledge, gradient boosting methods are a good first choice for creating an interpretable solution that works out of the box. In the next section, the relevant modeling steps will be demonstrated with code: data preparation, structuring into functions, fitting a model through the `tf.estimator` functionality, and interpretation of results.

How to do it...

We begin by loading the necessary packages:

```
import tensorflow as tf
import numpy as np
import pandas as pd
```

```
from IPython.display import clear_output
from matplotlib import pyplot as plt
import matplotlib.pyplot as plt
import seaborn as sns
sns_colors = sns.color_palette('colorblind')
from numpy.random import uniform, seed
from scipy.interpolate import griddata
from matplotlib.font_manager import FontProperties
from sklearn.metrics import roc_curve
```

In principle, categorical variables could be simply recoded into integers (using a function such as `LabelEncoder` from scikit-learn) and a gradient boosting model would work just fine – these minimal requirements on data preprocessing are one of the reasons behind the popularity of ensembles of trees. However, in this recipe, we want to focus on demonstrating the interpretability of the model and therefore we want to analyze individual indicator values. For that reason, we create a function performing one-hot encoding in a TF-friendly format:

```
def one_hot_cat_column(feature_name, vocab):
    return tf.feature_column.indicator_column(
    tf.feature_column.categorical_column_with_vocabulary_list(feature_name,
                                                    vocab))
```

As mentioned in the introduction, for this recipe we will be using the hotel cancellations dataset available from the following URL:

https://www.sciencedirect.com/science/article/pii/S2352340918315191

We choose this dataset because it is fairly realistic for a typical business prediction problem a reader might encounter: there's a time dimension present, and a mixture of numeric and categorical features. At the same time, it is fairly clean (no missing values), which means we can focus on the actual modeling and not on data wrangling:

```
xtrain = pd.read_csv('../input/hotel-booking-
                        demand/hotel_bookings.csv')
xtrain.head(3)
```

The dataset has a time dimension, so a natural training/validation split can be made on `reservation_status_date`:

```
xvalid = xtrain.loc[xtrain['reservation_status_date'] >= '2017-08-01']
xtrain = xtrain.loc[xtrain['reservation_status_date'] < '2017-08-01']
```

Separate the features from the target:

```
ytrain, yvalid = xtrain['is_canceled'], xvalid['is_canceled']
xtrain.drop('is_canceled', axis = 1, inplace = True)
xvalid.drop('is_canceled', axis = 1, inplace = True)
```

We separate the columns into numerical and categorical ones and encode them in the TF-expected format. We skip some columns that could perhaps improve the model performance, but due to their nature they introduce a risk of leakage: introducing information that might improve the model performance in training but will fail when predicting on unseen data. In our situation, one such variable is `arrival_date_year`: if the model uses this variable very strongly, it will fail if we present it with a dataset further into the future (where a specific value of the variable will obviously be absent).

We remove some additional variables from our training data – this step can either be conducted based on expert judgment prior to the modeling procedure, or it can be automated. The latter approach would involve running a small model and examining the global feature importance: if the results show one very important feature dominating over others, it is a potential source of leakage:

```python
xtrain.drop(['arrival_date_year','assigned_room_type', 'booking_changes',
'reservation_status', 'country', 'days_in_waiting_list'], axis =1, inplace
= True)

num_features = ["lead_time","arrival_date_week_number",
                "arrival_date_day_of_month",
                "stays_in_weekend_nights",
                "stays_in_week_nights","adults","children",
                "babies","is_repeated_guest", "previous_cancellations",
                "previous_bookings_not_canceled","agent","company",
                "required_car_parking_spaces",
                "total_of_special_requests", "adr"]


cat_features = ["hotel","arrival_date_month","meal","market_segment",
                "distribution_channel","reserved_room_type",
                "deposit_type","customer_type"]

def one_hot_cat_column(feature_name, vocab):
    return tf.feature_column.indicator_column(
        tf.feature_column.categorical_column_with_vocabulary_list(
                                            feature_name,
                                            vocab))
feature_columns = []
for feature_name in cat_features:
    # Need to one-hot encode categorical features.
    vocabulary = xtrain[feature_name].unique()
    feature_columns.append(one_hot_cat_column(feature_name, vocabulary))

for feature_name in num_features:
    feature_columns.append(tf.feature_column.numeric_column(feature_name,
                                        dtype=tf.float32))
```

The next step required is creating the input functions for the boosted trees algorithm: we specify how data will be read into our model for both training and inference. We use the `from_tensor_slices` method in the `tf.data` API to read in data directly from pandas:

```python
NUM_EXAMPLES = len(ytrain)

def make_input_fn(X, y, n_epochs=None, shuffle=True):

    def input_fn():

        dataset = tf.data.Dataset.from_tensor_slices((dict(X), y))
        if shuffle:

            dataset = dataset.shuffle(NUM_EXAMPLES)
        # For training, cycle thru dataset as many times as need (n_
epochs=None).
        dataset = dataset.repeat(n_epochs)
        # In memory training doesn't use batching.
        dataset = dataset.batch(NUM_EXAMPLES)
        return dataset
    return input_fn


# Training and evaluation input functions.
train_input_fn = make_input_fn(xtrain, ytrain)
eval_input_fn = make_input_fn(xvalid, yvalid, shuffle=False,
                                            n_epochs=1)
```

We can now build the actual BoostedTrees model. We set up a minimal list of parameters (`max_depth` being one of the most important ones) – the ones not specified in the definition are left at their default values, which can be found through the help functions in the documentation:

```python
params = {
  'n_trees': 125,
  'max_depth': 5,
  'n_batches_per_layer': 1,
  'center_bias': True
}

est = tf.estimator.BoostedTreesClassifier(feature_columns, **params)
# Train model.
est.train(train_input_fn, max_steps=100)
```

Once we have trained a model, we can evaluate the performance with respect to different metrics. `BoostedTreesClassifier` contains an `evaluate` method and the output covers a wide range of possible metrics; which ones are used for guidance depends on the specific application, but those outputted by default already allow us to evaluate the model from various angles (for example, if we are dealing with a highly imbalanced dataset, `auc` can be somewhat misleading and we should evaluate the loss as well). For a more detailed explanation, the reader is referred to documentation at `https://www.tensorflow.org/api_docs/python/tf/estimator/BoostedTreesClassifier`:

```
# Evaluation
results = est.evaluate(eval_input_fn)
pd.Series(results).to_frame()
```

The results you see should look like this:

	0
accuracy	0.741732
accuracy_baseline	0.916010
auc	0.646061
auc_precision_recall	0.200471
average_loss	0.521212
label/mean	0.083990
loss	0.521212
precision	0.135165
prediction/mean	0.348795
recall	0.384375
global_step	100.000000

```
pred_dicts = list(est.predict(eval_input_fn))
probs = pd.Series([pred['probabilities'][1] for pred in pred_dicts])
```

We can evaluate the results at different levels of generality – details of the difference between global and local are given as follows. Let's start with the **receiver operating characteristic** (**ROC**) curve: a graph showing the performance of a classification model at all possible classification thresholds. We plot the false positive rate versus the true positive rate: a random classifier would be a diagonal line from (0,0) to (1,1), and the further away we move from that scenario toward the upper-left corner, the better our classifier is:

```
fpr, tpr, _ = roc_curve(yvalid, probs)
plt.plot(fpr, tpr)
```

```
plt.title('ROC curve')
plt.xlabel('false positive rate')
plt.ylabel('true positive rate')
plt.xlim(0,); plt.ylim(0,); plt.show()
```

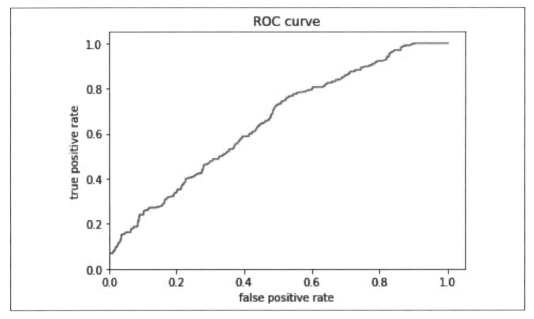

Figure 5.1: ROC for the trained classifier

Local interpretability refers to an understanding of a model's predictions at the individual example level: we will create and visualize per-instance contributions. This is particularly useful if model predictions need to be explained to audiences exhibiting technical cognitive diversity. We refer to these values as **directional feature contributions** (**DFCs**):

```
pred_dicts = list(est.experimental_predict_with_explanations(eval_input_
fn))

# Create DFC Pandas dataframe.
labels = yvalid.values
probs = pd.Series([pred['probabilities'][1] for pred in pred_dicts])
df_dfc = pd.DataFrame([pred['dfc'] for pred in pred_dicts])
df_dfc.describe().T
```

	count	mean	std	min	25%	50%	75%	max
arrival_date_week_number	3810.0	0.019350	0.022113	-0.030147	0.005745	0.014741	0.019361	0.13834
arrival_date_day_of_month	3810.0	0.014576	0.025335	-0.011630	0.000000	0.003322	0.004134	0.09222
lead_time	3810.0	0.005081	0.068627	-0.203443	-0.030246	0.015132	0.048495	0.15737
market_segment	3810.0	-0.011470	0.039524	-0.174266	-0.044574	-0.011785	0.025545	0.05854
agent	3810.0	0.004215	0.019723	-0.090495	-0.002943	0.002157	0.013018	0.08341
previous_cancellations	3810.0	-0.025231	0.020449	-0.070469	-0.039491	-0.026849	-0.009798	0.25100
adr	3810.0	0.015954	0.019125	-0.048982	0.001744	0.010666	0.027898	0.13844
total_of_special_requests	3810.0	-0.020157	0.051674	-0.093304	-0.051190	-0.035322	-0.005823	0.14547
deposit_type	3810.0	-0.021982	0.013524	-0.077839	-0.023315	-0.022245	-0.020574	0.14937
arrival_date_month	3810.0	0.010577	0.009856	-0.029990	0.005439	0.013877	0.017266	0.08978
customer_type	3810.0	-0.001571	0.034125	-0.128769	-0.009160	0.005580	0.017889	0.13140
required_car_parking_spaces	3810.0	-0.016367	0.037135	-0.159597	-0.016156	-0.007631	-0.003485	0.03503
adults	3810.0	-0.001510	0.003977	-0.028990	-0.003076	-0.001080	0.000000	0.06405
distribution_channel	3810.0	-0.002297	0.006363	-0.033720	-0.003365	-0.000672	0.001582	0.11527
children	3810.0	0.000147	0.003054	-0.014593	0.000000	0.000097	0.001040	0.01483
previous_bookings_not_canceled	3810.0	-0.000586	0.008589	-0.153374	-0.001013	0.000116	0.000240	0.08456
meal	3810.0	-0.000992	0.003895	-0.021380	-0.002687	-0.001077	-0.000020	0.07996
babies	3810.0	0.000000	0.000000	0.000000	0.000000	0.000000	0.000000	0.00000
company	3810.0	0.000000	0.000000	0.000000	0.000000	0.000000	0.000000	0.00000
hotel	3810.0	0.000000	0.000000	0.000000	0.000000	0.000000	0.000000	0.00000

The complete summary of the complete DFC DataFrame can be somewhat overwhelming at first glance, and in practice, one is most likely to focus on a subset of the columns. What we get in each row are summary statistics (`mean`, `std`, and so on) of the directional contributions of a feature (`arrival_date_week_number` in the first row, `arrival_date_day_of_month` for the second, and so on) across all observations in the validation set.

How it works...

The following code block demonstrates the steps necessary to extract the feature contributions to a prediction for a particular record. For convenience and reusability, we define a function plotting a chosen record first (for easier interpretation, we want to plot feature importances using different colors, depending on whether their contribution is positive or negative):

```
def _get_color(value):
    """To make positive DFCs plot green, negative DFCs plot red."""
    green, red = sns.color_palette()[2:4]
    if value >= 0: return green
    return red


def _add_feature_values(feature_values, ax):
    """Display feature's values on left of plot."""
    x_coord = ax.get_xlim()[0]
```

```
    OFFSET = 0.15
    for y_coord, (feat_name, feat_val) in enumerate(feature_values.
                                                items()):
        t = plt.text(x_coord, y_coord - OFFSET, '{}'.format(feat_val),
                                                size=12)
        t.set_bbox(dict(facecolor='white', alpha=0.5))
    from matplotlib.font_manager import FontProperties
    font = FontProperties()
    font.set_weight('bold')
    t = plt.text(x_coord, y_coord + 1 - OFFSET, 'feature\nvalue',
    fontproperties=font, size=12)


def plot_example(example):
  TOP_N = 8 # View top 8 features.
  sorted_ix = example.abs().sort_values()[-TOP_N:].index  # Sort by
magnitude.
  example = example[sorted_ix]
  colors = example.map(_get_color).tolist()
  ax = example.to_frame().plot(kind='barh',
                          color=[colors],
                          legend=None,
                          alpha=0.75,
                          figsize=(10,6))
  ax.grid(False, axis='y')
  ax.set_yticklabels(ax.get_yticklabels(), size=14)

  # Add feature values.
  _add_feature_values(xvalid.iloc[ID][sorted_ix], ax)
  return ax
```

With the boilerplate code defined, we plot the detailed graph for a specific record in a straightforward manner:

```
ID = 10
example = df_dfc.iloc[ID]  # Choose ith example from evaluation set.
TOP_N = 8  # View top 8 features.
sorted_ix = example.abs().sort_values()[-TOP_N:].index
ax = plot_example(example)
ax.set_title('Feature contributions for example {}\n pred: {:1.2f}; label:
{}'.format(ID, probs[ID], labels[ID]))
ax.set_xlabel('Contribution to predicted probability', size=14)
plt.show()
```

Which delivers the following output:

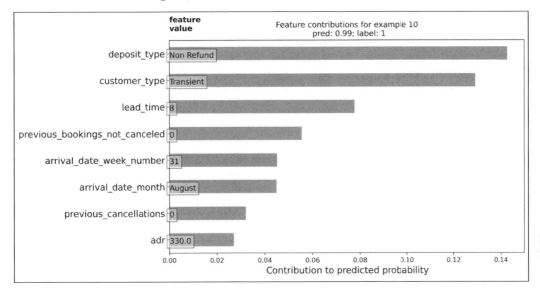

Figure 5.2: How different features contribute to predicted probabilities

Besides analyzing the feature relevance on the level of individual observation, we can also take a global (aggregate) view. Global interpretability refers to an understanding of the model as a whole: we will retrieve and visualize gain-based feature importances and permutation feature importances and also show aggregated DFCs.

Gain-based feature importances measure the loss change when splitting on a particular feature, while permutation feature importances are computed by evaluating the model performance on the evaluation set by shuffling each feature one by one and attributing the change in model performance to the shuffled feature.

In general, permutation feature importance is preferred to gain-based feature importance, though both methods can be unreliable in situations where potential predictor variables vary in their scale of measurement or their number of categories and when features are correlated.

The function calculating permutation importances is as follows:

```
def permutation_importances(est, X_eval, y_eval, metric, features):
    """Column by column, shuffle values and observe effect on eval set.

    source: http://explained.ai/rf-importance/index.html
    A similar approach can be done during training. See "Drop-column
importance"
    in the above article."""
    baseline = metric(est, X_eval, y_eval)
    imp = []
    for col in features:
```

```
        save = X_eval[col].copy()
        X_eval[col] = np.random.permutation(X_eval[col])
        m = metric(est, X_eval, y_eval)
        X_eval[col] = save
        imp.append(baseline - m)
    return np.array(imp)

def accuracy_metric(est, X, y):
    """TensorFlow estimator accuracy."""
    eval_input_fn = make_input_fn(X,
                                  y=y,
                                  shuffle=False,
                                  n_epochs=1)
    return est.evaluate(input_fn=eval_input_fn)['accuracy']
```

We use the following function to display the most relevant columns:

```
features = CATEGORICAL_COLUMNS + NUMERIC_COLUMNS
importances = permutation_importances(est, dfeval, y_eval, accuracy_metric,
                                      features)
df_imp = pd.Series(importances, index=features)

sorted_ix = df_imp.abs().sort_values().index
ax = df_imp[sorted_ix][-5:].plot(kind='barh', color=sns_colors[2],
figsize=(10, 6))
ax.grid(False, axis='y')
ax.set_title('Permutation feature importance')
plt.show()
```

Which gives you the following output:

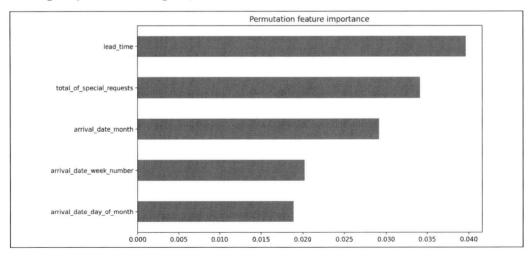

Figure 5.3: The permutation feature importance of different features

And we use the following function to display the gain feature importance columns in the same way:

```
importances = est.experimental_feature_importances(normalize=True)
df_imp = pd.Series(importances)

# Visualize importances.
N = 8
ax = (df_imp.iloc[0:N][::-1]
    .plot(kind='barh',
        color=sns_colors[0],
        title='Gain feature importances',
        figsize=(10, 6)))
ax.grid(False, axis='y')
```

Which gives you the following output:

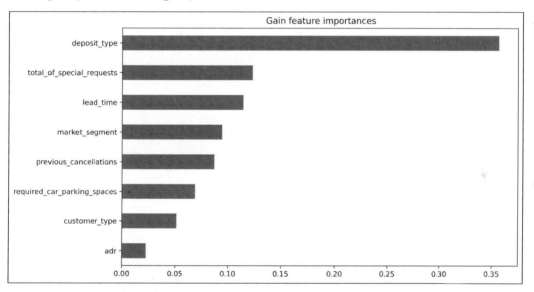

Figure 5.4: The gain feature importance of different features

The absolute values of DFCs can be averaged to understand the impact at a global level:

```
dfc_mean = df_dfc.abs().mean()
N = 8
sorted_ix = dfc_mean.abs().sort_values()[-N:].index  # Average and sort by
absolute.
ax = dfc_mean[sorted_ix].plot(kind='barh',
                        color=sns_colors[1],
                        title='Mean |directional feature contributions|',
                        figsize=(10, 6))
ax.grid(False, axis='y')
```

Which gives you the following output:

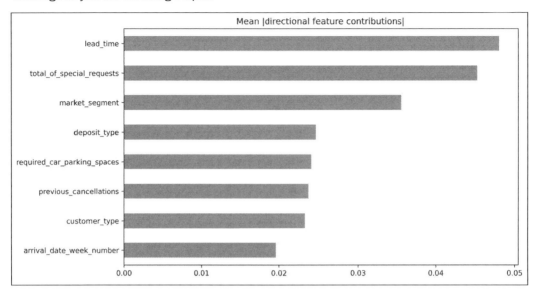

Figure 5.5: The mean directional feature contributions of different features

In this recipe, we have introduced the TF implementation of `GradientBoostingClassifier`: a flexible model architecture applicable to a wide range of tabular data problems. We built a model to solve a real business problem: predicting the probability that a customer might cancel their hotel booking and, in the process, we introduced all the relevant components of the TF Boosted Trees pipeline:

▶ Prepare the data for use with the model

▶ Configure the `GradientBoostingClassifier` with `tf.estimator`

▶ Evaluate the feature importance and model interpretability, both on a global and local level

See also

There is a plethora of articles introducing the gradient boosting family of algorithms:

▶ An excellent Medium post at `https://medium.com/analytics-vidhya/introduction-to-the-gradient-boosting-algorithm-c25c653f826b`

▶ The official XGBoost documentation: `https://xgboost.readthedocs.io/en/latest/tutorials/model.html`

▶ The LightGBM documentation: `https://papers.nips.cc/paper/6907-lightgbm-a-highly-efficient-gradient-boosting-decision-tree.pdf`

6
Neural Networks

In this chapter, we will introduce neural networks and how to implement them in TensorFlow. Most of the subsequent chapters will be based on neural networks, so learning how to use them in TensorFlow is very important.

Neural networks are currently breaking records in tasks such as image and speech recognition, reading handwriting, understanding text, image segmentation, dialog systems, autonomous car driving, and so much more. While some of these tasks will be covered in later chapters, it is important to introduce neural networks as a general-purpose, easy-to-implement machine learning algorithm, so that we can expand on it later.

The concept of a neural network has been around for decades. However, it only recently gained traction because we now have the computational power to train large networks because of advances in processing power, algorithm efficiency, and data sizes.

A neural network is, fundamentally, a sequence of operations applied to a matrix of input data. These operations are usually collections of additions and multiplications followed by the application of non-linear functions. One example that we have already seen is logistic regression, which we looked at in *Chapter 4, Linear Regression*. Logistic regression is the sum of partial slope-feature products followed by the application of the sigmoid function, which is non-linear. Neural networks generalize this a little more by allowing any combination of operations and non-linear functions, which includes the application of absolute values, maximums, minimums, and so on.

The most important trick to neural networks is called **backpropagation**. Backpropagation is a procedure that allows us to update model variables based on the learning rate and the output of the loss function. We used backpropagation to update our model variables in *Chapter 3, Keras*, and *Chapter 4, Linear Regression*.

Another important feature to take note of regarding neural networks is the non-linear activation function. Since most neural networks are just combinations of addition and multiplication operations, they will not be able to model non-linear datasets. To address this issue, we will use non-linear activation functions in our neural networks. This will allow the neural network to adapt to most non-linear situations.

It is important to remember that, as we have seen in many of the algorithms covered, neural networks are sensitive to the hyperparameters we choose. In this chapter, we will explore the impact of different learning rates, loss functions, and optimization procedures.

There are a few more resources I would recommend to you for learning about neural networks that cover the topic in greater depth and more detail:

- ▶ The seminal paper describing backpropagation is *Efficient Back Prop* by Yann LeCun et al. The PDF is located here: `http://yann.lecun.com/exdb/publis/pdf/lecun-98b.pdf`.

- ▶ CS231, *Convolutional Neural Networks for Visual Recognition*, by Stanford University. Class resources are available here: `http://cs231n.stanford.edu/`.

- ▶ CS224d, *Deep Learning for Natural Language Processing*, by Stanford University. Class resources are available here: `http://cs224d.stanford.edu/`.

- ▶ *Deep Learning*, a book by the MIT Press. Goodfellow, et al. 2016. The book is located here: `http://www.deeplearningbook.org`.

- ▶ The online book *Neural Networks and Deep Learning* by Michael Nielsen, which is located here: `http://neuralnetworksanddeeplearning.com/`.

- ▶ For a more pragmatic approach and introduction to neural networks, Andrej Karpathy has written a great summary with JavaScript examples called *A Hacker's Guide to Neural Networks*. The write-up is located here: `http://karpathy.github.io/neuralnets/`.

- ▶ Another site that summarizes deep learning well is called *Deep Learning for Beginners* by Ian Goodfellow, Yoshua Bengio, and Aaron Courville. The web page can be found here: `http://randomekek.github.io/deep/deeplearning.html`.

We will start by introducing the basic concepts of neural networking before working up to multilayer networks. In the last section, we will create a neural network that will learn how to play Tic-Tac-Toe.

In this chapter, we'll cover the following recipes:

- ▶ Implementing operational gates
- ▶ Working with gates and activation functions
- ▶ Implementing a one-layer neural network
- ▶ Implementing different layers

▶ Using a multilayer neural network

▶ Improving the predictions of linear models

▶ Learning to play Tic-Tac-Toe

The reader can find all of the code from this chapter online at https://github.com/PacktPublishing/Machine-Learning-Using-TensorFlow-Cookbook, and on the Packt repository at https://github.com/PacktPublishing/Machine-Learning-Using-TensorFlow-Cookbook.

Implementing operational gates

One of the most fundamental concepts of neural networks is its functioning as an operational gate. In this section, we will start with a multiplication operation as a gate, before moving on to consider nested gate operations.

Getting ready

The first operational gate we will implement is $f(x) = a \cdot x$:

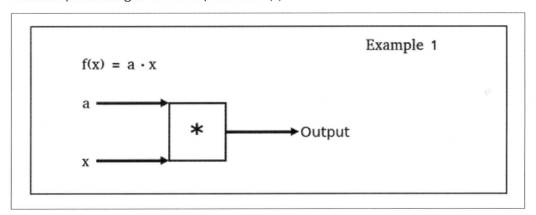

To optimize this gate, we declare the *a* input as a variable and *x* as the input tensor of our model. This means that TensorFlow will try to change the *a* value and not the *x* value. We will create the loss function as the difference between the output and the target value, which is 50.

The second, nested, operational gate will be $f(x) = a \cdot x + b$:

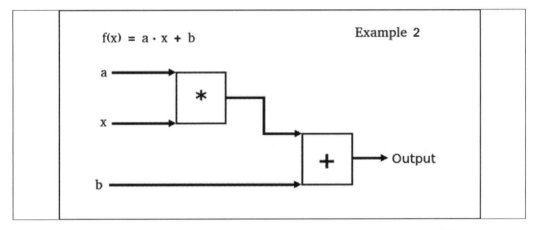

$$f(x) = a \cdot x + b$$

Example 2

Again, we will declare *a* and *b* as variables and *x* as the input tensor of our model. We optimize the output toward the target value of 50 again. The interesting thing to note is that the solution for this second example is not unique. There are many combinations of model variables that will allow the output to be 50. With neural networks, we do not care so much about the values of the intermediate model variables, but instead place more emphasis on the desired output.

How to do it...

To implement the first operational gate, $f(x) = a \cdot x$, in TensorFlow and train the output toward the value of 50, follow these steps:

1. Start off by loading TensorFlow as follows:
   ```
   import tensorflow as tf
   ```

2. Now we will need to declare our model variable and input data. We make our input data equal to the value 5, so that the multiplication factor to get 50 will be 10 (that is, 5*10=50), as follows:
   ```
   a = tf.Variable(4.)
   x_data = tf.keras.Input(shape=(1,))
   x_val = 5.
   ```

3. Next, we create a lambda layer that computes the operation, and we create a functional Keras model with the following input:
   ```
   multiply_layer = tf.keras.layers.Lambda(lambda x:tf.multiply(a, x))
   outputs = multiply_layer(x_data)
   model = tf.keras.Model(inputs=x_data, outputs=outputs,
   name="gate_1")
   ```

4. We will now declare our optimizing algorithm as the stochastic gradient descent as follows:

```
optimizer=tf.keras.optimizers.SGD(0.01)
```

5. We can now optimize our model output toward the desired value of 50. We will use the loss function as the L2 distance between the output and the desired target value of 50. We do this by continually feeding in the input value of 5 and backpropagating the loss to update the model variable toward the value of 10, shown as follows:

```
print('Optimizing a Multiplication Gate Output to 50.')
for i in range(10):

    # Open a GradientTape.
    with tf.GradientTape() as tape:

        # Forward pass.
        mult_output = model(x_val)

        # Loss value as the difference between
        # the output and a target value, 50.
        loss_value = tf.square(tf.subtract(mult_output, 50.))

    # Get gradients of loss with reference to the variable "a" to
adjust.
    gradients = tape.gradient(loss_value, a)

    # Update the variable "a" of the model.
    optimizer.apply_gradients(zip([gradients], [a]))

    print("{} * {} = {}".format(a.numpy(), x_val, a.numpy() * x_
val))
```

6. The preceding step should result in the following output:

```
Optimizing a Multiplication Gate Output to 50.
7.0 * 5.0 = 35.0
8.5 * 5.0 = 42.5
9.25 * 5.0 = 46.25
9.625 * 5.0 = 48.125
9.8125 * 5.0 = 49.0625
9.90625 * 5.0 = 49.5312
9.95312 * 5.0 = 49.7656
9.97656 * 5.0 = 49.8828
9.98828 * 5.0 = 49.9414
9.99414 * 5.0 = 49.9707
```

Next, we will do the same with the two-nested operational gate, $f(x) = a \cdot x + b$.

7. We will start in exactly the same way as the preceding example, but will initialize two model variables, a and b, as follows:

```python
import tensorflow as tf
# Initialize variables and input data
x_data = tf.keras.Input(dtype=tf.float32, shape=(1,))
x_val = 5.
a = tf.Variable(1., dtype=tf.float32)
b = tf.Variable(1., dtype=tf.float32)


# Add a layer which computes f(x) = a * x
multiply_layer = tf.keras.layers.Lambda(lambda x:tf.multiply(a, x))


# Add a layer which computes f(x) = b + x
add_layer = tf.keras.layers.Lambda(lambda x:tf.add(b, x))


res = multiply_layer(x_data)
outputs = add_layer(res)


# Build the model
model = tf.keras.Model(inputs=x_data, outputs=outputs,
name="gate_2")


# Optimizer
optimizer=tf.keras.optimizers.SGD(0.01)
```

8. We now optimize the model variables to train the output toward the target value of 50, shown as follows:

```python
print('Optimizing two Gate Output to 50.')
for i in range(10):

    # Open a GradientTape.
    with tf.GradientTape(persistent=True) as tape:

        # Forward pass.
        two_gate_output = model(x_val)

        # Loss value as the difference between
        # the output and a target value, 50.
        loss_value = tf.square(tf.subtract(two_gate_output, 50.))

    # Get gradients of loss with reference to
    # the variables "a" and "b" to adjust.
    gradients_a = tape.gradient(loss_value, a)
    gradients_b = tape.gradient(loss_value , b)
```

```
    # Update the variables "a" and "b" of the model.
    optimizer.apply_gradients(zip([gradients_a, gradients_b], [a,
b]))

    print("Step: {} ==> {} * {} + {}= {}".format(i, a.numpy(),
                                          x_val, b.numpy(),
                                          a.numpy()*x_val+b.
numpy())))
```

9. The preceding step should result in the following output:

```
Optimizing Two Gate Output to 50.
5.4 * 5.0 + 1.88 = 28.88
7.512 * 5.0 + 2.3024 = 39.8624
8.52576 * 5.0 + 2.50515 = 45.134
9.01236 * 5.0 + 2.60247 = 47.6643
9.24593 * 5.0 + 2.64919 = 48.8789
9.35805 * 5.0 + 2.67161 = 49.4619
9.41186 * 5.0 + 2.68237 = 49.7417
9.43769 * 5.0 + 2.68754 = 49.876
9.45009 * 5.0 + 2.69002 = 49.9405
9.45605 * 5.0 + 2.69121 = 49.9714
```

It is important to note here that the solution to the second example is not unique. This does not matter as much in neural networks, as all parameters are adjusted toward reducing the loss. The final solution here will depend on the initial values of a and b. If these were randomly initialized, instead of to the value of 1, we would see different ending values for the model variables for each iteration.

How it works...

We achieved the optimization of a computational gate via TensorFlow's implicit backpropagation. TensorFlow keeps track of our model's operations and variable values and makes adjustments in respect of our optimization algorithm specification and the output of the loss function.

We can keep expanding the operational gates while keeping track of which inputs are variables and which inputs are data. This is important to keep track of, because TensorFlow will change all variables to minimize the loss but not the data.

The implicit ability to keep track of the computational graph and update the model variables automatically with every training step is one of the great features of TensorFlow and what makes it so powerful.

Working with gates and activation functions

Now that we can link together operational gates, we want to run the computational graph output through an activation function. In this section, we will introduce common activation functions.

Getting ready

In this section, we will compare and contrast two different activation functions: **sigmoid** and **rectified linear unit** (**ReLU**). Recall that the two functions are given by the following equations:

$$sigmoid(x) = \sigma(x) = \frac{1}{1 + e^x}$$

$$ReLU(x) = \max(0, x)$$

In this example, we will create two one-layer neural networks with the same structure, except that one will feed through the sigmoid activation and one will feed through the ReLU activation. The loss function will be governed by the L2 distance from the value 0.75. We will randomly pull batch data and then optimize the output toward 0.75.

How to do it...

We proceed with the recipe as follows:

1. We will start by loading the necessary libraries. This is also a good point at which we can bring up how to set a random seed with TensorFlow. Since we will be using a random number generator from NumPy and TensorFlow, we need to set a random seed for both. With the same random seeds set, we should be able to replicate the results. We do this with the following input:

```
import tensorflow as tf
import numpy as np
import matplotlib.pyplot as plt
tf.random.set_seed(5)
np.random.seed(42)
```

2. Now we need to declare our batch size, model variables, and data model inputs. Our computational graph will consist of feeding in our normally distributed data into two similar neural networks that differ only by the activation function at the end, shown as follows:

```
batch_size = 50
x_data = tf.keras.Input(shape=(1,))
x_data = tf.keras.Input(shape=(1,))
```

```
a1 = tf.Variable(tf.random.normal(shape=[1,1], seed=5))
b1 = tf.Variable(tf.random.uniform(shape=[1,1], seed=5))
a2 = tf.Variable(tf.random.normal(shape=[1,1], seed=5))
b2 = tf.Variable(tf.random.uniform(shape=[1,1], seed=5))
```

3. Next, we'll declare our two models, the sigmoid activation model and the ReLU activation model, as follows:

```python
class MyCustomGateSigmoid(tf.keras.layers.Layer):

  def __init__(self, units, a1, b1):
    super(MyCustomGateSigmoid, self).__init__()
    self.units = units
    self.a1 = a1
    self.b1 = b1

  # Compute f(x) = sigmoid(a1 * x + b1)
  def call(self, inputs):
    return tf.math.sigmoid(inputs * self.a1 + self.b1)

# Add a layer which computes f(x) = sigmoid(a1 * x + b1)
my_custom_gate_sigmoid = MyCustomGateSigmoid(units=1, a1=a1, b1=b1)
output_sigmoid = my_custom_gate_sigmoid(x_data)

# Build the model
model_sigmoid = tf.keras.Model(inputs=x_data, outputs=output_
sigmoid, name="gate_sigmoid")

class MyCustomGateRelu(tf.keras.layers.Layer):

  def __init__(self, units, a2, b2):
    super(MyCustomGateRelu, self).__init__()
    self.units = units
    self.a2 = a2
    self.b2 = b2

  # Compute f(x) = relu(a2 * x + b2)
  def call(self, inputs):
    return tf.nn.relu(inputs * self.a2 + self.b2)

# Add a layer which computes f(x) = relu(a2 * x + b2)
my_custom_gate_relu = MyCustomGateRelu(units=1, a2=a2, b2=b2)
outputs_relu = my_custom_gate_relu(x_data)

# Build the model
```

```
model_relu = tf.keras.Model(inputs=x_data, outputs=outputs_relu,
name="gate_relu")
```

4. Now we need to declare our optimization algorithm and initialize our variables, shown as follows:

```
optimizer=tf.keras.optimizers.SGD(0.01)
```

5. Now we'll loop through our training for 750 iterations for both models, as shown in the following code block. The loss functions will be the average L2 norm between the model output and the value of 0.75. We will also save the loss output and the activation output values for plotting later on:

```
# Run loop across gate
print('\n Optimizing Sigmoid AND Relu Output to 0.75')
loss_vec_sigmoid = []
loss_vec_relu = []

activation_sigmoid = []
activation_relu = []

for i in range(500):

    rand_indices = np.random.choice(len(x), size=batch_size)
    x_vals = np.transpose([x[rand_indices]])
    # Open a GradientTape.
    with tf.GradientTape(persistent=True) as tape:

        # Forward pass.
        output_sigmoid = model_sigmoid(x_vals)
        output_relu = model_relu(x_vals)

        # Loss value as the difference as the difference between
        # the output and a target value, 0.75.
        loss_sigmoid = tf.reduce_mean(tf.square(tf.subtract(output_
sigmoid, 0.75)))
        loss_vec_sigmoid.append(loss_sigmoid)
        loss_relu = tf.reduce_mean(tf.square(tf.subtract(output_
relu, 0.75)))
        loss_vec_relu.append(loss_relu)


    # Get gradients of loss_sigmoid with reference to the variable
"a1" and "b1" to adjust.
    gradients_a1 = tape.gradient(loss_sigmoid, my_custom_gate_
sigmoid.a1)
```

```
    gradients_b1 = tape.gradient(loss_sigmoid , my_custom_gate_
sigmoid.b1)

    # Get gradients of loss_relu with reference to the variable "a2"
and "b2" to adjust.
    gradients_a2 = tape.gradient(loss_relu, my_custom_gate_relu.a2)
    gradients_b2 = tape.gradient(loss_relu , my_custom_gate_relu.b2)

    # Update the variable "a1" and "b1" of the model.
    optimizer.apply_gradients(zip([gradients_a1, gradients_b1], [my_
custom_gate_sigmoid.a1, my_custom_gate_sigmoid.b1]))

    # Update the variable "a2" and "b2" of the model.
    optimizer.apply_gradients(zip([gradients_a2, gradients_b2], [my_
custom_gate_relu.a2, my_custom_gate_relu.b2]))

    output_sigmoid = model_sigmoid(x_vals)
    output_relu = model_relu(x_vals)

    activation_sigmoid.append(np.mean(output_sigmoid))
    activation_relu.append(np.mean(output_relu))

    if i%50==0:
        print('sigmoid = ' + str(np.mean(output_sigmoid)) + ' relu =
' + str(np.mean(output_relu)))
```

6. To plot the loss and the activation outputs, we need to input the following code:

```
plt.plot(activation_sigmoid, 'k-', label='Sigmoid Activation')
plt.plot(activation_relu, 'r--', label='Relu Activation')
plt.ylim([0, 1.0])
plt.title('Activation Outputs')
plt.xlabel('Generation')
plt.ylabel('Outputs')
plt.legend(loc='upper right')
plt.show()
plt.plot(loss_vec_sigmoid, 'k-', label='Sigmoid Loss')
plt.plot(loss_vec_relu, 'r--', label='Relu Loss')
plt.ylim([0, 1.0])
plt.title('Loss per Generation')
plt.xlabel('Generation')
plt.ylabel('Loss')
plt.legend(loc='upper right')
plt.show()
```

The activation output needs to be plotted as shown in the following diagram:

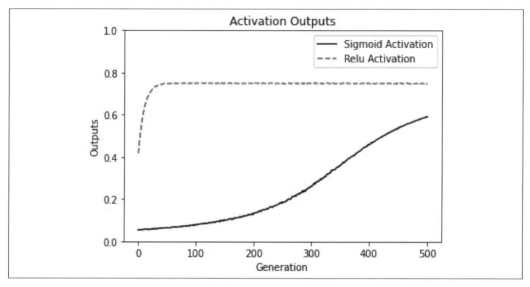

Figure 6.1: Computational graph outputs from the network with the sigmoid activation
and a network with the ReLU activation

The two neural networks work with a similar architecture and target (0.75) but with two
different activation functions, sigmoid and ReLU. It is important to notice how much more
rapidly the ReLU activation network converges to the desired target of 0.75 than the sigmoid
activation, as shown in the following diagram:

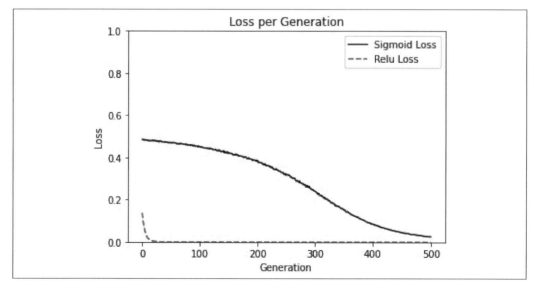

Figure 6.2: This figure depicts the loss value of the sigmoid and the ReLU activation networks.
Notice how extreme the ReLU loss is at the beginning of the iterations

How it works...

Because of the form of the ReLU activation function, it returns the value of zero much more often than the sigmoid function. We consider this behavior as a type of sparsity. This sparsity results in a speeding up of convergence, but a loss of controlled gradients. On the other hand, the sigmoid function has very well-controlled gradients and does not risk the extreme values that the ReLU activation does, as illustrated in the following table:

Activation function	Advantages	Disadvantages
Sigmoid	Less extreme outputs	Slower convergence
ReLU	Quick convergence	Extreme output values possible

There's more...

In this section, we compared the ReLU activation function and the sigmoid activation function for neural networks. There are many other activation functions that are commonly used for neural networks, but most fall into either one of two categories; the first category contains functions that are shaped like the sigmoid function, such as arctan, hypertangent, heaviside step, and so on; the second category contains functions that are shaped like the ReLU function, such as softplus, leaky ReLU, and so on. Most of what we discussed in this section about comparing the two functions will hold true for activations in either category. However, it is important to note that the choice of activation function has a big impact on the convergence and the output of neural networks.

Implementing a one-layer neural network

We have all of the tools needed to implement a neural network that operates on real data, so in this section, we will create a neural network with one layer that operates on the Iris dataset.

Getting ready

In this section, we will implement a neural network with one hidden layer. It will be important to understand that a fully connected neural network is based mostly on matrix multiplication. As such, it is important that the dimensions of the data and matrix are lined up correctly.

Since this is a regression problem, we will use **mean squared error** (**MSE**) as the loss function.

How to do it...

We proceed with the recipe as follows:

1. To create the computational graph, we'll start by loading the following necessary libraries:

    ```
    import matplotlib.pyplot as plt
    import numpy as np
    import tensorflow as tf
    from sklearn import datasets
    ```

2. Now we'll load the `Iris` data and store the length as the target value with the following code:

    ```
    iris = datasets.load_iris()
    x_vals = np.array([x[0:3] for x in iris.data])
    y_vals = np.array([x[3] for x in iris.data])
    ```

3. Since the dataset is smaller, we will want to set a seed to make the results reproducible, as follows:

    ```
    seed = 3
    tf.set_random_seed(seed)
    np.random.seed(seed)
    ```

4. To prepare the data, we'll create a 80-20 train-test split and normalize the x features to be between 0 and 1 via min-max scaling, shown as follows:

    ```
    train_indices = np.random.choice(len(x_vals), round(len(x_
    vals)*0.8), replace=False)
    test_indices = np.array(list(set(range(len(x_vals))) - set(train_
    indices)))
    x_vals_train = x_vals[train_indices]
    x_vals_test = x_vals[test_indices]
    y_vals_train = y_vals[train_indices]
    y_vals_test = y_vals[test_indices]

    def normalize_cols(m):
        col_max = m.max(axis=0)
        col_min = m.min(axis=0)
        return (m-col_min) / (col_max - col_min)

    x_vals_train = np.nan_to_num(normalize_cols(x_vals_train))
    x_vals_test = np.nan_to_num(normalize_cols(x_vals_test))
    ```

5. Now we will declare the batch size and the data model input with the following code:

```
batch_size = 50
x_data = tf.keras.Input(dtype=tf.float32, shape=(3,))
```

6. The important part is to declare our model variables with the appropriate shape. We can declare the size of our hidden layer to be any size we wish; in the following code block, we have set it to have five hidden nodes:

```
hidden_layer_nodes = 5
a1 = tf.Variable(tf.random.normal(shape=[3,hidden_layer_nodes],
seed=seed))
b1 = tf.Variable(tf.random.normal(shape=[hidden_layer_nodes],
seed=seed))
a2 = tf.Variable(tf.random.normal(shape=[hidden_layer_nodes,1],
seed=seed))
b2 = tf.Variable(tf.random.normal(shape=[1], seed=seed))
```

7. We'll now declare our model in two steps. The first step will be creating the hidden layer output and the second will be creating the final_output of the model, as follows:

 As a note, our model goes from three input features to five hidden nodes, and finally to one output value.

```
hidden_output = tf.keras.layers.Lambda(lambda x: tf.nn.relu(tf.
add(tf.matmul(x, a1), b1)))

final_output = tf.keras.layers.Lambda(lambda x: tf.nn.relu(tf.
add(tf.matmul(x, a2), b2)))

model = tf.keras.Model(inputs=x_data, outputs=output, name="1layer_
neural_network")
```

8. Now we'll declare our optimizing algorithm with the following code:

```
optimizer = tf.keras.optimizers.SGD(0.005)
```

9. Next, we loop through our training iterations. We'll also initialize two lists in which we can store our train and test_loss functions. In every loop, we also want to randomly select a batch from the training data for fitting to the model, shown as follows:

```
# First we initialize the loss vectors for storage.
loss_vec = []
test_loss = []
for i in range(500):
```

```
    rand_index = np.random.choice(len(x_vals_train), size=batch_
size)
    rand_x = x_vals_train[rand_index]
    rand_y = np.transpose([y_vals_train[rand_index]])

    # Open a GradientTape.
    with tf.GradientTape(persistent=True) as tape:

        # Forward pass.
        output = model(rand_x)

        # Apply loss function (MSE)
        loss = tf.reduce_mean(tf.square(rand_y - output))
        loss_vec.append(np.sqrt(loss))

    # Get gradients of loss with reference to the variables to
adjust.
    gradients_a1 = tape.gradient(loss, a1)
    gradients_b1 = tape.gradient(loss, b1)
    gradients_a2 = tape.gradient(loss, a2)
    gradients_b2 = tape.gradient(loss, b2)

    # Update the variables of the model.
    optimizer.apply_gradients(zip([gradients_a1, gradients_b1,
gradients_a2, gradients_b2], [a1, b1, a2, b2]))

    # Forward pass.
    output_test = model(x_vals_test)
    # Apply loss function (MSE) on test
    loss_test = tf.reduce_mean(tf.square(np.transpose([y_vals_test])
- output_test))
    test_loss.append(np.sqrt(loss_test))

    if (i+1)%50==0:
        print('Generation: ' + str(i+1) + '. Loss = ' + str(np.
mean(loss)))
        print('Generation: ' + str(i+1) + '. Loss = ' + str(temp_
loss))
```

10. We can plot the losses with `matplotlib` and the following code:

```
plt.plot(loss_vec, 'k-', label='Train Loss')
plt.plot(test_loss, 'r--', label='Test Loss')
plt.title('Loss (MSE) per Generation')
plt.xlabel('Generation')
plt.ylabel('Loss')
plt.legend(loc='upper right')
plt.show()
```

We proceed with the recipe by plotting the following diagram:

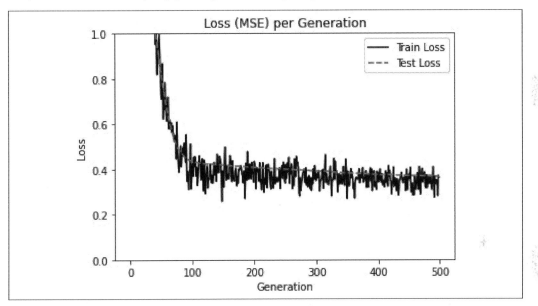

Figure 6.3: We plot the loss (MSE) of the train and test set

Note that we can also see that the train set loss is not as smooth as that in the test set. This is because of two reasons: the first is that we are using a smaller batch size than the test set, although not by much; the second cause is the fact that we are training on the train set, and the test set does not impact the variables of the model.

How it works...

Our model has now been visualized as a neural network diagram, as shown in the following diagram:

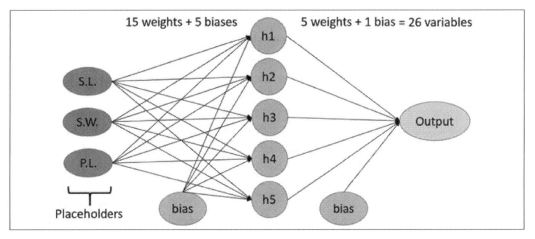

Figure 6.4: A neural network diagram

The preceding figure is a visualization of our neural network that has five nodes in the hidden layer. We are feeding in three values: the **sepal length** (**S.L.**), the **sepal width** (**S.W.**), and the **petal length** (**P.L.**). The target will be the petal width. In total, there will be 26 total variables in the model.

Implementing different layers

It is important to know how to implement different layers. In the preceding recipe, we implemented fully connected layers. In this recipe, we will further expand our knowledge of various layers.

Getting ready

We have explored how to connect data inputs and a fully connected hidden layer, but there are more types of layers available as built-in functions inside TensorFlow. The most popular layers that are used are convolutional layers and maxpool layers. We will show you how to create and use such layers with input data and with fully connected data. First, we will look at how to use these layers on one-dimensional data, and then on two-dimensional data.

While neural networks can be layered in any fashion, one of the most common designs is to use convolutional layers and fully connected layers to first create features. If we then have too many features, it is common to use a maxpool layer.

After these layers, non-linear layers are commonly introduced as activation functions. **Convolutional neural networks** (**CNNs**), which we will consider in *Chapter 8, Convolutional Neural Networks,* usually have convolutional, maxpool, and activation layers.

How to do it...

We will first look at one-dimensional data. We need to generate a random array of data for this task using the following steps:

1. We'll start by loading the libraries we need, as follows:

```
import tensorflow as tf
import numpy as np
```

2. Now we'll initialize some parameters and we'll create the input data layer with the following code:

```
data_size = 25
conv_size = 5
maxpool_size = 5
stride_size = 1
num_outputs = 5

x_input_1d = tf.keras.Input(dtype=tf.float32, shape=(data_size,1),
name="input_layer")
```

3. Next, we will define a convolutional layer, as follows:

 For our example data, we have a batch size of 1, a width of 1, a height of 25, and a channel size of 1. Also note that we can calculate the output dimensions of convolutional layers with the output_size=(W-F+2P)/S+1 formula, where W is the input size, F is the filter size, P is the padding size, and S is the stride size.

```
my_conv_output = tf.keras.layers.Conv1D(kernel_size=(conv_size),
                                         filters=data_size,
                                         strides=stride_size,
                                         padding="VALID",

name="convolution_layer")(x_input_1d)
```

4. Next, we add a ReLU activation layer, as follows:

```
my_activation_output = tf.keras.layers.ReLU(name="activation_layer")
(my_conv_output)
```

5. Now we'll add a maxpool layer. This layer will create a `maxpool` on a moving window across our one-dimensional vector. For this example, we will initialize it to have a width of 5, shown as follows:

 TensorFlow's `maxpool` arguments are very similar to those of the convolutional layer. While a `maxpool` argument does not have a filter, it does have size, stride, and padding options. Since we have a window of 5 with valid padding (no zero padding), then our output array will have 4 fewer entries.

```
my_maxpool_output = tf.keras.layers.MaxPool1D(strides=stride_size,

pool_size=maxpool_size,

                                            padding='VALID',

name="maxpool_layer")(my_activation_output)
```

6. The final layer that we will connect is the fully connected layer. Here, we will use a dense layer, as shown in the following code block:

```
my_full_output = tf.keras.layers.Dense(units=num_outputs,

name="fully_connected_layer")(my_maxpool_output)
```

7. Now we'll create the model, and print the output of each of the layers, as follows:

```
print('>>>> 1D Data <<<<')

model_1D = tf.keras.Model(inputs=x_input_1d, outputs=my_full_output,
name="model_1D")
model_1D.summary()

# Input
print('\n== input_layer ==')
print('Input = array of length %d' % (x_input_1d.shape.as_list()
[1]))

# Convolution
print('\n== convolution_layer ==')
print('Convolution w/ filter, length = %d, stride size = %d, results
in an array of length %d' %
      (conv_size,stride_size,my_conv_output.shape.as_list()[1]))
```

```
# Activation
print('\n== activation_layer ==')
print('Input = above array of length %d' % (my_conv_output.shape.
as_list()[1]))
print('ReLU element wise returns an array of length %d' % (my_
activation_output.shape.as_list()[1]))


# Max Pool
print('\n== maxpool_layer ==')
print('Input = above array of length %d' % (my_activation_output.
shape.as_list()[1]))
print('MaxPool, window length = %d, stride size = %d, results in the
array of length %d' %
    (maxpool_size,stride_size,my_maxpool_output.shape.as_list()
[1]))


# Fully Connected
print('\n== fully_connected_layer ==')
print('Input = above array of length %d' % (my_maxpool_output.shape.
as_list()[1]))
print('Fully connected layer on all 4 rows with %d outputs' %
    (my_full_output.shape.as_list()[1]))
```

8. The preceding step should result in the following output:

```
>>>> 1D Data <<<<
Model: "model_1D"


Layer (type)                  Output Shape          Param #
=================================================================
input_layer (InputLayer)      [(None, 25, 1)]        0

convolution_layer (Conv1D)    (None, 21, 25)         150

activation_layer (ReLU)       (None, 21, 25)         0

maxpool_layer (MaxPooling1D)  (None, 17, 25)         0

fully_connected_layer (Dense  (None, 17, 5)          130
=================================================================
Total params: 280
Trainable params: 280
Non-trainable params: 0
```

```
== input_layer ==
Input = array of length 25

== convolution_layer ==
Convolution w/ filter, length = 5, stride size = 1, results in an
array of length 21

== activation_layer ==
Input = above array of length 21
ReLU element wise returns an array of length 21

== maxpool_layer ==
Input = above array of length 21
MaxPool, window length = 5, stride size = 1, results in the array of
length 17

== fully_connected_layer ==
Input = above array of length 17
Fully connected layer on all 4 rows with 17 outputs
```

 One-dimensional data is very important to consider for neural networks. Time series, signal processing, and some text embeddings are considered to be one-dimensional and are frequently used in neural networks.

We will now consider the same types of layer in an equivalent order but for two-dimensional data:

1. We will start by initializing the variables, as follows:

```
row_size = 10
col_size = 10
conv_size = 2
conv_stride_size = 2
maxpool_size = 2
maxpool_stride_size = 1
num_outputs = 5
```

2. Then we will initialize our input data layer. Since our data has a height and width already, we just need to expand it in two dimensions (a batch size of 1, and a channel size of 1) as follows:

```
x_input_2d = tf.keras.Input(dtype=tf.float32, shape=(row_size,col_
size, 1), name="input_layer_2d")
```

3. Just as in the one-dimensional example, we now need to add a 2D convolutional layer. For the filter, we will use a random 2x2 filter, a stride of 2 in both directions, and valid padding (in other words, no zero padding). Because our input matrix is 10x10, our convolutional output will be 5x5, shown as follows:

```
my_convolution_output_2d =
tf.keras.layers.Conv2D(kernel_size=(conv_size),

filters=conv_size,

strides=conv_stride_size,
                                          padding="VALID",

name="convolution_layer_2d")(x_input_2d)
```

4. Next, we add a ReLU activation layer, as follows:

```
my_activation_output_2d = tf.keras.layers.ReLU(name="activation_
layer_2d")(my_convolution_output_2d)
```

5. Our maxpool layer is very similar to the one-dimensional case, except we have to declare a width and height for the maxpool window and the stride. In our case, we will use the same value for all spatial dimensions so we will set integer values, shown as follows:

```
my_maxpool_output_2d =
tf.keras.layers.MaxPool2D(strides=maxpool_stride_size,

pool_size=maxpool_size,
                                          padding='VALID',

name="maxpool_layer_2d")(my_activation_output_2d)
```

6. Our fully connected layer is very similar to the one-dimensional output. We use a dense layer, as follows:

```
my_full_output_2d = tf.keras.layers.Dense(units=num_outputs,

name="fully_connected_layer_2d")(my_maxpool_output_2d)
```

7. Now we'll create the model, and print the output of each of the layers, as follows:

```
print('>>>> 2D Data <<<<')

model_2D = tf.keras.Model(inputs=x_input_2d, outputs=my_full_
output_2d, name="model_2D")
model_2D.summary()

# Input
print('\n== input_layer ==')
```

```
print('Input = %s array' % (x_input_2d.shape.as_list()[1:3]))


# Convolution
print('\n== convolution_layer ==')
print('%s Convolution, stride size = [%d, %d] , results in the %s
array' %
      ([conv_size,conv_size],conv_stride_size,conv_stride_size,my_
convolution_output_2d.shape.as_list()[1:3]))


# Activation
print('\n== activation_layer ==')
print('Input = the above %s array' % (my_convolution_output_2d.
shape.as_list()[1:3]))
print('ReLU element wise returns the %s array' % (my_activation_
output_2d.shape.as_list()[1:3]))


# Max Pool
print('\n== maxpool_layer ==')
print('Input = the above %s array' % (my_activation_output_2d.shape.
as_list()[1:3]))
print('MaxPool, stride size = [%d, %d], results in %s array' %
      (maxpool_stride_size,maxpool_stride_size,my_maxpool_output_2d.
shape.as_list()[1:3]))


# Fully Connected
print('\n== fully_connected_layer ==')
print('Input = the above %s array' % (my_maxpool_output_2d.shape.
as_list()[1:3]))
print('Fully connected layer on all %d rows results in %s outputs' %
      (my_maxpool_output_2d.shape.as_list()[1],my_full_output_2d.
shape.as_list()[3]))


feed_dict = {x_input_2d: data_2d}
```

8. The preceding step should result in the following output:

```
>>>> 2D Data <<<<
Model: "model_2D"


Layer (type)                      Output Shape               Param #
=====================================================================
input_layer_2d (InputLayer)   [(None, 10, 10, 1)]            0


convolution_layer_2d (Conv2D  (None, 5, 5, 2)                10


activation_layer_2d (ReLU)     (None, 5, 5, 2)               0
```

```
maxpool_layer_2d (MaxPooling (None, 4, 4, 2)              0

fully_connected_layer_2d (De (None, 4, 4, 5)             15
=================================================================
Total params: 25
Trainable params: 25
Non-trainable params: 0


== input_layer ==
Input = [10, 10] array

== convolution_layer ==
[2, 2] Convolution, stride size = [2, 2] , results in the [5, 5]
array

== activation_layer ==
Input = the above [5, 5] array
ReLU element wise returns the [5, 5] array

== maxpool_layer ==
Input = the above [5, 5] array
MaxPool, stride size = [1, 1], results in [4, 4] array

== fully_connected_layer ==
Input = the above [4, 4] array
Fully connected layer on all 4 rows results in 5 outputs
```

How it works...

We should now know how to use the convolutional and maxpool layers in TensorFlow with one-dimensional and two-dimensional data. Regardless of the shape of the input, we ended up with outputs of the same size. This is important for illustrating the flexibility of neural network layers. This section should also impress upon us again the importance of shapes and sizes in neural network operations.

Using a multilayer neural network

We will now apply our knowledge of different layers to real data by using a multilayer neural network on the low birth weight dataset.

Getting ready

Now that we know how to create neural networks and work with layers, we will apply this methodology with the aim of predicting birth weights in the low birth weight dataset. We'll create a neural network with three hidden layers. The low birth weight dataset includes the actual birth weights and an indicator variable for whether the given birth weight is above or below 2,500 grams. In this example, we'll make the target the actual birth weight (regression) and then see what the accuracy is on the classification at the end. At the end, our model should be able to identify whether the birth weight will be <2,500 grams.

How to do it...

We proceed with the recipe as follows:

1. We will start by loading the libraries as follows:

```
import tensorflow as tf
import matplotlib.pyplot as plt
import csv
import random
import numpy as np
import requests
import os
```

2. We'll now load the data from the website using the `requests` module. After this, we will split the data into features of interest and the target value, shown as follows:

```
# name of data file
birth_weight_file = 'birth_weight.csv'

# download data and create data file if file does not exist in
current directory
if not os.path.exists(birth_weight_file):
    birthdata_url = https://github.com/PacktPublishing/Machine-
Learning-Using-TensorFlow-Cookbook/blob/master/ch6/06_Using_
Multiple_Layers/birth_weight.csv
    birth_file = requests.get(birthdata_url)
    birth_data = birth_file.text.split('\r\n')
    birth_header = birth_data[0].split('\t')
    birth_data = [[float(x) for x in y.split('\t') if
                                        len(x)>=1]
for y in birth_data[1:] if len(y)>=1]
    with open(birth_weight_file, "w") as f:
        writer = csv.writer(f)
        writer.writerows([birth_header])
        writer.writerows(birth_data)
```

```
        f.close()

# read birth weight data into memory
birth_data = []
with open(birth_weight_file, newline='') as csvfile:
    csv_reader = csv.reader(csvfile)
    birth_header = next(csv_reader)
    for row in csv_reader:
        birth_data.append(row)

birth_data = [[float(x) for x in row] for row in birth_data]


# Extract y-target (birth weight)
y_vals = np.array([x[8] for x in birth_data])

# Filter for features of interest
cols_of_interest = ['AGE', 'LWT', 'RACE', 'SMOKE', 'PTL', 'HT',
'UI']
x_vals = np.array([[x[ix] for ix, feature in enumerate(birth_header)
if feature in cols_of_interest] for x in birth_data])
```

3. To help with repeatability, we now need to set the random seed for both NumPy and TensorFlow. Then we declare our batch size as follows:

```
# make results reproducible
seed = 3
np.random.seed(seed)
tf.random.set_seed(seed)
# set batch size for training
batch_size = 150
```

4. Next, we split the data into an 80-20 train-test split. After this, we need to normalize our input features so that they are between 0 and 1 with min-max scaling, shown as follows:

```
train_indices = np.random.choice(len(x_vals), round(len(x_
vals)*0.8), replace=False)
test_indices = np.array(list(set(range(len(x_vals))) - set(train_
indices)))
x_vals_train = x_vals[train_indices]
x_vals_test = x_vals[test_indices]
y_vals_train = y_vals[train_indices]
y_vals_test = y_vals[test_indices]

# Record training column max and min for scaling of non-training
```

```
data
train_max = np.max(x_vals_train, axis=0)
train_min = np.min(x_vals_train, axis=0)

# Normalize by column (min-max norm to be between 0 and 1)
def normalize_cols(mat, max_vals, min_vals):
    return (mat - min_vals) / (max_vals - min_vals)

x_vals_train = np.nan_to_num(normalize_cols(x_vals_train, train_max,
train_min))
x_vals_test = np.nan_to_num(normalize_cols(x_vals_test, train_max,
train_min))
```

Normalizing input features is a common feature transformation and is especially useful for neural networks. It will help with convergence if our data is centered between 0 and 1 for the activation functions.

5. Since we have multiple layers that have similar initialized variables, we now need to create a function to initialize both the weights and the bias. We do that with the following code:

```
# Define Variable Functions (weights and bias)
def init_weight(shape, st_dev):
    weight = tf.Variable(tf.random.normal(shape, stddev=st_dev))
    return(weight)

def init_bias(shape, st_dev):
    bias = tf.Variable(tf.random.normal(shape, stddev=st_dev))
    return(bias)
```

6. We now need to initialize our input data layer. There will be seven input features. The output will be the birth weight in grams:

```
x_data = tf.keras.Input(dtype=tf.float32, shape=(7,))
```

7. The fully connected layer will be used three times for all three hidden layers. To prevent repeated code, we will create a layer function for use when we initialize our model, shown as follows:

```
# Create a fully connected layer:

def fully_connected(input_layer, weights, biases):

    return tf.keras.layers.Lambda(lambda x: tf.nn.relu(tf.add(tf.
matmul(x, weights), biases)))(input_layer)
```

8. Now it's time to create our model. For each layer (and output layer), we will initialize a weight matrix, bias matrix, and the fully connected layer. For this example, we will use hidden layers of sizes 25, 10, and 3:

 The model that we are using will have 522 variables to fit. To arrive at this number, we can see that between the data and the first hidden layer we have 7*25+25=200 variables. If we continue in this way and add them up, we'll have 200+260+33+4=497 variables. This is significantly larger than the nine variables that we used in the logistic regression model on this data.

```
#--------Create the first layer (25 hidden nodes)--------
weight_1 = init_weight(shape=[7,25], st_dev=5.0)
bias_1 = init_bias(shape=[25], st_dev=10.0)
layer_1 = fully_connected(x_data, weight_1, bias_1)

#--------Create second layer (10 hidden nodes)--------
weight_2 = init_weight(shape=[25, 10], st_dev=5.0)
bias_2 = init_bias(shape=[10], st_dev=10.0)
layer_2 = fully_connected(layer_1, weight_2, bias_2)

#--------Create third layer (3 hidden nodes)--------
weight_3 = init_weight(shape=[10, 3], st_dev=5.0)
bias_3 = init_bias(shape=[3], st_dev=10.0)
layer_3 = fully_connected(layer_2, weight_3, bias_3)

#--------Create output layer (1 output value)--------
weight_4 = init_weight(shape=[3, 1], st_dev=5.0)
bias_4 = init_bias(shape=[1], st_dev=10.0)
final_output = fully_connected(layer_3, weight_4, bias_4)

model = tf.keras.Model(inputs=x_data, outputs=final_output,
name="multiple_layers_neural_network")
```

9. We'll now declare our optimizer (using Adam optimization) and loop through our training iterations. We will use the L1 loss function (the absolute value). We'll also initialize two lists in which we can store our `train` and `test_loss` functions. In every loop, we also want to randomly select a batch from the training data for fitting to the model and print the status every 25 generations, shown as follows:

```
# Declare Adam optimizer
optimizer = tf.keras.optimizers.Adam(0.025)

# Training loop
```

```
loss_vec = []
test_loss = []
for i in range(200):
    rand_index = np.random.choice(len(x_vals_train), size=batch_
size)
    rand_x = x_vals_train[rand_index]
    rand_y = np.transpose([y_vals_train[rand_index]])

    # Open a GradientTape.
    with tf.GradientTape(persistent=True) as tape:

        # Forward pass.
        output = model(rand_x)

        # Apply Loss function (MSE)
        loss = tf.reduce_mean(tf.abs(rand_y - output))
        loss_vec.append(loss)

    # Get gradients of loss with reference to the weights and bias
variables to adjust.
    gradients_w1 = tape.gradient(loss, weight_1)
    gradients_b1 = tape.gradient(loss, bias_1)
    gradients_w2 = tape.gradient(loss, weight_2)
    gradients_b2 = tape.gradient(loss, bias_2)
    gradients_w3 = tape.gradient(loss, weight_3)
    gradients_b3 = tape.gradient(loss, bias_3)
    gradients_w4 = tape.gradient(loss, weight_4)
    gradients_b4 = tape.gradient(loss, bias_4)

    # Update the weights and bias variables of the model.
    optimizer.apply_gradients(zip([gradients_w1, gradients_b1,
gradients_w2, gradients_b2,
                                    gradients_w3, gradients_b3,
gradients_w4, gradients_b4],
                                    [weight_1, bias_1, weight_2,
bias_2, weight_3, bias_3, weight_4, bias_4]))

    # Forward pass.
    output_test = model(x_vals_test)
    # Apply Loss function (MSE) on test
    temp_loss = tf.reduce_mean(tf.abs(np.transpose([y_vals_test]) -
output_test))
    test_loss.append(temp_loss)

    if (i+1) % 25 == 0:
```

```
        print('Generation: ' + str(i+1) + '. Loss = ' + str(loss.
numpy()))
```

10. The preceding step should result in the following output:

```
Generation: 25. Loss = 1921.8002
Generation: 50. Loss = 1453.3898
Generation: 75. Loss = 987.57074
Generation: 100. Loss = 709.81696
Generation: 125. Loss = 508.625
Generation: 150. Loss = 541.36774
Generation: 175. Loss = 539.6093
Generation: 200. Loss = 441.64032
```

11. The following is a snippet of code that plots the train and test loss with `matplotlib`:

```
plt.plot(loss_vec, 'k-', label='Train Loss')
plt.plot(test_loss, 'r--', label='Test Loss')
plt.title('Loss per Generation')
plt.xlabel('Generation')
plt.ylabel('Loss')
plt.legend(loc='upper right')
plt.show()
```

We proceed with the recipe by plotting the following diagram:

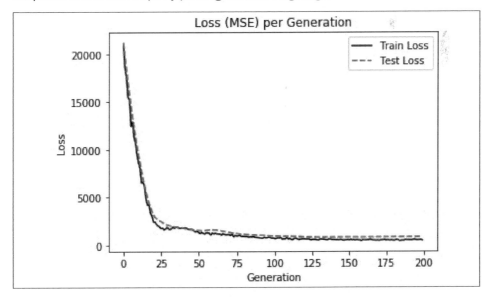

Figure 6.5: In the preceding figure, we plot the train and test losses for our neural network that we trained to predict birth weight in grams. Notice that we have arrived at a good model after approximately 30 generations

12. Now, we need to output the train and test regression results and turn them into classification results by creating an indicator for if they are above or below 2,500 grams. To find out the model's accuracy, we need to use the following code:

```
# Model Accuracy
actuals = np.array([x[0] for x in birth_data])
test_actuals = actuals[test_indices]
train_actuals = actuals[train_indices]
test_preds = model(x_vals_test)
train_preds = model(x_vals_train)
test_preds = np.array([1.0 if x < 2500.0 else 0.0 for x in test_
preds])
train_preds = np.array([1.0 if x < 2500.0 else 0.0 for x in train_
preds])
# Print out accuracies
test_acc = np.mean([x == y for x, y in zip(test_preds, test_
actuals)])
train_acc = np.mean([x == y for x, y in zip(train_preds, train_
actuals)])
print('On predicting the category of low birthweight from regression
output (<2500g):')
print('Test Accuracy: {}'.format(test_acc))
print('Train Accuracy: {}'.format(train_acc))
```

13. The preceding step should result in the following output:

```
Test Accuracy: 0.7631578947368421
Train Accuracy: 0.7880794701986755
```

As you can see, both the train set accuracy and the test set accuracy are quite good and the models learn without under- or overfitting.

How it works...

In this recipe, we created a regression neural network with three fully connected hidden layers to predict the birth weight of the low birth weight dataset. In the next recipe, we will try to improve our logistic regression by making it a multiple-layer, logistic-type neural network.

Improving the predictions of linear models

In this recipe, we will attempt to improve our logistic model by increasing the accuracy of the low birth weight prediction. We will use a neural network.

Getting ready

For this recipe, we will load the low birth weight data and use a neural network with two hidden fully connected layers with sigmoid activations to fit the probability of a low birth weight.

How to do it...

We proceed with the recipe as follows:

1. We start by loading the libraries and initializing our computational graph as follows:

    ```
    import matplotlib.pyplot as plt
    import numpy as np
    import tensorflow as tf
    import requests
    import os.path
    import csv
    ```

2. Next, we load, extract, and normalize our data as in the preceding recipe, except that here we are going to be using the low birth weight indicator variable as our target instead of the actual birth weight, shown as follows:

    ```
    # Name of data file
    birth_weight_file = 'birth_weight.csv'
    birthdata_url = 'https://github.com/PacktPublishing/Machine-
    Learning-Using-TensorFlow-Cookbook/blob/master/ch6/06_Using_
    Multiple_Layers/birth_weight.csv'

    # Download data and create data file if file does not exist in
    current directory
    if not os.path.exists(birth_weight_file):
        birth_file = requests.get(birthdata_url)
        birth_data = birth_file.text.split('\r\n')
        birth_header = birth_data[0].split('\t')
        birth_data = [[float(x) for x in y.split('\t') if len(x) >= 1]
                      for y in birth_data[1:] if len(y) >= 1]
        with open(birth_weight_file, "w") as f:
            writer = csv.writer(f)
            writer.writerows([birth_header])
            writer.writerows(birth_data)

    # read birth weight data into memory
    birth_data = []
    with open(birth_weight_file, newline='') as csvfile:
        csv_reader = csv.reader(csvfile)
    ```

```
        birth_header = next(csv_reader)
        for row in csv_reader:
            birth_data.append(row)

birth_data = [[float(x) for x in row] for row in birth_data]

# Pull out target variable
y_vals = np.array([x[0] for x in birth_data])
# Pull out predictor variables (not id, not target, and not
birthweight)
x_vals = np.array([x[1:8] for x in birth_data])

train_indices = np.random.choice(len(x_vals), round(len(x_
vals)*0.8), replace=False)
test_indices = np.array(list(set(range(len(x_vals))) - set(train_
indices)))
x_vals_train = x_vals[train_indices]
x_vals_test = x_vals[test_indices]
y_vals_train = y_vals[train_indices]
y_vals_test = y_vals[test_indices]

def normalize_cols(m, col_min=np.array([None]), col_max=np.
array([None])):
    if not col_min[0]:
        col_min = m.min(axis=0)
    if not col_max[0]:
        col_max = m.max(axis=0)
    return (m - col_min) / (col_max - col_min), col_min, col_max


x_vals_train, train_min, train_max = np.nan_to_num(normalize_cols(x_
vals_train))
x_vals_test, _, _ = np.nan_to_num(normalize_cols(x_vals_test, train_
min, train_max))
```

3. Next, we need to declare our batch size, our seed in order to have reproductible results, and our input data layer as follows:

```
batch_size = 90

seed = 98
np.random.seed(seed)
tf.random.set_seed(seed)

x_data = tf.keras.Input(dtype=tf.float64, shape=(7,))
```

4. As previously, we now need to declare functions that initialize a variable and a layer in our model. To create a better logistic function, we need to create a function that returns a logistic layer on an input layer. In other words, we will just use a fully connected layer and return a sigmoid element for each layer. It is important to remember that our loss function will have the final sigmoid included, so we want to specify on our last layer that we will not return the sigmoid of the output, shown as follows:

```
# Create variable definition
def init_variable(shape):
    return(tf.Variable(tf.random.normal(shape=shape,
dtype="float64", seed=seed)))



# Create a logistic layer definition
def logistic(input_layer, multiplication_weight, bias_weight,
activation = True):

    # We separate the activation at the end because the loss
function will
    # implement the last sigmoid necessary
    if activation:
        return tf.keras.layers.Lambda(lambda x: tf.nn.sigmoid(tf.
add(tf.matmul(x, multiplication_weight), bias_weight)))(input_layer)
    else:
        return tf.keras.layers.Lambda(lambda x: tf.add(tf.matmul(x,
multiplication_weight), bias_weight))(input_layer)
```

5. Now we will declare three layers (two hidden layers and an output layer). We will start by initializing a weight and bias matrix for each layer and defining the layer operations as follows:

```
# First logistic layer (7 inputs to 14 hidden nodes)
A1 = init_variable(shape=[7,14])
b1 = init_variable(shape=[14])
logistic_layer1 = logistic(x_data, A1, b1)

# Second logistic layer (14 hidden inputs to 5 hidden nodes)
A2 = init_variable(shape=[14,5])
b2 = init_variable(shape=[5])
logistic_layer2 = logistic(logistic_layer1, A2, b2)

# Final output layer (5 hidden nodes to 1 output)
A3 = init_variable(shape=[5,1])
b3 = init_variable(shape=[1])
final_output = logistic(logistic_layer2, A3, b3, activation=False)
```

```
# Build the model
model = tf.keras.Model(inputs=x_data, outputs=final_output,
name="improving_linear_reg_neural_network")
```

6. Next, we define a loss function (cross-entropy) and declare the optimization algorithm, as follows:

```
# Loss function (Cross Entropy Loss)
def cross_entropy(final_output, y_target):
    return tf.reduce_mean(tf.nn.sigmoid_cross_entropy_with_
logits(logits=final_output, labels=y_target))


# Declare optimizer
optimizer = tf.keras.optimizers.Adam(0.002)
```

Cross-entropy is a way of measuring distances between probabilities. Here, we want to measure the difference between certainty (0 or 1) and our model probability (0 < x < 1). TensorFlow implements cross-entropy with the built-in sigmoid function. This is also important as part of the hyperparameter tuning, as we are more likely to find the best loss function, learning rate, and optimization algorithm for the problem at hand. For brevity in this recipe, we do not include hyperparameter tuning.

7. In order to evaluate and compare our model to previous models, we need to create a prediction and accuracy operation on the graph. This will allow us to feed in the whole test set and determine the accuracy, as follows:

```
# Accuracy
def compute_accuracy(final_output, y_target):
    prediction = tf.round(tf.nn.sigmoid(final_output))
    predictions_correct = tf.cast(tf.equal(prediction, y_target),
tf.float32)
    return tf.reduce_mean(predictions_correct)
```

8. We are now ready to start our training loop. We will train for 1,500 generations and save the model loss and train and test accuracies for plotting later. Our training loop is started with the following code:

```
# Training Loop
loss_vec = []
train_acc = []
test_acc = []
for i in range(1500):
```

```
    rand_index = np.random.choice(len(x_vals_train), size=batch_
size)
    rand_x = x_vals_train[rand_index]
    rand_y = np.transpose([y_vals_train[rand_index]])

    # Open a GradientTape.
    with tf.GradientTape(persistent=True) as tape:

        # Forward pass.
        output = model(rand_x)

        # Apply loss function (Cross Entropy Loss)
        loss = cross_entropy(output, rand_y)
        loss_vec.append(loss)

    # Get gradients of loss with reference to the weights and bias
variables to adjust.
    gradients_A1 = tape.gradient(loss, A1)
    gradients_b1 = tape.gradient(loss, b1)
    gradients_A2 = tape.gradient(loss, A2)
    gradients_b2 = tape.gradient(loss, b2)
    gradients_A3 = tape.gradient(loss, A3)
    gradients_b3 = tape.gradient(loss, b3)

    # Update the weights and bias variables of the model.
    optimizer.apply_gradients(zip([gradients_A1, gradients_
b1,gradients_A2, gradients_b2, gradients_A3, gradients_b3],
                            [A1, b1, A2, b2, A3, b3]))

    temp_acc_train = compute_accuracy(model(x_vals_train),
np.transpose([y_vals_train]))
    train_acc.append(temp_acc_train)

    temp_acc_test = compute_accuracy(model(x_vals_test),
np.transpose([y_vals_test]))
    test_acc.append(temp_acc_test)

    if (i+1)%150==0:
        print('Loss = ' + str(loss.numpy()))
```

9. The preceding step should result in the following output:

```
Loss = 0.5885411040188063
Loss = 0.581099555117532
Loss = 0.6071769535895101
```

```
Loss = 0.5043174136225906
Loss = 0.5023625777095964
Loss = 0.485112570717733
Loss = 0.5906992621835641
Loss = 0.4280814147901789
Loss = 0.5425164697605331
Loss = 0.35608561907724867
```

10. The following code blocks illustrate how to plot the cross-entropy loss and train and test set accuracies with `matplotlib`:

```
# Plot loss over time
plt.plot(loss_vec, 'k-')
plt.title('Cross Entropy Loss per Generation')
plt.xlabel('Generation')
plt.ylabel('Cross Entropy Loss')
plt.show()
# Plot train and test accuracy
plt.plot(train_acc, 'k-', label='Train Set Accuracy')
plt.plot(test_acc, 'r--', label='Test Set Accuracy')
plt.title('Train and Test Accuracy')
plt.xlabel('Generation')
plt.ylabel('Accuracy')
plt.legend(loc='lower right')
plt.show()
```

We get the plot for cross-entropy loss per generation as follows:

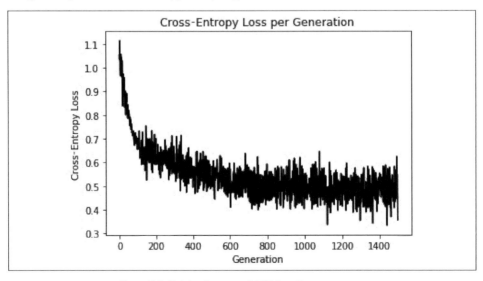

Figure 6.6: Training loss over 1,500 iterations

Within approximately 150 generations, we have reached a good model. As we continue to train, we can see that very little is gained over the remaining iterations, as shown in the following diagram:

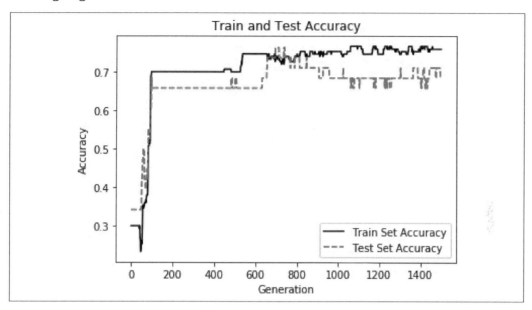

Figure 6.7: Accuracy for the train set and test set

As you can see in the preceding diagram, we arrived at a good model very quickly.

How it works...

When considering using neural networks to model data, you have to consider the advantages and disadvantages. While our model has converged faster than previous models, and perhaps with greater accuracy, this comes with a price; we are training many more model variables and there is a greater chance of overfitting. To check if overfitting is occurring, we look at the accuracy of the test and train sets. If the accuracy of the training set continues to increase while the accuracy on the test set stays the same or even decreases slightly, we can assume overfitting is occurring.

To combat underfitting, we can increase our model depth or train the model for more iterations. To address overfitting, we can add more data or add regularization techniques to our model.

It is also important to note that our model variables are not as interpretable as a linear model. Neural network models have coefficients that are harder to interpret than linear models, as they explain the significance of features within the model.

Learning to play Tic-Tac-Toe

To show how adaptable neural networks can be, we will now attempt to use a neural network in order to learn the optimal moves for Tic-Tac-Toe. We will approach this knowing that Tic-Tac-Toe is a deterministic game and that the optimal moves are already known.

Getting ready

To train our model, we will use a list of board positions followed by the optimal response for a number of different boards. We can reduce the amount of boards to train on by considering only board positions that are different with regard to symmetry. The non-identity transformations of a Tic-Tac-Toe board are a rotation (in either direction) of 90 degrees, 180 degrees, and 270 degrees, a horizontal reflection, and a vertical reflection. Given this idea, we will use a shortlist of boards with the optimal move, apply two random transformations, and then feed that into our neural network for learning.

 Since Tic-Tac-Toe is a deterministic game, it is worth noting that whoever goes first should either win or draw. We will hope for a model that can respond to our moves optimally and ultimately result in a draw.

If we denote Xs using 1, Os using -1, and empty spaces using 0, then the following diagram illustrates how we can consider a board position and an optimal move as a row of data:

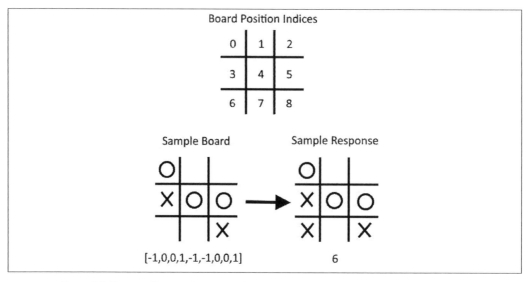

Figure 6.8: Here, we illustrate how to consider a board and an optimal move as a row of data.
Note that X = 1, 0 = -1, empty spaces are 0, and we start indexing at 0

In addition to the model loss, to check how our model is performing we will do two things. The first check we will perform is to remove a position and an optimal move row from our training set. This will allow us to see if the neural network model can generalize a move it hasn't seen before. The second way to evaluate our model is to actually play a game against it at the end.

The list of possible boards and optimal moves can be found in the GitHub directory for this recipe at `https://github.com/PacktPublishing/Machine-Learning-Using-TensorFlow-Cookbook/tree/master/ch6/08_Learning_Tic_Tac_Toe` and in the Packt repository at `https://github.com/PacktPublishing/Machine-Learning-Using-TensorFlow-Cookbook`.

How to do it...

We proceed with the recipe as follows:

1. We need to start by loading the necessary libraries for this script, as follows:

```
import tensorflow as tf
import matplotlib.pyplot as plt
import csv
import numpy as np
import random
```

2. Next, we declare the following batch size for training our model:

```
batch_size = 50
```

3. To make visualizing the boards a bit easier, we will create a function that outputs Tic-Tac-Toe boards with Xs and Os. This is done with the following code:

```
def print_board(board):
    symbols = ['O', ' ', 'X']
    board_plus1 = [int(x) + 1 for x in board]
    board_line1 = ' {} | {} |
                            {}'.format(symbols[board_plus1[0]],
                                       symbols[board_plus1[1]],
                                       symbols[board_plus1[2]])
    board_line2 = ' {} | {} |
                            {}'.format(symbols[board_plus1[3]],
                                       symbols[board_plus1[4]],
                                       symbols[board_plus1[5]])
    board_line3 = ' {} | {} |
                            {}'.format(symbols[board_plus1[6]],
                                       symbols[board_plus1[7]],
                                       symbols[board_plus1[8]])
    print(board_line1)
    print('_____')
    print(board_line2)
```

```
        print('_____')
        print(board_line3)
```

4. Now we have to create a function that will return a new board and an optimal response position under a transformation. This is done with the following code:

```
def get_symmetry(board, response, transformation):
    '''

    :param board: list of integers 9 long:
        opposing mark = -1
        friendly mark = 1
        empty space = 0
    :param transformation: one of five transformations on a
                                            board:
        rotate180, rotate90, rotate270, flip_v, flip_h
    :return: tuple: (new_board, new_response)
    '''

    if transformation == 'rotate180':
        new_response = 8 - response
        return board[::-1], new_response

    elif transformation == 'rotate90':
        new_response = [6, 3, 0, 7, 4, 1, 8, 5, 2].index(response)
        tuple_board = list(zip(*[board[6:9], board[3:6],
board[0:3]]))
        return [value for item in tuple_board for value in item],
new_response

    elif transformation == 'rotate270':
        new_response = [2, 5, 8, 1, 4, 7, 0, 3, 6].index(response)
        tuple_board = list(zip(*[board[0:3], board[3:6],
board[6:9]]))[::-1]
        return [value for item in tuple_board for value in item],
new_response

    elif transformation == 'flip_v':
        new_response = [6, 7, 8, 3, 4, 5, 0, 1, 2].index(response)
        return board[6:9] +  board[3:6] + board[0:3], new_response

    elif transformation == 'flip_h':
        # flip_h = rotate180, then flip_v
        new_response = [2, 1, 0, 5, 4, 3, 8, 7, 6].index(response)
        new_board = board[::-1]
        return new_board[6:9] +  new_board[3:6] + new_board[0:3],
new_response
```

```
        else:
            raise ValueError('Method not implmented.')
```

5. The list of boards and their optimal responses is in a `.csv` file in the directory available in the GitHub repository at `https://github.com/nfmcclure/tensorflow_cookbook` or the Packt repository at `https://github.com/PacktPublishing/TensorFlow-Machine-Learning-Cookbook-Second-Edition`. We will create a function that will load the file with the boards and responses and will store it as a list of tuples, as follows:

```
def get_moves_from_csv(csv_file):
    '''
    :param csv_file: csv file location containing the boards w/
responses
    :return: moves: list of moves with index of best response
    '''
    moves = []
    with open(csv_file, 'rt') as csvfile:
        reader = csv.reader(csvfile, delimiter=',')
        for row in reader:
            moves.append(([int(x) for x in
row[0:9]],int(row[9])))
    return moves
```

6. Now we need to tie everything together to create a function that will return a randomly transformed board and response. This is done with the following code:

```
def get_rand_move(moves, rand_transforms=2):
    # This function performs random transformations on a board.
    (board, response) = random.choice(moves)
    possible_transforms = ['rotate90', 'rotate180', 'rotate270',
'flip_v', 'flip_h']
    for i in range(rand_transforms):
        random_transform = random.choice(possible_transforms)
        (board, response) = get_symmetry(board, response, random_
transform)
    return board, response
```

7. Next, we load our data and create a training set as follows:

```
moves = get_moves_from_csv('base_tic_tac_toe_moves.csv')
# Create a train set:
train_length = 500
train_set = []
for t in range(train_length):
    train_set.append(get_rand_move(moves))
```

8. Remember that we want to remove one board and an optimal response from our training set to see if the model can generalize making the best move. The best move for the following board will be to play at index number 6:

```
test_board = [-1, 0, 0, 1, -1, -1, 0, 0, 1]
train_set = [x for x in train_set if x[0] != test_board]
```

9. We can now initialize the weights and bias and create our models:

```
def init_weights(shape):
    return tf.Variable(tf.random_normal(shape))


A1 = init_weights([9, 81])
bias1 = init_weights([81])
A2 = init_weights([81, 9])
bias2 = init_weights([9])
```

10. Now, we create our model. Note that we do not include the `softmax()` activation function in the following model because it is included in the loss function:

```
# Initialize input data
X = tf.keras.Input(dtype=tf.float32, batch_input_shape=[None, 9])
hidden_output = tf.keras.layers.Lambda(lambda x: tf.nn.sigmoid(tf.
add(tf.matmul(x, A1), bias1)))(X)
final_output = tf.keras.layers.Lambda(lambda x: tf.add(tf.matmul(x,
A2), bias2))(hidden_output)
model = tf.keras.Model(inputs=X, outputs=final_output, name="tic_
tac_toe_neural_network")
```

11. Next, we will declare our optimizer, as follows:

```
optimizer = tf.keras.optimizers.SGD(0.025)
```

12. We can now loop through the training of our neural network with the following code. Note that our `loss` function will be the average softmax of the final output logits (unstandardized output):

```
# Initialize variables
loss_vec = []
for i in range(10000):
    rand_indices = np.random.choice(range(len(train_set)), batch_
size, replace=False)
    batch_data = [train_set[i] for i in rand_indices]
    x_input = [x[0] for x in batch_data]
    y_target = np.array([y[1] for y in batch_data])

    # Open a GradientTape.
    with tf.GradientTape(persistent=True) as tape:
```

```
        # Forward pass.
        output = model(np.array(x_input, dtype=float))

        # Apply loss function (Cross Entropy Loss)
        loss = tf.reduce_mean(tf.nn.sparse_softmax_cross_entropy_
with_logits(logits=output, labels=y_target))
        loss_vec.append(loss)

    # Get gradients of loss with reference to the weights and bias
variables to adjust.
    gradients_A1 = tape.gradient(loss, A1)
    gradients_b1 = tape.gradient(loss, bias1)
    gradients_A2 = tape.gradient(loss, A2)
    gradients_b2 = tape.gradient(loss, bias2)

    # Update the weights and bias variables of the model.
    optimizer.apply_gradients(zip([gradients_A1, gradients_b1,
gradients_A2, gradients_b2],
                        [A1, bias1, A2, bias2]))

    if i % 500 == 0:
        print('Iteration: {}, Loss: {}'.format(i, loss))
```

13. The following is the code needed to plot the loss over the model training:

```
plt.plot(loss_vec, 'k-', label='Loss')
plt.title('Loss (MSE) per Generation')
plt.xlabel('Generation')
plt.ylabel('Loss')
plt.show()
```

We should get the following plot for the loss per generation:

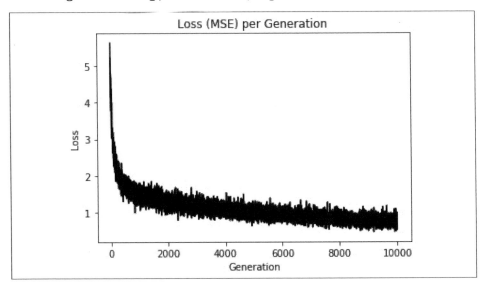

Figure 6.9: A Tic-Tac-Toe train set loss over 10,000 iterations

In the preceding diagram, we have plotted the loss over the training steps.

14. To test the model, we need to see how it performs on the test board that we removed from the training set. We are hoping that the model can generalize and predict the optimal index for moving, which will be index number 6. Most of the time the model will succeed, shown as follows:

```
test_boards = [test_board]
logits = model.predict(test_boards)
predictions = tf.argmax(logits, 1)
print(predictions)
```

15. The preceding step should result in the following output:

```
[6]
```

16. In order to evaluate our model, we need to play against our trained model. To do this, we have to create a function that will check for a win. This way, our program will know when to stop asking for more moves. This is done with the following code:

```
def check(board):
    wins = [[0,1,2], [3,4,5], [6,7,8], [0,3,6], [1,4,7], [2,5,8],
[0,4,8], [2,4,6]]
    for i in range(len(wins)):
        if
board[wins[i][0]]==board[wins[i][1]]==board[wins[i][2]]==1.:
            return 1
        elif
```

```
        board[wins[i][0]]==board[wins[i][1]]==board[wins[i][2]]==-1.:
                return 1
        return 0
```

17. Now we can loop through and play a game with our model. We start with a blank
    board (all zeros), we ask the user to input an index (0-8) of where to play, and we then
    feed that into the model for a prediction. For the model's move, we take the largest
    available prediction that is also an open space. From this game, we can see that our
    model is not perfect, as follows:

```
game_tracker = [0., 0., 0., 0., 0., 0., 0., 0., 0.]
win_logical = False
num_moves = 0
while not win_logical:
    player_index = input('Input index of your move (0-8): ')
    num_moves += 1
    # Add player move to game
    game_tracker[int(player_index)] = 1.

    # Get model's move by first getting all the logits for each
index
    [potential_moves] = model(np.array([game_tracker], dtype=float))
    # Now find allowed moves (where game tracker values = 0.0)
    allowed_moves = [ix for ix, x in enumerate(game_tracker) if x ==
0.0]
    # Find best move by taking argmax of logits if they are in
allowed moves
    model_move = np.argmax([x if ix in allowed_moves else -999.0
for ix, x in enumerate(potential_moves)])

    # Add model move to game
    game_tracker[int(model_move)] = -1.
    print('Model has moved')
    print_board(game_tracker)
    # Now check for win or too many moves
    if check(game_tracker) == -1 or num_moves >= 5:
        print('Game Over!')
        win_logical = True
    elif check(game_tracker) == 1:
        print('Congratulations, You won!')
        win_logical = True
```

18. The preceding step should result in the following interactive output:

```
Input index of your move (0-8):  4
Model has moved
   |   |
_____

   | X |
_____

   |   | 0
Input index of your move (0-8):  6
Model has moved
 0 |   |
_____

   | X |
_____

 X |   | 0
Input index of your move (0-8):  2
Model has moved
 0 |   | X
_____

   | X |
_____

 X | 0 | 0
Congratulations, You won!
```

As you can see, a human player beats the machine very quickly and easily.

How it works...

In this section, we trained a neural network to play Tic-Tac-Toe by feeding in board positions and a nine-dimensional vector, and predicted the optimal response. We only had to feed in a few possible Tic-Tac-Toe boards and apply random transformations to each board to increase the training set size.

To test our algorithm, we removed all instances of one specific board and saw whether our model could generalize to predict the optimal response. Finally, we played a sample game against our model. This model isn't perfect yet. Using more data or applying a more complex neural network architecture could be done to improve it. But the better thing to do is to change the type of learning: instead of using supervised learning, we're better off using a reinforcement learning-based approach.

7
Predicting with Tabular Data

Most of the available data that can be easily found is not composed of images or text documents, but it is instead made of relational tables, each one possibly containing numbers, dates, and short text, which can be all joined together. This is because of the widespread adoption of database applications based on the relational paradigm (data tables that can be combined together by the values of certain columns that act as joining keys). These tables are the main source of tabular data nowadays and because of that, there are certain challenges.

Here are the challenges commonly faced by **Deep Neural Networks** (**DNNs**) when applied to tabular data:

- ▶ Mixed features data types
- ▶ Data in a sparse format (there are more zeros than non-zero data), which is not the best for a DNN converging to an optimum solution
- ▶ No state-of-the-art architecture has emerged yet, there are just some various best practices
- ▶ Less data is available for a single problem than in a usual image recognition problem
- ▶ There's suspicion from non-technical people because DNNs are less interpretable than simpler machine learning algorithms for tabular data
- ▶ Often, DNNs are not the best-in-class solution for tabular data, because gradient boosting solutions (such as LightGBM, XGBoost, and CatBoost) might perform better

Even if these challenges seem quite difficult, simply do not get discouraged. The challenges when applying DNNs to tabular data are certainly serious, but on the other hand, so are the opportunities. Andrew Ng, Adjunct Professor at Stanford University and deep learning expert (`https://www.coursera.org/instructor/andrewng`), recently stated: *"Deep learning has seen tremendous adoption in consumer Internet companies with a huge number of users and thus big data, but for it to break into other industries where datasets sizes are smaller, we now need better techniques for small data."*

In this chapter, we introduce you to some of the best recipes for handling small, tabular data with TensorFlow. In doing so, we will be using TensorFlow, Keras, and two specialized machine learning packages: pandas (`https://pandas.pydata.org/`) and scikit-learn (`https://scikit-learn.org/stable/index.html`). In the previous chapters, we often used TensorFlow Datasets (`https://www.tensorflow.org/datasets`) and specialized layers for feature columns (`https://www.tensorflow.org/api_docs/python/tf/feature_column`). We could have reused them for this chapter, but then we would have missed some interesting transformations that only scikit-learn can provide, and doing cross-validation would have proved difficult.

Consider moreover that using scikit-learn makes sense if you are comparing the performance of different algorithms on a problem, and you need to standardize a data preparation pipeline not only for the TensorFlow model but also for other more classical machine learning and statistical models.

In order to install pandas and scikit-learn (if you are using Anaconda, they should already be on your system), please follow these guidelines:

- For pandas: `https://pandas.pydata.org/docs/getting_started/install.html`
- For scikit-learn: `https://scikit-learn.org/stable/install.html`

In this chapter, we will deal with a series of recipes focused on learning from tabular data, which is data arranged in the form of a table, where rows represent observations and columns are the observed values for each feature.

Tabular data is the common input data for most machine learning algorithms, but not a usual one for DNNs, since DNNs excel with other kinds of data, such as images and text.

Recipes for deep learning for tabular data require solving problems, such as data heterogeneity, which are not mainstream, and they require using many common machine learning strategies, such as cross-validation, which are not currently implemented in TensorFlow.

By the end of this chapter, you should have knowledge of the following:

- ▶ Processing numerical data
- ▶ Processing dates
- ▶ Processing categorical data
- ▶ Processing ordinal data
- ▶ Processing high-cardinality categorical data
- ▶ Wrapping up all the processing
- ▶ Setting up a data generator
- ▶ Creating custom activations for tabular data
- ▶ Running a test run on a difficult problem

Let's start immediately with how to deal with numerical data. You will be amazed by how these recipes can be effective with many tabular data problems.

Processing numerical data

We will start by preparing numerical data. You have numerical data when:

- ▶ Your data is expressed by a floating number
- ▶ Your data is an integer and it has a certain number of unique values (otherwise if there are only few values in sequence, you are dealing with an ordinal variable, such as a ranking)
- ▶ Your integer data is not representing a class or label (otherwise you are dealing with a categorical variable)

When working with numerical data, a few situations may affect the performance of a DNN when processing such data:

- ▶ Missing data (NULL or NaN values, or even INF values) that will prevent your DNN from working at all
- ▶ Constant values that will make computations slower and interfere with the bias each neuron in the network is already providing
- ▶ Skewed distribution
- ▶ Non-standardized data, especially data with extreme values

Before feeding numerical data to your neural network, you have to be sure that all these issues have been properly dealt with or you may encounter errors or a learning process that will not work.

Getting ready

In order to address all the potential issues, we will mostly be using specialized functions from scikit-learn. Before starting our recipe, we will import them into our environment:

```python
import numpy as np
import pandas as pd

try:
    from sklearn.impute import IterativeImputer
except:
    from sklearn.experimental import enable_iterative_imputer
    from sklearn.impute import IterativeImputer

from sklearn.ensemble import ExtraTreesRegressor
from sklearn.impute import SimpleImputer

from sklearn.preprocessing import StandardScaler, QuantileTransformer
from sklearn.feature_selection import VarianceThreshold

from sklearn.pipeline import Pipeline
```

In order to test our recipe we will use a simple 3x4 table, with some columns containing NaN values, and some constant columns that contain no NaN values:

```python
example = pd.DataFrame([[1, 2, 3, np.nan], [1, 3, np.nan, 4], [1, 2, 2, 2]],
columns = ['a', 'b', 'c', 'd'])
```

How to do it...

Our recipe will build a scikit-learn pipeline, based on our indications relative to:

- ▶ The minimum acceptable variance for a feature to be kept, or you may just be introducing unwanted constants into your network that may hinder the learning process (the `variance_threshold` parameter)

- ▶ What to use as a baseline strategy for imputing missing values (the `imputer` parameter, by default set to replace missing values with the mean of the feature) so that your input matrix will be completed and matrix multiplication will be possible (the basic computation in a neural network)

- ▶ Whether we should use a more sophisticated imputation strategy based on the missing values of all the numeric data (the `multivariate_imputer` parameter), because sometimes points are not missing at random and other variables may supply the information you need for a proper estimation

▶ Whether to add a binary feature denoting for each feature where the missing values were, which is a good strategy because you often find information also on missing patterns (the `add_indicator` parameter)

▶ Whether to transform the distribution of variables in order to force them to resemble a symmetric distribution (`quantile_transformer` parameter, set to `normal` by default) because your network will learn better from symmetrical data distributions

▶ Whether we should rescale our output based on the statistical normalization, that is, dividing by the standard deviation after having removed the mean (the `scaler` parameter, set to `True` by default)

Now, bearing all that in mind, let's build our pipeline as follows:

```
def assemble_numeric_pipeline(variance_threshold=0.0,
                              imputer='mean',
                              multivariate_imputer=False,
                              add_indicator=True,
                              quantile_transformer='normal',
                              scaler=True):
    numeric_pipeline = []
    if variance_threshold is not None:
        if isinstance(variance_threshold, float):
            numeric_pipeline.append(('var_filter',

VarianceThreshold(threshold=variance_threshold)))
        else:
            numeric_pipeline.append(('var_filter',
                                    VarianceThreshold()))
    if imputer is not None:
        if multivariate_imputer is True:
            numeric_pipeline.append(('imputer',

IterativeImputer(estimator=ExtraTreesRegressor(n_estimators=100, n_jobs=-2),

initial_strategy=imputer,

add_indicator=add_indicator)))
        else:
            numeric_pipeline.append(('imputer',
                                    SimpleImputer(strategy=imputer,

add_indicator=add_indicator)
                )
            )

    if quantile_transformer is not None:
```

```
        numeric_pipeline.append(('transformer',
                            QuantileTransformer(n_quantiles=100,

output_distribution=quantile_transformer,
                                        random_state=42)
                    )
                )

    if scaler is not None:
        numeric_pipeline.append(('scaler',
                            StandardScaler()
                    )
                )

    return Pipeline(steps=numeric_pipeline)
```

We can now create our numerical pipeline by specifying our transformation preferences:

```
numeric_pipeline =
assemble_numeric_pipeline(variance_threshold=0.0,
                        imputer='mean',
                        multivariate_imputer=False,
                        add_indicator=True,
                        quantile_transformer='normal',
                        scaler=True)
```

We can immediately try our new function on the example by applying first the `fit` and then the `transform` methods:

```
numeric_pipeline.fit(example)
np.round(numeric_pipeline.transform(example), 3)
```

Here is the resulting output NumPy array:

```
array([[-0.707,  1.225, -0.  , -0.707,  1.414],
       [ 1.414, -0.  ,  1.225,  1.414, -0.707],
       [-0.707, -1.225, -1.225, -0.707, -0.707]])
```

As you can see all the original data has been completely transformed, with all the missing values replaced.

How it works...

As we previously mentioned, we are using scikit-learn for comparability with other machine learning solutions and because there are a few unique scikit-learn functions involved in the building of this recipe:

- ▶ VarianceThreshold (https://scikit-learn.org/stable/modules/generated/sklearn.feature_selection.VarianceThreshold.html)
- ▶ IterativeImputer (https://scikit-learn.org/stable/modules/generated/sklearn.impute.IterativeImputer.html)
- ▶ SimpleImputer (https://scikit-learn.org/stable/modules/generated/sklearn.impute.SimpleImputer.html)
- ▶ QuantileTransformer (https://scikit-learn.org/stable/modules/generated/sklearn.preprocessing.QuantileTransformer.html)
- ▶ StandardScaler (https://scikit-learn.org/stable/modules/generated/sklearn.preprocessing.StandardScaler.html)
- ▶ Pipeline (https://scikit-learn.org/stable/modules/generated/sklearn.pipeline.Pipeline.html)

For each function, you will find a link pointing to the scikit-learn documentation with detailed information on how the function works. It is paramount to explain why the scikit-learn approach is so important for this recipe (and for the others you will find in this chapter).

When processing images or text, you usually don't need to define specific processes for respectively training and testing data. That's because you apply deterministic transformations to both. For instance, in images, you just divide the pixels' values by 255 in order to normalize them.

However, with tabular data you need transformations that are more complex and not deterministic at all because they involve learning and memorizing specific parameters. For instance, when imputing a missing value for a feature by using the mean, you have first to compute the mean from your training data. Then you have to reuse that exact value for any other new data you will apply the same imputation on (it won't work to compute again the mean on any new data because it could be from a slightly different distribution and may not match what your DNN has learned).

All of this involves keeping track of many parameters learned from your training data. scikit-learn may help you in that because when you use the `fit` method, it learns and stores away all the parameters it derives from training data. Using the `transform` method, you will apply the transformations with the learned-by-fit parameters on any new data (or on the very same training data).

There's more...

scikit-learn functions usually return a NumPy array. It is not a problem to label the resulting array using the input columns, if no further feature creation has occurred. Unfortunately, this is not the case because of the transformation pipeline we created:

▶ The variance threshold will remove features that are not useful

▶ Missing value imputation will create missing binary indicators

We can actually explore this by inspecting the fitted pipeline and finding out which columns have been removed and what has been added from the original data. A function can be created to do just that for us automatically:

```python
def derive_numeric_columns(df, pipeline):
    columns = df.columns
    if 'var_filter' in pipeline.named_steps:
        threshold = pipeline.named_steps.var_filter.threshold
        columns = columns[pipeline.named_steps.var_filter.
variances_>threshold]
    if 'imputer' in pipeline.named_steps:
        missing_cols = pipeline.named_steps.imputer.indicator_.features_
        if len(missing_cols) > 0:
            columns = columns.append(columns[missing_cols] + '_missing')
    return columns
```

When we try it on our example:

```python
derive_numeric_columns(example, numeric_pipeline)
```

We obtain a pandas index containing the remaining columns and the binary indicators (denoted by the name of the original feature and the _missing suffix):

```python
Index(['b', 'c', 'd', 'c_missing', 'd_missing'], dtype='object')
```

 Keeping track of your columns as you transform them can help you when you need to debug your transformed data and if you need to explain how your DNN works using tools such as shap (https://github.com/slundberg/shap) or lime (https://github.com/marcotcr/lime).

This recipe should suffice for all your needs with regard to numerical data. Now let's proceed to examine dates and times.

Processing dates

Dates are common in databases and, especially when processing the forecasting of future estimates (such as in sales forecasting), they can prove indispensable. Neural networks cannot process dates as they are, since they are often expressed as strings. Hence, you have to transform them by separating their numerical elements, and once you have split a date into its components, you have just numbers that can easily be dealt with by any neural network. Certain time elements, however, are cyclical (days, months, hours, days of the week) and lower and higher numbers are actually contiguous. Consequently, you need to use sine and cosine functions, which will render such cyclical numbers in a format that can be both understood and correctly interpreted by a DNN.

Getting ready

Since we need to code a class operating using the fit/transform operations that are typical of scikit-learn, we import the `BaseEstimator` and `TransformerMixin` classes from scikit-learn to inherit from. This inheritance will help us to make our recipe perfectly compatible with all other functions from scikit-learn:

```
from sklearn.base import BaseEstimator, TransformerMixin
```

For testing purposes, we also prepare an example dataset of dates in string form, using the day/month/year format:

```
example = pd.DataFrame({'date_1': ['04/12/2018', '05/12/2019',
                                   '07/12/2020'],
                        'date_2': ['12/5/2018', '15/5/2015',
                                   '18/5/2016'],
                        'date_3': ['25/8/2019', '28/8/2018',
                                   '29/8/2017']})
```

The provided example is quite short and simplistic, but it should illustrate all the relevant points as we work through it.

How to do it...

This time we will design a class of our own, `DateProcessor`. After being initialized, instances of this class can pick a pandas DataFrame and filter and process each date into a new DataFrame that can be processed by a DNN.

The process focuses on one date at a time, extracting days, days of the week, months, and years (additionally also hours and minutes), and transforming all cyclical time measures using sine and cosine transformations:

```python
class DateProcessor(BaseEstimator, TransformerMixin):
    def __init__(self, date_format='%d/%m/%Y', hours_secs=False):
        self.format = date_format
        self.columns = None
        self.time_transformations = [
            ('day_sin', lambda x: np.sin(2*np.pi*x.dt.day/31)),
            ('day_cos', lambda x: np.cos(2*np.pi*x.dt.day/31)),
            ('dayofweek_sin',
                    lambda x: np.sin(2*np.pi*x.dt.dayofweek/6)),
            ('dayofweek_cos',
                    lambda x: np.cos(2*np.pi*x.dt.dayofweek/6)),
            ('month_sin',
                    lambda x: np.sin(2*np.pi*x.dt.month/12)),
            ('month_cos',
                    lambda x: np.cos(2*np.pi*x.dt.month/12)),
            ('year',
                    lambda x: (x.dt.year - x.dt.year.min()
                        ) / (x.dt.year.max() - x.dt.year.min()))
        ]
        if hours_secs:
            self.time_transformations = [
                ('hour_sin',
                    lambda x: np.sin(2*np.pi*x.dt.hour/23)),
                ('hour_cos',
                    lambda x: np.cos(2*np.pi*x.dt.hour/23)),
                ('minute_sin',
                    lambda x: np.sin(2*np.pi*x.dt.minute/59)),
                ('minute_cos',
                    lambda x: np.cos(2*np.pi*x.dt.minute/59))
            ] + self.time_transformations

    def fit(self, X, y=None, **fit_params):
        self.columns = self.transform(X.iloc[0:1,:]).columns
        return self

    def transform(self, X, y=None, **fit_params):
        transformed = list()
        for col in X.columns:
            time_column = pd.to_datetime(X[col],
                                    format=self.format)
```

```
        for label, func in self.time_transformations:
            transformed.append(func(time_column))
            transformed[-1].name += '_' + label
    transformed = pd.concat(transformed, axis=1)
    return transformed

def fit_transform(self, X, y=None, **fit_params):
    self.fit(X, y, **fit_params)
    return self.transform(X)
```

Now that we have scripted down the recipe in the form of a `DateProcessor` class, let's explore more of its inner workings.

How it works...

The key to the entire class is the transformation operated by the pandas `to_datetime` function, which turns any string representing a date into the `datetime64[ns]` type.

 to_datetime works because you provide it a template (the format parameter) for turning strings into dates. For a complete guide on how to define such a template, please visit `https://docs.python.org/3/library/datetime.html#strftime-and-strptime-behavior`.

When you need to fit and transform your data, the class will automatically process all the dates into the right format and furthermore, perform transformations using sine and cosine functions:

```
DateProcessor().fit_transform(example)
```

Some resulting transformations will be obvious, but some others related to cyclical time may appear puzzling. Let's spend a bit of time exploring how they work and why.

There's more...

The class doesn't return the raw extraction of time elements such as the hour, the minute, or the day, but it transforms them using first a sine, then a cosine transformation. Let's plot how it transforms the 24 hours in order to get an better understanding of this recipe:

```
import matplotlib.pyplot as plt

sin_time = np.array([[t, np.sin(2*np.pi*t/23)] for t in range(0, 24)])
cos_time = np.array([[t, np.cos(2*np.pi*t/23)] for t in range(0, 24)])

plt.plot(sin_time[:,0], sin_time[:,1], label='sin hour')
```

```
plt.plot(cos_time[:,0], cos_time[:,1], label='cos hour')
plt.axhline(y=0.0, linestyle='--', color='lightgray')
plt.legend()
plt.show()
```

Here is the plot that you will obtain:

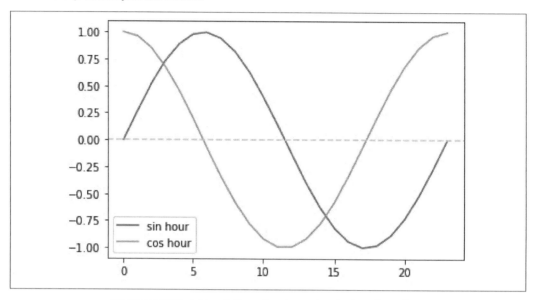

Figure 7.1: Plotting of hourly time after sine and cosine transformations

From the plot, we can figure out how the start and end of the day coincide, thus closing the time cycle. Each transformation also returns the same value for a couple of different hours. That's the reason why we should pick both sine and cosine together; if you use both, each point in time has a different tuple of sine and cosine values, and so you can detect exactly where you are in continuous time. This can also be explained visually by plotting the sine and cosine values in a scatter plot:

```
ax = plt.subplot()
ax.set_aspect('equal')
ax.set_xlabel('sin hour')
ax.set_ylabel('cos hour')
plt.scatter(sin_time[:,1], cos_time[:,1])
plt.show()
```

Here is the result:

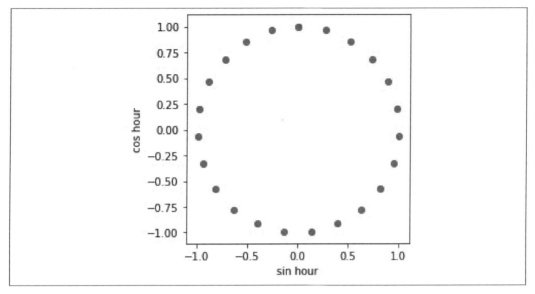

Figure 7.2: Combining the sine and cosine transformations of hourly time into a scatter plot

As in a clock, the hours are plotted in a circle, each one separate and distinct, yet in full cyclical continuity.

Processing categorical data

Strings usually represent categorical data in tabular data. Each unique value in a categorical feature represents a quality that refers to the example we are examining (hence, we consider this information to be **qualitative** whereas numerical information is **quantitative**). In statistical terms, each unique value is called a **level** and the categorical feature is called a **factor**. Sometimes you can find numeric codes used as categorical (identifiers), when the qualitative information has been previously encoded into numbers, but the way to deal with them doesn't change: the information is in numeric values but it should be treated as categorical.

Since you don't know how each unique value in a categorical feature is related to every other value present in the feature (if you jump ahead and group values together or order them you are basically expressing a hypothesis you have about the data), you can treat each of them as a value in itself. Hence, you can derive the idea of creating a binary feature from each unique categorical value. This process is called one-hot encoding and it is the most common data processing approach that can make categorical data usable by DNNs and other machine learning algorithms.

For instance, if you have a categorical variable containing the unique values of red, blue, and green, you can turn it into three distinct binary variables, each one representing uniquely a single value, as represented in the following schema:

Color		Color_red	Color_green	Color_blue
Red		1	0	0
Green		0	1	0
Blue		0	0	1

This approach presents a problem for DNNs, though. When your categorical variable has too many levels (conventionally more than 255), the resulting binary derived features are not only too numerous, making your dataset huge, but also carry little information since most of the numerical values will be just zeros (we call this situation **sparse data**). Sparse data is somewhat problematic for a DNN because backpropagation doesn't work optimally when there are too many zeros in the data since the lack of information can stop the signal from making a meaningful difference as it's sent back through the network.

We therefore distinguish between low-cardinality and high-cardinality categorical variables, on the basis of their number of unique values and process (by one-hot encoding) only those categorical variables that we consider to have low cardinality (conventionally if there are less than 255 unique values, but you can choose a lower threshold, such as 64, 32, or even 24).

Getting ready

We import the scikit-learn function for one-hot encoding and we prepare a simple example dataset containing categorical data both in string and numerical form:

```
from sklearn.preprocessing import OneHotEncoder

example = pd.DataFrame([['car', 1234], ['house', 6543],
                        ['tree', 3456]], columns=['object', 'code'])
```

Now we can proceed to the recipe.

How to do it...

We prepare a class that can turn numbers to strings, so, after using it, every numerical categorical feature will be processed in the same way as the strings. We then prepare our recipe, which is a scikit-learn pipeline that combines our string converter and one-hot encoding together (we won't forget to automatically deal with any missing values by converting them into unique values).

```
class ToString(BaseEstimator, TransformerMixin):
    def fit(self, X, y=None, **fit_params):
        return self
    def transform(self, X, y=None, **fit_params):
        return X.astype(str)
    def fit_transform(self, X, y=None, **fit_params):
        self.fit(X, y, **fit_params)
        return self.transform(X)


categorical_pipeline = Pipeline(steps=[
        ('string_converter', ToString()),
        ('imputer', SimpleImputer(strategy='constant',
                                  fill_value='missing')),
        ('onehot', OneHotEncoder(handle_unknown='ignore'))])
```

Though the code snippet is short, it indeed achieves quite a lot. Let's understand how it works.

How it works...

Like the other methods we've seen, we just fit and transform our example:

```
categorical_pipeline.fit_transform(example).todense()
```

Since the returned array will be sparse (a special format for datasets where zero values prevail), we can convert it back to our usual NumPy array format using the .todense method.

There's more...

One-hot encoding, by converting every categorical unique value into a variable of its own, produces many new features. In order to label them we have to inspect the scikit-learn one-hot encoding instance we used and extract the labels from it:

```
def derive_ohe_columns(df, pipeline):
    return [str(col) + '_' + str(lvl)
        for col, lvls in zip(df.columns,
        pipeline.named_steps.onehot.categories_) for lvl in lvls]
```

For instance, in our example, now we can figure out what each new feature represents by calling the following function:

```
derive_ohe_columns(example, categorical_pipeline)
```

The results provide us indication about both the original feature and the unique value represented by the binary variable:

```
['object_car',
 'object_house',
 'object_tree',
 'code_1234',
 'code_3456',
 'code_6543']
```

As you can see, the results provide an indication of both the original feature and the unique value represented by the binary variable.

Processing ordinal data

Ordinal data (for instance, rankings or star values in a review) is certainly more similar to numerical data than it is to categorical data, yet we have to first consider certain differences before dealing with it plainly as a number. The problem with categorical data is that you can process it as numerical data, but probably the distance between one point and the following one in the scale is different than the distance between the following one and the next (technically the steps could be different). This is because ordinal data doesn't represent quantities, but just ordering. On the other hand, we also treat it as categorical data, because categories are independent and we will lose the information implied in the ordering. The solution for ordinal data is simply to treat it as both a numerical and a categorical variable.

Getting ready

First, we need to import the `OrdinalEncoder` function from scikit-learn, which will help us in numerically recoding ordinal values, even when they are textual (such as the ordinal scale bad, neutral, and good):

```
from sklearn.preprocessing import OrdinalEncoder
```

We can then prepare our example using two features containing ordinal information recorded as strings:

```
example = pd.DataFrame([['first', 'very much'],
                        ['second', 'very little'],
                        ['third', 'average']],
                       columns = ['rank', 'importance'])
```

Again, the example is just a toy dataset, but it should allow us to test the functionalities demonstrated by this recipe.

How to do it...

At this point, we can prepare two pipelines. The first pipeline will be working on the ordinal data by turning it into ordered numeric (this transformation will preserve the ordering of the original feature). The second transformation one-hot encodes the ordinal data (a transformation that will preserve the step information between ordinal grades, but not their ordering). As with the date transformation in the recipe *Processing dates*, earlier in this chapter, just two pieces of information derived from your original data will be enough for you to process ordinal data in a DNN:

```
oe = OrdinalEncoder(categories=[['first', 'second', 'third'],
                    ['very much', 'average', 'very little']])


categorical_pipeline = Pipeline(steps=[
            ('string_converter', ToString()),
            ('imputer', SimpleImputer(strategy='constant',
                                      fill_value='missing')),
            ('onehot', OneHotEncoder(handle_unknown='ignore'))])
```

As this recipe is mainly composed of a scikit-learn pipeline, it should be quite familiar to you. Let's delve into it to understand more of its workings.

How it works...

All you have to do is to operate the transformations separately and then stack the resulting vectors together:

```
np.hstack((oe.fit_transform(example), categorical_pipeline.fit_
transform(example).todense()))
```

Here is the result from our example:

```
matrix([[0., 0., 1., 0., 0., 0., 0., 1.],
        [1., 2., 0., 1., 0., 0., 1., 0.],
        [2., 1., 0., 0., 1., 1., 0., 0.]])
```

Columns can be easily derived using the `derive_ohe_columns` function that we have seen before:

```
example.columns.tolist() + derive_ohe_columns(example, categorical_
pipeline)
```

Here is the list containing the transformed column names:

```
['rank',
 'importance',
```

```
    'rank_first',
    'rank_second',
    'rank_third',
    'importance_average',
    'importance_very little',
    'importance_very much']
```

By combining the variables covering the numerical part and the unique values of an ordinal variable, we should now be able to utilize all the real information from our data.

Processing high-cardinality categorical data

When processing high-cardinality categorical features, we can use the previously mentioned one-hot encoding strategy. However, we may encounter problems because the resulting matrix is too sparse (many zero values), thus preventing our DNN from converging to a good solution, or making the dataset unfeasible to handle (because sparse matrices made dense can occupy a large amount of memory).

The best solution instead is to pass them to our DNN as numerically labeled features and let a Keras embedding layer take care of them (https://www.tensorflow.org/api_docs/python/tf/keras/layers/Embedding). An embedding layers is just a matrix of weights that can convert the high-cardinality categorical input into a lower-dimensionality numerical output. It is basically a weighted linear combination whose weights are optimized to convert categories into numbers that can best help the prediction process.

Under the hood, the embedding layer converts your categorical data into one-hot-encoded vectors that become the input of a small neural network. The purpose of this small neural network is just to mix and combine the inputs together into a smaller output layer. The one-hot encoding performed by the layer works only on numerically labeled categories (no strings), so it is paramount to transform our high-cardinality categorical data in the correct way.

The scikit-learn package provides the LabelEncoder function as a possible solution, but this method presents some problems, because it cannot handle previously unseen categories, nor can it properly work in a fit/transform regime. Our recipe has to wrap it up and make it suitable for producing the correct input and information for a Keras embedding layer.

Getting ready

In this recipe, we will need to redefine the LabelEncoder function from scikit-learn and make it suitable for a fit/transform process:

```
from sklearn.preprocessing import LabelEncoder
```

Since we need to simulate a high-cardinality categorical variable, we will use random unique values (made of letters and digits) created by a simple script. That will allow us to test a larger number of examples, too:

```
import string
import random

def random_id(length=8):
    voc = string.ascii_lowercase + string.digits
    return ''.join(random.choice(voc) for i in range(length))

example = pd.DataFrame({'high_cat_1': [random_id(length=2)
                                       for i in range(500)],
                        'high_cat_2': [random_id(length=3)
                                       for i in range(500)],
                        'high_cat_3': [random_id(length=4)
                                       for i in range(500)]})
```

This is the output of our random example generator:

	high_cat_1	high_cat_2	high_cat_3
0	7z	30i	r1ms
1	6w	ycy	08bj
2	ki	idv	jb5e
3	2v	fz0	qzut
4	ea	fwq	ytsg
...	...	...	...
495	kt	4nq	51te
496	si	2qs	zpz4
497	fb	gpm	urz5
498	3k	pfl	iuzc
499	l2	mu9	jnby

500 rows × 3 columns

The first column contains a two-letter code, the second uses three letters, and the last one four letters.

How to do it...

In this recipe, we will prepare another scikit-learn class. It extends the existing `LabelEncoder` function because it automatically handles missing values. It keeps records of the mapping between the original categorical values and their resulting numeric equivalents and at transformation time, it can handle previously unseen categories, labeling them as unknown:

```
class LEncoder(BaseEstimator, TransformerMixin):

    def __init__(self):
        self.encoders = dict()
```

```
            self.dictionary_size = list()
            self.unk = -1

    def fit(self, X, y=None, **fit_params):
        for col in range(X.shape[1]):
            le = LabelEncoder()
            le.fit(X.iloc[:, col].fillna('_nan'))
            le_dict = dict(zip(le.classes_,
                                le.transform(le.classes_)))

            if '_nan' not in le_dict:
                max_value = max(le_dict.values())
                le_dict['_nan'] = max_value

            max_value = max(le_dict.values())
            le_dict['_unk'] = max_value

            self.unk = max_value
            self.dictionary_size.append(len(le_dict))
            col_name = X.columns[col]
            self.encoders[col_name] = le_dict

        return self

    def transform(self, X, y=None, **fit_params):
        output = list()
        for col in range(X.shape[1]):
            col_name = X.columns[col]
            le_dict = self.encoders[col_name]
            emb = X.iloc[:, col].fillna('_nan').apply(lambda x:
                            le_dict.get(x, le_dict['_unk'])).values
            output.append(pd.Series(emb,
                            name=col_name).astype(np.int32))
        return output

    def fit_transform(self, X, y=None, **fit_params):
        self.fit(X, y, **fit_params)
        return self.transform(X)
```

Like the other classes we've seen so far, LEncoder has a fitting method that stores information for future uses and a transform method that applies transformations based on the information previously stored after fitting it to the training data.

How it works...

After instancing our label encoder, we simply fit and transform our example, turning each categorical feature into a sequence of numeric labels:

```
le = LEncoder()
le.fit_transform(example)
```

After all the coding to complete the recipe, the execution of this class is indeed simple and straightforward.

There's more...

In order for the Keras embeddings layers to work properly, we need to specify the input size of our high-cardinality categorical variable. By accessing the le.dictionary_size in our examples, we had 412, 497, and 502 distinct values in our example variables:

```
le.dictionary_size
```

In our examples, we had 412, 497, and 502 distinct values, respectively, in our example variables:

```
[412, 497, 502]
```

This number includes the **missing** and **unknown** labels, even if there were no missing or unknown elements in the examples we fitted.

Wrapping up all the processing

Now that we have completed the recipes relating to processing different kinds of tabular data, in this recipe we will be wrapping everything together in a class that can easily handle all the fit/transform operations with a pandas DataFrame as input and explicit specifications of what columns to process and how.

Getting ready

Since we will combine multiple transformations, we will take advantage of the FeatureUnion function from scikit-learn, a function that can concatenate them together easily:

```
from sklearn.pipeline import FeatureUnion
```

As a testing dataset, we will then simply combine all our previously used test data:

```
example = pd.concat([
pd.DataFrame([[1, 2, 3, np.nan], [1, 3, np.nan, 4],[1, 2, 2, 2]],
             columns = ['a', 'b', 'c', 'd']),
pd.DataFrame({'date_1': ['04/12/2018', '05/12/2019','07/12/2020'],
              'date_2': ['12/5/2018', '15/5/2015', '18/5/2016'],
              'date_3': ['25/8/2019', '28/8/2018', '29/8/2017']}),
pd.DataFrame([['first', 'very much'], ['second', 'very little'],
              ['third', 'average']],
             columns = ['rank', 'importance']),
pd.DataFrame([['car', 1234], ['house', 6543], ['tree', 3456]],
             columns=['object', 'code']),
pd.DataFrame({'high_cat_1': [random_id(length=2)
                             for i in range(3)],
              'high_cat_2': [random_id(length=3)
                             for i in range(3)],
              'high_cat_3': [random_id(length=4)
                             for i in range(3)]})
], axis=1)
```

As for as our toy dataset, we just combine all the datasets we have used up to now.

How to do it...

The wrapper class of this recipe has been split into parts, in order to help you to inspect and study the code better. The first part comprises the initialization, which effectively incorporates all the recipes we have seen so far in this chapter:

```
class TabularTransformer(BaseEstimator, TransformerMixin):

    def instantiate(self, param):
        if isinstance(param, str):
            return [param]
        elif isinstance(param, list):
            return param
        else:
            return None

    def __init__(self, numeric=None, dates=None,
                 ordinal=None, cat=None, highcat=None,
                 variance_threshold=0.0, missing_imputer='mean',
                 use_multivariate_imputer=False,
                 add_missing_indicator=True,
```

```
                quantile_transformer='normal', scaler=True,
                ordinal_categories='auto',
                date_format='%d/%m/%Y', hours_secs=False):

    self.numeric = self.instantiate(numeric)
    self.dates = self.instantiate(dates)
    self.ordinal = self.instantiate(ordinal)
    self.cat  = self.instantiate(cat)
    self.highcat = self.instantiate(highcat)
    self.columns = None
    self.vocabulary = None
```

After having recorded all the key parameters of the wrappers, we proceed to examine all the individual parts of it. Please don't forget that all these code snippets are part of the same __init__ method and that we are simply re-using the recipes we have seen previously, therefore for any details of these code snippets, just refer to the previous recipes.

Here we record the numeric pipeline:

```
    self.numeric_process = assemble_numeric_pipeline(
            variance_threshold=variance_threshold,
            imputer=missing_imputer,
            multivariate_imputer=use_multivariate_imputer,
            add_indicator=add_missing_indicator,
            quantile_transformer=quantile_transformer,
            scaler=scaler)
```

After that, we record the pipeline processing time-related features:

```
    self.dates_process = DateProcessor(
            date_format=date_format, hours_secs=hours_secs)
```

Now it is the turn of ordinal variables:

```
    self.ordinal_process = FeatureUnion(
            [('ordinal',
            OrdinalEncoder(categories=ordinal_categories)),
            ('categorial',
            Pipeline(steps=[('string_converter', ToString()),
            ('imputer',
            SimpleImputer(strategy='constant',
                        fill_value='missing')),
            ('onehot',
            OneHotEncoder(handle_unknown='ignore'))])))])
```

We close with the categorical pipelines, both the low-and high-categorical ones:

```
        self.cat_process = Pipeline(steps=[
            ('string_converter', ToString()),
            ('imputer', SimpleImputer(strategy='constant',
                                      fill_value='missing')),
            ('onehot', OneHotEncoder(handle_unknown='ignore'))])

        self.highcat_process = LEncoder()
```

The next part regards the fitting. Depending on the different variable types available, the appropriate fit process will be applied and the newly processed or generated columns will be recorded in the .columns index list:

```
    def fit(self, X, y=None, **fit_params):
        self.columns = list()
        if self.numeric:
            self.numeric_process.fit(X[self.numeric])
            self.columns += derive_numeric_columns(
                            X[self.numeric],
                            self.numeric_process).to_list()
        if self.dates:
            self.dates_process.fit(X[self.dates])
            self.columns += self.dates_process.columns.to_list()
        if self.ordinal:
            self.ordinal_process.fit(X[self.ordinal])
            self.columns += self.ordinal + derive_ohe_columns(
                        X[self.ordinal],
                        self.ordinal_process.transformer_list[1][1])
        if self.cat:
            self.cat_process.fit(X[self.cat])
            self.columns += derive_ohe_columns(X[self.cat],
                                               self.cat_process)
        if self.highcat:
            self.highcat_process.fit(X[self.highcat])
            self.vocabulary = dict(zip(self.highcat,
                            self.highcat_process.dictionary_size))
            self.columns = [self.columns, self.highcat]
        return self
```

The `transform` method provides all the transformations and matrix joining in order to return a list of arrays containing, as their first element, the numerical parts of the processed data, followed by the numerical label vectors representing the high-cardinality categorical variables:

```python
def transform(self, X, y=None, **fit_params):
    flat_matrix = list()
    if self.numeric:
        flat_matrix.append(
                self.numeric_process.transform(X[self.numeric])
                            .astype(np.float32))
    if self.dates:
        flat_matrix.append(
                self.dates_process.transform(X[self.dates])
                            .values
                            .astype(np.float32))
    if self.ordinal:
        flat_matrix.append(
                self.ordinal_process.transform(X[self.ordinal])
                            .todense()
                            .astype(np.float32))
    if self.cat:
        flat_matrix.append(
                self.cat_process.transform(X[self.cat])
                            .todense()
                            .astype(np.float32))
    if self.highcat:
        cat_vectors = self.highcat_process.transform(
                                        X[self.highcat])

        if len(flat_matrix) > 0:
            return [np.hstack(flat_matrix)] + cat_vectors
        else:
            return cat_vectors
    else:
        return np.hstack(flat_matrix)
```

Finally, we set the `fit_transform` method, which sequentially executes the fit and transform operations:

```python
def fit_transform(self, X, y=None, **fit_params):
    self.fit(X, y, **fit_params)
    return self.transform(X)
```

Now that we have finished wrapping everything together, we can take a look at how it works.

How it works...

In our test, we assign the list of column names to variables depending on their type:

```
numeric_vars = ['a', 'b', 'c', 'd']
date_vars = ['date_1', 'date_2', 'date_3']
ordinal_vars = ['rank', 'importance']
cat_vars = ['object', 'code']
highcat_vars = ['high_cat_1', 'high_cat_2', 'high_cat_3']

tt = TabularTransformer(numeric=numeric_vars, dates=date_vars,
                        ordinal=ordinal_vars, cat=cat_vars,
                        highcat=highcat_vars)
```

After having instantiated the `TabularTransformer`, and mapped the variables we need to be processed to their type, we proceed to fit and transform our example dataset:

```
input_list = tt.fit_transform(example)
```

The result is a list of NumPy arrays. We can iterate through them and print their shape in order to check how the output is composed:

```
print([(item.shape, item.dtype) for item in input_list])
```

The printed result reports a larger array as its first element (the combined result of all processes except the high-cardinality categorical one):

```
[((3, 40), dtype('float32')), ((3,), dtype('int32')), ((3,),
dtype('int32')), ((3,), dtype('int32'))]
```

Our DNN can now expect a list as input, where the first element is a numerical matrix and the following elements are vectors to be sent to categorical embeddings layers.

There's more...

In order to be able to retrace each column and vector name, the `TabularTransformer` has a `columns` method, `tt.columns`, that can be invoked. The `TabularTransformer` can also call `tt.vocabulary` for information about the dimensionality of the categorical variables, which is necessary in order to correctly set the input shape of the embeddings layers in the network. The returned result is a dictionary in which the column name is the key and the dictionary size is the value:

```
{'high_cat_1': 5, 'high_cat_2': 5, 'high_cat_3': 5}
```

Now that we have these two methods for tracking down variable names (`tt.columns`) and defining the vocabulary of high-cardinality variables (`tt.vocabulary`), we are just a step away from a complete deep leaning framework for deep learning processing of tabular data.

Setting up a data generator

We are just missing one key ingredient before we try our framework out on a difficult test task. The previous recipe presented a `TabularTransformer` that can effectively turn a pandas DataFrame into numerical arrays that a DNN can process. Yet, the recipe can only deal with all the data at once. The next step is to provide a way to create batches of the data of different sizes. This could be accomplished using `tf.data` or a Keras generator and, since previously in the book we have already explored quite a few examples with `tf.data`, this time we will prepare the code for a Keras generator that's capable of generating random batches on the fly when our DNN is learning.

Getting ready

Our generator will inherit from the `Sequence` class:

```
from tensorflow.keras.utils import Sequence
```

The `Sequence` class is the base object for fitting a sequence of data and it requires you to implement custom __getitem__ (which will return a complete batch) and __len__ (which will report how many batches are necessary to complete an epoch) methods.

How to do it...

We now script a new class called `DataGenerator` that inherits from the Keras `Sequence` class:

```
class DataGenerator(Sequence):

    def __init__(self, X, y,
                    tabular_transformer=None,
                    batch_size=32,
                    shuffle=False,
                    dict_output=False
                    ):

        self.X = X
        self.y = y
        self.tbt = tabular_transformer
        self.tabular_transformer = tabular_transformer
        self.batch_size = batch_size
```

```python
        self.shuffle = shuffle
        self.dict_output = dict_output
        self.indexes = self._build_index()
        self.on_epoch_end()
        self.item = 0

    def _build_index(self):
        return np.arange(len(self.y))

    def on_epoch_end(self):
        if self.shuffle:
            np.random.shuffle(self.indexes)

    def __len__(self):
        return int(len(self.indexes) / self.batch_size) + 1

    def __iter__(self):
        for i in range(self.__len__()):
            self.item = i
            yield self.__getitem__(index=i)

        self.item = 0

    def __next__(self):
        return self.__getitem__(index=self.item)

    def __call__(self):
        return self.__iter__()

    def __data_generation(self, selection):
        if self.tbt is not None:
            if self.dict_output:
                dct = {'input_'+str(j) : arr for j,
                        arr in enumerate(
                    self.tbt.transform(self.X.iloc[selection, :]))}
                return dct, self.y[selection]
            else:
                return self.tbt.transform(
                    self.X.iloc[selection, :]), self.y[selection]
        else:
            return self.X.iloc[selection, :], self.y[selection]

    def __getitem__(self, index):
        indexes = self.indexes[
```

```
                index*self.batch_size:(index+1)*self.batch_size]
        samples, labels = self.__data_generation(indexes)
        return samples, labels, [None]
```

The generator is now set up. Let's proceed to the next section and explore how it works in more detail.

How it works...

Apart from the __init__ method, which instantiates the internal variables of the class, the DataGenerator class consists of these methods:

- ▶ _build_index: This creates an index of the provided data
- ▶ on_epoch_end: At the end of each epoch, this method will randomly shuffle the data
- ▶ __len__: This reports how many batches are required to complete an epoch
- ▶ __iter__: This renders the class an iterable
- ▶ __next__: This calls the next batch
- ▶ __call__: This returns the __iter__ method call
- ▶ __data_generation: Where the TabularTransformer operates on data batches, returning the transformed output (returning it as a list of arrays or as a dictionary of arrays)
- ▶ __getitem__: This splits the data into batches and calls the __data_generation method for the transformations

This completes the final piece of the puzzle. Using the last two recipes you can fully transform and deliver to a TensorFlow model any mixed variable tabular dataset to a TensorFlow model, just by filling in a few parameters. In the next two recipes we will provide you with some specific tricks to make our DNN work better with tabular data, and we'll look at a fully fledged example from a famous Kaggle competition.

Creating custom activations for tabular data

With images and text, it is more difficult to backpropagate errors in DNNs working on tabular data because the data is sparse. While the ReLU activation function is used widely, new activation functions have been found to work better in such cases and can improve the network performances. These activations functions are SeLU, GeLU, and Mish. Since SeLU is already present in Keras and TensorFlow (see https://www.tensorflow.org/api_docs/python/tf/keras/activations/selu and https://www.tensorflow.org/api_docs/python/tf/nn/selu), in this recipe we'll use the GeLU and Mish activation functions.

Getting ready

You need the usual imports:

```
from tensorflow import keras as keras
import numpy as np
import matplotlib.pyplot as plt
```

We've added `matplotlib`, so we can plot how these new activation functions work and get an idea of the reason for their efficacy.

How to do it...

GeLU and Mish are defined by their mathematics, which you can find in their original papers:

▶ *Gaussian Error Linear Units (GELUs)*: https://arxiv.org/abs/1606.08415

▶ *Mish, A Self Regularized Non-Monotonic Neural Activation Function*: https://arxiv.org/abs/1908.08681

Here are the formulas translated into code:

```
def gelu(x):
    return 0.5 * x * (1 + tf.tanh(tf.sqrt(2 / np.pi) *
                      (x + 0.044715 * tf.pow(x, 3))))


keras.utils.get_custom_objects().update(
                         {'gelu': keras.layers.Activation(gelu)})
def mish(inputs):
    return inputs * tf.math.tanh(tf.math.softplus(inputs))


keras.utils.get_custom_objects().update(
                         {'mish': keras.layers.Activation(mish)})
```

The interesting part of the recipe is that `get_custom_objects` is a function that allows you to record your new functions in custom TensorFlow objects and then easily recall them as strings in layer parameters. You can find more information about how custom objects work in Keras by having a look at the TensorFlow documentation: https://www.tensorflow.org/api_docs/python/tf/keras/utils/get_custom_objects.

How it works...

We can get an idea of how these two activation functions work by plotting positive and negative inputs against their outputs. A few commands from matplotlib will help us with the visualization:

```
gelu_vals = list()
mish_vals = list()
abscissa = np.arange(-4, 1, 0.1)
for val in abscissa:
    gelu_vals.append(gelu(tf.cast(val, tf.float32)).numpy())
    mish_vals.append(mish(tf.cast(val, tf.float32)).numpy())

plt.plot(abscissa, gelu_vals, label='gelu')
plt.plot(abscissa, mish_vals, label='mish')
plt.axvline(x=0.0, linestyle='--', color='darkgray')
plt.axhline(y=0.0, linestyle='--', color='darkgray')
plt.legend()
plt.show()
```

After running the code, you should get the following plot:

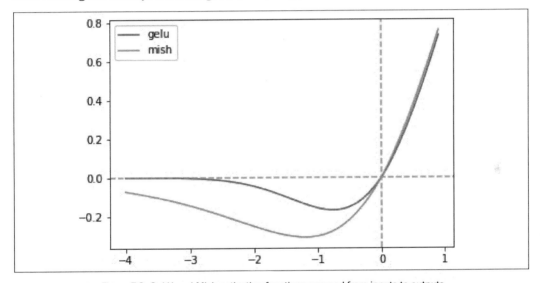

Figure 7.3: GeLU and Mish activation functions mapped from inputs to outputs

As with the ReLU activation function, inputs from zero onward are just identically mapped as output (preserving linearity in the positive activations). The interesting thing happens when the input is below zero, actually, because it is not suppressed as happens with ReLU. In both the GeLU and Mish activation functions, the output is a dampened transformation of the negative input that recedes to zero when the input is very negative. This prevents both the case of dying neurons, because negative inputs can still pass information, and the case of saturated neurons, because overly negative values are turned off.

With different strategies, negative input is therefore processed and propagated both by the GeLU and Mish activations functions. This allows a defined gradient from negative inputs, which doesn't cause harm to the network.

Running a test on a difficult problem

Throughout the chapter, we have provided recipes to handle tabular data in a successful way. Each recipe is not actually a solution in itself, but a piece of a puzzle. When the pieces are combined you can get excellent results and in this last recipe, we will demonstrate how to assemble all the recipes together to successfully complete a difficult Kaggle challenge.

The Kaggle competition, *Amazon.com – Employee Access Challenge* (`https://www.kaggle.com/c/amazon-employee-access-challenge`), is a competition that's notable for the high-cardinality variables involved and is a solid benchmark that's used to compare gradient boosting algorithms. The aim of the competition is to develop a model that can predict whether an Amazon employee should be given access to a specific resource based on their role and activities. The answer should be given as likelihood. As predictors, you have different ID codes corresponding to the type of resource you are evaluating access to, the role of the employee in the organization, and the referring manager.

Getting ready

As usual, we start by importing TensorFlow and Keras:

```
import tensorflow as tf
import tensorflow.keras as keras
```

Using sequential-based data generators may trigger some errors in TensorFlow 2.2. This is due to eager execution and, as a precaution, we have to disable it for this recipe:

```
tf.compat.v1.disable_eager_execution()
```

In order to get hold of the Amazon dataset, the best and fastest way is to install **CatBoost**, a gradient boosting algorithm that uses the dataset as a benchmark. If it is not already present in your installed environment, you easily install it using the `pip install catboost` command:

```
from catboost.datasets import amazon

X, Xt = amazon()

y = X["ACTION"].apply(lambda x: 1 if x == 1 else 0).values
X.drop(["ACTION"], axis=1, inplace=True)
```

Since the test data (uploaded into the Xt variable) has an unlabeled target variable, we will be using just the training data in the X variable.

How to do it...

As a first step, we will define the DNN architecture for this problem. Since the problem involves only categorical variables with high cardinality, we start setting an input and an embedding layer for each feature.

We first define an input for each feature, where the data flows into the network, and then each input is directed into its respective embedding layer. The size of the input is based on the number of unique values of the feature, and the size of the output is based on the logarithm of the input size. The output of each embedding is then passed to a spatial dropout (since the embedding layer will return a matrix, the spatial dropout will blank out entire columns of the matrix) and then flattened. Finally, all the flattened results are concatenated into a single layer. From there on, the data has to pass through two dense layers with dropout before reaching the output response node, a sigmoid activated node that will return a probability as an answer:

```python
def dnn(categorical_variables, categorical_counts,
        feature_selection_dropout=0.2, categorical_dropout=0.1,
        first_dense = 256, second_dense = 256,
        dense_dropout = 0.2,
        activation_type=gelu):

    categorical_inputs = []
    categorical_embeddings = []

    for category in categorical_variables:
        categorical_inputs.append(keras.layers.Input(
                shape=[1], name=category))
        category_counts = categorical_counts[category]
        categorical_embeddings.append(
            keras.layers.Embedding(category_counts+1,
                    int(np.log1p(category_counts)+1),
                    name = category +
                        "_embed")(categorical_inputs[-1]))

    def flatten_dropout(x, categorical_dropout):
        return keras.layers.Flatten()(
            keras.layers.SpatialDropout1D(categorical_dropout)(x))

    categorical_logits = [flatten_dropout(cat_emb,
                            categorical_dropout)
```

```
                          for cat_emb in categorical_embeddings]
        categorical_concat = keras.layers.Concatenate(
                    name = "categorical_concat")(categorical_logits)

        x = keras.layers.Dense(first_dense,
                        activation=activation_type)(categorical_concat)
        x = keras.layers.Dropout(dense_dropout)(x)
        x = keras.layers.Dense(second_dense,
                        activation=activation_type)(x)
        x = keras.layers.Dropout(dense_dropout)(x)
        output = keras.layers.Dense(1, activation="sigmoid")(x)
        model = keras.Model(categorical_inputs, output)

        return model
```

The architecture works only with categorical data. It takes each categorical input (expecting a single integer code) and fits it into an embedding layer, whose output is a reduced dimensionality vector (whose dimensions are computed using the heuristic `int(np.log1p(category_counts)+1)`). It applies a `SpatialDropout1D` and finally it flattens the output. `SpatialDropout1D` removes all the connections in a row of the output matrix from all channels, thus effectively dropping some information from the embedding. All the outputs of all the categorical variables are then concatenated and passed on to a series of dense layers with GeLU activations and dropout. It all ends with a single sigmoid node (so you can get the emission of a probability in the range [0,1]).

After defining the architecture, we define the score functions, taking them from scikit-learn and converting them for use in Keras using the `tf.py_function` from TensorFlow (`https://www.tensorflow.org/api_docs/python/tf/py_function`), a wrapper that can turn any function into a once-differentiable TensorFlow operation that can be executed eagerly.

As score functions, we use the average precision and the ROC AUC. Both of these can help us figure out how we are performing on a binary classification by telling us how closely the predicted probabilities resemble the true values. More on ROC AUC and average precision can be found in the scikit-learn documentation at `https://scikit-learn.org/stable/modules/generated/sklearn.metrics.average_precision_score.html` and `https://scikit-learn.org/stable/modules/generated/sklearn.metrics.roc_auc_score.html#sklearn.metrics.roc_auc_score`.

We also instantiate a simple plotting function that can plot selected error and score measures as recorded during the training both on the training and validation sets:

```
from sklearn.metrics import average_precision_score, roc_auc_score

def mAP(y_true, y_pred):
    return tf.py_function(average_precision_score,
                        (y_true, y_pred), tf.double)
```

```
def auc(y_true, y_pred):
    try:
        return tf.py_function(roc_auc_score,
                                (y_true, y_pred), tf.double)
    except:
        return 0.5

def compile_model(model, loss, metrics, optimizer):
    model.compile(loss=loss, metrics=metrics, optimizer=optimizer)
    return model

def plot_keras_history(history, measures):
    """
    history: Keras training history
    measures = list of names of measures
    """
    rows = len(measures) // 2 + len(measures) % 2
    fig, panels = plt.subplots(rows, 2, figsize=(15, 5))
    plt.subplots_adjust(top = 0.99, bottom=0.01,
                        hspace=0.4, wspace=0.2)
    try:
        panels = [item for sublist in panels for item in sublist]
    except:
        pass
    for k, measure in enumerate(measures):
        panel = panels[k]
        panel.set_title(measure + ' history')
        panel.plot(history.epoch, history.history[measure],
                    label="Train "+measure)
        panel.plot(history.epoch, history.history["val_"+measure],
                    label="Validation "+measure)
        panel.set(xlabel='epochs', ylabel=measure)
        panel.legend()

    plt.show(fig)
```

At this point, you need to set up the training phase. Given the limited number of examples and your need to test your solution, using cross-validation is the best choice. The `StratifiedKFold` function from scikit-learn will provide you with the right tool for the job.

In `StratifiedKFold`, your data is randomly (you can provide a seed value for reproducibility) split into *k* parts, each one with the same proportion of the target variable as is found in the original data.

These *k* splits are used to generate *k* training tests that can help you infer the performance of the DNN architecture you have set up. In fact, *k* times over, *all but one* of the splits are used to train your model and the one kept apart is left out for testing each time. This ensures that you have *k* tests made on splits that have not been used for training.

This approach, especially when dealing with only a few training examples, is preferable to picking up a single test set to verify your models on, because by sampling a test set you could find a sample that is differently distributed from your train set. Moreover, by using a single test set, you also risk overfitting your test set. If you repeatedly test different solutions, eventually you may find a solution that fits the test set very well but is not a generalizable solution in itself.

Let's put it into practice here:

```python
from sklearn.model_selection import StratifiedKFold

SEED = 0
FOLDS = 3
BATCH_SIZE = 512

skf = StratifiedKFold(n_splits=FOLDS,
                      shuffle=True,
                      random_state=SEED)

roc_auc = list()
average_precision = list()
categorical_variables = X.columns.to_list()

for fold, (train_idx, test_idx) in enumerate(skf.split(X, y)):

    tt = TabularTransformer(highcat = categorical_variables)

    tt.fit(X.iloc[train_idx])
    categorical_levels = tt.vocabulary

    model = dnn(categorical_variables,
                categorical_levels,
                feature_selection_dropout=0.1,
                categorical_dropout=0.1,
                first_dense=64,
                second_dense=64,
                dense_dropout=0.1,
                activation_type=mish)

    model = compile_model(model,
```

```
                            keras.losses.binary_crossentropy,
                            [auc, mAP],
                            tf.keras.optimizers.Adam(learning_rate=0.0001))

    train_batch = DataGenerator(X.iloc[train_idx],
                                y[train_idx],
                                tabular_transformer=tt,
                                batch_size=BATCH_SIZE,
                                shuffle=True)

    val_X, val_y = tt.transform(X.iloc[test_idx]), y[test_idx]

    history = model.fit(train_batch,
                        validation_data=(val_X, val_y),
                        epochs=30,
                        class_weight=[1.0,
                                (np.sum(y==0) / np.sum(y==1))],
                        verbose=2)

    print("\nFOLD %i" % fold)
    plot_keras_history(history, measures=['auc', 'loss'])

    preds = model.predict(val_X, verbose=0,
                        batch_size=1024).flatten()

    roc_auc.append(roc_auc_score(y_true=val_y, y_score=preds))
    average_precision.append(average_precision_score(
                                y_true=val_y, y_score=preds))

print(f"mean cv roc auc {np.mean(roc_auc):0.3f}")
print(f"mean cv ap {np.mean(average_precision):0.3f}")
```

The script runs a training and validation test for each fold and stores the results that will help you correctly evaluate the performances of your DNN for tabular data.

How it works...

Each fold will print a plot detailing how the DNN performed, both on log-loss and ROC AUC, for the training and the validation sample:

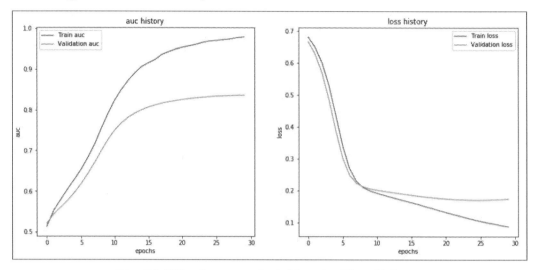

Figure 7.4: DNN performance on the training set and the validation set

All the folds have a similar trajectory, with a significant decoupling of the train and validation curves after 5 epochs and a widening gap after 15 epochs, implying a certain overfitting during the training phase. By modifying your DNN architecture, and changing parameters such as the learning rate or the optimization algorithm, you can safely experiment to try to achieve better results because the cross-validation procedure ensures that you are making the right decisions.

8

Convolutional Neural Networks

Convolutional Neural Networks (**CNNs**) are responsible for the major breakthroughs in image recognition made in the past few years. In this chapter, we will cover the following topics:

- ▶ Implementing a simple CNN
- ▶ Implementing an advanced CNN
- ▶ Retraining existing CNN models
- ▶ Applying StyleNet and the neural style project
- ▶ Implementing DeepDream

 As a reminder, the reader can find all of the code for this chapter available online here: `https://github.com/PacktPublishing/Machine-Learning-Using-TensorFlow-Cookbook`, as well as the Packt repository: `https://github.com/PacktPublishing/Machine-Learning-Using-TensorFlow-Cookbook`.

Introduction

In the previous chapters, we discussed **Dense Neural Networks** (**DNNs**) in which each neuron of a layer is connected to each neuron of the adjacent layer. In this chapter, we will focus on a special type of neural network that performs well for image classification: CNNs.

A CNN is a combination of two components: a feature extractor module followed by a trainable classifier. The first component includes a stack of convolution, activation, and pooling layers. A DNN does the classification. Each neuron in a layer is connected to those in the next layer.

In mathematics, a convolution is a function that is applied over the output of another function. In our case, we will consider using a matrix multiplication (filter) across an image. For our purposes, we find an image to be a matrix of numbers. These numbers may represent pixels or even image attributes. The convolution operation we will apply to these matrices involves moving a filter of fixed width across the image and using element-wise multiplication to get our result.

See the following diagram for a conceptual understanding of how image convolution can work:

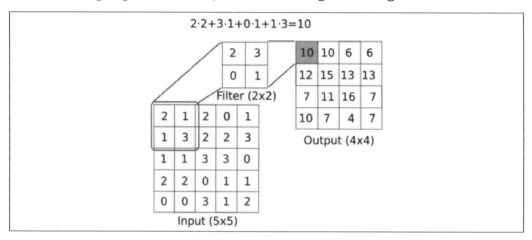

Figure 8.1: Application of a 2x2 convolutional filter across a 5x5 input matrix producing a new 4x4 feature layer

In *Figure 8.1*, we see how a convolutional filter applied across an image (length by width by depth) operates to create a new feature layer. Here, we have a *2x2* convolutional filter, working in the valid spaces of the *5x5* input with a stride of 1 in both directions. The result is a *4x4* matrix. This new feature layer highlights the areas in the input image that activate the filter the most.

CNNs also have other operations that fulfill more requirements, such as introducing non-linearities (ReLU), or aggregating parameters (max pooling, average pooling), and other similar operations. The preceding diagram is an example of applying a convolution operation on a *5x5* array with the convolutional filter being a *2x2* matrix. The step size is 1 and we only consider valid placements. The trainable variables in this operation will be the *2x2* filter weights.

After a convolution, it is common to follow up with an aggregation operation, such as max pooling. The pooling operation goal is to reduce the number of parameters, computation loads, and memory usage. The maximum pooling preserves only the strongest features.

The following diagram provides an example of how max pooling operates. In this example, it has a *2x2* region with a stride of 2 in both directions:

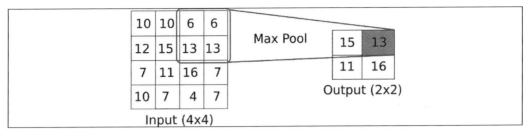

Figure 8.2: Application of a max pooling operation on a 4x4 input image

Figure 8.2 shows how a max pooling operation could operate. Here, we have a *2x2* window, running on the valid spaces of a *4x4* input with a stride of 2 in both directions. The result is a *2x2* matrix, which is simply the maximum value of each region.

Although we will start by creating our own CNN for image recognition, I recommend using existing architectures, as we will do in the remainder of the chapter.

It is common to take a pre-trained network and retrain it with a new dataset and a new fully connected layer at the end. This method is beneficial because we don't have to train a model from scratch; we just have to fine-tune a pre-trained model for our novel task. We will illustrate it in the *Retraining existing CNN models* recipe later in the chapter, where we will retrain an existing architecture to improve on our CIFAR-10 predictions.

Without any further delay, let's start immediately with how to implement a simple CNN.

Implementing a simple CNN

In this recipe, we will develop a CNN based on the LeNet-5 architecture, which was first introduced in 1998 by Yann LeCun et al. for handwritten and machine-printed character recognition.

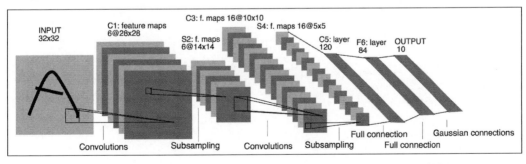

Figure 8.3: LeNet-5 architecture – Original image published in [LeCun et al., 1998]

This architecture consists of two sets of CNNs composed of convolution-ReLU-max pooling operations used for feature extraction, followed by a flattening layer and two fully connected layers to classify the images.

Our goal will be to improve upon our accuracy in predicting MNIST digits.

Getting ready

To access the MNIST data, Keras provides a package (tf.keras.datasets) that has excellent dataset-loading functionalities. (Note that TensorFlow also provides its own collection of ready-to-use datasets with the TF Datasets API.) After loading the data, we will set up our model variables, create the model, train the model in batches, and then visualize loss, accuracy, and some sample digits.

How to do it...

Perform the following steps:

1. First, we'll load the necessary libraries and start a graph session:

```
import matplotlib.pyplot as plt
import numpy as np
import tensorflow as tf
```

2. Next, we will load the data and reshape the images in a four-dimensional matrix:

```
(x_train, y_train), (x_test, y_test) = tf.keras.datasets.mnist.
load_data()
# Reshape
x_train = x_train.reshape(-1, 28, 28, 1)
x_test = x_test.reshape(-1, 28, 28, 1)
#Padding the images by 2 pixels
x_train = np.pad(x_train, ((0,0),(2,2),(2,2),(0,0)), 'constant')
x_test = np.pad(x_test, ((0,0),(2,2),(2,2),(0,0)), 'constant')
```

Note that the MNIST dataset downloaded here includes training and test datasets. These datasets are composed of the grayscale images (integer arrays with shape (num_sample, 28,28)) and the labels (integers in the range 0-9). We pad the images by 2 pixels since in the LeNet-5 paper input images were *32x32*.

3. Now, we will set the model parameters. Remember that the depth of the image (number of channels) is 1 because these images are grayscale. We'll also set up a seed to have reproducible results:

```
image_width = x_train[0].shape[0]
image_height = x_train[0].shape[1]
num_channels = 1 # grayscale = 1 channel

seed = 98
np.random.seed(seed)
tf.random.set_seed(seed)
```

4. We'll declare our training data variables and our test data variables. We will have different batch sizes for training and evaluation. You may change these, depending on the physical memory that is available for training and evaluating:

```
batch_size = 100
evaluation_size = 500
epochs = 300
eval_every = 5
```

5. We'll normalize our images to change the values of all pixels to a common scale:

```
x_train = x_train / 255
x_test = x_test/ 255
```

6. Now we'll declare our model. We will have the feature extractor module composed of two convolutional/ReLU/max pooling layers followed by the classifier with fully connected layers. Also, to get the classifier to work, we flatten the output of the feature extractor module so we can use it in the classifier. Note that we use a softmax activation function at the last layer of the classifier. Softmax turns numeric output (logits) into probabilities that sum to one:

```
input_data = tf.keras.Input(dtype=tf.float32, shape=(image_
width,image_height, num_channels), name="INPUT")

# First Conv-ReLU-MaxPool Layer
conv1 = tf.keras.layers.Conv2D(filters=6,
                               kernel_size=5,
                               padding='VALID',
                               activation="relu",
                               name="C1")(input_data)

max_pool1 = tf.keras.layers.MaxPool2D(pool_size=2,
                                      strides=2,
                                      padding='SAME',
                                      name="S1")(conv1)
```

```python
# Second Conv-ReLU-MaxPool Layer
conv2 = tf.keras.layers.Conv2D(filters=16,
                               kernel_size=5,
                               padding='VALID',
                               strides=1,
                               activation="relu",
                               name="C3")(max_pool1)


max_pool2 = tf.keras.layers.MaxPool2D(pool_size=2,
                                      strides=2,
                                      padding='SAME',
                                      name="S4")(conv2)

# Flatten Layer
flatten = tf.keras.layers.Flatten(name="FLATTEN")(max_pool2)


# First Fully Connected Layer
fully_connected1 = tf.keras.layers.Dense(units=120,
                                         activation="relu",
                                         name="F5")(flatten)

# Second Fully Connected Layer
fully_connected2 = tf.keras.layers.Dense(units=84,
                                         activation="relu",
                                         name="F6")(fully_
connected1)

# Final Fully Connected Layer
final_model_output = tf.keras.layers.Dense(units=10,
                                           activation="softmax",
                                           name="OUTPUT"
                                           )(fully_connected2)


model = tf.keras.Model(inputs= input_data, outputs=final_model_
output)
```

7. Next, we will compile the model using an Adam (Adaptive Moment Estimation) optimizer. Adam uses adaptive learning rates and momentum that allow us to get to local minima faster, and so converge faster. As our targets are integers and not in a one-hot-encoded format, we will use the sparse categorical cross-entropy loss function. Then we will also add an accuracy metric to determine how accurate the model is on each batch:

```
model.compile(
    optimizer="adam",
    loss="sparse_categorical_crossentropy",
    metrics=["accuracy"]
```

8. Next, we print a string summary of our network:

```
model.summary()
```

Layer (type)	Output Shape	Param #
INPUT (InputLayer)	[(None, 32, 32, 1)]	0
C1 (Conv2D)	(None, 28, 28, 6)	156
S1 (MaxPooling2D)	(None, 14, 14, 6)	0
C3 (Conv2D)	(None, 10, 10, 16)	2416
S4 (MaxPooling2D)	(None, 5, 5, 16)	0
FLATTEN (Flatten)	(None, 400)	0
F5 (Dense)	(None, 120)	48120
F6 (Dense)	(None, 84)	10164
OUTPUT (Dense)	(None, 10)	850

```
Total params: 61,706
Trainable params: 61,706
Non-trainable params: 0
```

Figure 8.4: The LeNet-5 architecture

The LeNet-5 model has 7 layers and contains 61,706 trainable parameters. So, let's go to train the model.

9. We can now start training our model. We loop through the data in randomly chosen batches. Every so often, we choose to evaluate the model on the train and test batches and record the accuracy and loss. We can see that, after 300 epochs, we quickly achieve 96-97% accuracy on the test data:

```
train_loss = []
train_acc = []
test_acc = []
for i in range(epochs):
    rand_index = np.random.choice(len(x_train), size=batch_size)
    rand_x = x_train[rand_index]
    rand_y = y_train[rand_index]

    history_train = model.train_on_batch(rand_x, rand_y)

    if (i+1) % eval_every == 0:
        eval_index = np.random.choice(len(x_test), size=evaluation_
size)
        eval_x = x_test[eval_index]
        eval_y = y_test[eval_index]

        history_eval = model.evaluate(eval_x,eval_y)

        # Record and print results
        train_loss.append(history_train[0])
        train_acc.append(history_train[1])
        test_acc.append(history_eval[1])
        acc_and_loss = [(i+1), history_train
 [0], history_train[1], history_eval[1]]
        acc_and_loss = [np.round(x,2) for x in acc_and_loss]
        print('Epoch # {}. Train Loss: {:.2f}. Train Acc (Test Acc):
{:.2f} ({:.2f})'.format(*acc_and_loss))
```

10. This results in the following output:

```
Epoch # 5. Train Loss: 2.19. Train Acc (Test Acc): 0.23 (0.34)
Epoch # 10. Train Loss: 2.01. Train Acc (Test Acc): 0.59 (0.58)
Epoch # 15. Train Loss: 1.71. Train Acc (Test Acc): 0.74 (0.73)
Epoch # 20. Train Loss: 1.32. Train Acc (Test Acc): 0.73 (0.77)
...
Epoch # 290. Train Loss: 0.18. Train Acc (Test Acc): 0.95 (0.94)
Epoch # 295. Train Loss: 0.13. Train Acc (Test Acc): 0.96 (0.96)
Epoch # 300. Train Loss: 0.12. Train Acc (Test Acc): 0.95 (0.97)
```

11. The following is the code to plot the loss and accuracy using `Matplotlib`:

```
# Matlotlib code to plot the loss and accuracy
eval_indices = range(0, epochs, eval_every)
# Plot loss over time
plt.plot(eval_indices, train_loss, 'k-')
plt.title('Loss per Epoch')
plt.xlabel('Epoch')
plt.ylabel('Loss')
plt.show()

# Plot train and test accuracy
plt.plot(eval_indices, train_acc, 'k-', label='Train Set Accuracy')
plt.plot(eval_indices, test_acc, 'r--', label='Test Set Accuracy')
plt.title('Train and Test Accuracy')
plt.xlabel('Epoch')
plt.ylabel('Accuracy')
plt.legend(loc='lower right')
plt.show()
```

We then get the following plots:

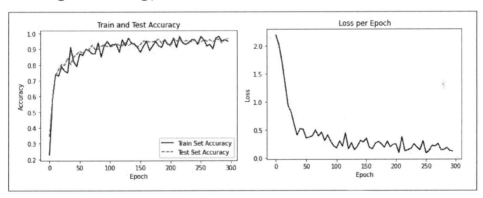

Figure 8.5: The left plot is the train and test set accuracy across our 300 training epochs.
The right plot is the softmax loss value over 300 epochs.

12. If we want to plot a sample of the latest batch results, here is the code to plot a sample consisting of six of the latest results:

```
# Plot some samples and their predictions
actuals = y_test[30:36]
preds = model.predict(x_test[30:36])
predictions = np.argmax(preds,axis=1)
images = np.squeeze(x_test[30:36])

Nrows = 2
```

```
Ncols = 3
for i in range(6):
    plt.subplot(Nrows, Ncols, i+1)
    plt.imshow(np.reshape(images[i], [32,32]), cmap='Greys_r')
    plt.title('Actual: ' + str(actuals[i]) + ' Pred: ' +
str(predictions[i]),
                          fontsize=10)
    frame = plt.gca()
    frame.axes.get_xaxis().set_visible(False)
    frame.axes.get_yaxis().set_visible(False)

plt.show()
```

We get the following output for the code above:

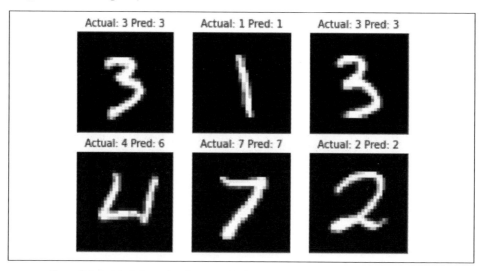

Figure 8.6: A plot of six random images with the actual and predicted values in the title.
The lower-left picture was predicted to be a 6, when in fact it is a 4.

Using a simple CNN, we achieved a good result in accuracy and loss for this dataset.

How it works...

We increased our performance on the MNIST dataset and built a model that quickly
achieves about 97% accuracy while training from scratch. Our features extractor module
is a combination of convolutions, ReLU, and max pooling. Our classifier is a stack of fully
connected layers. We trained in batches of size 100 and looked at the accuracy and loss
across the epochs. Finally, we also plotted six random digits and found that the model
prediction fails to predict one image. The model predicts a 6 when in fact it's a 4.

CNN does very well with image recognition. Part of the reason for this is that the convolutional layer creates its low-level features that are activated when they come across a part of the image that is important. This type of model creates features on its own and uses them for prediction.

There's more...

In the past few years, CNN models have made vast strides in image recognition. Many novel ideas are being explored and new architectures are discovered very frequently. A vast repository of scientific papers in this field is a repository website called arXiv.org (`https://arxiv.org/`), which is created and maintained by Cornell University. arXiv.org includes some very recent articles in many areas, including computer science and computer science subfields such as computer vision and image recognition (`https://arxiv.org/list/cs.CV/recent`).

See also

Here is a list of some great resources you can use to learn about CNNs:

- Stanford University has a great wiki here: `http://scarlet.stanford.edu/teach/index.php/An_Introduction_to_Convolutional_Neural_Networks`
- *Deep Learning* by Michael Nielsen, found here: `http://neuralnetworksanddeeplearning.com/chap6.html`
- *An Introduction to Convolutional Neural Networks* by Jianxin Wu, found here: `https://pdfs.semanticscholar.org/450c/a19932fcef1ca6d0442cbf52fec38fb9d1e5.pdf`
- *LeNet-5, convolutional neural networks* by Yann LeCun: `http://yann.lecun.com/exdb/lenet/`
- *Gradient-Based Learning Applied to Document Recognition* by Yann LeCun et al.: `http://yann.lecun.com/exdb/publis/pdf/lecun-01a.pdf`

Implementing an advanced CNN

It is crucial to be able to extend CNN models for image recognition so that we understand how to increase the depth of the network. This way, we may increase the accuracy of our predictions if we have enough data. Extending the depth of CNN networks is done in a standard fashion: we just repeat the convolution, max pooling, and ReLU in series until we are satisfied with the depth. Many of the more accurate image recognition networks operate in this fashion.

Loading and preprocessing data may cause a big headache: most image datasets will be too large to fit into memory, but image preprocessing will be needed to improve the performance of the model. What we can do with TensorFlow is use the `tf.data` API to create an input pipeline. This API contains a set of utilities for loading and preprocessing data. Using it, we will instantiate a `tf.data.Dataset` object from the CIFAR-10 dataset (downloaded through the Keras dataset API `tf.keras.datasets`), combine consecutive elements of this dataset into batches, and apply transformations to each image. Also, with image recognition data, it is common to randomly perturb the image before sending it through for training. Here, we will randomly crop, flip, and change the brightness.

Getting ready

In this recipe, we will implement a more advanced method of reading image data and use a larger CNN to do image recognition on the CIFAR-10 dataset (`https://www.cs.toronto.edu/~kriz/cifar.html`). This dataset has 60,000 *32x32* images that fall into exactly one of 10 possible classes. The potential labels for the pictures are airplane, automobile, bird, cat, deer, dog, frog, horse, ship, and truck. Please also refer to the first bullet point in the *See also* section.

The official TensorFlow `tf.data` tutorial is available under the *See also* section at the end of this recipe.

How to do it...

Perform the following steps:

1. To start with, we load the necessary libraries:

```
import matplotlib.pyplot as plt
import numpy as np
import tensorflow as tf
from tensorflow import keras
```

2. Now we'll declare some dataset and model parameters and then some image transformation parameters, such as what size the random cropped images will take:

```
# Set dataset and model parameters
batch_size = 128
buffer_size= 128
epochs=20

#Set transformation parameters
crop_height = 24
crop_width = 24
```

3. Now we'll get the train and test images from the CIFAR-10 dataset using the `keras.datasets` API. This API provides few toy datasets where data fits in memory, so the data is expressed in NumPy arrays (the core Python library for scientific computing):

```
(x_train, y_train), (x_test, y_test) = tf.keras.datasets.cifar10.
load_data()
```

4. Next, we'll create a train and a test TensorFlow dataset from the NumPy arrays using `tf.data.Dataset`, so we can build a flexible and efficient pipeline for images using the `tf.data` API:

```
dataset_train = tf.data.Dataset.from_tensor_slices((x_train, y_
train))
dataset_test = tf.data.Dataset.from_tensor_slices((x_test, y_test))
```

5. We'll define a reading function that will load and distort the images slightly for training with TensorFlow's built-in image modification functions:

```
# Define CIFAR reader
def read_cifar_files(image, label):

    final_image = tf.image.resize_with_crop_or_pad(image, crop_
width, crop_height)
    final_image = image / 255

    # Randomly flip the image horizontally, change the brightness
and contrast
    final_image = tf.image.random_flip_left_right(final_image)
    final_image = tf.image.random_brightness(final_image,max_
delta=0.1)
    final_image = tf.image.random_contrast(final_image,lower=0.5,
upper=0.8)

    return final_image, label
```

6. Now that we have an image pipeline function and two TensorFlow datasets, we can initialize both the training image pipeline and the test image pipeline:

```
dataset_train_processed = dataset_train.shuffle(buffer_size).
batch(batch_size).map(read_cifar_files)
dataset_test_processed = dataset_test.batch(batch_size).map(lambda
image,label: read_cifar_files(image, label, False))
```

 Note that, in this example, our input data fits in memory so we use the `from_tensor_slices()` method to convert all the images into `tf.Tensor`. But the `tf.data` API allows processing large datasets that do not fit in memory. The iteration over the dataset happens in a streaming fashion.

7. Next, we can create our sequential model. The model we will use has two convolutional layers followed by three fully connected layers. The two convolutional layers will create 64 features each. The first fully connected layer will connect the second convolutional layer with 384 hidden nodes. The second fully connected operation will connect those 384 hidden nodes to 192 hidden nodes. The final hidden layer operation will then connect the 192 nodes to the 10 output classes we are trying to predict. We will use the softmax function at the last layer because a picture can only take on exactly one category, so the output should be a probability distribution over the 10 targets:

```
model = keras.Sequential(
    [# First Conv-ReLU-Conv-ReLU-MaxPool Layer
    tf.keras.layers.Conv2D(input_shape=[32,32,3],
                            filters=32,
                            kernel_size=3,
                            padding='SAME',
                            activation="relu",
                            kernel_initializer='he_uniform',
                            name="C1"),
    tf.keras.layers.Conv2D(filters=32,
                            kernel_size=3,
                            padding='SAME',
                            activation="relu",
                            kernel_initializer='he_uniform',
                            name="C2"),
    tf.keras.layers.MaxPool2D((2,2),
                            name="P1"),
    tf.keras.layers.Dropout(0.2),
    # Second Conv-ReLU-Conv-ReLU-MaxPool Layer
    tf.keras.layers.Conv2D(filters=64,
                            kernel_size=3,
                            padding='SAME',
                            activation="relu",
                            kernel_initializer='he_uniform',
                            name="C3"),
    tf.keras.layers.Conv2D(filters=64,
                            kernel_size=3,
                            padding='SAME',
                            activation="relu",
                            kernel_initializer='he_uniform',
                            name="C4"),
```

```
        tf.keras.layers.MaxPool2D((2,2),
                                  name="P2"),
      tf.keras.layers.Dropout(0.2),
    # Third Conv-ReLU-Conv-ReLU-MaxPool Layer
     tf.keras.layers.Conv2D(filters=128,
                            kernel_size=3,
                            padding='SAME',
                            activation="relu",
                            kernel_initializer='he_uniform',
                            name="C5"),
    tf.keras.layers.Conv2D(filters=128,
                           kernel_size=3,
                           padding='SAME',
                           activation="relu",
                           kernel_initializer='he_uniform',
                           name="C6"),
      tf.keras.layers.MaxPool2D((2,2),
                                name="P3"),
      tf.keras.layers.Dropout(0.2),
      # Flatten Layer
      tf.keras.layers.Flatten(name="FLATTEN"),
      # Fully Connected Layer
      tf.keras.layers.Dense(units=128,
                            activation="relu",
                            name="D1"),
    tf.keras.layers.Dropout(0.2),
    # Final Fully Connected Layer
    tf.keras.layers.Dense(units=10,
                          activation="softmax",
                          name="OUTPUT")
    ])
```

8. Now we'll compile our model. Our loss will be the categorical cross-entropy loss. We add an accuracy metric that takes in the predicted logits from the model and the actual targets and returns the accuracy for recording statistics on the train/test sets. We also run the summary method to print a summary page:

```
model.compile(loss="sparse_categorical_crossentropy",
    metrics=["accuracy"]
)
model.summary()
```

```
Model: "sequential_1"

Layer (type)                  Output Shape              Param #
=================================================================
C1 (Conv2D)                   (None, 32, 32, 32)        896

C2 (Conv2D)                   (None, 32, 32, 32)        9248

P1 (MaxPooling2D)             (None, 16, 16, 32)        0

dropout_2 (Dropout)           (None, 16, 16, 32)        0

C3 (Conv2D)                   (None, 16, 16, 64)        18496

C4 (Conv2D)                   (None, 16, 16, 64)        36928

P2 (MaxPooling2D)             (None, 8, 8, 64)          0

dropout_3 (Dropout)           (None, 8, 8, 64)          0

C5 (Conv2D)                   (None, 8, 8, 128)         73856

C6 (Conv2D)                   (None, 8, 8, 128)         147584

P3 (MaxPooling2D)             (None, 4, 4, 128)         0

dropout_4 (Dropout)           (None, 4, 4, 128)         0

FLATTEN (Flatten)             (None, 2048)              0

D1 (Dense)                    (None, 128)               262272

dropout_5 (Dropout)           (None, 128)               0

OUTPUT (Dense)                (None, 10)                1290
=================================================================
Total params: 550,570
Trainable params: 550,570
Non-trainable params: 0
```

Figure 8.7: The model summary is composed of 3 VGG blocks
(a VGG – Visual Geometry Group – block is a sequence of convolutional layers,
followed by a max pooling layer for spatial downsampling), followed by a classifier.

9. We now fit the model, looping through our training and test input pipelines. We will save the training loss and the test accuracy:

```
history = model.fit(dataset_train_processed,
                    validation_data=dataset_test_processed,
                    epochs=epochs)
```

10. Finally, here is some `Matplotlib` code that will plot the loss and test accuracy throughout the training:

```
# Print loss and accuracy
# Matlotlib code to plot the loss and accuracy
epochs_indices = range(0, 10, 1)
```

```
# Plot loss over time
plt.plot(epochs_indices, history.history["loss"], 'k-')
plt.title('Softmax Loss per Epoch')
plt.xlabel('Epoch')
plt.ylabel('Softmax Loss')
plt.show()

# Plot accuracy over time
plt.plot(epochs_indices, history.history["val_accuracy"], 'k-')
plt.title('Test Accuracy per Epoch')
plt.xlabel('Epoch')
plt.ylabel('Accuracy')
plt.show()
```

We get the following plots for this recipe:

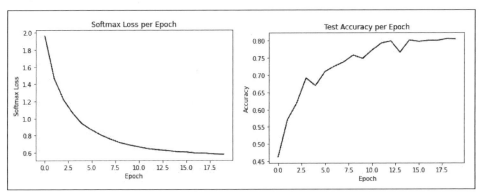

Figure 8.8: The training loss is on the left and the test accuracy is on the right.
For the CIFAR-10 image recognition CNN, we were able to achieve a model
that reaches around 80% accuracy on the test set.

How it works...

After we downloaded the CIFAR-10 data, we established an image pipeline. We used this train and test pipeline to try to predict the correct category of the images. By the end, the model had achieved around 80% accuracy on the test set. We can achieve better accuracy by using more data, fine-tuning the optimizers, or adding more epochs.

See also

► For more information about the CIFAR-10 dataset, please see *Learning Multiple Layers of Features from Tiny Images*, Alex Krizhevsky, 2009: `https://www.cs.toronto.edu/~kriz/learning-features-2009-TR.pdf`.

▶ The tf.data TensorFlow tutorial: https://www.tensorflow.org/guide/data.

▶ Introduction to Keras for Engineers (data loading and preprocessing): https://keras.io/getting_started/intro_to_keras_for_engineers/#data-loading-amp-preprocessing.

Retraining existing CNN models

Training a new image recognition model from scratch requires a lot of time and computational power. If we can take a pre-trained network and retrain it with our images, it may save us computational time. For this recipe, we will show how to use a pre-trained TensorFlow image recognition model and fine-tune it to work on a different set of images.

We will illustrate how to use transfer learning from a pre-trained network for CIFAR-10. The idea is to reuse the weights and structure of the prior model from the convolutional layers and retrain the fully connected layers at the top of the network. This method is called **fine-tuning**.

Getting ready

The CNN network we are going to employ uses a very popular architecture called **Inception**. The Inception CNN model was created by Google and has performed very well on many image recognition benchmarks. For details, see the paper referenced in the second bullet point of the *See also* section.

The main Python script we will cover shows how to get CIFAR-10 image data and transform it into the Inception retraining format. After that, we will reiterate how to train the Inception v3 network on our images.

How to do it...

Perform the following steps:

1. We'll start by loading the necessary libraries:

```
import tensorflow as tf
from tensorflow import keras

from tensorflow.keras.applications.inception_v3 import InceptionV3
from tensorflow.keras.applications.inception_v3 import preprocess_
input, decode_predictions
```

2. We'll now set the parameters used later by the tf.data.Dataset API:

```
batch_size = 32
buffer_size= 1000
```

3. Now, we'll download the CIFAR-10 data, and we'll also declare the 10 categories to reference when saving the images later on:

```
(x_train, y_train), (x_test, y_test) = tf.keras.datasets.cifar10.
load_data()

objects = ['airplane', 'automobile', 'bird', 'cat', 'deer',
           'dog', 'frog', 'horse', 'ship', 'truck']
```

4. Then, we'll initialize the data pipeline using `tf.data.Dataset` for the train and test datasets:

```
dataset_train = tf.data.Dataset.from_tensor_slices((x_train, y_
train))
dataset_test = tf.data.Dataset.from_tensor_slices((x_test, y_test))
```

5. Inception v3 is pretrained on the ImageNet dataset, so our CIFAR-10 images must match the format of these images. The width and height expected should be no smaller than 75, so we will resize our images to *75x75* spatial size. Then, the images should be normalized, so we will apply the inception preprocessing task (the `preprocess_input` method) on each image.

```
def preprocess_cifar10(img, label):
    img = tf.cast(img, tf.float32)
    img = tf.image.resize(img, (75, 75))

    return tf.keras.applications.inception_v3.preprocess_input(img) ,
label

dataset_train_processed = dataset_train.shuffle(buffer_size).
batch(batch_size).map(preprocess_cifar10)
dataset_test_processed = dataset_test.batch(batch_size).
map(preprocess_cifar10)
```

6. Now, we will create our model based on the InceptionV3 model. We will load the InceptionV3 model using the `tensorflow.keras.applications` API. This API contains pre-trained deep learning models that can be used for prediction, feature extraction, and fine-tuning. Then, we will load the weights without the classification head.

```
inception_model = InceptionV3(
    include_top=False,
    weights="imagenet",
    input_shape=(75,75,3)
)
```

7. We build our own model on top of the InceptionV3 model by adding a classifier with three fully connected layers.

```
x = inception_model.output
x= keras.layers.GlobalAveragePooling2D()(x)
x = keras.layers.Dense(1024, activation="relu")(x)
x = keras.layers.Dense(128, activation="relu")(x)
output = keras.layers.Dense(10, activation="softmax")(x)


model=keras.Model(inputs=inception_model.input, outputs = output)
```

8. We'll set the base layers in Inception as not trainable. Only the classifier weights will be updated during the back-propagation phase (not the Inception weights):

```
for inception_layer in inception_model.layers:
    inception_layer.trainable= False
```

9. Now we'll compile our model. Our loss will be the categorical cross-entropy loss. We add an accuracy metric that takes in the predicted logits from the model and the actual targets and returns the accuracy for recording statistics on the train/test sets:

```
model.compile(optimizer="adam", loss="sparse_categorical_
crossentropy", metrics=["accuracy"])
```

10. We'll now fit the model, looping through our training and test input pipelines:

```
model.fit(x=dataset_train_processed ,
          validation_data=dataset_test_processed)
```

11. By the end, the model had achieved around 63% accuracy on the test set:

```
loss: 1.1316 - accuracy: 0.6018 - val_loss: 1.0361 - val_accuracy:
0.6366...
```

How it works...

After we downloaded the CIFAR-10 data, we established an image pipeline to convert the images into the required Inception format. We added a classifier on top of the InceptionV3 model and trained it to predict the correct category of the CIFAR-10 images. By the end, the model had achieved around 63% accuracy on the test set. Remember that we are fine-tuning the model and retraining the fully connected layers at the top to fit our 10-category data.

▶ TensorFlow Inception-v3 documentation: `https://www.tensorflow.org/api_docs/python/tf/keras/applications/inception_v3`

▶ Keras Applications documentation: `https://keras.io/api/applications/`

▶ GoogLeNet Inception-v3 paper: `https://arxiv.org/abs/1512.00567`

Applying StyleNet and the neural style project

Once we have an image recognition CNN trained, we can use the network itself for some interesting data and image processing. StyleNet is a procedure that attempts to learn an image style from one picture and apply it to a second picture while keeping the second image structure (or content) intact. To do so, we have to find intermediate CNN nodes that correlate strongly with a style, separately from the content of the image.

StyleNet is a procedure that takes two images and applies the style of one image to the content of the second image. It is based on a famous paper by Leon Gatys in 2015, *A Neural Algorithm of Artistic Style* (refer to the first bullet point under the next *See also* section). The authors found a property in some CNNs containing intermediate layers. Some of them seem to encode the style of a picture, and some others its content. To this end, if we train the style layers on the style picture and the content layers on the original image, and back-propagate those calculated losses, we can change the original image to be more like the style image.

Getting ready

This recipe is an adapted version of the official TensorFlow neural style transfer, which is available under the *See also* section at the end of this recipe.

To accomplish this, we will use the network recommended by Gatys in *A Neural Algorithm of Artistic Style*; called **imagenet-vgg-19**.

How to do it...

Perform the following steps:

1. First, we'll start our Python script by loading the necessary libraries:

```
import imageio
import numpy as np
from skimage.transform import resize
import tensorflow as tf
```

```
import matplotlib.pyplot as plt
import matplotlib as mpl
import IPython.display as display
import PIL.Image
```

2. Then we can declare the locations of our two images: the original image and the style image. For our purposes, we will use the cover image of this book for the original image; for the style image, we will use *Starry Night* by Vincent van Gogh. Feel free to use any two pictures you want here. If you choose to use these pictures, they are available on the book's GitHub site, `https://github.com/PacktPublishing/Machine-Learning-Using-TensorFlow-Cookbook` (navigate to the StyleNet section):

```
content_image_file = 'images/book_cover.jpg'
style_image_file = 'images/starry_night.jpg'
```

3. Now we'll load the two images with `scipy` and change the style image to fit the content image dimensions:

```
# Read the images
content_image = imageio.imread(content_image_file)
style_image = imageio.imread(style_image_file)
content_image = tf.image.convert_image_dtype(content_image,
tf.float32)
style_image = tf.image.convert_image_dtype(style_image, tf.float32)

# Get shape of target and make the style image the same
target_shape = content_image.shape
style_image = resize(style_image, target_shape)
```

4. Then, we'll display the content and style images:

```
mpl.rcParams['figure.figsize'] = (12,12)
mpl.rcParams['axes.grid'] = False

plt.subplot(1, 2, 1)
plt.imshow(content_image)
plt.title("Content Image")

plt.subplot(1, 2, 2)
plt.imshow(style_image)
plt.title("Style Image")
```

Figure 8.9: Example content and style images

5. Now, we will load the VGG-19 model pre-trained on ImageNet without the classification head. We will use the `tensorflow.keras.applications` API. This API contains pre-trained deep learning models that can be used for prediction, feature extraction, and fine-tuning.

```
vgg = tf.keras.applications.VGG19(include_top=False,
weights='imagenet')
vgg.trainable = False
```

6. Next, we'll display the VGG-19 architecture:

```
[layer.name for layer in vgg.layers]
```

7. In neural style transfer, we want to apply the style of one image to the content of another image. A CNN is composed of several convolutional and pooling layers. The convolutional layers extract complex features and the pooling layers give spatial information. Gatys' paper recommends a few strategies for assigning intermediate layers to the content and style images. While we should keep `block4_conv2` for the content image, we can try different combinations of the other `blockX_conv1` layer outputs for the style image:

```
content_layers = ['block4_conv2', 'block5_conv2']
style_layers = ['block1_conv1', 'block2_conv1', 'block3_conv1',
'block4_conv1', 'block5_conv1']

num_content_layers = len(content_layers)
num_style_layers = len(style_layers)
```

8. While the values of the intermediate feature maps represent the content of an image, the style can be described by the means and correlations across these feature maps. Here, we define the Gram matrix to capture the style of an image. The Gram matrix measures the degree of correlation between each of the feature maps. This computation is done on each intermediate feature map and gets only information about the texture of an image. Note that we lose information about its spatial structure.

```
def gram_matrix(input_tensor):
  result = tf.linalg.einsum('bijc,bijd->bcd', input_tensor, input_
tensor)
  input_shape = tf.shape(input_tensor)
  num_locations = tf.cast(input_shape[1]*input_shape[2], tf.float32)
  return result/(num_locations)
```

9. Next, we build a model that returns style and content dictionaries that contain the name of each layer and associated content/style tensors. The Gram matrix is applied on the style layers:

```
class StyleContentModel(tf.keras.models.Model):
  def __init__(self, style_layers, content_layers):
    super(StyleContentModel, self).__init__()

    self.vgg = tf.keras.applications.VGG19(include_top=False,
weights='imagenet')

    outputs = [vgg.get_layer(name).output for name in style_layers +
content_layers]
    self.vgg = tf.keras.Model([vgg.input], outputs)
    self.style_layers = style_layers
    self.content_layers = content_layers
    self.num_style_layers = len(style_layers)
    self.vgg.trainable = False

  def call(self, inputs):
    "Expects float input in [0,1]"
    inputs = inputs*255.0
    inputs = inputs[tf.newaxis, :]
    preprocessed_input =
tf.keras.applications.vgg19.preprocess_input(inputs)
    outputs = self.vgg(preprocessed_input)
    style_outputs, content_outputs =
(outputs[:self.num_style_layers],

outputs[self.num_style_layers:])

    style_outputs = [gram_matrix(style_output)
```

```
                    for style_output in style_outputs]

        content_dict = {content_name:value
                        for content_name, value
                        in zip(self.content_layers, content_outputs)}

        style_dict = {style_name:value
                      for style_name, value
                      in zip(self.style_layers, style_outputs)}

        return {'content':content_dict, 'style':style_dict}
```

10. Set the style and content target values. They will be used in the loss computation:

```
extractor = StyleContentModel(style_layers, content_layers)
style_targets = extractor(style_image)['style']
content_targets = extractor(content_image)['content']
```

11. Adam and LBFGS usually have the same error and converge quickly but LBFGS is better than Adam with larger images. While the paper recommends using LBFGS, as our images are small, we will choose the Adam optimizer.

```
#Optimizer configuration
learning_rate = 0.05
beta1 = 0.9
beta2 = 0.999

opt = tf.optimizers.Adam(learning_rate=learning_rate, beta_1=beta1,
beta_2=beta2)
```

12. Next, we compute the total loss as a weighted sum of the content and the style losses:

```
content_weight = 5.0
style_weight = 1.0
```

13. The content loss will compare our original image and our current image (through the content layer features). The style loss will compare the style features we have pre-computed with the style features from the input image. The third and final loss term will help smooth out the image. We use total variation loss here to penalize dramatic changes in neighboring pixels, as follows:

```
def style_content_loss(outputs):
    style_outputs = outputs['style']
    content_outputs = outputs['content']
```

```
        style_loss = tf.add_n([tf.reduce_mean((style_outputs[name]-
    style_targets[name])**2)
                            for name in style_outputs.keys()])
    style_loss *= style_weight / num_style_layers

        content_loss = tf.add_n([tf.reduce_mean((content_outputs[name]-
    content_targets[name])**2)
                            for name in content_outputs.keys()])
    content_loss *= content_weight / num_content_layers
    loss = style_loss + content_loss
    return loss
```

14. Next, we declare a utility function. As we have a float image, we need to keep the pixel values between 0 and 1:

```
def clip_0_1(image):
  return tf.clip_by_value(image, clip_value_min=0.0, clip_value_
max=1.0)
```

15. Now, we declare another utility function to convert a tensor to an image:

```
def tensor_to_image(tensor):
  tensor = tensor*255
  tensor = np.array(tensor, dtype=np.uint8)
  if np.ndim(tensor)>3:
    assert tensor.shape[0] == 1
    tensor = tensor[0]
  return PIL.Image.fromarray(tensor)
```

16. Next, we use gradient tape to run the gradient descent, generate our new image, and display it, as follows:

```
epochs = 100

image = tf.Variable(content_image)

for generation in range(epochs):

    with tf.GradientTape() as tape:
        outputs = extractor(image)
        loss = style_content_loss(outputs)

    grad = tape.gradient(loss, image)
    opt.apply_gradients([(grad, image)])
    image.assign(clip_0_1(image))
```

```
    print(".", end='')

display.display(tensor_to_image(image))
```

Figure 8.10: Using the StyleNet algorithm to combine the book cover image with Starry Night

Note that a different style of emphasis can be used by changing the content and style weighting.

How it works...

We first loaded the two images, then loaded the pre-trained network weights and assigned layers to the content and style images. We calculated three loss functions: a content image loss, a style loss, and a total variation loss. Then we trained random noise pictures to use the style of the style image and the content of the original image. Style transfer can be used in photo and video editing applications, games, art, virtual reality, and so on. For example, at the 2019 Game Developers Conference, Google introduced Stadia to change a game's art in real time. A clip of it live in action is available under the last bullet of the *See also* section at the end of this recipe.

See also

▶ *A Neural Algorithm of Artistic Style* by Gatys, Ecker, Bethge. 2015: `https://arxiv.org/abs/1508.06576`

▶ A well-recommended video of a presentation by Leon Gatys at CVPR 2016 (*Computer Vision and Pattern Recognition*) can be viewed here: `https://www.youtube.com/watch?v=UFffxcCQMPQ`

▶ To view the original TensorFlow code for the neural style transfer process, please see `https://www.tensorflow.org/tutorials/generative/style_transfer`

▶ To go deeper inside the theory, please see `https://towardsdatascience.com/neural-style-transfer-tutorial-part-1-f5cd3315fa7f`

▶ Google Stadia – Style Transfer ML: `https://stadiasource.com/article/2/Stadia-Introducing-Style-Transfer-ML-GDC2019`

Implementing DeepDream

Another use for trained CNNs is exploiting the fact that some intermediate nodes detect features of labels (for instance, a cat's ear, or a bird's feather). Using this fact, we can find ways to transform any image to reflect those node features for any node we choose. This recipe is an adapted version of the official TensorFlow DeepDream tutorial (refer to the first bullet point in the next *See also* section). Feel free to visit the Google AI blog post written by DeepDream's creator, named Alexander Mordvintsev (second bullet point in the next *See also* section). The hope is that we can prepare you to use the DeepDream algorithm to explore CNNs, and features created in them.

Getting ready

Originally, this technique was invented to better understand how a CNN sees. The goal of DeepDream is to over-interpret the patterns that the model detects and generate inspiring visual content with surreal patterns. This algorithm is a new kind of psychedelic art.

How to do it...

Perform the following steps:

1. To get started with DeepDream, we'll start by loading the necessary libraries:

```
import numpy as np
import PIL.Image
import imageio
```

```
import matplotlib.pyplot as plt
import matplotlib as mpl
import tensorflow as tf
import IPython.display as display
```

2. We'll prepare the image to dreamify. We'll read the original image, reshape it to 500 maximum dimensions, and display it:

```
# Read the images
original_img_file = path + 'images/book_cover.jpg'
original_img = imageio.imread(original_img_file)

# Reshape to 500 max dimension
new_shape = tf.cast((500, 500 * original_img.shape[1] / original_
img.shape[0]), tf.int32)
original_img = tf.image.resize(original_img, new_shape,
method='nearest').numpy()

# Display the image
mpl.rcParams['figure.figsize'] = (20,6)
mpl.rcParams['axes.grid'] = False

plt.imshow(original_img)
plt.title("Original Image")
```

3. We'll load the Inception model pre-trained on ImageNet without the classification head. We will use the `tf.keras.applications` API:

```
inception_model = tf.keras.applications.InceptionV3(include_
top=False, weights='imagenet')
```

4. We summarize the model. We can note that the Inception model is quite large:

```
inception_model.summary()
```

5. Next, we will select the convolutional layers to use for DeepDream processing later. In a CNN, the earlier layers extract basic features such as edges, shapes, textures, and so on, while the deeper layers extract high-level features such as clouds, trees, or birds. To create a DeepDream image, we will focus on the layers where the convolutions are mixed. Now, we'll create the feature extraction model with the two mixed layers as outputs:

```
names = ['mixed3', 'mixed5']
layers = [inception_model.get_layer(name).output for name in names]
deep_dream_model = tf.keras.Model(inputs=inception_model.input,
outputs=layers)
```

6. Now we will define the loss function that returns the sum of all output layers:

```
def compute_loss(img, model):
  # Add a dimension to the image to have a batch of size 1.
  img_batch = tf.expand_dims(img, axis=0)

  # Apply the model to the images and get the outputs to retrieve
the activation.
  layer_activations = model(img_batch)

  # Compute the loss for each layer
  losses = []
  for act in layer_activations:
    loss = tf.math.reduce_mean(act)
    losses.append(loss)

  return  tf.reduce_sum(losses)
```

7. We declare two utility functions that undo the scaling and display a processed image:

```
def deprocess(img):
  img = 255*(img + 1.0)/2.0
  return tf.cast(img, tf.uint8)

def show(img):
  display.display(PIL.Image.fromarray(np.array(img)))
```

8. We'll now apply the gradient ascent process. In DeepDream, we don't minimize the loss using gradient descent, but we maximize the activation of these layers by maximizing their loss via gradient ascent. So, we'll over-interpret the patterns that the model detects, and we'll generate inspiring visual content with surreal patterns:

```
def run_deep_dream(image, steps=100, step_size=0.01):
    # Apply the Inception preprocessing
    image = tf.keras.applications.inception_v3.preprocess_
input(image)
    image = tf.convert_to_tensor(image)

    loss = tf.constant(0.0)
    for n in tf.range(steps):
        # We use gradient tape to track TensorFlow computations
        with tf.GradientTape() as tape:
            # We use watch to force TensorFlow to track the image
            tape.watch(image)
            # We compute the loss
            loss = compute_loss(image, deep_dream_model)
```

```python
        # Compute the gradients
        gradients = tape.gradient(loss, image)

        # Normalize the gradients.
        gradients /= tf.math.reduce_std(gradients) + 1e-8

        # Perform the gradient ascent by directly adding the
gradients to the image
        image = image + gradients*step_size
        image = tf.clip_by_value(image, -1, 1)

        # Display the intermediate image
        if (n % 100 ==0):
            display.clear_output(wait=True)
            show(deprocess(image))
            print ("Step {}, loss {}".format(n, loss))

    # Display the final image
    result = deprocess(image)
    display.clear_output(wait=True)
    show(result)

    return result
```

9. Then, we will run DeepDream on the original image:

```python
dream_img = run_deep_dream(image=original_img,
                          steps=100, step_size=0.01)
```

The output is as follows:

Figure 8.11: DeepDream applied to the original image

While the result is good, it could be better! We notice that the image output is noisy; the patterns seem to be applied at the same granularity and the output is in low resolution.

10. To make images better, we can use the concept of octaves. We perform gradient ascent on the same image resized multiple times (each step of increasing the size of an image is an octave improvement). Using this process, the detected features at a smaller scale could be applied to patterns at higher scales with more details.

```
OCTAVE_SCALE = 1.30

image = tf.constant(np.array(original_img))
base_shape = tf.shape(image)[:-1]
float_base_shape = tf.cast(base_shape, tf.float32)

for n in range(-2, 3):
    # Increase the size of the image
    new_shape = tf.cast(float_base_shape*(OCTAVE_SCALE**n),
tf.int32)
    image = tf.image.resize(image, new_shape).numpy()

    # Apply deep dream
    image = run_deep_dream(image=image, steps=50, step_size=0.01)

# Display output
display.clear_output(wait=True)
image = tf.image.resize(image, base_shape)
image = tf.image.convert_image_dtype(image/255.0, dtype=tf.uint8)
show(image)
```

The output is as follows:

Figure 8.12: DeepDream with the concept of octaves applied to the original image

By using the concept of octaves, things get rather interesting: the output is less noisy and the network amplifies the patterns it sees better.

There's more...

We urge the reader to use the official DeepDream tutorials as a source of further information, and also to visit the original Google research blog post on DeepDream (refer to the following *See also* section).

See also

- ▶ The TensorFlow tutorial on DeepDream: `https://www.tensorflow.org/tutorials/generative/deepdream`
- ▶ The original Google research blog post on DeepDream: `https://research.googleblog.com/2015/06/inceptionism-going-deeper-into-neural.html`

9
Recurrent Neural Networks

Recurrent Neural Networks (**RNNs**) are the primary modern approach for modeling data that is sequential in nature. The word "recurrent" in the name of the architecture class refers to the fact that the output of the current step becomes the input to the next one (and potentially further ones as well). At each element in the sequence, the model considers both the current input and what it "remembers" about the preceding elements.

Natural Language Processing (**NLP**) tasks are one of the primary areas of application for RNNs: if you are reading through this very sentence, you are picking up the context of each word from the words that came before it. NLP models based on RNNs can build on this approach to achieve generative tasks, such as novel text creation, as well as predictive ones such as sentiment classification or machine translation.

In this chapter, we'll cover the following topics:

- ▶ Text generation
- ▶ Sentiment classification
- ▶ Time series – stock price prediction
- ▶ Open-domain question answering

The first topic we'll tackle is text generation: it demonstrates quite easily how we can use an RNN to generate novel content, and can therefore serve as a gentle introduction to RNNs.

Text generation

One of the best-known applications used to demonstrate the strength of RNNs is generating novel text (we will return to this application later, in the chapter on Transformer architectures).

In this recipe, we will use a **Long Short-Term Memory** (**LSTM**) architecture—a popular variant of RNNs—to build a text generation model. The name LSTM comes from the motivation for their development: "vanilla" RNNs struggled with long dependencies (known as the vanishing gradient problem) and the architectural solution of LSTM solved that. LSTM models achieve that by maintaining a cell state, as well as a "carry" to ensure that the signal (in the form of a gradient) is not lost as the sequence is processed. At each time step, the LSTM model considers the current word, the carry, and the cell state jointly.

The topic itself is not that trivial, but for practical purposes, full comprehension of the structural design is not essential. It suffices to keep in mind that an LSTM cell allows past information to be reinjected at a later point in time.

We will train our model on the NYT comment and headlines dataset (`https://www.kaggle.com/aashita/nyt-comments`) and will use it to generate new headlines. We chose this dataset for its moderate size (the recipe should be reproducible without access to a powerful workstation) and availability (Kaggle is freely accessible, unlike some data sources accessible only via paywall).

How to do it...

As usual, first we import the necessary packages.

```
import tensorflow as tf
from tensorflow import keras

# keras module for building LSTM
from keras.preprocessing.sequence import pad_sequences
from keras.layers import Embedding, LSTM, Dense
from keras.preprocessing.text import Tokenizer
from keras.callbacks import EarlyStopping
from keras.models import Sequential
import keras.utils as ku
```

We want to make sure our results are reproducible – due to the nature of the interdependencies within the Python deep learning universe, we need to initialize multiple random mechanisms.

```
import pandas as pd
import string, os
```

```
import warnings
warnings.filterwarnings("ignore")
warnings.simplefilter(action='ignore', category=FutureWarning)
```

The next step involves importing the necessary functionality from Keras itself:

```
from keras.preprocessing.sequence import pad_sequences
from keras.layers import Embedding, LSTM, Dense
from keras.preprocessing.text import Tokenizer
from keras.callbacks import EarlyStopping
from keras.models import Sequential
import keras.utils as ku
```

Finally, it is typically convenient—if not always in line with what purists deem best practice—to customize the level of warnings displayed in the execution of our code. It is mainly to deal with ubiquitous warnings around assigning value to a subset of a DataFrame: clean demonstration is more important in the current context than sticking to the coding standards expected in a production environment:

```
import warnings
warnings.filterwarnings("ignore")
warnings.simplefilter(action='ignore', category=FutureWarning)
```

We shall define some functions that will streamline the code later on. First, let's clean the text:

```
def clean_text(txt):
    txt = "".join(v for v in txt if v not in string.punctuation).lower()
    txt = txt.encode("utf8").decode("ascii",'ignore')
    return txt
```

Let's use a wrapper around the built-in TensorFlow tokenizer as follows:

```
def get_sequence_of_tokens(corpus):
    ## tokenization
    tokenizer.fit_on_texts(corpus)
    total_words = len(tokenizer.word_index) + 1

    ## convert data to sequence of tokens
    input_sequences = []
    for line in corpus:
        token_list = tokenizer.texts_to_sequences([line])[0]
        for i in range(1, len(token_list)):
            n_gram_sequence = token_list[:i+1]
            input_sequences.append(n_gram_sequence)
    return input_sequences, total_words
```

A frequently useful step is to wrap up a model-building step inside a function:

```python
def create_model(max_sequence_len, total_words):
    input_len = max_sequence_len - 1
    model = Sequential()

    model.add(Embedding(total_words, 10, input_length=input_len))

    model.add(LSTM(100))

    model.add(Dense(total_words, activation='softmax'))

    model.compile(loss='categorical_crossentropy', optimizer='adam')

    return model
```

The following is some boilerplate for padding the sequences (the utility of this will become clearer in the course of the recipe):

```python
def generate_padded_sequences(input_sequences):
    max_sequence_len = max([len(x) for x in input_sequences])
    input_sequences = np.array(pad_sequences(input_sequences,
                        maxlen=max_sequence_len, padding='pre'))

    predictors, label = input_sequences[:,:-1],input_sequences[:,-1]
    label = ku.to_categorical(label, num_classes=total_words)
    return predictors, label, max_sequence_len
```

Finally, we create a function that will be used to generate text from our fitted model:

```python
def generate_text(seed_text, next_words, model, max_sequence_len):
    for _ in range(next_words):
        token_list = tokenizer.texts_to_sequences([seed_text])[0]
        token_list = pad_sequences([token_list],
                    maxlen=max_sequence_len-1, padding='pre')
        predicted = model.predict_classes(token_list, verbose=0)

        output_word = ""
        for word,index in tokenizer.word_index.items():
            if index == predicted:
                output_word = word
                break
        seed_text += " "+output_word
    return seed_text.title()
```

The next step is to load our dataset (the `break` clause serves as a fast way to only pick up articles and not comment datasets):

```
curr_dir = '../input/'
all_headlines = []
for filename in os.listdir(curr_dir):
    if 'Articles' in filename:
        article_df = pd.read_csv(curr_dir + filename)
        all_headlines.extend(list(article_df.headline.values))
        break

all_headlines[:10]
```

We can inspect the first few elements as follows:

```
['The Opioid Crisis Foretold',
 'The Business Deals That Could Imperil Trump',
 'Adapting to American Decline',
 'The Republicans' Big Senate Mess',
 'States Are Doing What Scott Pruitt Won't',
 'Fake Pearls, Real Heart',
 'Fear Beyond Starbucks',
 'Variety: Puns and Anagrams',
 'E.P.A. Chief's Ethics Woes Have Echoes in His Past',
 'Where Facebook Rumors Fuel Thirst for Revenge']
```

As is usually the case with real-life text data, we need to clean the input text. For simplicity, we perform only the basic preprocessing: punctuation removal and conversion of all words to lowercase:

```
corpus = [clean_text(x) for x in all_headlines]
```

This is what the top 10 rows look like after the cleaning operation:

```
corpus[:10]

['the opioid crisis foretold',
 'the business deals that could imperil trump',
 'adapting to american decline',
 'the republicans big senate mess',
 'states are doing what scott pruitt wont',
 'fake pearls real heart',
 'fear beyond starbucks',
 'variety puns and anagrams',
 'epa chiefs ethics woes have echoes in his past',
 'where facebook rumors fuel thirst for revenge']
```

The next step is tokenization. Language models require input data in the form of sequences—given a sequence of words (tokens), the generation task boils down to predicting the next most likely token in the context. We can utilize the built-in tokenizer from the `preprocessing` module of Keras.

After cleaning up, we tokenize the input text: this is a process of extracting individual tokens (words or terms) from a corpus. We utilize the built-in tokenizer to retrieve the tokens and their respective indices. Each document is converted into a series of tokens:

```
tokenizer = Tokenizer()

inp_sequences, total_words = get_sequence_of_tokens(corpus)

inp_sequences[:10]
[[1, 708],
 [1, 708, 251],
 [1, 708, 251, 369],
 [1, 370],
 [1, 370, 709],
 [1, 370, 709, 29],
 [1, 370, 709, 29, 136],
 [1, 370, 709, 29, 136, 710],
 [1, 370, 709, 29, 136, 710, 10],
 [711, 5]]
```

The vectors like `[1,708]`, `[1,708, 251]` represent the n-grams generated from the input data, where an integer is an index of the token in the overall vocabulary generated from the corpus.

We have transformed our dataset into a format of sequences of tokens—possibly of different lengths. There are two choices: go with RaggedTensors (which are a slightly more advanced topic in terms of usage) or equalize the lengths to adhere to the standard requirement of most RNN models. For the sake of simplicity of presentation, we proceed with the latter solution: padding sequences shorter than the threshold using the `pad_sequence` function. This step is easily combined with formatting the data into predictors and labels:

```
predictors, label, max_sequence_len =
                          generate_padded_sequences(inp_sequences)
```

We utilize a simple LSTM architecture using the Sequential API:

1. Input layer: takes the tokenized sequence

2. LSTM layer: generates the output using LSTM units – we take 100 as a default value for the sake of demonstration, but the parameter (along with several others) is customizable

3. Dropout layer: we regularize the LSTM output to reduce the risk of overfitting

4. Output layer: generates the most likely output token:

```
model = create_model(max_sequence_len, total_words)
model.summary()
```

Layer (type)	Output Shape	Param #
embedding_1 (Embedding)	(None, 23, 10)	31340
lstm_1 (LSTM)	(None, 100)	44400
dense_1 (Dense)	(None, 3134)	316534

```
Total params: 392,274
Trainable params: 392,274
Non-trainable params: 0
```

We can now train our model using the standard Keras syntax:

```
model.fit(predictors, label, epochs=100, verbose=2)
```

Now that we have a fitted model, we can examine its performance: how good are the headlines generated by our LSTM based on a seed text? We achieve this by tokenizing the seed text, padding the sequence, and passing it into the model to obtain our predictions:

```
print (generate_text("united states", 5, model, max_sequence_len))

United States Shouldnt Sit Still An Atlantic

print (generate_text("president trump", 5, model, max_sequence_len))

President Trump Vs Congress Bird Moving One

print (generate_text("joe biden", 8, model, max_sequence_len))

Joe Biden Infuses The Constitution Invaded Canada Unique Memorial Award

print (generate_text("india and china", 8, model, max_sequence_len))

India And China Deal And The Young Think Again To It

print (generate_text("european union", 4, model, max_sequence_len))

European Union Infuses The Constitution Invaded
```

As you can see, even with a relatively simple setup (a moderately sized dataset and a vanilla model), we can generate text that looks somewhat realistic. Further fine-tuning would of course allow for more sophisticated content, which is a topic we will cover in *Chapter 10, Transformers.*

See also

There are multiple excellent resources online for learning about RNNs:

▶ For an excellent introduction – with great examples – see the post by Andrej Karpathy: `http://karpathy.github.io/2015/05/21/rnn-effectiveness/`

▶ A curated list of resources (tutorials, repositories) can be found at `https://github.com/kjw0612/awesome-rnn`

▶ Another great introduction can be found at `https://medium.com/@humble_bee/rnn-recurrent-neural-networks-lstm-842ba7205bbf`

Sentiment classification

A popular task in NLP is sentiment classification: based on the content of a text snippet, identify the sentiment expressed therein. Practical applications include analysis of reviews, survey responses, social media comments, or healthcare materials.

We will train our network on the Sentiment140 dataset introduced in `https://www-cs.stanford.edu/people/alecmgo/papers/TwitterDistantSupervision09.pdf`, which contains 1.6 million tweets annotated with three classes: negative, neutral, and positive. In order to avoid issues with locale, we standardize the encoding (this part is best done from the console level and not inside the notebook). The logic is the following: the original dataset contains raw text that—by its very nature—can contain non-standard characters (such as emojis, which are obviously common in social media communication). We want to convert the text to UTF8—the de facto standard for NLP in English. The fastest way to do it is by using a Linux command-line functionality:

▶ Iconv is a standard tool for conversion between encodings

▶ The -f and -t flags denote the input encoding and the target one, respectively

▶ -o specifies the output file:

```
iconv -f LATIN1 -t UTF8 training.1600000.processed.noemoticon.csv -o
training_cleaned.csv
```

How to do it...

We begin by importing the necessary packages as follows:

```
import json
import tensorflow as tf
import csv
import random
import numpy as np
import pandas as pd
import matplotlib.pyplot as plt


from tensorflow.keras.preprocessing.text import Tokenizer
from tensorflow.keras.preprocessing.sequence import pad_sequences
from tensorflow.keras.utils import to_categorical
from tensorflow.keras import regularizers
```

Next, we define the hyperparameters of our model:

- ▶ The embedding dimension is the size of word embedding we will use. In this recipe, we will use GloVe: an unsupervised learning algorithm trained on aggregated word co-occurrence statistics from a combined corpus of Wikipedia and Gigaword. The resulting vectors for (English) words give us an efficient way of representing text and are commonly referred to as embeddings.

- ▶ `max_length` and `padding_type` are parameters specifying how we pad the sequences (see previous recipe).

- ▶ `training_size` specifies the size of the target corpus.

- ▶ `test_portion` defines the proportion of the data we will use as a holdout.

- ▶ `dropout_val` and `nof_units` are hyperparameters for the model:

```
embedding_dim = 100
max_length = 16
trunc_type='post'
padding_type='post'
oov_tok = "<OOV>"
training_size=160000
test_portion=.1

num_epochs = 50

dropout_val = 0.2
nof_units = 64
```

Let's encapsulate the model creation step into a function. We define a fairly simple one for our classification task—an embedding layer, followed by regularization and convolution, pooling, and then the RNN layer:

```python
def create_model(dropout_val, nof_units):


    model = tf.keras.Sequential([
    tf.keras.layers.Embedding(vocab_size+1, embedding_dim, input_
length=max_length, weights=[embeddings_matrix], trainable=False),
        tf.keras.layers.Dropout(dropout_val),
        tf.keras.layers.Conv1D(64, 5, activation='relu'),
        tf.keras.layers.MaxPooling1D(pool_size=4),
        tf.keras.layers.LSTM(nof_units),
        tf.keras.layers.Dense(1, activation='sigmoid')
        ])
    model.compile(loss='binary_crossentropy',optimizer='adam',
                    metrics=['accuracy'])

    return model
```

Collect the content of the corpus we will train on:

```python
num_sentences = 0

with open("../input/twitter-sentiment-clean-dataset/training_cleaned.csv")
as csvfile:
    reader = csv.reader(csvfile, delimiter=',')
    for row in reader:
        list_item=[]
        list_item.append(row[5])
        this_label=row[0]
        if this_label=='0':
            list_item.append(0)
        else:
            list_item.append(1)
        num_sentences = num_sentences + 1
        corpus.append(list_item)
```

Convert to sentence format:

```python
sentences=[]
labels=[]
random.shuffle(corpus)
for x in range(training_size):
    sentences.append(corpus[x][0])
    labels.append(corpus[x][1])
```

Tokenize the sentences:

```
tokenizer = Tokenizer()
tokenizer.fit_on_texts(sentences)
word_index = tokenizer.word_index
vocab_size = len(word_index)
sequences = tokenizer.texts_to_sequences(sentences)
```

Normalize the sentence lengths with padding (see previous section):

```
padded = pad_sequences(sequences, maxlen=max_length, padding=padding_type,
truncating=trunc_type)
```

Divide the dataset into training and holdout sets:

```
split = int(test_portion * training_size)
test_sequences = padded[0:split]
training_sequences = padded[split:training_size]
test_labels = labels[0:split]
training_labels = labels[split:training_size]
```

A crucial step in using RNN-based models for NLP applications is the `embeddings` matrix:

```
embeddings_index = {};
with open('../input/glove6b/glove.6B.100d.txt') as f:
    for line in f:
        values = line.split();
        word = values[0];
        coefs = np.asarray(values[1:], dtype='float32');
        embeddings_index[word] = coefs;

embeddings_matrix = np.zeros((vocab_size+1, embedding_dim));
for word, i in word_index.items():
    embedding_vector = embeddings_index.get(word);
    if embedding_vector is not None:
        embeddings_matrix[i] = embedding_vector;
```

With all the preparations completed, we can set up the model:

```
model = create_model(dropout_val, nof_units)
model.summary()

Model: "sequential"
```

```
Layer (type)                    Output Shape            Param #
=================================================================
embedding (Embedding)           (None, 16, 100)         13877100

dropout (Dropout)               (None, 16, 100)         0

conv1d (Conv1D)                 (None, 12, 64)          32064

max_pooling1d (MaxPooling1D)    (None, 3, 64)           0

lstm (LSTM)                     (None, 64)              33024

dense (Dense)                   (None, 1)               65
=================================================================
Total params: 13,942,253
Trainable params: 65,153
Non-trainable params: 13,877,100
```

Training is performed in the usual way:

```
num_epochs = 50
history = model.fit(training_sequences, training_labels, epochs=num_epochs,
validation_data=(test_sequences, test_labels), verbose=2)

Train on 144000 samples, validate on 16000 samples
Epoch 1/50
144000/144000 - 47s - loss: 0.5685 - acc: 0.6981 - val_loss: 0.5454 - val_
acc: 0.7142
Epoch 2/50
144000/144000 - 44s - loss: 0.5296 - acc: 0.7289 - val_loss: 0.5101 - val_
acc: 0.7419
Epoch 3/50
144000/144000 - 42s - loss: 0.5130 - acc: 0.7419 - val_loss: 0.5044 - val_
acc: 0.7481
Epoch 4/50
144000/144000 - 42s - loss: 0.5017 - acc: 0.7503 - val_loss: 0.5134 - val_
acc: 0.7421
Epoch 5/50
144000/144000 - 42s - loss: 0.4921 - acc: 0.7563 - val_loss: 0.5025 - val_
acc: 0.7518
Epoch 6/50
144000/144000 - 42s - loss: 0.4856 - acc: 0.7603 - val_loss: 0.5003 - val_
acc: 0.7509
```

We can also assess the quality of our model visually:

```
acc = history.history['acc']
val_acc = history.history['val_acc']
loss = history.history['loss']
val_loss = history.history['val_loss']
epochs = range(len(acc))

plt.plot(epochs, acc, 'r', label='Training accuracy')
plt.plot(epochs, val_acc, 'b', label='Validation accuracy')
plt.title('Training and validation accuracy')
plt.legend()
plt.figure()

plt.plot(epochs, loss, 'r', label='Training Loss')
plt.plot(epochs, val_loss, 'b', label='Validation Loss')
plt.title('Training and validation loss')
plt.legend()

plt.show()
```

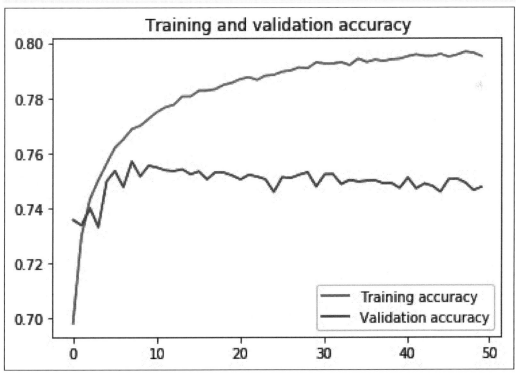

Figure 9.1: Training versus validation accuracy over epochs

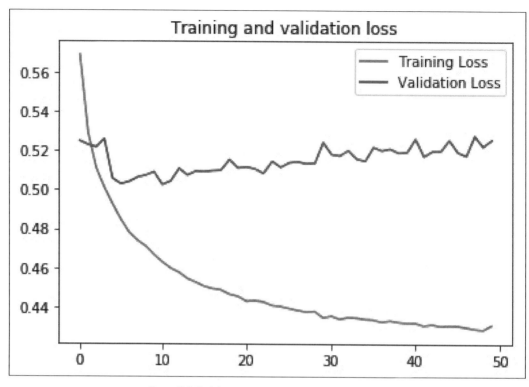

Figure 9.2: Training versus validation loss over epochs

As we can see from both graphs, the model already achieves good performance after a limited number of epochs and it stabilizes after that, with only minor fluctuations. Potential improvements would involve early stopping, and extending the size of the dataset.

See also

Readers interested in the applications of RNNs to sentiment classification can investigate the following resources:

- ▶ TensorFlow documentation tutorial: `https://www.tensorflow.org/tutorials/text/text_classification_rnn`

- ▶ `https://link.springer.com/chapter/10.1007/978-3-030-28364-3_49` is one of many articles demonstrating the application of RNNs to sentiment detection and it contains an extensive list of references

- ▶ GloVe documentation can be found at `https://nlp.stanford.edu/projects/glove/`

Stock price prediction

Sequential models such as RNNs are naturally well suited to time series prediction—and one of the most advertised applications is the prediction of financial quantities, especially prices of different financial instruments. In this recipe, we demonstrate how to apply LSTM to the problem of time series prediction. We will focus on the price of Bitcoin—the most popular cryptocurrency.

A disclaimer is in order: this is a demonstration example on a popular dataset. It is not intended as investment advice of any kind; building a reliable time series prediction model applicable in finance is a challenging endeavor, outside the scope of this book.

How to do it...

We begin by importing the necessary packages:

```
import numpy as np
import pandas as pd
from matplotlib import pyplot as plt

from keras.models import Sequential
from keras.layers import Dense
from keras.layers import LSTM

from sklearn.preprocessing import MinMaxScaler
```

The general parameters for our task are the future horizon of our prediction and the hyperparameter for the network:

```
prediction_days = 30
nof_units =4
```

As before, we will encapsulate our model creation step in a function. It accepts a single parameter, `units`, which is the dimension of the inner cells in LSTM:

```
def create_model(nunits):

    # Initialising the RNN
    regressor = Sequential()

    # Adding the input layer and the LSTM layer
    regressor.add(LSTM(units = nunits, activation = 'sigmoid', input_shape
= (None, 1)))
```

```
    # Adding the output layer
    regressor.add(Dense(units = 1))

    # Compiling the RNN
    regressor.compile(optimizer = 'adam', loss = 'mean_squared_error')

    return regressor
```

We can now proceed to load the data, with the usual formatting of the timestamp. For the sake of our demonstration, we will predict the average daily price—hence the grouping operation:

```
# Import the dataset and encode the date
df = pd.read_csv("../input/bitcoin-historical-data/bitstampUSD_1-min_
data_2012-01-01_to_2020-09-14.csv")
df['date'] = pd.to_datetime(df['Timestamp'],unit='s').dt.date
group = df.groupby('date')
Real_Price = group['Weighted_Price'].mean()
```

The next step is to split the data into training and test periods:

```
df_train= Real_Price[:len(Real_Price)-prediction_days]
df_test= Real_Price[len(Real_Price)-prediction_days:]
```

Preprocessing could theoretically be avoided, but it tends to help convergence in practice:

```
training_set = df_train.values
training_set = np.reshape(training_set, (len(training_set), 1))

sc = MinMaxScaler()
training_set = sc.fit_transform(training_set)
X_train = training_set[0:len(training_set)-1]
y_train = training_set[1:len(training_set)]
X_train = np.reshape(X_train, (len(X_train), 1, 1))
```

Fitting the model is straightforward:

```
regressor = create_model(nunits = nof_unit)

regressor.fit(X_train, y_train, batch_size = 5, epochs = 100)

Epoch 1/100
3147/3147 [==============================] - 6s 2ms/step - loss: 0.0319
Epoch 2/100
3147/3147 [==============================] - 3s 928us/step - loss: 0.0198
```

```
Epoch 3/100
3147/3147 [==============================] - 3s 985us/step - loss: 0.0089
Epoch 4/100
3147/3147 [==============================] - 3s 1ms/step - loss: 0.0023
Epoch 5/100
3147/3147 [==============================] - 3s 886us/step - loss: 3.3583e-
04
Epoch 6/100
3147/3147 [==============================] - 3s 957us/step - loss: 1.0990e-
04
Epoch 7/100
3147/3147 [==============================] - 3s 830us/step - loss: 1.0374e-
04
Epoch 8/100
```

With a fitted model we can generate a prediction over the forecast horizon, keeping in mind the need to invert our normalization so that the values are back on the original scale:

```
test_set = df_test.values
inputs = np.reshape(test_set, (len(test_set), 1))
inputs = sc.transform(inputs)
inputs = np.reshape(inputs, (len(inputs), 1, 1))
predicted_BTC_price = regressor.predict(inputs)
predicted_BTC_price = sc.inverse_transform(predicted_BTC_price)
```

This is what our forecasted results look like:

```
plt.figure(figsize=(25,15), dpi=80, facecolor='w', edgecolor='k')
ax = plt.gca()
plt.plot(test_set, color = 'red', label = 'Real BTC Price')
plt.plot(predicted_BTC_price, color = 'blue', label = 'Predicted BTC
Price')
plt.title('BTC Price Prediction', fontsize=40)
df_test = df_test.reset_index()
x=df_test.index
labels = df_test['date']
plt.xticks(x, labels, rotation = 'vertical')
for tick in ax.xaxis.get_major_ticks():
    tick.label1.set_fontsize(18)
for tick in ax.yaxis.get_major_ticks():
    tick.label1.set_fontsize(18)
plt.xlabel('Time', fontsize=40)
plt.ylabel('BTC Price(USD)', fontsize=40)
plt.legend(loc=2, prop={'size': 25})
plt.show()
```

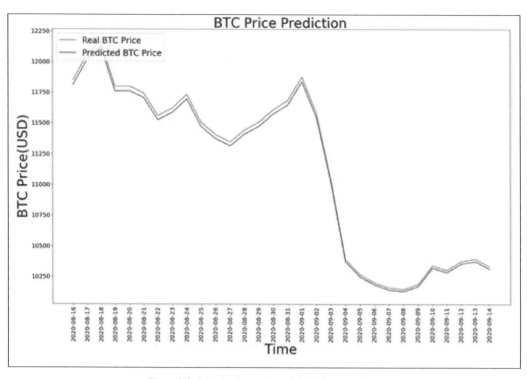

Figure 9.3: Actual price and predicted price over time

Overall, it is clear that even a simple model can generate a reasonable prediction—with an important caveat: this approach only works as long as the environment is stationary, that is, the nature of the relationship between past and present values remains stable over time. Regime changes and sudden interventions might have a dramatic impact on the price, if for example a major jurisdiction were to restrict the usage of cryptocurrencies (as has been the case over the last decade). Such occurrences can be modeled, but they require more elaborate approaches to feature engineering and are outside the scope of this chapter.

Open-domain question answering

Question-answering (QA) systems aim to emulate the human process of searching for information online, with machine learning methods employed to improve the accuracy of the provided answers. In this recipe, we will demonstrate how to use RNNs to predict long and short responses to questions about Wikipedia articles. We will use the Google Natural Questions dataset, along with which an excellent visualization helpful for understanding the idea behind QA can be found at `https://ai.google.com/research/NaturalQuestions/ visualization`.

The basic idea can be summarized as follows: for each article-question pair, you must predict/ select long- and short-form answers to the question drawn *directly from the article*:

▶ A long answer would be a longer section of text that answers the question—several sentences or a paragraph.

▶ A short answer might be a sentence or phrase, or even in some cases a simple YES/NO. The short answers are always contained within, or a subset of, one of the plausible long answers.

▶ A given article can (and very often will) allow for both long *and* short answers, depending on the question.

The recipe presented in this chapter is adapted from code made public by Xing Han Lu: https://www.kaggle.com/xhlulu.

How to do it...

As usual, we start by loading the necessary packages. This time we are using the fasttext embeddings for our representation (available from `https://fasttext.cc/`). Other popular choices include GloVe (used in the sentiment detection section) and ELMo (`https://allennlp.org/elmo`). There is no clearly superior one in terms of performance on NLP tasks, so we'll switch our choices as we go to demonstrate the different possibilities:

```
import os
import json
import gc
import pickle

import numpy as np
import pandas as pd
from tqdm import tqdm_notebook as tqdm
from tensorflow.keras.models import Model
from tensorflow.keras.layers import Input, Dense, Embedding,
SpatialDropout1D, concatenate, Masking
from tensorflow.keras.layers import LSTM, Bidirectional,
GlobalMaxPooling1D, Dropout
from tensorflow.keras.preprocessing import text, sequence
from tqdm import tqdm_notebook as tqdm
import fasttext
from tensorflow.keras.models import load_model
```

The general settings are as follows:

```
embedding_path = '/kaggle/input/fasttext-crawl-300d-2m-with-subword/crawl-
300d-2m-subword/crawl-300d-2M-subword.bin'
```

Our next step is to add some boilerplate code to streamline the code flow later. Since the task at hand is a little more involved than in the previous instances (or less intuitive), we wrap up more of the preparation work inside the dataset building functions. Due to the size of the dataset, we only load a subset of the training data and sample the negative-labeled data:

```python
def build_train(train_path, n_rows=200000, sampling_rate=15):
    with open(train_path) as f:
        processed_rows = []

        for i in tqdm(range(n_rows)):
            line = f.readline()
            if not line:
                break

            line = json.loads(line)

            text = line['document_text'].split(' ')
            question = line['question_text']
            annotations = line['annotations'][0]


            for i, candidate in enumerate(line['long_answer_candidates']):
                label = i == annotations['long_answer']['candidate_index']

                start = candidate['start_token']
                end = candidate['end_token']

                if label or (i % sampling_rate == 0):
                    processed_rows.append({
                        'text': " ".join(text[start:end]),
                        'is_long_answer': label,
                        'question': question,
                        'annotation_id': annotations['annotation_id']
                    })

        train = pd.DataFrame(processed_rows)

        return train

def build_test(test_path):
    with open(test_path) as f:
        processed_rows = []

        for line in tqdm(f):
            line = json.loads(line)
```

```
            text = line['document_text'].split(' ')
            question = line['question_text']
            example_id = line['example_id']

            for candidate in line['long_answer_candidates']:
                start = candidate['start_token']
                end = candidate['end_token']

                processed_rows.append({
                    'text': " ".join(text[start:end]),
                    'question': question,
                    'example_id': example_id,
                    'sequence': f'{start}:{end}'

                })

        test = pd.DataFrame(processed_rows)

    return test
```

With the next function, we train a Keras tokenizer to encode the text and questions into a list of integers (tokenization), then pad them to a fixed length to form a single NumPy array for text and another for questions:

```
def compute_text_and_questions(train, test, tokenizer):
    train_text = tokenizer.texts_to_sequences(train.text.values)
    train_questions = tokenizer.texts_to_sequences(train.question.values)
    test_text = tokenizer.texts_to_sequences(test.text.values)
    test_questions = tokenizer.texts_to_sequences(test.question.values)

    train_text = sequence.pad_sequences(train_text, maxlen=300)
    train_questions = sequence.pad_sequences(train_questions)
    test_text = sequence.pad_sequences(test_text, maxlen=300)
    test_questions = sequence.pad_sequences(test_questions)

    return train_text, train_questions, test_text, test_questions
```

As usual with RNN-based models for NLP, we need an embeddings matrix:

```
def build_embedding_matrix(tokenizer, path):
    embedding_matrix = np.zeros((tokenizer.num_words + 1, 300))
    ft_model = fasttext.load_model(path)

    for word, i in tokenizer.word_index.items():
```

```
            if i >= tokenizer.num_words - 1:
                break
            embedding_matrix[i] = ft_model.get_word_vector(word)

    return embedding_matrix
```

Next is our model construction step, wrapped up in a function:

1. We build two 2-layer bidirectional LSTMs; one to read the questions, and one to read the text

2. We concatenate the output and pass it to a fully connected layer

3. We use sigmoid on the output:

```
def build_model(embedding_matrix):
    embedding = Embedding(
        *embedding_matrix.shape,
        weights=[embedding_matrix],
        trainable=False,
        mask_zero=True
    )

    q_in = Input(shape=(None,))
    q = embedding(q_in)
    q = SpatialDropout1D(0.2)(q)
    q = Bidirectional(LSTM(100, return_sequences=True))(q)
    q = GlobalMaxPooling1D()(q)


    t_in = Input(shape=(None,))
    t = embedding(t_in)
    t = SpatialDropout1D(0.2)(t)
    t = Bidirectional(LSTM(150, return_sequences=True))(t)
    t = GlobalMaxPooling1D()(t)

    hidden = concatenate([q, t])
    hidden = Dense(300, activation='relu')(hidden)
    hidden = Dropout(0.5)(hidden)
    hidden = Dense(300, activation='relu')(hidden)
    hidden = Dropout(0.5)(hidden)

    out1 = Dense(1, activation='sigmoid')(hidden)

    model = Model(inputs=[t_in, q_in], outputs=out1)
    model.compile(loss='binary_crossentropy', optimizer='adam')
```

```
        return model
```

With the toolkit that we've defined, we can construct the datasets as follows:

```
directory = '../input/tensorflow2-question-answering/'
train_path = directory + 'simplified-nq-train.jsonl'
test_path = directory + 'simplified-nq-test.jsonl'


train = build_train(train_path)
test = build_test(test_path)
```

This is what the dataset looks like:

```
train.head()
```

	text	is_long_answer	question	annotation_id
0	<Table> <Tr> <Td> </Td> <Td> { hide) This art...	False	which is the most common use of opt-in e-mail ...	593165450220027640
1	<Tr> <Td> <Ul> <Li> Pay - per - click </Li> <L...	False	which is the most common use of opt-in e-mail ...	593165450220027640
2	<P> Email marketing has evolved rapidly alongs...	False	which is the most common use of opt-in e-mail ...	593165450220027640
3	<Li> Advertisers can reach substantial numbers...	False	which is the most common use of opt-in e-mail ...	593165450220027640
4	<P> A common example of permission marketing i...	True	which is the most common use of opt-in e-mail ...	593165450220027640

```
tokenizer = text.Tokenizer(lower=False, num_words=80000)


for text in tqdm([train.text, test.text, train.question, test.question]):
    tokenizer.fit_on_texts(text.values)


train_target = train.is_long_answer.astype(int).values


train_text, train_questions, test_text, test_questions = compute_text_and_
questions(train, test, tokenizer)
del train
```

We can now construct the model itself:

```
embedding_matrix = build_embedding_matrix(tokenizer, embedding_path)


model = build_model(embedding_matrix)
model.summary()


Model: "functional_1"
```

Layer (type)	Output Shape	Param #	Connected to
input_1 (InputLayer)	[(None, None)]	0	
input_2 (InputLayer)	[(None, None)]	0	
embedding (Embedding)	(None, None, 300)	24000300	input_1[0][0]
			input_2[0][0]
spatial_dropout1d (SpatialDropo	(None, None, 300)	0	embedding[0][0]
spatial_dropout1d_1 (SpatialDro	(None, None, 300)	0	embedding[1][0]
bidirectional (Bidirectional)	(None, None, 200)	320800	spatial_dropout1d[0][0]
bidirectional_1 (Bidirectional)	(None, None, 300)	541200	spatial_dropout1d_1[0][0]
global_max_pooling1d (GlobalMax	(None, 200)	0	bidirectional[0][0]
global_max_pooling1d_1 (GlobalM	(None, 300)	0	bidirectional_1[0][0]
concatenate (Concatenate)	(None, 500)	0	global_max_pooling1d[0][0]
			global_max_pooling1d_1[0][0]

dense (Dense) concatenate[0][0]	(None, 300)	150300	
dropout (Dropout) [0]	(None, 300)	0	dense[0]
dense_1 (Dense) [0]	(None, 300)	90300	dropout[0]
dropout_1 (Dropout) [0]	(None, 300)	0	dense_1[0]
dense_2 (Dense) dropout_1[0][0]	(None, 1)	301	

```
================================================================
========================
Total params: 25,103,201
Trainable params: 1,102,901
Non-trainable params: 24,000,300
```

The fitting is next, and that proceeds in the usual manner:

```
train_history = model.fit(
    [train_text, train_questions],
    train_target,
    epochs=2,
    validation_split=0.2,
    batch_size=1024
)
```

Now, we can build a test set to have a look at our generated answers:

```
directory = '/kaggle/input/tensorflow2-question-answering/'
test_path = directory + 'simplified-nq-test.jsonl'
test = build_test(test_path)
submission = pd.read_csv("../input/tensorflow2-question-answering/sample_
submission.csv")

test_text, test_questions = compute_text_and_questions(test, tokenizer)
```

We generate the actual predictions:

```
test_target = model.predict([test_text, test_questions], batch_size=512)

test['target'] = test_target

result = (
    test.query('target > 0.3')
    .groupby('example_id')
    .max()
    .reset_index()
    .loc[:, ['example_id', 'PredictionString']]
)

result.head()
```

	example_id	PredictionString
0	-1028916936938579349	321:389
1	-1074129516932871805	1891:1965
2	-1114334749483663139	744:3809
3	-1152268629614456016	317:367
4	-1220107454853145579	141:211

As you can see, LSTM allows us to handle fairly abstract tasks such as answering different types of questions. The bulk of the work in this recipe was around formatting the data into a suitable input format, and then postprocessing the results—the actual modeling occurs in a very similar fashion to that in the preceding chapters.

Summary

In this chapter, we have demonstrated the different capabilities of RNNs. They can handle diverse tasks with a sequential component (text generation and classification, time series prediction, and QA) within a unified framework. In the next chapter, we shall introduce transformers: an important architecture class that made it possible to reach new state-of-the-art results with NLP problems.

10
Transformers

Transformers are deep learning architectures introduced by Google in 2017 that are designed to process sequential data for downstream tasks such as translation, question answering, or text summarization. In this manner, they aim to solve a similar problem to RNNs discussed in *Chapter 9, Recurrent Neural Networks*, but Transformers have a significant advantage as they do not require processing the data in order. Among other advantages, this allows a higher degree of parallelization and therefore faster training.

Due to their flexibility, Transformers can be pretrained on large bodies of unlabeled data and then finetuned for other tasks. Two main groups of such pretrained models are **Bidirectional Encoder Representations from Transformers** (**BERTs**) and **Generative Pretrained Transformers** (**GPTs**).

In this chapter, we will cover the following topics:

- ▶ Text generation
- ▶ Sentiment analysis
- ▶ Text classification: sarcasm detection
- ▶ Question answering

We'll begin by demonstrating the text generation capabilities of GPT-2 – one of the most popular Transformer architectures usable by a broader audience. While sentiment analysis can be handled by RNNs as well (as demonstrated in the previous chapter), it is the generative capabilities that most clearly demonstrate the impact of introducing Transformers into the Natural Language Processing stack.

Text generation

The first GPT model was introduced in a 2018 paper by Radford et al. from OpenAI – it demonstrated how a generative language model can acquire knowledge and process long-range dependencies thanks to pretraining on a large, diverse corpus of contiguous text. Two successor models (trained on more extensive corpora) were released in the following years: GPT-2 in 2019 (1.5 billion parameters) and GPT-3 in 2020 (175 billion parameters). In order to strike a balance between demonstration capabilities and computation requirements, we will be working with GPT-2 – as of the time of writing, access to the GPT-3 API is limited.

We'll begin by demonstrating how to generate your own text based on a prompt given to the GPT-2 model without any finetuning.

How do we go about it?

We will be making use of the excellent Transformers library created by Hugging Face (https://huggingface.co/). It abstracts away several components of the building process, allowing us to focus on the model performance and intended performance.

As usual, we begin by loading the required packages:

```
#get deep learning basics
import tensorflow as tf
```

One of the advantages of the Transformers library – and a reason for its popularity, undoubtedly – is how easily we can download a specific model (and also define the appropriate tokenizer):

```
from transformers import TFGPT2LMHeadModel, GPT2Tokenizer
tokenizer = GPT2Tokenizer.from_pretrained("gpt2-large")
GPT2 = TFGPT2LMHeadModel.from_pretrained("gpt2-large", pad_token_
id=tokenizer.eos_token_id)
```

It is usually a good idea to fix the random seed to ensure the results are reproducible:

```
# settings

#for reproducability
SEED = 34
tf.random.set_seed(SEED)

#maximum number of words in output text
MAX_LEN = 70
```

For a proper description of the decoder architecture within Transformers, please refer to the *See also* section at the end of this section – for now, let us focus on the fact that how we decode is one of the most important decisions when using a GPT-2 model. Below, we review some of the methods that can be utilized.

With **greedy search**, the word with the highest probability is predicted as the next word in the sequence:

```
input_sequence = "There are times when I am really tired of people, but I feel lonely too."
```

Once we have our input sequence, we encode it and then call a decode method:

```
# encode context the generation is conditioned on
input_ids = tokenizer.encode(input_sequence, return_tensors='tf')

# generate text until the output length (which includes the context length)
reaches 70
greedy_output = GPT2.generate(input_ids, max_length = MAX_LEN)

print("Output:\n" + 100 * '-')
print(tokenizer.decode(greedy_output[0], skip_special_tokens = True))

Output:
----------------------------------------------------------------------
-----------------------
There are times when I am really tired of people, but I feel lonely too. I
feel like I'm alone in the world. I feel like I'm alone in my own body. I
feel like I'm alone in my own mind. I feel like I'm alone in my own heart.
I feel like I'm alone in my own mind
```

As you can see, the results leave some room for improvement: the model starts repeating itself, because the high-probability words mask the less-likely ones so they cannot explore more diverse combinations.

A simple remedy is **beam search**: we keep track of the alternative variants, so that more comparisons are possible:

```
# set return_num_sequences > 1
beam_outputs = GPT2.generate(
    input_ids,
    max_length = MAX_LEN,
    num_beams = 5,
    no_repeat_ngram_size = 2,
    num_return_sequences = 5,
```

```
        early_stopping = True
)

print('')
print("Output:\n" + 100 * '-')

# now we have 5 output sequences
for i, beam_output in enumerate(beam_outputs):
        print("{}: {}".format(i, tokenizer.decode(beam_output, skip_special_
        tokens=True)))

Output:
----------------------------------------------------------------------------
---------------------------
0: There are times when I am really tired of people, but I feel lonely too.
I don't know what to do with myself."

"I feel like I can't do anything right now," she said. "I'm so tired."
1: There are times when I am really tired of people, but I feel lonely too.
I don't know what to do with myself."

"I feel like I can't do anything right now," she says. "I'm so tired."
2: There are times when I am really tired of people, but I feel lonely too.
I don't know what to do with myself."

"I feel like I can't do anything right now," she says. "I'm not sure what
I'm supposed to be doing with my life."
3: There are times when I am really tired of people, but I feel lonely too.
I don''t know what to do with myself.""

"I feel like I can't do anything right now," she says. "I'm not sure what
I'm supposed to be doing."
4: There are times when I am really tired of people, but I feel lonely too.
I don't know what to do with myself."

"I feel like I can't do anything right now," she says. "I'm not sure what I
should do."
```

This is definitely more diverse – the message is the same, but at least the formulations look a little different from a style point of view.

Next, we can explore sampling – indeterministic decoding. Instead of following a strict path to find the end text with the highest probability, we rather randomly pick the next word by its conditional probability distribution. This approach risks producing incoherent ramblings, so we make use of the `temperature` parameter, which affects the probability mass distribution:

```
# use temperature to decrease the sensitivity to low probability candidates
sample_output = GPT2.generate(
                        input_ids,
                        do_sample = True,
                        max_length = MAX_LEN,
                        top_k = 0,
                        temperature = 0.2
)

print("Output:\n" + 100 * '-')
print(tokenizer.decode(sample_output[0], skip_special_tokens = True))
```

```
Output:
--------------------------------------------------------------------
------------------------
There are times when I am really tired of people, but I feel lonely too.
I feel like I'm alone in my own world. I feel like I'm alone in my own
life. I feel like I'm alone in my own mind. I feel like I'm alone in my own
heart. I feel like I'm alone in my own
```

Waxing poetic a bit. What happens if we increase the temperature?

```
sample_output = GPT2.generate(
                        input_ids,
                        do_sample = True,
                        max_length = MAX_LEN,
                        top_k = 0,
                        temperature = 0.8
)

print("Output:\n" + 100 * '-')
print(tokenizer.decode(sample_output[0], skip_special_tokens = True))
```

```
Output:
--------------------------------------------------------------------
------------------------
There are times when I am really tired of people, but I feel lonely too.
I find it strange how the people around me seem to be always so nice. The
only time I feel lonely is when I'm on the road. I can't be alone with my
thoughts.

What are some of your favourite things to do in the area
```

This is getting more interesting, although it still feels a bit like a train of thought – which is perhaps to be expected, given the content of our prompt. Let's explore some more ways to tune the output.

In **Top-K sampling**, the top *k* most likely next words are selected and the entire probability mass is shifted to these *k* words. So instead of increasing the chances of high-probability words occurring and decreasing the chances of low-probability words, we just remove low-probability words altogether:

```
#sample from only top_k most likely words
sample_output = GPT2.generate(
                            input_ids,
                            do_sample = True,
                            max_length = MAX_LEN,
                            top_k = 50
)


print("Output:\n" + 100 * '-')
print(tokenizer.decode(sample_output[0], skip_special_tokens = True),
'...')

Output:
-----------------------------------------------------------------------------
-------------------------------
There are times when I am really tired of people, but I feel lonely too. I
go to a place where you can feel comfortable. It's a place where you can
relax. But if you're so tired of going along with the rules, maybe I won't
go. You know what? Maybe if I don't go, you won''t ...
```

This seems like a step in the right direction. Can we do better?

Top-P sampling (also known as nucleus sampling) is similar to Top-K, but instead of choosing the top *k* most likely words, we choose the smallest set of words whose total probability is larger than *p*, and then the entire probability mass is shifted to the words in this set. The main difference here is that with Top-K sampling, the size of the set of words is static (obviously), whereas in Top-P sampling, the size of the set can change. To use this sampling method, we just set top_k = 0 and choose a top_p value:

```
#sample only from 80% most likely words
sample_output = GPT2.generate(
                            input_ids,
                            do_sample = True,
                            max_length = MAX_LEN,
                            top_p = 0.8,
                            top_k = 0
)


print("Output:\n" + 100 * '-')
print(tokenizer.decode(sample_output[0], skip_special_tokens = True),
'...')
```

```
Output:
------------------------------------------------------------------------------
------------------------
There are times when I am really tired of people, but I feel lonely too. I
feel like I should just be standing there, just sitting there. I know I'm
not a danger to anybody. I just feel alone." ...
```

We can combine both approaches:

```
#combine both sampling techniques
sample_outputs = GPT2.generate(
                        input_ids,
                        do_sample = True,
                        max_length = 2*MAX_LEN,
#to test how long we can generate and it be coherent
                        #temperature = .7,
                        top_k = 50,
                        top_p = 0.85,
                        num_return_sequences = 5

)

print("Output:\n" + 100 * '-')
for i, sample_output in enumerate(sample_outputs):
    print("{}: {}...".format(i, tokenizer.decode(sample_output, skip_
    special_tokens = True)))
    print('')
```

```
Output:
------------------------------------------------------------------------------
------------------------
0: There are times when I am really tired of people, but I feel lonely too.
I don't feel like I am being respected by my own country, which is why I am
trying to change the government."

In a recent video posted to YouTube, Mr. Jaleel, dressed in a suit and
tie, talks about his life in Pakistan and his frustration at his treatment
by the country's law enforcement agencies. He also describes how he met
a young woman from California who helped him organize the protest in
Washington.

"She was a journalist who worked with a television channel in Pakistan,"
Mr. Jaleel says in the video. "She came to my home one day,...

1: There are times when I am really tired of people, but I feel lonely
too. It's not that I don't like to be around other people, but it's just
something I have to face sometimes.
```

What is your favorite thing to eat?

The most favorite thing I have eaten is chicken and waffles. But I love rice, soups, and even noodles. I also like to eat bread, but I like it a little bit less.

What is your ideal day of eating?

It varies every day. Sometimes I want to eat at home, because I'm in a house with my family. But then sometimes I just have to have some sort...

2: There are times when I am really tired of people, but I feel lonely too. I think that there is something in my heart that is trying to be a better person, but I don't know what that is."

So what can be done?

"I want people to take the time to think about this," says Jorja, who lives in a small town outside of Boston.

She has been thinking a lot about her depression. She wants to make a documentary about it, and she wants to start a blog about it.

"I want to make a video to be a support system for people who are going through the same thing I was going through...

3: There are times when I am really tired of people, but I feel lonely too.

I want to be able to take good care of myself. I am going to be a very good person, even if I am lonely.

So, if it's lonely, then I will be happy. I will be a person who will be able to have good care of myself.

I have made this wish.

What is my hope? What is my goal? I want to do my best to be able to meet it, but…

"Yuu, what are you saying, Yuu?"

"Uwa, what is it?"

I...

4: There are times when I am really tired of people, but I feel lonely too. The only person I really love is my family. It's just that I'm not alone."

-Juan, 24, a student

A study from the European Economic Area, a free trade area between the EU and Iceland, showed that there are 2.3 million EU citizens living in Iceland. Another survey in 2014 showed that 1.3 million people in Iceland were employed.

The government is committed to making Iceland a country where everyone can live and work.

"We are here to help, not to steal," said one of the people who drove up in a Volkswagen.

...

Clearly, the more-sophisticated method's settings can give us pretty impressive results. Let's explore this avenue more – we'll use the prompts taken from OpenAI's GPT-2 website, where they feed them to a full-sized GPT-2 model. This comparison will give us an idea of how well we are doing with a local (smaller) model compared to a full one that was used for the original demos:

```python
MAX_LEN = 500

prompt1 = 'In a shocking finding, scientist discovered a herd of unicorns
living in a remote, previously unexplored valley, in the Andes Mountains.
Even more surprising to the researchers was the fact that the unicorns
spoke perfect English.'

input_ids = tokenizer.encode(prompt1, return_tensors='tf')

sample_outputs = GPT2.generate(
                        input_ids,
                        do_sample = True,
                        max_length = MAX_LEN,
#to test how long we can generate and it be coherent
                        #temperature = .8,
                        top_k = 50,
                        top_p = 0.85
                        #num_return_sequences = 5
)

print("Output:\n" + 100 * '-')
```

```
for i, sample_output in enumerate(sample_outputs):
    print("{}: {}...".format(i, tokenizer.decode(sample_output, skip_
    special_tokens = True)))
    print('')
```

Output:

```
--------------------------------------------------------------------------
------------------------
```

0: In a shocking finding, scientist discovered a herd of unicorns living in a remote, previously unexplored valley, in the Andes Mountains. Even more surprising to the researchers was the fact that the unicorns spoke perfect English.

This is the first time a herd of unicorns have been discovered in the Andes Mountains, a vast region stretching from the Himalayas to the Andes River in Bolivia.

According to the BBC, the unicorns were spotted by a small group of researchers on a private expedition, but they were the only ones that came across the bizarre creatures.

It was later learned that these were not the wild unicorns that were spotted in the wild in recent years, but rather a domesticated variety of the species.

Although they do not speak English, they do carry their own unique language, according to the researchers, who have named it "Ungla."

The herd of unicorns, which was discovered by a small group of researchers, is the first of its kind discovered in the Andes Mountains. It is thought that the herd of wild unicorns were introduced to the area hundreds of years ago by a local rancher who was attempting to make a profit from the animals.

Although they do not speak English, they do carry their own unique language, according to the researchers, who have named it "Ungla."

The researchers claim that the unicorns have only been sighted in the Andes Mountains, where they can be seen throughout the mountains of South America.

While the unicorns do not speak English, they do carry their own unique language, according to the researchers, who have named it "Ungla."

Ungla is a highly intelligent, cooperative species with a high level of social and cognitive complexity, and is capable of displaying sophisticated behaviors.

They are a particularly unique species, because they are capable of surviving in extreme conditions for long periods of time and without being fed or watered.

The team believes that the species was probably domesticated in the Andes Mountains, where it could not survive in its natural habitat.

"We can see from the genetics that the animals were probably domesticated in the Andes Mountains where they could not survive in their natural habitat and with water and food sources," said Professor David Catt, from the University of Cambridge, who led the study.

"So these were animals that would have been...

For comparison, this is the output from a complete model:

Output:

0: In a shocking finding, scientist discovered a herd of unicorns living in a remote, previously unexplored valley, in the Andes Mountains. Even more surprising to the researchers was the fact that the unicorns spoke perfect English.

*"This is not only a scientific finding; it is also a very important finding because it will enable us to further study the phenomenon," said Dr. Jorge Llamas, from the **National Institute of Anthropology and History (INAH)** in Colombia, in a statement.*

"We have previously found that humans have used human voices to communicate with the animals. In this case, the animals are communicating with us. In other words, this is a breakthrough in the field of animal communication," added Llamas...

In another example, it seems like the trepidations of the model authors were justified: GPT-2 can in fact generate fake news stories.

```
prompt2 = 'Miley Cyrus was caught shoplifting from Abercrombie and Fitch on
Hollywood Boulevard today.'

input_ids = tokenizer.encode(prompt2, return_tensors='tf')

sample_outputs = GPT2.generate(
                            input_ids,
                            do_sample = True,
                            max_length = MAX_LEN,
#to test how long we can generate and it be coherent
                            #temperature = .8,
                            top_k = 50,
```

```
                    top_p = 0.85
                    #num_return_sequences = 5
)

print("Output:\n" + 100 * '-')
for i, sample_output in enumerate(sample_outputs):
    print("{}: {}...".format(i, tokenizer.decode(sample_output, skip_
    special_tokens = True)))
    print('')
```

Output:

0: Miley Cyrus was caught shoplifting from Abercrombie and Fitch on
Hollywood Boulevard today. In a video captured by one of her friends, the
singer is seen grabbing her bag, but then quickly realizing the merchandise
she has to leave is too expensive to be worth a $1.99 purchase.

The video has already gone viral, and while the celebrity is certainly
guilty of breaking the law (even if she can't be accused of stealing for
a second time), there's one aspect of the situation that should make the
most sense. It's just like the shopping situation in the movie The Fast and
the Furious, where Michael Corleone is caught in possession of counterfeit
designer clothing.

This time around, though, the situation involves Cyrus. It's not a copy,
per se. It's actually a replica, a pair of a black and white Nike Air Force
1s, a colorway she wore in her music video.

It seems that the actress is caught by a friend who had gotten her a pair
of those sneakers when she was in school, so this is no surprise to her.
After all, there was a video of her stealing from her own store back in
2012, when she was a freshman at New York University.

It's not that there's anything wrong with the product. If the merchandise
is in good shape, that's all that matters. But there are a few things that
should come to mind when it comes to these shoes.

For one, the fabric is incredibly thin. The fabric is so thin that the
upper actually makes the shoes look like they're made of leather. There's
even a thin layer of plastic between the upper and the shoe.

Secondly, the material isn't even a shoe. It's just a piece of leather.
It's not actually a leather shoe at all, even though it's made of the same
material as the other items on the show. It's just a piece of leather. And
it's not the kind of leather that would actually hold up in a fight.

```
This is something that should be familiar to anyone who's ever shopped at
the store. If you go into the store looking for a pair of new Nike Air
Force 1s, and the salesperson is just selling you a piece of leather,
you're going to get disappointed. That's the nature of these shoes.

In addition to the aforementioned "stolen" footwear, Miley Cyrus...
```

Output:

0: Miley Cyrus was caught shoplifting from Abercrombie and Fitch on Hollywood Boulevard today. The star was spotted trying on three dresses before attempting to walk out of the store.

Abercrombie is one of a number of stores the star has frequented.

The singer was spotted walking into Abercrombie & Fitch in West Hollywood just after noon this afternoon before leaving the store.

The star is currently in the middle of a tour of Australia and New Zealand for her X Factor appearance on February 28....

What about riffing off literature classics like Tolkien?

```
prompt3 = 'Legolas and Gimli advanced on the orcs, raising their weapons
with a harrowing war cry'

input_ids = tokenizer.encode(prompt3, return_tensors='tf')

sample_outputs = GPT2.generate(
                        input_ids,
                        do_sample = True,
                        max_length = MAX_LEN,
#to test how long we can generate and it be coherent
                        #temperature = .8,
                        top_k = 50,
                        top_p = 0.85
                        #num_return_sequences = 5
)

print("Output:\n" + 100 * '-')
for i, sample_output in enumerate(sample_outputs):
    print("{}: {}...".format(i, tokenizer.decode(sample_output, skip_
    special_tokens = True)))
    print('')
```

```
Output:
------------------------------------------------------------------------
------------------------------
0: Legolas and Gimli advanced on the orcs, raising their weapons with a
harrowing war cry, and they roared their battle cries as they charged the
orcs with their spears and arrows. They reached the front of the line,
where the enemy were gathered, and they fell upon them with a hail of fire
and arrows, slaying many orcs and wounding others. The battle raged on
for a long time, and eventually the two sides met and fought for a long
time more. The orcs fell and the two armies were victorious. The orcs were
killed and the two armies were victorious.

The two armies fought one last time in battle. Gimli slew many of the orcs
and led his men to safety. They went to the city and took it. When they
returned, Sauron's servants were waiting to kill them. The two armies
fought again, and the battle raged on for a long time more. Gimli slew many
of the orcs and led his men to safety. They went to the city and took it.
When they returned, Sauron's servants were waiting to kill them. The two
armies fought again, and the battle raged on for a long time more. Gimli
slew many of the orcs and led his men to safety. They went to the city and
took it. When they returned, Sauron's servants were waiting to kill them.
The two armies fought again, and the battle raged on for a long time more.
Gimli slew many of the orcs and led his men to safety. They went to the
city and took it. When they returned, Sauron's servants were waiting to
kill them. The two armies fought again, and the battle raged on for a long
time more. Gimli slew many of the orcs and led his men to safety. They went
to the city and took it. When they returned, Sauron's servants were waiting
to kill them. The two armies fought again, and the battle raged on for a
long time more. Gimli slew many of the orcs and led his men to safety. They
went to the city and took it. When they returned, Sauron's servants were
waiting to kill them. The two armies fought again, and the battle raged
on for a long time more. Gimli slew many of the orcs and led his men to
safety. They went to the city and took it. When they returned, Sauron's
servants were waiting to kill them. The two armies fought again, and the
battle raged on for a...
```

Output:

0: Legolas and Gimli advanced on the orcs, raising their weapons with a harrowing war cry.

Then the orcs made their move.

The Great Orc Warband advanced at the sound of battle. They wore their weapons proudly on their chests, and they looked down upon their foes.

In the distance, the orcs could be heard shouting their orders in a low voice.

But the battle was not yet over. The orcs' axes and hammers slammed into the enemy ranks as though they were an army of ten thousand warriors, and their axes made the orcs bleed.

In the midst of the carnage, the Elven leader Aragorn cried out: "Come, brave. Let us fight the orcs!"

As you can see from the examples above, a GPT-2 model working out of the box (without finetuning) can already generate plausible-looking long-form text. Assessing the future impact of this technology on the field of communication remains an open and highly controversial issue: on the one hand, there is fully justified fear of fake news proliferation (see the Miley Cyrus story above). This is particularly concerning because large-scale automated detection of generated text is an extremely challenging topic. On the other hand, GPT-2 text generation capabilities can be helpful for creative types: be it style experimentation or parody, an AI-powered writing assistant can be a tremendous help.

See also

There are multiple excellent resources online for text generation with GPT-2:

▶ The original OpenAI post that introduced the model:

`https://openai.com/blog/better-language-models/`

▶ Top GPT-2 open source projects:

`https://awesomeopensource.com/projects/gpt-2`

▶ Hugging Face documentation:

`https://huggingface.co/blog/how-to-generate`

`https://huggingface.co/transformers/model_doc/gpt2.html`

Sentiment analysis

In this section, we'll demonstrate how DistilBERT – a lightweight version of BERT – can be used to handle a common problem of sentiment analysis. We will be using data from a Kaggle competition (`https://www.kaggle.com/c/tweet-sentiment-extraction`): given a tweet and the sentiment (positive, neutral, or negative), participants needed to identify the part of the tweet that defines that sentiment. Sentiment analysis is typically employed in business as part of a system that helps data analysts gauge public opinion, conduct detailed market research, and track customer experience. An important application is medical: the effect of different treatments on patients' moods can be evaluated based on their communication patterns.

How do we go about it?

As usual, we begin by loading the necessary packages.

```
import pandas as pd
import re
import numpy as np
np.random.seed(0)
import matplotlib.pyplot as plt
%matplotlib inline
import keras
from keras.preprocessing.sequence import pad_sequences
from keras.layers import Input, Dense, LSTM, GRU, Embedding
from keras.layers import Activation, Bidirectional, GlobalMaxPool1D,
GlobalMaxPool2D, Dropout
from keras.models import Model
from keras import initializers, regularizers, constraints, optimizers,
layers
from keras.preprocessing import text, sequence
from keras.callbacks import ModelCheckpoint
from keras.callbacks import EarlyStopping
from keras.optimizers import RMSprop, adam
import nltk
from nltk.corpus import stopwords
from nltk.tokenize import word_tokenize
from nltk.stem import WordNetLemmatizer,PorterStemmer
import seaborn as sns
import transformers
from transformers import AutoTokenizer
from tokenizers import BertWordPieceTokenizer
from keras.initializers import Constant
from keras.wrappers.scikit_learn import KerasClassifier
from sklearn.model_selection import GridSearchCV
from sklearn.metrics import accuracy_score
from collections import Counter

stop=set(stopwords.words('english'))

import os
```

In order to streamline the code, we define some helper functions for cleaning the text: we remove website links, starred-out NSFW terms, and emojis.

```
def basic_cleaning(text):
    text=re.sub(r'https?://www\.\S+\.com','',text)
```

```python
    text=re.sub(r'[^A-Za-z|\s]','',text)
    text=re.sub(r'\*+','swear',text) #capture swear words that are **** out
    return text


def remove_html(text):
    html=re.compile(r'<.*?>')
    return html.sub(r'',text)


# Reference : https://gist.github.com/slowkow/7a7f61f495e3dbb7e3d767f97bd73
04b
def remove_emoji(text):
    emoji_pattern = re.compile("["
                        u"\U0001F600-\U0001F64F"  # emoticons
                        u"\U0001F300-\U0001F5FF"  # symbols &
pictographs
                        u"\U0001F680-\U0001F6FF"  # transport & map
symbols
                        u"\U0001F1E0-\U0001F1FF"  # flags (iOS)
                        u"\U00002702-\U000027B0"
                        u"\U000024C2-\U0001F251"
                        "]+", flags=re.UNICODE)
    return emoji_pattern.sub(r'', text)


def remove_multiplechars(text):
    text = re.sub(r'(.)\1{3,}',r'\1', text)
    return text



def clean(df):
    for col in ['text']:#,'selected_text']:
        df[col]=df[col].astype(str).apply(lambda x:basic_cleaning(x))
        df[col]=df[col].astype(str).apply(lambda x:remove_emoji(x))
        df[col]=df[col].astype(str).apply(lambda x:remove_html(x))
        df[col]=df[col].astype(str).apply(lambda x:remove_multiplechars(x))

    return df

def fast_encode(texts, tokenizer, chunk_size=256, maxlen=128):
    tokenizer.enable_truncation(max_length=maxlen)
    tokenizer.enable_padding(max_length=maxlen)
    all_ids = []

    for i in range(0, len(texts), chunk_size):
        text_chunk = texts[i:i+chunk_size].tolist()
        encs = tokenizer.encode_batch(text_chunk)
```

```
        all_ids.extend([enc.ids for enc in encs])

    return np.array(all_ids)

def preprocess_news(df,stop=stop,n=1,col='text'):
    '''Function to preprocess and create corpus'''
    new_corpus=[]
    stem=PorterStemmer()
    lem=WordNetLemmatizer()
    for text in df[col]:
        words=[w for w in word_tokenize(text) if (w not in stop)]

        words=[lem.lemmatize(w) for w in words if(len(w)>n)]

        new_corpus.append(words)

    new_corpus=[word for l in new_corpus for word in l]
    return new_corpus
```

Load the data.

```
df = pd.read_csv('/kaggle/input/tweet-sentiment-extraction/train.csv')
df.head()
```

textID	text	selected_text	sentiment
cb774db0d1	I`d have responded, if I were going	I`d have responded, if I were going	neutral
549e992a42	Sooo SAD I will miss you here in San Diego!!!	Sooo SAD	negative
088c60f138	my boss is bullying me...	bullying me	negative
9642c003ef	what interview! leave me alone	leave me alone	negative
358bd9e861	Sons of ****, why couldn`t they put them on t...	Sons of ****,	negative

Figure 10.1: Sample of the tweet sentiment analysis data

The snapshot above demonstrates a sample of the data we will focus our analysis on: the complete text, the key phrase, and its associated sentiment (positive, negative, or neutral).

We proceed with fairly standard preprocessing of the data:

1. `basic_cleaning` – to remove website URLs and non-characters and to replace * swear words with the word swear.

2. `remove_html`.

3. `remove_emojis`.

4. `remove_multiplechars` – this is for when there are more than 3 characters in a row in a word, for example, wayyyyy. The function removes all but one of the letters.

```
df.dropna(inplace=True)

df_clean = clean(df)
```

As for labels, we one-hot encode the targets, tokenize them, and convert them into sequences.

```
df_clean_selection = df_clean.sample(frac=1)
X = df_clean_selection.text.values
y = pd.get_dummies(df_clean_selection.sentiment)

tokenizer = text.Tokenizer(num_words=20000)
tokenizer.fit_on_texts(list(X))
list_tokenized_train = tokenizer.texts_to_sequences(X)
X_t = sequence.pad_sequences(list_tokenized_train, maxlen=128)
```

DistilBERT is a light version of BERT: it has 40 pct fewer parameters, but achieves 97% of the performance. For the purpose of this recipe, we will use it primarily for its tokenizer and an embedding matrix. Although the matrix is trainable, we shall not utilize this option, in order to reduce the training time.

```
tokenizer = transformers.AutoTokenizer.from_pretrained("distilbert-base-
uncased")  ## change it to commit

# Save the loaded tokenizer locally
save_path = '/kaggle/working/distilbert_base_uncased/'
if not os.path.exists(save_path):
    os.makedirs(save_path)
tokenizer.save_pretrained(save_path)

# Reload it with the huggingface tokenizers library
fast_tokenizer = BertWordPieceTokenizer('distilbert_base_uncased/vocab.
txt', lowercase=True)
fast_tokenizer

X = fast_encode(df_clean_selection.text.astype(str), fast_tokenizer,
maxlen=128)

transformer_layer = transformers.TFDistilBertModel.from_
pretrained('distilbert-base-uncased')

embedding_size = 128 input_ = Input(shape=(100,))

inp = Input(shape=(128, ))

embedding_matrix=transformer_layer.weights[0].numpy()
```

```
x = Embedding(embedding_matrix.shape[0], embedding_matrix.
shape[1],embeddings_initializer=Constant(embedding_matrix),trainable=False)
(inp)
```

We proceed with the usual steps for defining a model.

```
x = Bidirectional(LSTM(50, return_sequences=True))(x)
x = Bidirectional(LSTM(25, return_sequences=True))(x)
x = GlobalMaxPool1D()(x) x = Dropout(0.5)(x)
x = Dense(50, activation='relu', kernel_regularizer='L1L2')(x)
x = Dropout(0.5)(x)
x = Dense(3, activation='softmax')(x)
model_DistilBert = Model(inputs=[inp], outputs=x)

model_DistilBert.compile(loss='categorical_crossentropy',optimizer='adam',m
etrics=['accuracy'])

model_DistilBert.summary()

Model: "model_1"
```

Layer (type)	Output Shape	Param #
input_2 (InputLayer)	(None, 128)	0
embedding_1 (Embedding)	(None, 128, 768)	23440896
bidirectional_1 (Bidirection	(None, 128, 100)	327600
bidirectional_2 (Bidirection	(None, 128, 50)	25200
global_max_pooling1d_1 (Glob	(None, 50)	0
dropout_1 (Dropout)	(None, 50)	0
dense_1 (Dense)	(None, 50)	2550
dropout_2 (Dropout)	(None, 50)	0
dense_2 (Dense)	(None, 3)	153

```
Total params: 23,796,399
Trainable params: 355,503
Non-trainable params: 23,440,896
```

We can now fit the model:

```
model_DistilBert.fit(X,y,batch_size=32,epochs=10,validation_split=0.1)

Train on 24732 samples, validate on 2748 samples
Epoch 1/10
24732/24732 [==============================] - 357s 14ms/step - loss:
1.0516 - accuracy: 0.4328 - val_loss: 0.8719 - val_accuracy: 0.5466
Epoch 2/10
24732/24732 [==============================] - 355s 14ms/step - loss:
0.7733 - accuracy: 0.6604 - val_loss: 0.7032 - val_accuracy: 0.6776
Epoch 3/10
24732/24732 [==============================] - 355s 14ms/step - loss:
0.6668 - accuracy: 0.7299 - val_loss: 0.6407 - val_accuracy: 0.7354
Epoch 4/10
24732/24732 [==============================] - 355s 14ms/step - loss:
0.6310 - accuracy: 0.7461 - val_loss: 0.5925 - val_accuracy: 0.7478
Epoch 5/10
24732/24732 [==============================] - 347s 14ms/step - loss:
0.6070 - accuracy: 0.7565 - val_loss: 0.5817 - val_accuracy: 0.7529
Epoch 6/10
24732/24732 [==============================] - 343s 14ms/step - loss:
0.5922 - accuracy: 0.7635 - val_loss: 0.5817 - val_accuracy: 0.7584
Epoch 7/10
24732/24732 [==============================] - 343s 14ms/step - loss:
0.5733 - accuracy: 0.7707 - val_loss: 0.5922 - val_accuracy: 0.7638
Epoch 8/10
24732/24732 [==============================] - 343s 14ms/step - loss:
0.5547 - accuracy: 0.7832 - val_loss: 0.5767 - val_accuracy: 0.7627
Epoch 9/10
24732/24732 [==============================] - 346s 14ms/step - loss:
0.5350 - accuracy: 0.7870 - val_loss: 0.5767 - val_accuracy: 0.7584
Epoch 10/10
24732/24732 [==============================] - 346s 14ms/step - loss:
0.5219 - accuracy: 0.7955 - val_loss: 0.5994 - val_accuracy: 0.7580
```

As we can see from the above output, the model converges quite rapidly and achieves a reasonable accuracy of 76% on the validation set already after 10 iterations. Further finetuning of hyperparameters and longer training can improve the performance, but even at this level, a trained model – for example, through the use of TensorFlow Serving – can provide a valuable addition to the sentiment analysis logic of a business application.

See also

The best starting point is the documentation by Hugging Face: `https://curiousily.com/posts/sentiment-analysis-with-bert-and-hugging-face-using-pytorch-and-python/`.

Open-domain question answering

Given a passage of text and a question related to that text, the idea of **Question Answering (QA)** is to identify the subset of the passage that answers the question. It is one of many tasks where Transformer architectures have been applied successfully. The Transformers library has a number of pretrained models for QA that can be applied even in the absence of a dataset to finetune on (a form of zero-shot learning).

However, different models might fail at different examples and it might be useful to examine the reasons. In this section, we'll demonstrate the TensorFlow 2.0 GradientTape functionality: it allows us to record operations on a set of variables we want to perform automatic differentiation on. To explain the model's output on a given input, we can:

- ▶ One-hot encode the input – unlike integer tokens (typically used in this context), a one-hot-encoding representation is differentiable
- ▶ Instantiate GradientTape and watch our input variable
- ▶ Compute a forward pass through the model
- ▶ Get the gradients of the output of interest (for example, a specific class logit) with respect to the *watched* input
- ▶ Use the normalized gradients as explanations

The code in this section is adapted from the results published by Fast Forward Labs: `https://experiments.fastforwardlabs.com/`.

How do we go about it?

```
import os
import zipfile
import shutil
import urllib.request
import logging
import lzma
import json
import matplotlib.pyplot as plt
import numpy as np
import pandas as pd
```

```
import time

import tensorflow as tf
from transformers import AutoTokenizer, TFAutoModelForQuestionAnswering,
TFBertForMaskedLM, TFBertForQuestionAnswering
```

As usual, we need some boilerplate: begin with a function for fetching pretrained QA models.

```
def get_pretrained_squad_model(model_name):

    model, tokenizer = None, None

    if model_name == "distilbertsquad1":
        tokenizer = AutoTokenizer.from_pretrained("distilbert-base-cased-
distilled-squad",use_fast=True)
        model = TFBertForQuestionAnswering.from_pretrained("distilbert-
base-cased-distilled-squad", from_pt=True)

    elif model_name == "distilbertsquad2":
        tokenizer = AutoTokenizer.from_pretrained("twmkn9/distilbert-base-
uncased-squad2",use_fast=True)
        model = TFAutoModelForQuestionAnswering.from_pretrained("twmkn9/
distilbert-base-uncased-squad2", from_pt=True)

    elif model_name == "bertsquad2":
        tokenizer = AutoTokenizer.from_pretrained("deepset/bert-base-cased-
squad2",use_fast=True)
        model = TFBertForQuestionAnswering.from_pretrained("deepset/bert-
base-cased-squad2", from_pt=True)

    elif model_name == "bertlargesquad2":
        tokenizer = AutoTokenizer.from_pretrained("bert-base-uncased",use_
fast=True)
        model = TFBertForQuestionAnswering.from_pretrained("deepset/bert-
large-uncased-whole-word-masking-squad2", from_pt=True)

    elif model_name == "albertbasesquad2":
        tokenizer = AutoTokenizer.from_pretrained("twmkn9/albert-base-v2-
squad2",use_fast=True)
        model = TFBertForQuestionAnswering.from_pretrained("twmkn9/albert-
base-v2-squad2", from_pt=True)

    elif model_name == "distilrobertasquad2":
        tokenizer = AutoTokenizer.from_pretrained("twmkn9/distilroberta-
base-squad2",use_fast=True)
        model = TFBertForQuestionAnswering.from_pretrained("twmkn9/
```

```
distilroberta-base-squad2", from_pt=True)

    elif model_name == "robertasquad2":
        tokenizer = AutoTokenizer.from_pretrained("deepset/roberta-base-
squad2",use_fast=True)
        model = TFAutoModelForQuestionAnswering.from_pretrained("deepset/
roberta-base-squad2", from_pt=True)

    elif model_name == "bertlm":

        tokenizer = AutoTokenizer.from_pretrained("bert-base-uncased",
                                                  use_fast=True)
        model = TFBertForMaskedLM.from_pretrained("bert-base-uncased",
                                                  from_pt=True)

    return model, tokenizer
```

Identify the span of the answer.

```
def get_answer_span(question, context, model, tokenizer):
    inputs = tokenizer.encode_plus(question, context, return_tensors="tf",
add_special_tokens=True, max_length=512)
    answer_start_scores, answer_end_scores = model(inputs)
    answer_start = tf.argmax(answer_start_scores, axis=1).numpy()[0]
    answer_end = (tf.argmax(answer_end_scores, axis=1) + 1).numpy()[0]
    print(tokenizer.convert_tokens_to_string(inputs["input_ids"][0][answer_
start:answer_end]))

    return answer_start, answer_end
```

We need some functions for data preparation.

```
def clean_tokens(gradients, tokens, token_types):

    """

    Clean the tokens and gradients gradients
    Remove "[CLS]","[CLR]", "[SEP]" tokens
    Reduce (mean) gradients values for tokens that are split ##
    """

    token_holder = []
    token_type_holder = []
    gradient_holder = []
    i = 0
```

```
    while i < len(tokens):
        if (tokens[i] not in ["[CLS]","[CLR]", "[SEP]"]):
            token = tokens[i]
            conn = gradients[i]
            token_type = token_types[i]

            if i < len(tokens)-1 :
                if tokens[i+1][0:2] == "##":
                    token = tokens[i]
                    conn = gradients[i]
                    j = 1
                    while i < len(tokens)-1 and tokens[i+1][0:2] == "##":
                        i +=1
                        token += tokens[i][2:]
                        conn += gradients[i]
                        j+=1
                    conn = conn /j
            token_holder.append(token)
            token_type_holder.append(token_type)
            gradient_holder.append(conn)

        i +=1

    return  gradient_holder,token_holder, token_type_holder

def get_best_start_end_position(start_scores, end_scores):

    answer_start = tf.argmax(start_scores, axis=1).numpy()[0]
    answer_end = (tf.argmax(end_scores, axis=1) + 1).numpy()[0]
    return answer_start, answer_end

def get_correct_span_mask(correct_index, token_size):

    span_mask = np.zeros((1, token_size))
    span_mask[0, correct_index] = 1
    span_mask = tf.constant(span_mask, dtype='float32')

    return span_mask

def get_embedding_matrix(model):

    if "DistilBert" in type(model).__name__:
        return model.distilbert.embeddings.word_embeddings
    else:
        return model.bert.embeddings.word_embeddings
```

```python
def get_gradient(question, context, model, tokenizer):

    """Return gradient of input (question) wrt to model output span
prediction

    Args:
        question (str): text of input question
        context (str): text of question context/passage
        model (QA model): Hugging Face BERT model for QA transformers.
modeling_tf_distilbert.TFDistilBertForQuestionAnswering, transformers.
modeling_tf_bert.TFBertForQuestionAnswering
        tokenizer (tokenizer): transformers.tokenization_bert.
BertTokenizerFast

    Returns:
            (tuple): (gradients, token_words, token_types, answer_text)
    """
    embedding_matrix = get_embedding_matrix(model)
    encoded_tokens =  tokenizer.encode_plus(question, context, add_special_
tokens=True, return_token_type_ids=True, return_tensors="tf")
    token_ids = list(encoded_tokens["input_ids"].numpy()[0])
    vocab_size = embedding_matrix.get_shape()[0]

    # convert token ids to one hot. We can't differentiate wrt to int token
ids hence the need for one hot representation

    token_ids_tensor = tf.constant([token_ids], dtype='int32')
    token_ids_tensor_one_hot = tf.one_hot(token_ids_tensor, vocab_size)


    with tf.GradientTape(watch_accessed_variables=False) as tape:

        # (i) watch input variable
        tape.watch(token_ids_tensor_one_hot)

        # multiply input model embedding matrix; allows us do backprop wrt
one hot input
        inputs_embeds = tf.matmul(token_ids_tensor_one_hot,embedding_
matrix)

        # (ii) get prediction
        start_scores,end_scores = model({"inputs_embeds": inputs_embeds,
"token_type_ids": encoded_tokens["token_type_ids"], "attention_mask":
encoded_tokens["attention_mask"] })
        answer_start, answer_end = get_best_start_end_position(start_
scores, end_scores)
```

```
        start_output_mask = get_correct_span_mask(answer_start, len(token_
    ids))

        end_output_mask = get_correct_span_mask(answer_end, len(token_ids))


        # zero out all predictions outside of the correct span positions;
    we want to get gradients wrt to just these positions
        predict_correct_start_token = tf.reduce_sum(start_scores *
                                        start_output_mask)
        predict_correct_end_token = tf.reduce_sum(end_scores *
                                        end_output_mask)


        # (iii) get gradient of input with respect to both start and end
    output
        gradient_non_normalized = tf.norm(
            tape.gradient([predict_correct_start_token, predict_correct_
    end_token], token_ids_tensor_one_hot),axis=2)


        # (iv) normalize gradient scores and return them as "explanations"
        gradient_tensor = (
            gradient_non_normalized /
            tf.reduce_max(gradient_non_normalized)
        )
        gradients = gradient_tensor[0].numpy().tolist()

        token_words = tokenizer.convert_ids_to_tokens(token_ids)
        token_types = list(encoded_tokens["token_type_ids"].numpy()[0])
        answer_text = tokenizer.decode(token_ids[answer_start:answer_end])

        return  gradients,  token_words, token_types,answer_text


def explain_model(question, context, model, tokenizer, explain_method =
"gradient"):
    if explain_method == "gradient":
        return get_gradient(question, context, model, tokenizer)
```

And finally plotting:

```
def plot_gradients(tokens, token_types, gradients, title):

    """ Plot  explanations
    """
    plt.figure(figsize=(21,3))
    xvals = [ x + str(i) for i,x in enumerate(tokens)]
```

```
    colors =  [ (0,0,1, c) for c,t in zip(gradients, token_types) ]
    edgecolors = [ "black" if t==0 else (0,0,1, c)  for c,t in
zip(gradients, token_types) ]
    # colors =  [  ("r" if t==0 else "b")  for c,t in zip(gradients, token_
types) ]
    plt.tick_params(axis='both', which='minor', labelsize=29)
    p = plt.bar(xvals, gradients, color=colors, linewidth=1,
edgecolor=edgecolors)
    plt.title(title)
    p=plt.xticks(ticks=[i for i in range(len(tokens))], labels=tokens,
fontsize=12,rotation=90)
```

We'll compare the performance of a small set of models across a range of questions.

```
questions = [
    { "question": "what is the goal of the fourth amendment?  ", "context":
"The Fourth Amendment of the U.S. Constitution provides that '[t]he right
of the people to be secure in their persons, houses, papers, and effects,
against unreasonable searches and seizures, shall not be violated, and
no Warrants shall issue, but upon probable cause, supported by Oath or
affirmation, and particularly describing the place to be searched, and the
persons or things to be seized.'The ultimate goal of this provision is to
protect people's right to privacy and freedom from unreasonable intrusions
by the government. However, the Fourth Amendment does not guarantee
protection from all searches and seizures, but only those done by the
government and deemed unreasonable under the law." },
    { "question": ""what is the taj mahal made of?", "context": "The Taj
Mahal is an ivory-white marble mausoleum on the southern bank of the river
Yamuna in the Indian city of Agra. It was commissioned in 1632 by the
Mughal emperor Shah Jahan (reigned from 1628 to 1658) to house the tomb of
his favourite wife, Mumtaz Mahal; it also houses the tomb of Shah Jahan
himself. The tomb is the centrepiece of a 17-hectare (42-acre) complex,
which includes a mosque and a guest house, and is set in formal gardens
bounded on three sides by a crenellated wall. Construction of the mausoleum
was essentially completed in 1643, but work continued on other phases of
the project for another 10 years. The Taj Mahal complex is believed to
have been completed in its entirety in 1653 at a cost estimated at the time
to be around 32 million rupees, which in 2020 would be approximately 70
billion rupees (about U.S. $916 million). The construction project employed
some 20,000 artisans under the guidance of a board of architects led by the
court architect to the emperor. The Taj Mahal was designated as a UNESCO
World Heritage Site in 1983 for being the jewel of Muslim art in India and
one of the universally admired masterpieces of the world's heritage. It is
regarded by many as the best example of Mughal architecture and a symbol of
India's rich history. The Taj Mahal attracts 7-8 million visitors a year
and in 2007, it was declared a winner of the New 7 Wonders of the World
(2000-2007) initiative." },
```

```
    { "question": "Who ruled macedonia ", "context": "Macedonia was an
ancient kingdom on the periphery of Archaic and Classical Greece, and
later the dominant state of Hellenistic Greece. The kingdom was founded
and initially ruled by the Argead dynasty, followed by the Antipatrid and
Antigonid dynasties. Home to the ancient Macedonians, it originated on the
northeastern part of the Greek peninsula. Before the 4th century BC, it was
a small kingdom outside of the area dominated by the city-states of Athens,
Sparta and Thebes, and briefly subordinate to Achaemenid Persia" },
    { "question": "what are the symptoms of COVID-19", "context":
"COVID-19 is the infectious disease caused by the most recently discovered
coronavirus. This new virus and disease were unknown before the outbreak
began in Wuhan, China, in December 2019. The most common symptoms of
COVID-19 are fever, tiredness, and dry cough. Some patients may have aches
and pains, nasal congestion, runny nose, sore throat or diarrhea. These
symptoms are usually mild and begin gradually. Some people become infected
but don't develop any symptoms and don't feel unwell. Most people (about
80%) recover from the disease without needing special treatment. Around 1
out of every 6 people who gets COVID-19 becomes seriously ill and develops
difficulty breathing. Older people, and those with underlying medical
problems like high blood pressure, heart problems or diabetes, are more
likely to develop serious illness. People with fever, cough and difficulty
breathing should seek medical attention." },
]
```

```python
model_names = ["distilbertsquad1","distilbertsquad2","bertsquad2","bertlarg
esquad2"]
result_holder = []
for model_name in model_names:
    bqa_model, bqa_tokenizer = get_pretrained_squad_model(model_name)

    for row in questions:

        start_time = time.time()
        question, context = row["question"], row["context"]
        gradients, tokens, token_types, answer  = explain_model(question,
context, bqa_model, bqa_tokenizer)
        elapsed_time = time.time() - start_time
        result_holder.append({"question": question,  "context":context,
"answer": answer, "model": model_name, "runtime": elapsed_time})

result_df = pd.DataFrame(result_holder)
```

Format the results for easier inspection.

```python
question_df = result_df[result_df["model"] == "bertsquad2"].reset_index()
[["question"]]
df_list = [question_df]
```

```
for model_name in model_names:

    sub_df = result_df[result_df["model"] == model_name].reset_index()
[["answer", "runtime"]]
    sub_df.columns = [ (col_name + "_" + model_name)  for col_name in
                                                    sub_df.columns]

    df_list.append(sub_df)


jdf = pd.concat(df_list, axis=1)
answer_cols = ["question"] + [col for col in jdf.columns if 'answer' in col]
jdf[answer_cols]
```

	question	answer_distilbertsquad1	answer_distilbertsquad2	answer_bertsquad2	answer_bertlargesquad2
0	what is the goal of the fourth amendment?	? [SEP] The Fourth Amendment of the U. S. Cons...	to protect people's right to privacy and fre...	protect people's right to privacy and freedo...	to protect people's right to privacy and fre...
1	what is the taj mahal made of?	to	ivory - white marble	ivory - white marble	ivory - white marble
2	Who ruled macedonia	to	argead dynasty	the Argead dynasty	the kingdom was founded and initially ruled by...
3	what are the symptoms of COVID-19	##rhea. These symptoms are usually mild and be...	fever, tiredness, and dry cough	fever, tiredness, and dry cough	fever, tiredness, and dry cough

Figure 10.2: Sample records demonstrating the answers generated by different models

As we can observe from the results data, even on this sample dataset there are marked differences between the models:

▶ DistilBERT (SQUAD1) can answer 5/8 questions, 2 correct

▶ DistilBERT (SQUAD2) can answer 7/8 questions, 7 correct

▶ BERT base can answer 5/8 questions, 5 correct

▶ BERT large can answer 7/8 questions, 7 correct

```
runtime_cols = [col for col in jdf.columns if 'runtime' in col]
mean_runtime = jdf[runtime_cols].mean()
print("Mean runtime per model across 4 question/context pairs")
print(mean_runtime)

Mean runtime per model across 4 question/context pairs
runtime_distilbertsquad1     0.202405
runtime_distilbertsquad2     0.100577
runtime_bertsquad2           0.266057
runtime_bertlargesquad2      0.386156
dtype: float64
```

Based on the results above, we can gain some insight into the workings of BERT-based QA models:

▶ In a situation where a BERT model fails to produce an answer (for example, it only gives CLS), almost none of the input tokens have high normalized gradient scores. This suggests room for improvement in terms of the metrics used – going beyond explanation scores and potentially combining them with model confidence scores to gain a more complete overview of the situation.

▶ Analyzing the performance difference between the base and large variants of the BERT model suggests that the trade-off (better performance versus longer inference time) should be investigated further.

▶ Taking into account the potential issues with our selection of the evaluation dataset, a possible conclusion is that DistilBERT (trained on SQuAD2) performs better than base BERT – which highlights issues around using SQuAD1 as a benchmark.

11
Reinforcement Learning with TensorFlow and TF-Agents

TF-Agents is a library for **reinforcement learning** (**RL**) in **TensorFlow** (**TF**). It makes the design and implementation of various algorithms easier by providing a number of modular components corresponding to the core parts of an RL problem:

▶ An agent operates in an **environment** and learns by processing signals received every time it chooses an action. In TF-Agents, an environment is typically implemented in Python and wrapped in a TF wrapper to enable efficient parallelization.

▶ A **policy** maps an observation from the environment into a distribution over actions.

▶ A **driver** executes a policy in an environment for a specified number of steps (also called **episodes**).

▶ A **replay buffer** is used to store experience (agent trajectories in action space, along with associated rewards) of executing a policy in an environment; the buffer content is queried for a subset of trajectories during training.

The basic idea is to cast each of the problems we discuss as a RL problem, and then map the components into TF-Agents counterparts. In this chapter, we will show how TF-Agents can be used to solve some simple RL problems:

▶ The GridWorld problem

▶ The OpenAI Gym environment

▶ Multi-armed bandits for content personalization

The best way to start our demonstration of RL capabilities in TF-Agents is with a toy problem: GridWorld is a good choice due to its intuitive geometry and easy-to-interpret action but, despite this simplicity, it constitutes a proper objective, where we can investigate the optimal paths an agent takes to achieve the goal.

GridWorld

The code in this section is adapted from `https://github.com/sachag678`.

We begin by demonstrating the basic TF-Agents functionality in the GridWorld environment. RL problems are best studied in the context of either games (where we have a clearly defined set of rules and fully observable context), or toy problems such as GridWorld. Once the basic concepts are clearly defined in a simplified but non-straightforward environment, we can move to progressively more challenging situations.

The first step is to define a GridWorld environment: this is a 6x6 square board, where the agent starts at (0,0), the finish is at (5,5), and the goal of the agent is to find the path from the start to the finish. Possible actions are moves up/down/left/right. If the agent lands on the finish, it receives a reward of 100, and the game terminates after 100 steps if the end was not reached by the agent. An example of the GridWorld "map" is provided here:

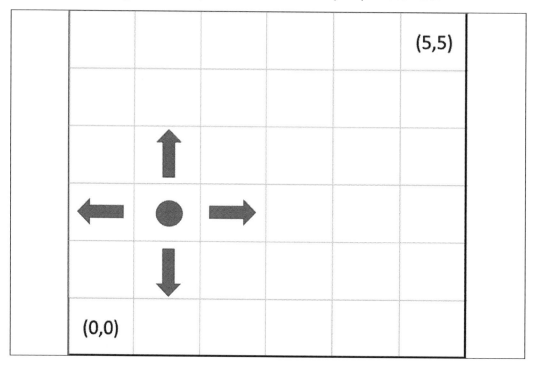

Figure 11.1: The GridWorld "map"

Now we understand what we're working with, let's build a model to find its way around the GridWorld from **(0,0)** to **(5,5)**.

How do we go about it?

As usual, we begin by loading the necessary libraries:

```
import tensorflow as tf
import numpy as np
from tf_agents.environments import py_environment, tf_environment, tf_py_
environment, utils, wrappers, suite_gym
from tf_agents.specs import array_spec
from tf_agents.trajectories import trajectory,time_step as ts

from tf_agents.agents.dqn import dqn_agent
from tf_agents.networks import q_network
from tf_agents.drivers import dynamic_step_driver
from tf_agents.metrics import tf_metrics, py_metrics
from tf_agents.policies import random_tf_policy
from tf_agents.replay_buffers import tf_uniform_replay_buffer
from tf_agents.utils import common
from tf_agents.drivers import py_driver, dynamic_episode_driver
from tf_agents.utils import common

import matplotlib.pyplot as plt
```

TF-Agents is a library under active development, so, despite our best efforts to keep the code up to date, certain imports might need to be modified by the time you are running this code.

A crucial step is defining the environment that our agent will be operating in. Inheriting from the `PyEnvironment` class, we specify the init method (action and observation definitions), conditions for resetting/terminating the state, and the mechanics for moving:

```
class GridWorldEnv(py_environment.PyEnvironment):

# the _init_ contains the specifications for action and observation
    def __init__(self):
        self._action_spec = array_spec.BoundedArraySpec(
            shape=(), dtype=np.int32, minimum=0, maximum=3, name='action')
        self._observation_spec = array_spec.BoundedArraySpec(
            shape=(4,), dtype=np.int32, minimum=[0,0,0,0],
                        maximum=[5,5,5,5], name='observation')
        self._state=[0,0,5,5] #represent the (row, col, frow, fcol) of the
player and the finish
        self._episode_ended = False
```

```
    def action_spec(self):
        return self._action_spec

    def observation_spec(self):
        return self._observation_spec

# once the same is over, we reset the state
    def _reset(self):
        self._state=[0,0,5,5]
        self._episode_ended = False
        return ts.restart(np.array(self._state, dtype=np.int32))

# the _step function handles the state transition by applying an action to
the current state to obtain a new one
    def _step(self, action):

        if self._episode_ended:
            return self.reset()

        self.move(action)

        if self.game_over():
            self._episode_ended = True

        if self._episode_ended:
            if self.game_over():
                reward = 100
            else:
                reward = 0
            return ts.termination(np.array(self._state, dtype=np.int32),
            reward)
        else:
            return ts.transition(
                np.array(self._state, dtype=np.int32), reward=0,
                discount=0.9)

    def move(self, action):
        row, col, frow, fcol = self._state[0],self._state[1],self._
        state[2],self._state[3]
        if action == 0: #down
            if row - 1 >= 0:
                self._state[0] -= 1
        if action == 1: #up
```

```
                if row + 1 < 6:
                    self._state[0] += 1
            if action == 2: #left
                if col - 1 >= 0:
                    self._state[1] -= 1
            if action == 3: #right
                if col + 1 < 6:
                    self._state[1] += 1


    def game_over(self):
        row, col, frow, fcol = self._state[0],self._state[1],self._
        state[2],self._state[3]
        return row==frow and col==fcol

def compute_avg_return(environment, policy, num_episodes=10):

    total_return = 0.0
    for _ in range(num_episodes):

        time_step = environment.reset()
        episode_return = 0.0

        while not time_step.is_last():
            action_step = policy.action(time_step)
            time_step = environment.step(action_step.action)
            episode_return += time_step.reward
            total_return += episode_return

    avg_return = total_return / num_episodes
    return avg_return.numpy()[0]

def collect_step(environment, policy):
    time_step = environment.current_time_step()
    action_step = policy.action(time_step)
    next_time_step = environment.step(action_step.action)
    traj = trajectory.from_transition(time_step, action_step, next_time_step)

    # Add trajectory to the replay buffer
    replay_buffer.add_batch(traj)
```

We have the following preliminary setup:

```
# parameter settings

num_iterations = 10000
```

```
initial_collect_steps = 1000
collect_steps_per_iteration = 1
replay_buffer_capacity = 100000
fc_layer_params = (100,)
batch_size = 128 #
learning_rate = 1e-5
log_interval = 200
num_eval_episodes = 2
eval_interval = 1000
```

We begin by creating the environments and wrapping them to ensure that they terminate after 100 steps:

```
train_py_env = wrappers.TimeLimit(GridWorldEnv(), duration=100)
eval_py_env = wrappers.TimeLimit(GridWorldEnv(), duration=100)


train_env = tf_py_environment.TFPyEnvironment(train_py_env)
eval_env = tf_py_environment.TFPyEnvironment(eval_py_env)
```

For this recipe, we will be using a **Deep Q-Network** (**DQN**) agent. This means that we need to define the network and the associated optimizer first:

```
q_net = q_network.QNetwork(
        train_env.observation_spec(),
        train_env.action_spec(),
        fc_layer_params=fc_layer_params)

optimizer = tf.compat.v1.train.AdamOptimizer(learning_rate=learning_rate)
```

As indicated above, the TF-Agents library is under active development. The current version works with TF > 2.3, but it was originally written for TensorFlow 1.x. The code used in this adaptation was developed using a previous version, so for the sake of backward compatibility, we require a less-than-elegant workaround, such as the following:

```
train_step_counter = tf.compat.v2.Variable(0)
```

Define the agent:

```
tf_agent = dqn_agent.DqnAgent(
        train_env.time_step_spec(),
        train_env.action_spec(),
        q_network=q_net,
        optimizer=optimizer,
        td_errors_loss_fn = common.element_wise_squared_loss,
        train_step_counter=train_step_counter)
```

```
tf_agent.initialize()

eval_policy = tf_agent.policy
collect_policy = tf_agent.collect_policy
```

As a next step, we create the replay buffer and replay observer. The former is used for storing the (action, observation) pairs for training:

```
replay_buffer = tf_uniform_replay_buffer.TFUniformReplayBuffer(
        data_spec = tf_agent.collect_data_spec,
        batch_size = train_env.batch_size,
        max_length = replay_buffer_capacity)

print("Batch Size: {}".format(train_env.batch_size))

replay_observer = [replay_buffer.add_batch]

train_metrics = [
            tf_metrics.NumberOfEpisodes(),
            tf_metrics.EnvironmentSteps(),
            tf_metrics.AverageReturnMetric(),
            tf_metrics.AverageEpisodeLengthMetric(),
]
```

We then create a dataset from our buffer so that it can be iterated over:

```
dataset = replay_buffer.as_dataset(
            num_parallel_calls=3,
            sample_batch_size=batch_size,
        num_steps=2).prefetch(3)
```

The final bit of preparation involves creating a driver that will simulate the agent in the game and store the (state, action, reward) tuples in the replay buffer, along with storing a number of metrics:

```
driver = dynamic_step_driver.DynamicStepDriver(
            train_env,
            collect_policy,
            observers=replay_observer + train_metrics,
        num_steps=1)

iterator = iter(dataset)

print(compute_avg_return(eval_env, tf_agent.policy, num_eval_episodes))
```

```
tf_agent.train = common.function(tf_agent.train)
tf_agent.train_step_counter.assign(0)

final_time_step, policy_state = driver.run()
```

Having finished the preparatory groundwork, we can run the driver, draw experience from the dataset, and use it to train the agent. For monitoring/logging purposes, we print the loss and average return at specific intervals:

```
episode_len = []
step_len = []
for i in range(num_iterations):
    final_time_step, _ = driver.run(final_time_step, policy_state)

    experience, _ = next(iterator)
    train_loss = tf_agent.train(experience=experience)
    step = tf_agent.train_step_counter.numpy()

    if step % log_interval == 0:
        print('step = {0}: loss = {1}'.format(step, train_loss.loss))
        episode_len.append(train_metrics[3].result().numpy())
        step_len.append(step)
        print('Average episode length: {}'.format(train_metrics[3].
                                                 result().numpy()))

    if step % eval_interval == 0:
        avg_return = compute_avg_return(eval_env, tf_agent.policy,
                                        num_eval_episodes)
        print('step = {0}: Average Return = {1}'.format(step, avg_return))
```

Once the code executes successfully, you should observe output similar to the following:

```
step = 200: loss = 0.27092617750167847 Average episode length:
96.5999984741211 step = 400: loss = 0.08925052732229233 Average episode
length: 96.5999984741211 step = 600: loss = 0.04888586699962616 Average
episode length: 96.5999984741211 step = 800: loss = 0.04527277499437332
Average episode length: 96.5999984741211 step = 1000: loss =
0.04451741278171539 Average episode length: 97.5999984741211 step = 1000:
Average Return = 0.0 step = 1200: loss = 0.02019939199090004 Average
episode length: 97.5999984741211 step = 1400: loss = 0.02462056837975979
Average episode length: 97.5999984741211 step = 1600: loss =
0.013112186454236507 Average episode length: 97.5999984741211 step = 1800:
loss = 0.004257255233824253 Average episode length: 97.5999984741211 step =
2000: loss = 78.85380554199219 Average episode length: 100.0 step = 2000:
```

```
Average Return = 0.0 step = 2200: loss = 0.010012316517531872 Average
episode length: 100.0 step = 2400: loss = 0.009675763547420502 Average
episode length: 100.0 step = 2600: loss = 0.00445540901273489 Average
episode length: 100.0 step = 2800: loss = 0.0006154756410978734
```

While detailed, the output of the training routine is not that well suited for reading by a human. However, we can visualize the progress of our agent instead:

```
plt.plot(step_len, episode_len)
plt.xlabel('Episodes')
plt.ylabel('Average Episode Length (Steps)')
plt.show()
```

Which will deliver us the following graph:

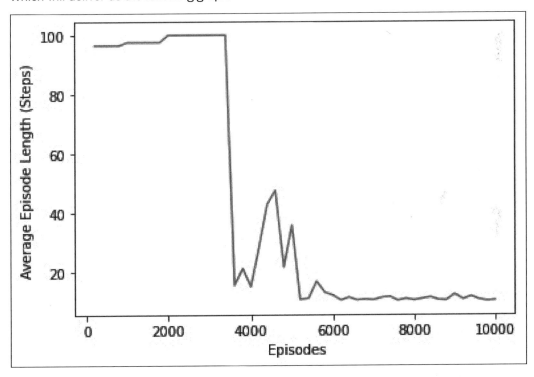

Figure 11.2: Average episode length over number of episodes

The graph demonstrates the progress in our model: after the first 4,000 episodes, there is a massive drop in the average episode length, indicating that it takes our agent less and less time to reach the ultimate objective.

See also

Documentation for customized environments can be found at `https://www.tensorflow.org/agents/tutorials/2_environments_tutorial`.

RL is a huge field and even a basic introduction is beyond the scope of this book, but for those interested in learning more, the best recommendation is the classic Sutton and Barto book: `http://incompleteideas.net/book/the-book.html`

CartPole

In this section, we will make use of Open AI Gym, a set of environments containing non-trivial elementary problems that can be solved using RL approaches. We'll use the CartPole environment. The objective of the agent is to learn how to keep a pole balanced on a moving cart, with possible actions including a movement to the left or to the right:

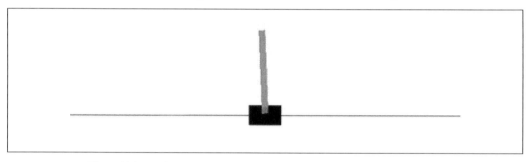

Figure 11.3: The CartPole environment, with the black cart balancing a long pole

Now we understand our environment, let's build a model to balance a pole.

How do we go about it?

We begin by installing some prerequisites and importing the necessary libraries. The installation part is mostly required to ensure that we can generate visualizations of the trained agent's performance:

```
!sudo apt-get install -y xvfb ffmpeg
!pip install gym
!pip install 'imageio==2.4.0'
!pip install PILLOW
!pip install pyglet
!pip install pyvirtualdisplay
!pip install tf-agents
```

```
from __future__ import absolute_import, division, print_function

import base64
import imageio
import IPython
import matplotlib
import matplotlib.pyplot as plt
import numpy as np
import PIL.Image
import pyvirtualdisplay

import tensorflow as tf

from tf_agents.agents.dqn import dqn_agent
from tf_agents.drivers import dynamic_step_driver
from tf_agents.environments import suite_gym
from tf_agents.environments import tf_py_environment
from tf_agents.eval import metric_utils
from tf_agents.metrics import tf_metrics
from tf_agents.networks import q_network
from tf_agents.policies import random_tf_policy
from tf_agents.replay_buffers import tf_uniform_replay_buffer
from tf_agents.trajectories import trajectory
from tf_agents.utils import common
tf.compat.v1.enable_v2_behavior()

# Set up a virtual display for rendering OpenAI gym environments.
display = pyvirtualdisplay.Display(visible=0, size=(1400, 900)).start()
```

As before, there are some hyperparameters of our toy problem that we define:

```
num_iterations = 20000

initial_collect_steps = 100
collect_steps_per_iteration = 1
replay_buffer_max_length = 100000

# parameters of the neural network underlying at the core of an agent
batch_size = 64
learning_rate = 1e-3
log_interval = 200

num_eval_episodes = 10
eval_interval = 1000
```

Next, we proceed with function definitions for our problem. Start by computing the average return for a policy in our environment over a fixed period (measured by the number of episodes):

```
def compute_avg_return(environment, policy, num_episodes=10):

  total_return = 0.0
  for _ in range(num_episodes):

    time_step = environment.reset()
    episode_return = 0.0

    while not time_step.is_last():
      action_step = policy.action(time_step)
      time_step = environment.step(action_step.action)
      episode_return += time_step.reward
    total_return += episode_return

  avg_return = total_return / num_episodes
  return avg_return.numpy()[0]
```

Boilerplate code for collecting a single step and the associated data aggregation are as follows:

```
def collect_step(environment, policy, buffer):
  time_step = environment.current_time_step()
  action_step = policy.action(time_step)
  next_time_step = environment.step(action_step.action)
  traj = trajectory.from_transition(time_step, action_step, next_time_step)

  # Add trajectory to the replay buffer
  buffer.add_batch(traj)

def collect_data(env, policy, buffer, steps):
  for _ in range(steps):
    collect_step(env, policy, buffer)
```

If a picture is worth a thousand words, then surely a video must be even better. In order to visualize the performance of our agent, we need a function that renders the actual animation:

```
def embed_mp4(filename):
  """Embeds an mp4 file in the notebook."""
  video = open(filename,'rb').read()
  b64 = base64.b64encode(video)
  tag = '''
```

```
<video width="640" height="480" controls>
  <source src="data:video/mp4;base64,{0}" type="video/mp4">
Your browser does not support the video tag.
</video>'''.format(b64.decode())


return IPython.display.HTML(tag)

def create_policy_eval_video(policy, filename, num_episodes=5, fps=30):
  filename = filename + ".mp4"
  with imageio.get_writer(filename, fps=fps) as video:
    for _ in range(num_episodes):
      time_step = eval_env.reset()
      video.append_data(eval_py_env.render())
      while not time_step.is_last():
        action_step = policy.action(time_step)
        time_step = eval_env.step(action_step.action)
        video.append_data(eval_py_env.render())
  return embed_mp4(filename)
```

With the preliminaries out of the way, we can now proceed to actually setting up our environment:

```
env_name = 'CartPole-v0'
env = suite_gym.load(env_name)
env.reset()
```

In the CartPole environment, the following applies:

- An observation is an array of four floats:
  - ❏ The position and velocity of the cart
  - ❏ The angular position and velocity of the pole

- The reward is a scalar float value
- An action is a scalar integer with only two possible values:
  - ❏ 0 – "move left"
  - ❏ 1 – "move right"

As before, split the training and evaluation environments and apply the wrappers:

```
train_py_env = suite_gym.load(env_name)
eval_py_env = suite_gym.load(env_name)


train_env = tf_py_environment.TFPyEnvironment(train_py_env)
eval_env = tf_py_environment.TFPyEnvironment(eval_py_env)
```

Define the network forming the backbone of the learning algorithm in our agent: a neural network predicting the expected returns of all actions (commonly referred to as Q-values in RL literature) given an observation of the environment as input:

```
fc_layer_params = (100,)

q_net = q_network.QNetwork(
    train_env.observation_spec(),
    train_env.action_spec(),
    fc_layer_params=fc_layer_params)

optimizer = tf.compat.v1.train.AdamOptimizer(learning_rate=learning_rate)

train_step_counter = tf.Variable(0)
```

With this, we can instantiate a DQN agent:

```
agent = dqn_agent.DqnAgent(
    train_env.time_step_spec(),
    train_env.action_spec(),
    q_network=q_net,
    optimizer=optimizer,
    td_errors_loss_fn=common.element_wise_squared_loss,
    train_step_counter=train_step_counter)

agent.initialize()
```

Set up the policies – the main one used for evaluation and deployment, and the secondary one that is utilized for data collection:

```
eval_policy = agent.policy
collect_policy = agent.collect_policy
```

In order to have an admittedly not very sophisticated comparison, we will also create a random policy (as the name suggests, it acts randomly). This demonstrates an important point, however: a policy can be created independently of an agent:

```
random_policy = random_tf_policy.RandomTFPolicy(train_env.time_step_spec(),
    train_env.action_spec())
```

To get an action from a policy, we call the `policy.action(time_step)` method. The `time_step` contains the observation from the environment. This method returns a policy step, which is a named tuple with three components:

▶ **Action**: the action to be taken (move left or move right)
▶ **State**: used for stateful (RNN-based) policies

▶ **Info**: auxiliary data, such as the log probabilities of actions:

```
example_environment = tf_py_environment.TFPyEnvironment(
    suite_gym.load('CartPole-v0'))

time_step = example_environment.reset()
```

The replay buffer tracks the data collected from the environment, which is used for training:

```
replay_buffer = tf_uniform_replay_buffer.TFUniformReplayBuffer(
    data_spec=agent.collect_data_spec,
    batch_size=train_env.batch_size,
    max_length=replay_buffer_max_length)
```

For most agents, collect_data_spec is a named tuple called **Trajectory**, containing the specs for observations, actions, rewards, and other items.

We now make use of our random policy to explore the environment:

```
collect_data(train_env, random_policy, replay_buffer, initial_collect_
steps)
```

The replay buffer can now be accessed by an agent by means of a pipeline. Since our DQN agent needs both the current and the next observation to calculate the loss, the pipeline samples two adjacent rows at a time (num_steps = 2):

```
dataset = replay_buffer.as_dataset(
    num_parallel_calls=3,
    sample_batch_size=batch_size,
    num_steps=2).prefetch(3)

iterator = iter(dataset)
```

During the training part, we switch between two steps, collecting data from the environment and using it to train the DQN:

```
agent.train = common.function(agent.train)

# Reset the train step
agent.train_step_counter.assign(0)

# Evaluate the agent's policy once before training.
avg_return = compute_avg_return(eval_env, agent.policy, num_eval_episodes)
returns = [avg_return]
```

```
for _ in range(num_iterations):

  # Collect a few steps using collect_policy and save to the replay buffer.
  collect_data(train_env, agent.collect_policy, replay_buffer, collect_
steps_per_iteration)

  # Sample a batch of data from the buffer and update the agent's network.
  experience, unused_info = next(iterator)
  train_loss = agent.train(experience).loss

  step = agent.train_step_counter.numpy()

  if step % log_interval == 0:
    print('step = {0}: loss = {1}'.format(step, train_loss))

  if step % eval_interval == 0:
    avg_return = compute_avg_return(eval_env, agent.policy, num_eval_episodes)
    print('step = {0}: Average Return = {1}'.format(step, avg_return))
    returns.append(avg_return)
```

A (partial) output of the code block is given here. By way of a quick reminder, step is the iteration in the training process, loss is the value of the loss function in the deep network driving the logic behind our agent, and Average Return is the reward at the end of the current run:

```
step = 200: loss = 4.396056175231934
step = 400: loss = 7.12950325012207
step = 600: loss = 19.0213623046875
step = 800: loss = 45.954856872558594
step = 1000: loss = 35.900394439697266
step = 1000: Average Return = 21.399999618530273
step = 1200: loss = 60.97482681274414
step = 1400: loss = 8.678962707519531
step = 1600: loss = 13.465248107910156
step = 1800: loss = 42.33995056152344
step = 2000: loss = 42.936370849609375
step = 2000: Average Return = 21.799999237060547
```

Each iteration consists of 200 time steps and keeping the pole up gives a reward of 1, so our maximum reward per episode is 200:

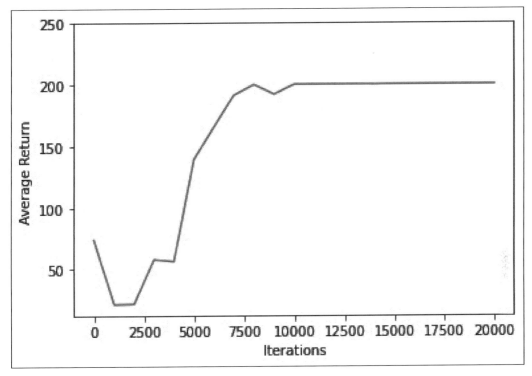

Figure 11.4: Average return over number of iterations

As you can see from the preceding graph, the agent takes about 10 thousand iterations to discover a successful policy (with some hits and misses, as the U-shaped pattern of reward in that part demonstrates). After that, the reward stabilizes and the algorithm is able to successfully complete the task each time.

We can also observe the performance of our agents in a video. As regards the random policy, you can try the following:

```
create_policy_eval_video(random_policy, "random-agent")
```

And as regards the trained one, you can try the following:

```
create_policy_eval_video(agent.policy, "trained-agent")
```

See also

Open AI Gym environment documentation can be found at https://gym.openai.com/.

MAB

In probability theory, a **multi-armed bandit** (**MAB**) problem refers to a situation where a limited set of resources must be allocated between competing choices in such a manner that some form of long-term objective is maximized. The name originated from the analogy that was used to formulate the first version of the model. Imagine we have a gambler facing a row of slot machines who has to decide which ones to play, how many times, and in what order. In RL, we formulate it as an agent that wants to balance exploration (acquisition of new knowledge) and exploitation (optimizing decisions based on experience already acquired). The objective of this balancing is the maximization of a total reward over a period of time.

An MAB is a simplified RL problem: an action taken by the agent does not influence the subsequent state of the environment. This means that there is no need to model state transitions, credit rewards to past actions, or plan ahead to get to rewarding states. The goal of an MAB agent is to determine a policy that maximizes the cumulative reward over time.

The main challenge is an efficient approach to the exploration-exploitation dilemma: if we always try to exploit the action with the highest expected rewards, there is a risk we miss out on better actions that could have been uncovered with more exploration.

The setup used in this example is adapted from the Vowpal Wabbit tutorial at `https://vowpalwabbit.org/tutorials/cb_simulation.html`.

In this section, we will simulate the problem of personalizing online content: Tom and Anna go to a website at different times of the day and are shown an article. Tom likes politics in the morning and music in the afternoon, while Anna prefers sport or politics in the morning and politics in the afternoon. Casting the problem in MAB terms, this means the following:

▶ The context is a pair {user, time of day}

▶ Possible actions are news topics {politics, sport, music, food}

▶ The reward is 1 if a user is shown content they find interesting at this time, and 0 otherwise

The objective is to maximize the reward measured through the **clickthrough rate** (**CTR**) of the users.

How do we go about it?

As usual, we begin by loading the necessary packages:

```
!pip install tf-agents

import abc
import numpy as np
```

```
import tensorflow as tf

from tf_agents.agents import tf_agent
from tf_agents.drivers import driver
from tf_agents.environments import py_environment
from tf_agents.environments import tf_environment
from tf_agents.environments import tf_py_environment
from tf_agents.policies import tf_policy
from tf_agents.specs import array_spec
from tf_agents.specs import tensor_spec
from tf_agents.trajectories import time_step as ts
from tf_agents.trajectories import trajectory
from tf_agents.trajectories import policy_step
tf.compat.v1.reset_default_graph()
tf.compat.v1.enable_resource_variables()
tf.compat.v1.enable_v2_behavior()
nest = tf.compat.v2.nest

from tf_agents.bandits.agents import lin_ucb_agent
from tf_agents.bandits.environments import stationary_stochastic_py_
environment as sspe
from tf_agents.bandits.metrics import tf_metrics
from tf_agents.drivers import dynamic_step_driver
from tf_agents.replay_buffers import tf_uniform_replay_buffer

import matplotlib.pyplot as plt
```

We then define some hyperparameters that will be used later:

```
batch_size = 2

num_iterations = 100
steps_per_loop = 1
```

The first function we need is a context sampler to generate observations coming from the environment. Since we have two users and two parts of the day, it comes down to generating two-element binary vectors:

```
def context_sampling_fn(batch_size):

  def _context_sampling_fn():
    return np.random.randint(0, 2, [batch_size, 2]).astype(np.float32)
  return _context_sampling_fn
```

Next, we define a generic function for calculating the reward per arm:

```
class CalculateReward(object):

    """A class that acts as linear reward function when called."""
    def __init__(self, theta, sigma):
        self.theta = theta
        self.sigma = sigma
    def __call__(self, x):
        mu = np.dot(x, self.theta)
        #return np.random.normal(mu, self.sigma)
        return (mu > 0) + 0
```

We can use the function to define the rewards per arm. They reflect the set of preferences described at the beginning of this recipe:

```
arm0_param = [2, -1]
arm1_param = [1, -1]
arm2_param = [-1, 1]
arm3_param = [ 0, 0]



arm0_reward_fn = CalculateReward(arm0_param, 1)
arm1_reward_fn = CalculateReward(arm1_param, 1)
arm2_reward_fn = CalculateReward(arm2_param, 1)
arm3_reward_fn = CalculateReward(arm3_param, 1)
```

The final part of our function's setup involves a calculation of the optimal rewards for a given context:

```
def compute_optimal_reward(observation):
    expected_reward_for_arms = [
        tf.linalg.matvec(observation, tf.cast(arm0_param, dtype=tf.float32)),
        tf.linalg.matvec(observation, tf.cast(arm1_param, dtype=tf.float32)),
        tf.linalg.matvec(observation, tf.cast(arm2_param, dtype=tf.float32)),
        tf.linalg.matvec(observation, tf.cast(arm3_param, dtype=tf.float32))
    ]
    optimal_action_reward = tf.reduce_max(expected_reward_for_arms, axis=0)

    return optimal_action_reward
```

For the sake of this example, we assume that the environment is stationary; in other words, the preferences do not change over time (which does not need to be the case in a practical scenario, depending on your time horizon of interest):

```
environment = tf_py_environment.TFPyEnvironment(
    sspe.StationaryStochasticPyEnvironment(
        context_sampling_fn(batch_size),
        [arm0_reward_fn, arm1_reward_fn, arm2_reward_fn, arm3_reward_fn],
        batch_size=batch_size))
```

We are now ready to instantiate an agent implementing a bandit algorithm. We use a predefined LinUCB class; as usual, we define the observation (two elements representing the user and the time of day), time step, and action specification (one of four possible types of content):

```
observation_spec = tensor_spec.TensorSpec([2], tf.float32)
time_step_spec = ts.time_step_spec(observation_spec)
action_spec = tensor_spec.BoundedTensorSpec(
    dtype=tf.int32, shape=(), minimum=0, maximum=2)

agent = lin_ucb_agent.LinearUCBAgent(time_step_spec=time_step_spec,
                                     action_spec=action_spec)
```

A crucial component of the MAB setup is regret, which is defined as the difference between an actual reward collected by the agent and the expected reward of an **oracle policy**:

```
regret_metric = tf_metrics.RegretMetric(compute_optimal_reward)
```

We can now commence the training of our agent. We run the trainer loop for num_iterations and execute steps_per_loop in each step. Finding the appropriate values for those parameters is usually about striking a balance between the recent nature of updates and training efficiency:

```
replay_buffer = tf_uniform_replay_buffer.TFUniformReplayBuffer(
    data_spec=agent.policy.trajectory_spec,
    batch_size=batch_size,
    max_length=steps_per_loop)

observers = [replay_buffer.add_batch, regret_metric]

driver = dynamic_step_driver.DynamicStepDriver(
    env=environment,
    policy=agent.collect_policy,
    num_steps=steps_per_loop * batch_size,
    observers=observers)

regret_values = []

for _ in range(num_iterations):
```

```
driver.run()
loss_info = agent.train(replay_buffer.gather_all())
replay_buffer.clear()
regret_values.append(regret_metric.result())
```

We can visualize the results of our experiment by plotting the regret (negative reward) over subsequent iterations of the algorithm:

```
plt.plot(regret_values)
plt.ylabel('Average Regret')
plt.xlabel('Number of Iterations')
```

Which will plot the following graph for us:

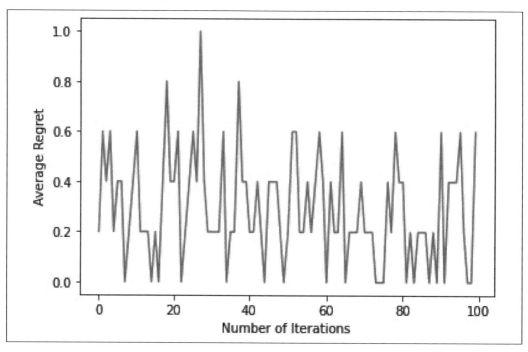

Figure 11.5: Performance of a trained UCB agent over time

As the preceding graph demonstrates, after an initial period of learning (indicating a spike in regret around iteration 30), the agent keeps getting better at serving the desired content. There is a lot of variation going on, which shows that even in a simplified setting – two users – efficient personalization remains a challenge. Possible avenues of improvement could involve longer training or adapting a DQN agent so that more sophisticated logic can be employed for prediction.

See also

An extensive collection of bandits and related environments can be found in the *TF-Agents documentation repository*: https://github.com/tensorflow/agents/tree/master/tf_agents/bandits/agents/examples/v2.

Readers interested in contextual multi-armed bandits are encouraged to follow the relevant chapters from the book by *Sutton and Barto*: https://web.stanford.edu/class/psych209/Readings/SuttonBartoIPRLBook2ndEd.pdf.

12

Taking TensorFlow to Production

Throughout this book, we have seen that TensorFlow is capable of implementing many models, but there is more that TensorFlow can do. This chapter will show you a few of those things. In this chapter, we will cover the following topics:

- ▶ Visualizing graphs in TensorBoard
- ▶ Managing hyperparameter tuning with TensorBoard's HParams
- ▶ Implementing unit tests using tf.test
- ▶ Using multiple executors
- ▶ Parallelizing TensorFlow using tf.distribute.strategy
- ▶ Saving and restoring a TensorFlow model
- ▶ Using TensorFlow Serving

We'll start by showing how to use the various aspects of TensorBoard, a capability that comes with TensorFlow. This tool allows us to visualize summary metrics, graphs, and images even while our model is training. Next, we will show you how to write code that is ready for production use with a focus on unit tests, training distribution across multiple processing units, and efficient model saving and loading. Finally, we will address a machine learning serving solution by hosting a model as REST endpoints.

Visualizing Graphs in TensorBoard

Monitoring and troubleshooting machine learning algorithms can be a daunting task, especially if you have to wait a long time for the training to complete before you know the results. To work around this, TensorFlow includes a computational graph visualization tool called **TensorBoard**. With TensorBoard, we can visualize graphs and important values (loss, accuracy, batch training time, and so on) even during training.

Getting ready

To illustrate the various ways we can use TensorBoard, we will reimplement the MNIST model from *The Introductory CNN Model* recipe in *Chapter 8, Convolutional Neural Networks*. Then, we'll add the TensorBoard callback and fit the model. We will show how to monitor numerical values, histograms of sets of values, how to create an image in TensorBoard, and how to visualize TensorFlow models.

How to do it...

1. First, we'll load the libraries necessary for the script:

```
import tensorflow as tf
import numpy as np
import datetime
```

2. We'll now reimplement the MNIST model:

```
(x_train, y_train), (x_test, y_test) = tf.keras.datasets.mnist.
load_data()

x_train = x_train.reshape(-1, 28, 28, 1)
x_test = x_test.reshape(-1, 28, 28, 1)

# Padding the images by 2 pixels since in the paper input images
were 32x32
x_train = np.pad(x_train, ((0,0),(2,2),(2,2),(0,0)), 'constant')
x_test = np.pad(x_test, ((0,0),(2,2),(2,2),(0,0)), 'constant')

# Normalize
x_train = x_train / 255
x_test = x_test/ 255

# Set model parameters
image_width = x_train[0].shape[0]
image_height = x_train[0].shape[1]
num_channels = 1 # grayscale = 1 channel
```

```python
# Training and Test data variables
batch_size = 100
evaluation_size = 500
generations = 300
eval_every = 5

# Set for reproducible results
seed = 98
np.random.seed(seed)
tf.random.set_seed(seed)

# Declare the model
input_data = tf.keras.Input(dtype=tf.float32, shape=(image_
width,image_height, num_channels), name="INPUT")

# First Conv-ReLU-MaxPool Layer
conv1 = tf.keras.layers.Conv2D(filters=6,
                               kernel_size=5,
                               padding='VALID',
                               activation="relu",
                               name="C1")(input_data)

max_pool1 = tf.keras.layers.MaxPool2D(pool_size=2,
                                      strides=2,
                                      padding='SAME',
                                      name="S1")(conv1)

# Second Conv-ReLU-MaxPool Layer
conv2 = tf.keras.layers.Conv2D(filters=16,
                               kernel_size=5,
                               padding='VALID',
                               strides=1,
                               activation="relu",
                               name="C3")(max_pool1)

max_pool2 = tf.keras.layers.MaxPool2D(pool_size=2,
                                      strides=2,
                                      padding='SAME',
                                      name="S4")(conv2)

# Flatten Layer
flatten = tf.keras.layers.Flatten(name="FLATTEN")(max_pool2)
```

```
# First Fully Connected Layer
fully_connected1 = tf.keras.layers.Dense(units=120,
                                          activation="relu",
                                          name="F5")(flatten)

# Second Fully Connected Layer
fully_connected2 = tf.keras.layers.Dense(units=84,
                                          activation="relu",
                                          name="F6")(fully_
connected1)

# Final Fully Connected Layer
final_model_output = tf.keras.layers.Dense(units=10,
                                           activation="softmax",
                                           name="OUTPUT"
                                           )(fully_connected2)


model = tf.keras.Model(inputs= input_data, outputs=final_model_
output)
```

3. Next, we will compile the model with the sparse categorical cross-entropy loss and the Adam optimizer. Then, we'll display the summary:

```
model.compile(
    optimizer="adam",
    loss="sparse_categorical_crossentropy",
    metrics=["accuracy"]
)
model.summary()
```

4. We will create a timestamped subdirectory for each run. The summary writer will write the TensorBoard logs to this folder:

```
log_dir="logs/experiment-" + datetime.datetime.now().
strftime("%Y%m%d-%H%M%S")
```

5. Next, we will instantiate a `TensorBoard` callback and pass it to the `fit` method. All logs during the training phase will be stored in this directory and can be viewed instantly in TensorBoard:

```
tensorboard_callback =
tf.keras.callbacks.TensorBoard(log_dir=log_dir,

write_images=True,

histogram_freq=1 )

model.fit(x=x_train,
          y=y_train,
          epochs=5,
          validation_data=(x_test, y_test),
          callbacks=[tensorboard_callback])
```

6. We then start the `TensorBoard` application by running the following command:

```
$ tensorboard --logdir="logs"
```

7. Then we navigate in our browser to the following link: `http://127.0.0.0:6006`. We can specify a different port if needed by passing, for example, a `--port 6007` command (for running on port 6007). We can also start TensorBoard within the notebook through the `%tensorboard --logdir="logs"` command line. Remember that TensorBoard will be viewable as your program is running.

8. We can quickly and easily visualize and compare metrics of several experiments during the model training through TensorBoard's scalars view. By default, TensorBoard writes the metrics and losses every epoch. We can update this frequency by batch using the following argument: `update_freq='batch'`. We can also visualize model weights as images with the argument `write_images=True` or display bias and weights with histograms (computing every epoch) using `histogram_freq=1`.

9. Here is a screenshot of the scalars view:

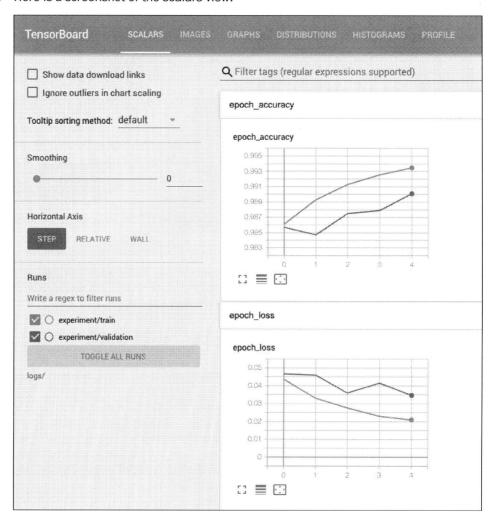

Figure 12.1: Training and test loss decrease over time while the training and test accuracy increase

10. Here, we show how to visualize weights and bias with a histogram summary. With this dashboard, we can plot many histogram visualizations of all the values of a non-scalar tensor (such as weights and bias) at different points in time. So, we can see how the values have changed over time:

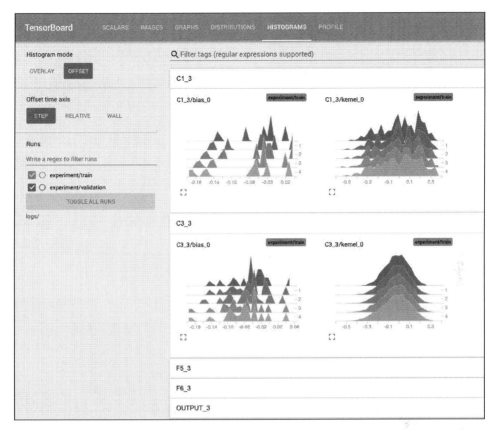

Figure 12.2: The Histograms view to visualize weights and bias in TensorBoard

11. Now, we will visualize the TensorFlow model through TensorFlow's Graphs dashboard, which shows the model using different views. This dashboard allows visualizing the op-level graph but also the conceptual graph. The op-level displays the Keras model with extra edges to other computation nodes, whereas the conceptual graph displays only the Keras model. These views allow quickly examining and comparing our intended design and understanding the TensorFlow model structure.

12. Here, we show how to visualize the op-level graph:

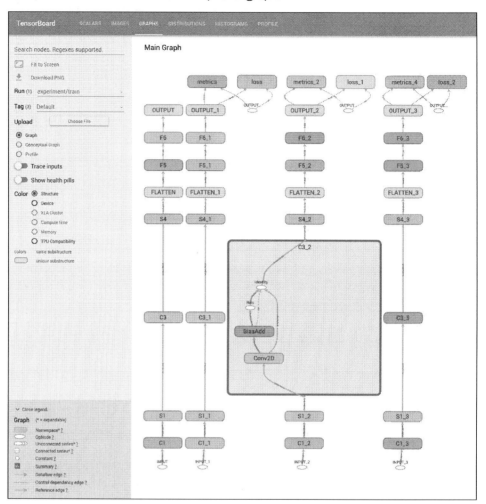

Figure 12.3: The op-level graph in TensorBoard

13. By adding the TensorBoard callback, we can visualize the loss, the metrics, model weights as images, and so on. But we can also use the `tf.summary` module for writing summary data that can be visualized in TensorFlow. First, we have to create a `FileWriter` and then, we can write histogram, scalar, text, audio, or image summaries. Here, we'll write images using the Image Summary API and visualize them in TensorBoard:

```
# Create a FileWriter for the timestamped log directory.
file_writer = tf.summary.create_file_writer(log_dir)

with file_writer.as_default():
```

```
# Reshape the images and write image summary.
images = np.reshape(x_train[0:10], (-1, 32, 32, 1))
tf.summary.image("10 training data examples", images, max_
outputs=10, step=0)
```

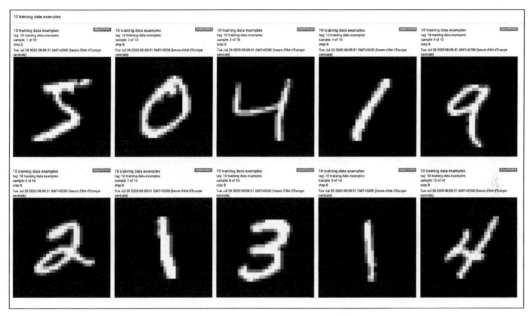

Figure 12.4: Visualize images in TensorBoard

Be careful of writing image summaries too often to TensorBoard. For example, if we were to write an image summary every generation for 10,000 generations, that would generate 10,000 images worth of summary data. This tends to eat up disk space very quickly.

How it works...

In this section, we implemented a CNN model on the MNIST dataset. We added a TensorBoard callback and fitted the model. Then, we used TensorFlow's visualization tool, which enables you to monitor numerical values and histograms of sets of values, to visualize the model graph, and so on.

Remember that we can launch TensorBoard through a command line as in the recipe but we can also launch it within a notebook by using the %tensorboard magic line.

See also

For some references on the TensorBoard API, visit the following websites:

► The official TensorBoard guide: `https://www.tensorflow.org/tensorboard/get_started`

► The TensorFlow summary API: `https://www.tensorflow.org/api_docs/python/tf/summary`

There's more...

TensorBoard.dev is a free managed service provided by Google. The aim is to easily host, track, and share machine learning experiments with anyone. After we launch our experiments, we just have to upload our TensorBoard logs to the TensorBoard server. Then, we share the link and anyone who has the link can view our experiments. Note not to upload sensitive data because uploaded TensorBoard datasets are public and visible to everyone.

Managing Hyperparameter tuning with TensorBoard's HParams

Tuning hyperparameters in a machine learning project can be a real pain. The process is iterative and can take a long time to test all the hyperparameter combinations. But fortunately, HParams, a TensorBoard plugin, comes to the rescue. It allows testing to find the best combination of hyperparameters.

Getting ready

To illustrate how the HParams plugin works, we will use a sequential model implementation on the MNIST dataset. We'll configure HParams and compare several hyperparameter combinations in order to find the best hyperparameter optimization.

How to do it...

1. First, we'll load the libraries necessary for the script:

```
import tensorflow as tf
from tensorboard.plugins.hparams import api as hp
import numpy as np
import datetime
```

2. Next, we'll load and prepare the MNIST dataset:

```
(x_train, y_train), (x_test, y_test) = tf.keras.datasets.mnist.
load_data()

# Normalize
x_train = x_train / 255
x_test = x_test/ 255

## Set model parameters
image_width = x_train[0].shape[0]
image_height = x_train[0].shape[1]
num_channels = 1 # grayscale = 1 channel
```

3. Then, for each hyperparameter, we'll define the list or the interval of values to test. In this section, we'll go over three hyperparameters: the number of units per layer, the dropout rate, and the optimizer:

```
HP_ARCHITECTURE_NN = hp.HParam('archi_nn',
hp.Discrete(['128,64','256,128']))
HP_DROPOUT = hp.HParam('dropout', hp.RealInterval(0.0, 0.1))
HP_OPTIMIZER = hp.HParam('optimizer', hp.Discrete(['adam', 'sgd']))
```

4. The model will be a sequential model with five layers: a flatten layer, followed by a dense layer, a dropout layer, another dense layer, and the output layer with 10 units. The train function takes as an argument the HParams dictionary that contains a combination of hyperparameters. As we use a Keras model, we add an HParams Keras callback on the fit method to monitor each experiment. For each experiment, the plugin will log the hyperparameter combinations, losses, and metrics. We can add a summary File Writer if we want to monitor other information:

```
def train_model(hparams, experiment_run_log_dir):

    nb_units = list(map(int, hparams[HP_ARCHITECTURE_NN].
split(",")))

    model = tf.keras.models.Sequential()
    model.add(tf.keras.layers.Flatten(name="FLATTEN"))
    model.add(tf.keras.layers.Dense(units=nb_units[0],
activation="relu", name="D1"))
    model.add(tf.keras.layers.Dropout(hparams[HP_DROPOUT],
name="DROP_OUT"))
    model.add(tf.keras.layers.Dense(units=nb_units[1],
activation="relu", name="D2"))
    model.add(tf.keras.layers.Dense(units=10, activation="softmax",
name="OUTPUT"))
```

```
        model.compile(
            optimizer=hparams[HP_OPTIMIZER],
            loss="sparse_categorical_crossentropy",
            metrics=["accuracy"]
        )

        tensorboard_callback = tf.keras.callbacks.TensorBoard(log_
dir=experiment_run_log_dir)
        hparams_callback = hp.KerasCallback(experiment_run_log_dir,
hparams)

        model.fit(x=x_train,
                  y=y_train,
                  epochs=5,
                  validation_data=(x_test, y_test),
                  callbacks=[tensorboard_callback, hparams_callback]
                  )
    model = tf.keras.Model(inputs= input_data, outputs=final_model_
output)
```

5. Next, we'll iterate on all the hyperparameters:

```
for archi_nn in HP_ARCHITECTURE_NN.domain.values:
    for optimizer in HP_OPTIMIZER.domain.values:
        for dropout_rate in (HP_DROPOUT.domain.min_value, HP_
DROPOUT.domain.max_value):
            hparams = {
                HP_ARCHITECTURE_NN : archi_nn,
                HP_OPTIMIZER: optimizer,
                HP_DROPOUT : dropout_rate
            }

            experiment_run_log_dir="logs/experiment-" + datetime.
datetime.now().strftime("%Y%m%d-%H%M%S")

            train_model(hparams, experiment_run_log_dir)
```

6. We then start the TensorBoard application by running this command:

```
$ tensorboard --logdir="logs"
```

7. Then, we can quickly and easily visualize the results (hyperparameters and metrics) in the HParams table view. Filters and sorting can be applied on the left pane if needed:

Trial ID	Show Metrics	archi_nn	optimizer	dropout	train.epoch_accuracy	validation.epoch_accuracy	train.epoch_loss	validation.epoch_loss
06716f8851f586f…	☐	128,64	adam	0.10000	0.98042	0.97550	0.059984	0.081189
5cbf9612fba561ff…	☐	256,128	sgd	0.0000	0.95150	0.95410	0.17082	0.15873
6c342a2fbe24c27…	☐	256,128	adam	0.0000	0.98890	0.97720	0.035187	0.078059
6ff73a352256eb8…	☐	128,64	sgd	0.10000	0.94260	0.95260	0.19803	0.16271
b271d8fedf6d7df…	☐	128,64	adam	0.0000	0.98673	0.97820	0.042307	0.074075
bd8e413d70c8df6…	☐	256,128	adam	0.10000	0.98453	0.97870	0.048126	0.068502
ced96c9c31fd2af…	☐	256,128	sgd	0.10000	0.94917	0.95570	0.17816	0.15441
dfdf30a386ec262…	☐	128,64	sgd	0.0000	0.94867	0.94910	0.17970	0.16948

Figure 12.5: The HParams table view visualized in TensorBoard

8. On the parallel coordinates view, each axis represents a hyperparameter or a metric and each run is represented by a line. This visualization allows the quick identification of the best hyperparameter combination:

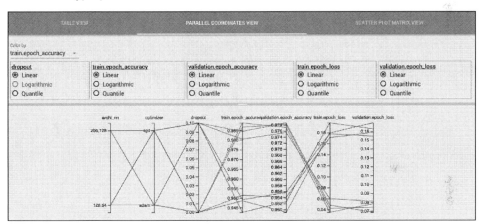

Figure 12.6: The HParams parallel coordinates view visualized in TensorBoard

Using TensorBoard HParams is a simple and insightful way to identify the best hyperparameters and also to manage your experiments with TensorFlow.

See also

For a reference on the HParams TensorBoard plugin, visit the following website:

▶ The official TensorBoard guide: `https://www.tensorflow.org/tensorboard/hyperparameter_tuning_with_hparams`

Implementing unit tests

Testing code results in faster prototyping, more efficient debugging, faster changing, and makes it easier to share code. TensorFlow 2.0 provides the `tf.test` module and we will cover it in this recipe.

Getting ready

When programming a TensorFlow model, it helps to have unit tests to check the functionality of the program. This helps us because when we want to make changes to a program unit, tests will make sure those changes do not break the model in unknown ways. In Python, the main test framework is `unittest` but TensorFlow provides its own test framework. In this recipe, we will create a custom layer class. We will implement a unit test to illustrate how to write it in TensorFlow.

How to do it...

1. First, we need to load the necessary libraries as follows:

```
import tensorflow as tf
import numpy as np
```

2. Then, we need to declare our custom gate that applies the function f(x) = a1 * x + b1:

```
class MyCustomGate(tf.keras.layers.Layer):

    def __init__(self, units, a1, b1):
        super(MyCustomGate, self).__init__()
        self.units = units
        self.a1 = a1
        self.b1 = b1

    # Compute f(x) = a1 * x + b1
    def call(self, inputs):
        return inputs * self.a1 + self.b1
```

3. Next, we create our unit test class that inherits from the `tf.test.TestCase` class. The setup method is a hook method that is called before every `test` method. The `assertAllEqual` method checks that the expected and the computed outputs have the same values:

```
class MyCustomGateTest(tf.test.TestCase):

    def setUp(self):
```

```
        super(MyCustomGateTest, self).setUp()
        # Configure the layer with 1 unit, a1 = 2 et b1=1
        self.my_custom_gate = MyCustomGate(1,2,1)

    def testMyCustomGateOutput(self):
        input_x = np.array([[1,0,0,1],
                            [1,0,0,1]])
        output = self.my_custom_gate(input_x)
        expected_output = np.array([[3,1,1,3], [3,1,1,3]])

        self.assertAllEqual(output, expected_output)
```

4. Now we need a `main()` function in our script, to run all unit tests:

```
tf.test.main()
```

5. From the terminal, run the following command. We should get the following output:

```
$ python3 01_implementing_unit_tests.py
...
[        OK ] MyCustomGateTest.testMyCustomGateOutput
[ RUN       ] MyCustomGateTest.test_session
[   SKIPPED ] MyCustomGateTest.test_session
------------------------------------------------------------------
---
Ran 2 tests in 0.016s

OK (skipped=1)
```

We implemented one test and it passed. Don't worry about the two `test_session` tests – they are phantom tests.

Note that many assertions tailored to TensorFlow are available in the `tf.test` API.

How it works...

In this section, we implemented a TensorFlow unit test using the `tf.test` API that is very similar to the Python unit test. Remember that unit testing helps assure us that code will function as expected, provides confidence in sharing code, and makes reproducibility more accessible.

See also

For a reference on the `tf.test` module, visit the following website:

▶ The official TensorFlow test API: `https://www.tensorflow.org/api_docs/python/tf/test`

Using multiple executors

You will be aware that there are many features of TensorFlow, including computational graphs that lend themselves naturally to being computed in parallel. Computational graphs can be split over different processors as well as in processing different batches. We will address how to access different processors on the same machine in this recipe.

Getting ready

In this recipe, we will show you how to access multiple devices on the same system and train on them. A device is a CPU or an accelerator unit (GPUs, TPUs) where TensorFlow can run operations. This is a very common occurrence: along with a CPU, a machine may have one or more GPUs that can share the computational load. If TensorFlow can access these devices, it will automatically distribute the computations to multiple devices via a greedy process. However, TensorFlow also allows the program to specify which operations will be on which device via a name scope placement.

In this recipe, we will show you different commands that will allow you to access various devices on your system; we'll also demonstrate how to find out which devices TensorFlow is using. Remember that some functions are still experimental and are subject to change.

How to do it...

1. In order to find out which devices TensorFlow is using for which operations, we will activate the logs for device placement by setting `tf.debugging.set_log_device_placement` to `True`. If a TensorFlow operation is implemented for CPU and GPU devices, the operation will be executed by default on a GPU device if a GPU is available:

```
tf.debugging.set_log_device_placement(True)

a = tf.constant([1.0, 2.0, 3.0, 4.0, 5.0, 6.0], shape=[2, 3],
name='a')
b = tf.constant([1.0, 2.0, 3.0, 4.0, 5.0, 6.0], shape=[3, 2],
name='b')
c = tf.matmul(a, b)
```

```
Executing op Reshape in device /job:localhost/replica:0/task:0/
device:GPU:0
Executing op Reshape in device /job:localhost/replica:0/task:0/
device:GPU:0
Executing op MatMul in device /job:localhost/replica:0/task:0/
device:GPU:0
```

2. We can also use the tensor device attribute that returns the name of the device on which this tensor will be assigned:

```
a = tf.constant([1.0, 2.0, 3.0, 4.0, 5.0, 6.0], shape=[2, 3],
name='a')
print(a.device)
b = tf.constant([1.0, 2.0, 3.0, 4.0, 5.0, 6.0], shape=[3, 2],
name='b')
print(b.device)

Executing op Reshape in device /job:localhost/replica:0/task:0/
device:GPU:0
Executing op MatMul in device /job:localhost/replica:0/task:0/
device:GPU:0
```

3. By default, TensorFlow automatically decides how to distribute computations across computing devices (CPUs and GPUs) and sometimes we need to select the device to use by creating a device context with the `tf.device` function. Each operation executed in this context will use the selected device:

```
tf.debugging.set_log_device_placement(True)
with tf.device('/device:CPU:0'):
    a = tf.constant([1.0, 2.0, 3.0, 4.0, 5.0, 6.0], shape=[2, 3],
name='a')
    b = tf.constant([1.0, 2.0, 3.0, 4.0, 5.0, 6.0], shape=[3, 2],
name='b')
    c = tf.matmul(a, b)

Executing op Reshape in device /job:localhost/replica:0/task:0/
device:CPU:0
Executing op Reshape in device /job:localhost/replica:0/task:0/
device:CPU:0
Executing op MatMul in device /job:localhost/replica:0/task:0/
device:CPU:0
```

4. If we move the `matmul` operation out of the context, this operation will be executed on a GPU device if it's available:

```
tf.debugging.set_log_device_placement(True)
with tf.device('/device:CPU:0'):
    a = tf.constant([1.0, 2.0, 3.0, 4.0, 5.0, 6.0], shape=[2, 3],
name='a')
    b = tf.constant([1.0, 2.0, 3.0, 4.0, 5.0, 6.0], shape=[3, 2],
name='b')
c = tf.matmul(a, b)

Executing op Reshape in device /job:localhost/replica:0/task:0/
device:CPU:0
Executing op Reshape in device /job:localhost/replica:0/task:0/
device:CPU:0
Executing op MatMul in device /job:localhost/replica:0/task:0/
device:GPU:0
```

5. When using GPUs, TensorFlow automatically takes up a large portion of the GPU memory. While this is usually desired, we can take steps to be more careful with GPU memory allocation. While TensorFlow never releases GPU memory, we can slowly grow its allocation to the maximum limit (only when needed) by setting a GPU memory growth option. Note that physical devices cannot be modified after being initialized:

```
gpu_devices = tf.config.list_physical_devices('GPU')
if gpu_devices:
    try:
        tf.config.experimental.set_memory_growth(gpu_devices[0],
True)
    except RuntimeError as e:
        # Memory growth cannot be modified after GPU has been
initialized
        print(e)
```

6. If we want to put a hard limit on the GPU memory used by TensorFlow, we can also create a virtual GPU device and set the maximum memory limit (in MB) to allocate on this virtual GPU. Note that virtual devices cannot be modified after being initialized:

```
gpu_devices = tf.config.list_physical_devices('GPU')
if gpu_devices:
    try:
tf.config.experimental.set_virtual_device_configuration(gpu_
devices[0],
                                              [tf.config.
experimental.VirtualDeviceConfiguration(memory_limit=1024)])
    except RuntimeError as e:
        # Memory growth cannot be modified after GPU has been
```

```
initialized
        print(e)
```

7. We can also simulate virtual GPU devices with a single physical GPU. This is done with the following code:

```
gpu_devices = tf.config.list_physical_devices('GPU')
if gpu_devices:
    try:

tf.config.experimental.set_virtual_device_configuration(gpu_
devices[0],

[tf.config.experimental.VirtualDeviceConfiguration(memory_
limit=1024),

tf.config.experimental.VirtualDeviceConfiguration(memory_limit=1024) ])
    except RuntimeError as e:
        # Memory growth cannot be modified after GPU has been
initialized
        print(e)
```

8. Sometimes we may need to write robust code that can determine whether it is running with the GPU available or not. TensorFlow has a built-in function that can test whether the GPU is available. This is helpful when we want to write code that takes advantage of the GPU when it is available and assign specific operations to it. This is done with the following code:

```
if tf.test.is_built_with_cuda():
    <Run GPU specific code here>
```

9. If we need to assign specific operations, say, to the GPU, we input the following code. This will perform simple calculations and assign operations to the main CPU and the two auxiliary GPUs:

```
if tf.test.is_built_with_cuda():
    with tf.device('/cpu:0'):
        a = tf.constant([1.0, 3.0, 5.0], shape=[1, 3])
        b = tf.constant([2.0, 4.0, 6.0], shape=[3, 1])

        with tf.device('/gpu:0'):
            c = tf.matmul(a,b)
            c = tf.reshape(c, [-1])

        with tf.device('/gpu:1'):
            d = tf.matmul(b,a)
            flat_d = tf.reshape(d, [-1])
```

```
            combined = tf.multiply(c, flat_d)
        print(combined)
```

```
Num GPUs Available:  2
Executing op Reshape in device /job:localhost/replica:0/task:0/
device:CPU:0
Executing op Reshape in device /job:localhost/replica:0/task:0/
device:CPU:0
Executing op MatMul in device /job:localhost/replica:0/task:0/
device:GPU:0
Executing op Reshape in device /job:localhost/replica:0/task:0/
device:GPU:0
Executing op MatMul in device /job:localhost/replica:0/task:0/
device:GPU:1
Executing op Reshape in device /job:localhost/replica:0/task:0/
device:GPU:1
Executing op Mul in device /job:localhost/replica:0/task:0/
device:CPU:0
tf.Tensor([  88.  264.  440.  176.  528.  880.  264.  792. 1320.],
shape=(9,), dtype=float32)
```

We can see that the first two operations have been performed on the main CPU, the next two on the first auxiliary GPU, and the last two on the second auxiliary GPU.

How it works...

When we want to set specific devices on our machine for TensorFlow operations, we need to know how TensorFlow refers to such devices. Device names in TensorFlow follow the following conventions:

Device	Device name
Main CPU	/device:CPU:0
Main GPU	/GPU:0
Second GPU	/job:localhost/replica:0/task:0/device:GPU:1
Third GPU	/job:localhost/replica:0/task:0/device:GPU:2

Remember that TensorFlow considers a CPU as a unique processor even if the processor is a multi-core processor. All cores are wrapped in /device:CPU:0, that is to say, TensorFlow does indeed use multiple CPU cores by default.

There's more...

Fortunately, running TensorFlow in the cloud is now easier than ever. Many cloud computation service providers offer GPU instances that have a main CPU and a powerful GPU alongside it. Note that an easy way to have a GPU is to run the code in Google Colab and set the GPU as the hardware accelerator in the notebook settings.

Parallelizing TensorFlow

Training a model can be very time-consuming. Fortunately, TensorFlow offers several distributed strategies to speed up the training, whether for a very large model or a very large dataset. This recipe will show us how to use the TensorFlow distributed API.

Getting ready

The TensorFlow distributed API allows us to distribute the training by replicating the model into different nodes and training on different subsets of data. Each strategy supports a hardware platform (multiple GPUs, multiple machines, or TPUs) and uses either a synchronous or asynchronous training strategy. In synchronous training, each worker trains over different batches of data and aggregates their gradients at each step. While in the asynchronous mode, each worker is independently training over the data and the variables are updated asynchronously. Note that for the moment, TensorFlow only supports data parallelism described above and according to the roadmap, it will soon support model parallelism. This paradigm is used when the model is too large to fit on a single device and needs to be distributed over many devices. In this recipe, we will go over the mirrored strategy provided by this API.

How to do it...

1. First, we'll load the libraries necessary for this recipe as follows:
```
import tensorflow as tf
import tensorflow_datasets as tfds
```

2. We will create two virtual GPUs:
```
# Create two virtual GPUs
gpu_devices = tf.config.list_physical_devices('GPU')
if gpu_devices:
    try:

tf.config.experimental.set_virtual_device_configuration(gpu_
devices[0],
```

```
[tf.config.experimental.VirtualDeviceConfiguration(memory_
limit=1024),

tf.config.experimental.VirtualDeviceConfiguration(memory_limit=1024) ])
    except RuntimeError as e:
        # Memory growth cannot be modified after GPU has been
initialized
        print(e)
```

3. Next, we will load the MNIST dataset via the `tensorflow_datasets` API as follows:

```
datasets, info = tfds.load('mnist', with_info=True, as_
supervised=True)
mnist_train, mnist_test = datasets['train'], datasets['test']
```

4. Then, we will prepare the data:

```
def normalize_img(image, label):
  """Normalizes images: `uint8` -> `float32`."""
  return tf.cast(image, tf.float32) / 255., label

mnist_train = mnist_train.map(
    normalize_img, num_parallel_calls=tf.data.experimental.AUTOTUNE)
mnist_train = mnist_train.cache()
mnist_train = mnist_train.shuffle(info.splits['train'].num_examples)
mnist_train = mnist_train.prefetch(tf.data.experimental.AUTOTUNE)

mnist_test = mnist_test.map(
    normalize_img, num_parallel_calls=tf.data.experimental.AUTOTUNE)
mnist_test = mnist_test.cache()
mnist_test = mnist_test.prefetch(tf.data.experimental.AUTOTUNE)
```

5. We are now ready to apply a mirrored strategy. The goal of this strategy is to replicate the model across all GPUs on the same machine. Each model is trained on different batches of data and a synchronous training strategy is applied:

```
mirrored_strategy = tf.distribute.MirroredStrategy()
```

6. Next, we check that we have two devices corresponding to the two virtual GPUs created at the beginning of this recipe as follows:

```
print('Number of devices: {}'.format(mirrored_strategy.num_replicas_
in_sync))
```

7. Then, we'll define the value of the batch size. The batch size given to the dataset is the global batch size. The global batch size is the sum of all batch sizes of every replica. So, we had to compute the global batch size using the number of replicas:

```
BATCH_SIZE_PER_REPLICA = 128
```

```
BATCH_SIZE = BATCH_SIZE_PER_REPLICA * mirrored_strategy.num_
replicas_in_sync

mnist_train = mnist_train.batch(BATCH_SIZE)
mnist_test = mnist_test.batch(BATCH_SIZE)
```

8. Next, we'll define and compile our model using the mirrored strategy scope. Note that all variables created inside the scope are mirrored across all replicas:

```
with mirrored_strategy.scope():
    model = tf.keras.Sequential()
    model.add(tf.keras.layers.Flatten(name="FLATTEN"))
    model.add(tf.keras.layers.Dense(units=128 , activation="relu",
name="D1"))
    model.add(tf.keras.layers.Dense(units=64 , activation="relu",
name="D2"))
    model.add(tf.keras.layers.Dense(units=10, activation="softmax",
name="OUTPUT"))

    model.compile(
        optimizer="sgd",
        loss="sparse_categorical_crossentropy",
        metrics=["accuracy"]
    )
```

9. Once the compilation is over, we can fit the previous model as we would normally:

```
model.fit(mnist_train,
          epochs=10,
          validation_data= mnist_test
          )
```

Using a strategy scope is the only thing you have to do to distribute your training.

How it works...

Using the distributed TensorFlow API is quite easy. All you have to do is to assign the scope. Then, operations can be manually or automatically assigned to workers. Note that we can easily switch between strategies.

Here's a brief overview of some distributed strategies:

►   The TPU strategy is like the mirrored strategy but it runs on TPUs.

►   The Multiworker Mirrored strategy is very similar to the mirrored strategy but the model is trained across several machines, potentially with multiple GPUs. We have to specify the cross-device communication.

- ▶ The Central Storage strategy uses a synchronous mode on one machine with multiple GPUs. Variables aren't mirrored but placed on the CPU and operations are replicated into all local GPUs.
- ▶ The Parameter Server strategy is implemented on a cluster of machines. Some machines have a worker role and others have a parameter server role. The workers compute and the parameter servers store the variable of the model.

See also

For some references on the `tf.distribute.Strategy` module, visit the following websites:

- ▶ Distributed training with TensorFlow: `https://www.tensorflow.org/guide/distributed_training`
- ▶ The `tf.distribute` API: `https://www.tensorflow.org/api_docs/python/tf/distribute`

There's more...

In this recipe, we've just gotten over the mirrored strategy and we've executed our program eagerly with the Keras API. Note that the TensorFlow distributed API works better when used in graph mode than in eager mode.

This API moves quickly so feel free to consult the official documentation to know which distributed strategies are supported in which scenarios (the Keras API, a custom training loop, or the Estimator API).

Saving and restoring a TensorFlow model

If we want to use our machine learning model in production or reuse our trained model for a transfer learning task, we have to store our model. In this section, we will outline some methods for storing and restoring the weights or the whole model.

Getting ready

In this recipe, we want to summarize various ways to store a TensorFlow model. We will cover the best way to save and restore an entire model, only the weights, and model checkpoints.

How to do it...

1. We start by loading the necessary libraries:

```
import tensorflow as tf
```

2. Next, we'll build an MNIST model using the Keras Sequential API:

```
(x_train, y_train), (x_test, y_test) = tf.keras.datasets.mnist.
load_data()

# Normalize
x_train = x_train / 255
x_test = x_test/ 255

model = tf.keras.Sequential()
model.add(tf.keras.layers.Flatten(name="FLATTEN"))
model.add(tf.keras.layers.Dense(units=128 , activation="relu",
name="D1"))
model.add(tf.keras.layers.Dense(units=64 , activation="relu",
name="D2"))
model.add(tf.keras.layers.Dense(units=10, activation="softmax",
name="OUTPUT"))

model.compile(optimizer="sgd",
              loss="sparse_categorical_crossentropy",
              metrics=["accuracy"]
             )

model.fit(x=x_train,
          y=y_train,
          epochs=5,
          validation_data=(x_test, y_test)
          )
```

3. Then, we will use the recommended format to save an entire model on disk named the SavedModel format. This format saves the model graph and variables:

```
model.save("SavedModel")
```

4. A directory named `SavedModel` is created on disk. It contains a TensorFlow program,the `saved_model.pb` file; the `variables` directory, which contains the exact value of all parameters; and the `assets` directory, which contains files used by the TensorFlow graph:

```
SavedModel
|_ assets
|_ variables
|_ saved_model.pb
```

Note that the `save()` operation also takes other parameters. Extra directories can be created based on the model complexity and the signatures and options passed to the save method.

5. Next, we'll restore our saved model:

```
model2 = tf.keras.models.load_model("SavedModel")
```

6. If we prefer to save the model in the H5 format, we can either pass a filename that ends in .h5 or add the `save_format="h5"` argument:

```
model.save("SavedModel.h5")
model.save("model_save", save_format="h5")
```

7. We can also use a `ModelCheckpoint` callback in order to save an entire model or just the weights into a checkpoint structure at some intervals. This callback is added to the `callback` argument in the `fit` method. In the configuration below, the model weights will be stored at each epoch:

```
checkpoint_callback = tf.keras.callbacks.
ModelCheckpoint(filepath="./checkpoint",save_weights_only=True,
save_freq='epoch')

model.fit(x=x_train,
          y=y_train,
          epochs=5,
          validation_data=(x_test, y_test),
          callbacks=[checkpoint_callback]
          )
```

8. We can load the entire model or only the weights later in order to continue the training. Here, we will reload the weights:

```
model.load_weights("./checkpoint")
```

Now, you're ready to save and restore an entire model, only the weights, or model checkpoints.

How it works...

In this section, we provided several ways to store and restore an entire model or only the weights. That allows you to put a model into production or avoids retraining a full model from scratch. We have also seen how to store a model during the training process and after it.

For some references on this topic, visit the following websites:

▶ The official training checkpoints guide: `https://www.tensorflow.org/guide/checkpoint`

▶ The official SavedModel format guide: `https://www.tensorflow.org/guide/saved_model`

▶ The `tf.saved_model` API: `https://www.tensorflow.org/api_docs/python/tf/saved_model/save`

▶ The Keras Model Checkpoint API: `https://www.tensorflow.org/api_docs/python/tf/keras/callbacks/ModelCheckpoint`

Using TensorFlow Serving

In this section, we will show you how to serve machine learning models in production. We will use the TensorFlow Serving components of the **TensorFlow Extended** (**TFX**) platform. TFX is an MLOps tool that builds complete, end-to-end machine learning pipelines for scalable and high-performance model tasks. A TFX pipeline is composed of a sequence of components for data validation, data transformation, model analysis, and model serving. In this recipe, we will focus on the last component, which can support model versioning, multiple models, and so on.

Getting ready

We'll start this section by encouraging you to read through the official documentation and the short tutorials on the TFX site, available at `https://www.tensorflow.org/tfx`.

For this example, we will build an MNIST model, save it, download the TensorFlow Serving Docker image, run it, and send POST requests to the REST server in order to get some image predictions.

How to do it...

1. Here, we will start in the same way as before, by loading the necessary libraries:

```
import tensorflow as tf
import numpy as np
import requests
import matplotlib.pyplot as plt
import json
```

2. We'll build an MNIST model using the Keras Sequential API:

```
(x_train, y_train), (x_test, y_test) = tf.keras.datasets.mnist.
load_data()

# Normalize
x_train = x_train / 255
x_test = x_test/ 255

model = tf.keras.Sequential()
model.add(tf.keras.layers.Flatten(name="FLATTEN"))
model.add(tf.keras.layers.Dense(units=128 , activation="relu",
name="D1"))
model.add(tf.keras.layers.Dense(units=64 , activation="relu",
name="D2"))
model.add(tf.keras.layers.Dense(units=10, activation="softmax",
name="OUTPUT"))

model.compile(optimizer="sgd",
            loss="sparse_categorical_crossentropy",
            metrics=["accuracy"]
            )

model.fit(x=x_train,
        y=y_train,
        epochs=5,
        validation_data=(x_test, y_test)
        )
```

3. Then, we will save our model as the SavedModel format and create a directory for each version of our model. TensorFlow Serving wants a specific tree structure and models saved into SavedModel format. Each model version should be exported to a different subdirectory under a given path. So, we can easily specify the version of a model we want to use when we call the server to do predictions:

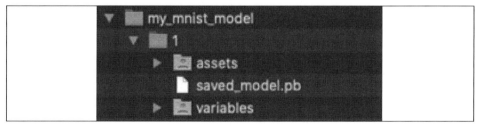

Figure 12.7: A screenshot of the directory structure that TensorFlow Serving expects

The preceding screenshot shows the desired directory structure. In it, we have our defined data directory, `my_mnist_model`, followed by our model-version number, 1. In the version number directory, we save our protobuf model and a `variables` folder that contains the desired variables to save.

 We should be aware that inside our data directory, TensorFlow Serving will look for integer folders. TensorFlow Serving will automatically boot up and grab the model under the largest integer number. This means that to deploy a new model, we need to label it version 2 and stick it under a new folder that is also labeled 2. TensorFlow Serving will then automatically pick up the model.

4. Then, we'll install TensorFlow Serving by using Docker. We encourage readers to visit the official Docker documentation to get Docker installation instructions if needed.

    The first step is to pull the latest TensorFlow Serving Docker image:

    ```
    $ docker pull tensorflow/serving
    ```

5. Now, we'll start a Docker container: publish the REST API port 8501 to our host's port 8501, take the previously created model, `my_mnist_model`, bind it to the model base path, `/models/my_mnist_model`, and fill in the environment variable `MODEL_NAME` with `my_mnist_model`:

    ```
    $ docker run -p 8501:8501 \
       --mount type=bind,source="$(pwd)/my_mnist_model/",target=/models/my_mnist_model \
       -e MODEL_NAME=my_mnist_model -t tensorflow/serving
    ```

6. Then, we will display the images to predict:

    ```
    num_rows = 4
    num_cols = 3
    plt.figure(figsize=(2*2*num_cols, 2*num_rows))
    for row in range(num_rows):
        for col in range(num_cols):
            index = num_cols * row + col
            image = x_test[index]
            true_label = y_test[index]
            plt.subplot(num_rows, 2*num_cols, 2*index+1)
            plt.imshow(image.reshape(28,28), cmap="binary")
            plt.axis('off')
            plt.title('\n\n It is a {}'.format(y_test[index]),
    fontdict={'size': 16})
    plt.tight_layout()
    plt.show()
    ```

It is a 7

It is a 2

It is a 1

It is a 0

It is a 4

It is a 1

It is a 4

It is a 9

It is a 5

It is a 9

It is a 0

It is a 6

7. We can now submit binary data to the `<host>:8501` and get back the JSON response showing the results. We can do this via any machine and with any programming language. It is very useful to not have to rely on the client to have a local copy of TensorFlow.

   Here, we will send POST predict requests to our server and pass the images. The server will return 10 probabilities for each image corresponding to the probability for each digit between 0 and 9:

```
json_request = '{{ "instances" : {} }}'.format(x_test[0:12].
tolist())
resp = requests.post('http://localhost:8501/v1/models/my_mnist_
model:predict', data=json_request, headers = {"content-type":
"application/json"})

print('response.status_code: {}'.format(resp.status_code))
print('response.content: {}'.format(resp.content))

predictions = json.loads(resp.text)['predictions']
```

8. Then, we will display the prediction results for our images:

```
num_rows = 4
num_cols = 3
plt.figure(figsize=(2*2*num_cols, 2*num_rows))
for row in range(num_rows):
    for col in range(num_cols):
        index = num_cols * row + col
        image = x_test[index]
        predicted_label = np.argmax(predictions[index])
        true_label = y_test[index]
        plt.subplot(num_rows, 2*num_cols, 2*index+1)
        plt.imshow(image.reshape(28,28), cmap="binary")
        plt.axis('off')
        if predicted_label == true_label:
            color = 'blue'
        else:
            color = 'red'
        plt.title('\n\n The model predicts a {} \n and it is a
{}'.format(predicted_label, true_label), fontdict={'size': 16},
color=color)
plt.tight_layout()
plt.show()
```

Now, let's look at a visual representation of 16 predictions:

The model predicts a 7 and it is a 7

7

The model predicts a 2 and it is a 2

2

The model predicts a 1 and it is a 1

/

The model predicts a 0 and it is a 0

0

The model predicts a 4 and it is a 4

4

The model predicts a 1 and it is a 1

/

The model predicts a 4 and it is a 4

4

The model predicts a 9 and it is a 9

9

The model predicts a 6 and it is a 5

5

The model predicts a 9 and it is a 9

9

The model predicts a 0 and it is a 0

0

The model predicts a 6 and it is a 6

6

How it works...

Machine learning teams focus on creating machine learning models and operations teams focus on deploying models. MLOps applies DevOps principles to machine learning. It brings the best practices of software development (commenting, documentation, versioning, testing, and so on) to data science. MLOps is about removing the barriers between the machine learning teams that produce models and the operations teams that deploy models.

In this recipe, we only focus on serving models using the TFX Serving component but TFX is an MLOps tool that builds complete, end-to-end machine learning pipelines. We can only encourage the reader to explore this platform.

There are also many other solutions available that may be used to serve a model, such as Kubeflow, Django/Flask, or managed cloud services such as AWS SageMaker, GCP AI Platform, or Azure ML.

There's more...

Links to tools and resources for architectures not covered in this chapter are as follows:

- ▶ **Using TensorFlow Serving with Docker**: https://www.tensorflow.org/serving/docker
- ▶ **Using TensorFlow Serving with Kubernetes**: https://www.tensorflow.org/tfx/serving/serving_kubernetes
- ▶ **Installing TensorFlow Serving**: https://www.tensorflow.org/tfx/tutorials/serving/rest_simple
- ▶ **TensorFlow extended**: https://www.tensorflow.org/tfx
- ▶ **Kubeflow – The machine learning toolkit for Kubernetes**: https://www.kubeflow.org/
- ▶ **GCP AI Platform**: https://cloud.google.com/ai-platform
- ▶ **AWS SageMaker**: https://aws.amazon.com/fr/sagemaker/
- ▶ **Azure ML**: https://azure.microsoft.com/services/machine-learning/

Share your experience

Thank you for taking the time to read this book. If you enjoyed this book, help others to find it. Leave a review at https://www.amazon.com/dp/1800208863

Packt>

Other Books You May Enjoy

If you enjoyed this book, you may be interested in these other books by Packt:

Python Machine Learning - Third Edition

Sebastian Raschka, Vahid Mirjalili

ISBN: 978-1-78995-575-0

- ▸ Master the frameworks, models, and techniques that enable machines to 'learn' from data
- ▸ Use scikit-learn for machine learning and TensorFlow for deep learning
- ▸ Apply machine learning to image classification, sentiment analysis, intelligent web applications, and more
- ▸ Build and train neural networks, GANs, and other models
- ▸ Discover best practices for evaluating and tuning models
- ▸ Predict continuous target outcomes using regression analysis
- ▸ Dig deeper into textual and social media data using sentiment analysis

Deep Learning with TensorFlow 2 and Keras - Second Edition

Antonio Gulli, Amita Kapoor, Sujit Pal

ISBN: 978-1-83882-341-2

- Build machine learning and deep learning systems with TensorFlow 2 and the Keras API
- Use Regression analysis, the most popular approach to machine learning
- Understand ConvNets (convolutional neural networks) and how they are essential for deep learning systems such as image classifiers
- Use GANs (generative adversarial networks) to create new data that fits with existing patterns
- Discover RNNs (recurrent neural networks) that can process sequences of input intelligently, using one part of a sequence to correctly interpret another
- Apply deep learning to natural human language and interpret natural language texts to produce an appropriate response
- Train your models on the cloud and put TF to work in real environments
- Explore how Google tools can automate simple ML workflows without the need for complex modeling

Advanced Deep Learning with TensorFlow 2 and Keras - Second Edition

Rowel Atienza

ISBN: 978-1-83882-165-4

- ▸ Use mutual information maximization techniques to perform unsupervised learning
- ▸ Use segmentation to identify the pixel-wise class of each object in an image
- ▸ Identify both the bounding box and class of objects in an image using object detection
- ▸ Learn the building blocks for advanced techniques - MLPss, CNN, and RNNs
- ▸ Understand deep neural networks - including ResNet and DenseNet
- ▸ Understand and build autoregressive models – autoencoders, VAEs, and GANs
- ▸ Discover and implement deep reinforcement learning methods

Packt is searching for authors like you

If you're interested in becoming an author for Packt, please visit `authors.packtpub.com` and apply today. We have worked with thousands of developers and tech professionals, just like you, to help them share their insight with the global tech community. You can make a general application, apply for a specific hot topic that we are recruiting an author for, or submit your own idea.

Index

Printed in Great Britain
by Amazon